THE ORDEAL
OF ELIZABETH MARSH

In Defiance of Oligarchy: The Tory Party, 1714–1760
Lewis Namier
Britons: Forging the Nation, 1707–1837
Captives: Britain, Empire and the World, 1600–1850

THE ORDEAL

of

ELIZABETH MARSH

A Woman in World History

LINDA COLLEY

Harper*Press*

An Imprint of HarperCollins*Publishers*

HarperCollins*Publishers*
77–85 Fulham Palace Road,
Hammersmith, London W6 8JB
www.harpercollins.co.uk

Published by HarperCollins*Publishers* 2007

1

A catalogue record for this book is available
from the British Library

ISBN 13 978–0–00–719218–2
ISBN 10 0–00–719218–5

Endpaper illustration
© The Trustees of the British Museum

Maps by Peter Wilkinson

Set in PostScript Linotype Adobe Caslon with
Castellar Display by Rowland Phototypesetting Ltd,
Bury St Edmunds, Suffolk

Printed and bound in Great Britain by
Clays Ltd, St Ives plc

This book is proudly printed on paper which contains wood
from well managed forests, certified in accordance with
the rules of the Forest Stewardship Council.
For more information about FSC,
please visit www.fsc-uk.org

Mixed Sources
Product group from well-managed
forests and other controlled sources
www.fsc.org Cert no. SW-COC-1806
© 1996 Forest Stewardship Council
FSC

Jan Colley's book

CONTENTS

PLATES

Admiral Sir Edward Hughes, watercolour in Madras style, *c.*1783 *(The British Library, London)*

Hamburg, engraving by Johann Georg, *c.*1750 *(AKG Images, London)*

'A view of a section of the Port of Barcelona including Moorish and European merchants and their ships'. Eighteenth-century engraving by Moulinier *(Mary Evans Picture Library, London)*

The Lower Crisp in Florida as it now is *(By kind courtesy of Professor Dan Schafer)*

The Upper Crisp *(By kind courtesy of Professor Dan Schafer)*

'Examination of a bankrupt before his creditors in the Court of King's Bench, Guildhall', by Augustus Charles Pugin and Thomas Rowlandson *(Guildhall Library, City of London)*

Money lenders in Calcutta *(Courtesy of The Lewis Walpole Library, Yale University)*

'In India on the March', by Samuel Davis *(Yale Center for British Art, Paul Mellon Collection, USA/Bridgeman Art Library, London)*

'Procession at the Great Temple of Jagannath, Puri', British school, *c.*1818–20 *(The British Library, London)*

Lockleys, the Hertfordshire mansion acquired by Elizabeth Marsh's daughter and Sir George Shee *(Reproduced by kind permission of Hertfordshire Archives and Local Studies. Document ref: D/Eof/7)*

Captain John Henry Crisp, Elizabeth Marsh's half-Indian grandson *(The British Library, London)*

Preparing for the scientific expedition to Sumatra at the Madras observatory *(The British Library, London)*

TEXT ILLUSTRATIONS

MAPS

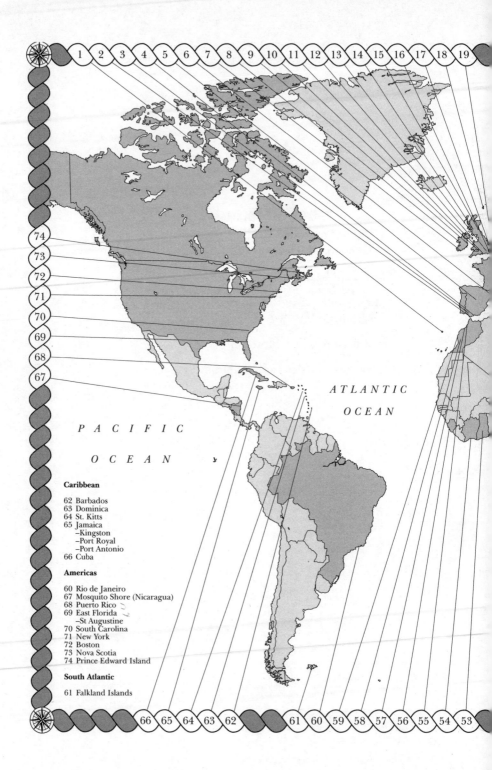

PACIFIC

OCEAN

ATLANTIC

OCEAN

Caribbean

62 Barbados
63 Dominica
64 St. Kitts
65 Jamaica
　　–Kingston
　　–Port Royal
　　–Port Antonio
66 Cuba

Americas

60 Rio de Janeiro
67 Mosquito Shore (Nicaragua)
68 Puerto Rico
69 East Florida
　　–St Augustine
70 South Carolina
71 New York
72 Boston
73 Nova Scotia
74 Prince Edward Island

South Atlantic

61 Falkland Islands

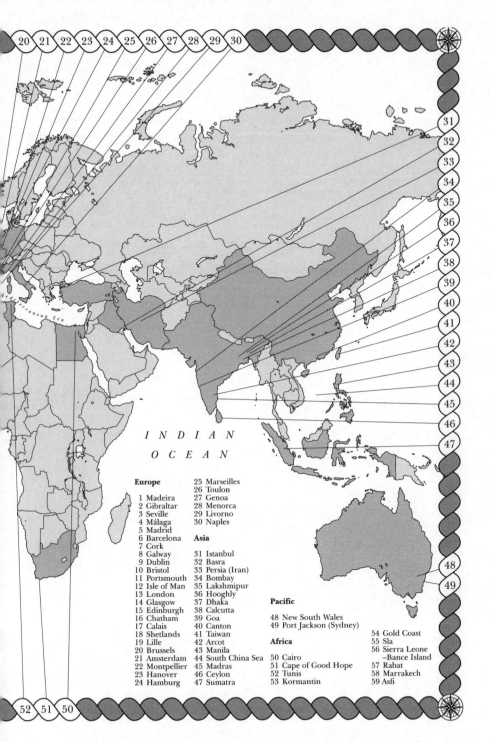

Europe

1 Madeira
2 Gibraltar
3 Seville
4 Málaga
5 Madrid
6 Barcelona
7 Cork
8 Galway
9 Dublin
10 Bristol
11 Portsmouth
12 Isle of Man
13 London
14 Glasgow
15 Edinburgh
16 Chatham
17 Calais
18 Shetlands
19 Lille
20 Brussels
21 Amsterdam
22 Montpellier
23 Hanover
24 Hamburg
25 Marseilles
26 Toulon
27 Genoa
28 Menorca
29 Livorno
30 Naples

Asia

31 Istanbul
32 Basra
33 Persia (Iran)
34 Bombay
35 Lakshmipur
36 Hooghly
37 Dhaka
38 Calcutta
39 Goa
40 Canton
41 Taiwan
42 Arcot
43 Manila
44 South China Sea
45 Madras
46 Ceylon
47 Sumatra

Pacific

48 New South Wales
49 Port Jackson (Sydney)

Africa

50 Cairo
51 Cape of Good Hope
52 Tunis
53 Kormantin
54 Gold Coast
55 Sla
56 Sierra Leone
 –Bance Island
57 Rabat
58 Marrakech
59 Asfi

The world – as Elizabeth Marsh and her extended family experienced it

CONVENTIONS

Place names have changed radically since Elizabeth Marsh's lifetime, especially in regions of the world that have previously been colonized or fought over by contending states. Many names remain contested. In this book, I generally use the names that are most current today: hence Dhaka and Menorca, rather than Dacca and Minorca. Some now-discarded place names possess so much historical resonance, however, that I have judged it inappropriate to update them. Thus I refer to Calcutta in these pages, not Kolkata.

For the transliteration of Arabic terms and phrases, I have drawn on the *Encyclopaedia of Islam* and on the advice of expert friends. Making sense of the mangled Anglo-Indian terminology employed in Elizabeth Marsh's Indian Journal has been made easier by the University of Chicago's online version of *Hobson-Jobson*.

In order to convey the fluctuating fortunes of the main characters in this book, I provide estimates at times of what they were worth in terms of today's purchasing power. I have drawn these estimates from the 'How much is that?' site on EH.net.

Before 1752, the British followed the Julian calendar and dated the beginning of the New Year from 25 March, not 1 January. Thus the captain's log of the *Kingston*, the ship on which Milbourne Marsh set out from Portsmouth for Jamaica, has it readying for sail in early 1731. But in terms of the modern Gregorian calendar, it was early in 1732 that the *Kingston* was got ready; and I have used the modern-style year throughout the text and endnotes. When quoting from original manuscripts in the text, I have modernized spelling, extended abbreviations, and altered punctuation whenever the sense has seemed to demand it. Books cited in the endnotes are published in London unless otherwise stated. I describe at the beginning of the notes the other conventions I employ in the course of them.

INTRODUCTION

'I search for Eliza every where: I discover, I discern some of her
features . . . But what is become of her who united them all?'
ABBÉ RAYNAL

THIS IS A BIOGRAPHY that crosses boundaries, and it tells three
connected stories. The first is the career of a remarkable but barely
known woman, Elizabeth Marsh, who lived from 1735 to 1785, and
who travelled farther and more dangerously by sea and in four
continents than any female contemporary for whom records survive. The second story is concerned with members of her extended
family, her parents, uncle, brothers, husband, children, multiple
cousins and other, more distant, kin. Because of the nature of
their occupations, their migrations and their ideas, these people
played vital roles in fostering Elizabeth Marsh's own conspicuous
mobility. They also helped to connect her, in both constructive
and traumatic ways, with some of the most transformative forces
of her age. For this is not just an account of an individual and
a family: it is also, and thirdly, a global story. Elizabeth Marsh's
existence coincided with a distinctive and markedly violent phase
of world history, in which connections between continents and
oceans broadened and altered in multiple ways. These changes in
the global landscape repeatedly shaped and distorted Elizabeth
Marsh's personal progress. So this book charts a world in a life
and a life in the world. It is also an argument for re-casting and
re-evaluating biography as a way of deepening our understanding
of the global past.

Her Life

Elizabeth Marsh's life is at once startlingly atypical and widely revealing, strange and representative. She was conceived in Jamaica, and may have been of mixed racial parentage. Her voyage *in utero* across the Atlantic from Kingston to England was the first of many oceanic journeys on her part, and inaugurated a life that was shaped as much by water as dry land, and that even on shore was spent in a succession of cosmopolitan ports and riverside cities. As a child, Elizabeth Marsh moved between Portsmouth and Chatham and the lower decks of Royal Navy warships at sail. Migrating with her family to the Mediterranean in 1755, she lived first in Menorca, and then – after a French invasion drove them out – in Gibraltar. Taken to Morocco in 1756 by force, but also as a consequence of her own actions, she was one of the first nominal Europeans to have a sustained personal encounter with its then acting Sultan, Sidi Muhammad, penetrating to the heart of his palace complex at Marrakech, and barely escaping sexual enslavement. The under-educated daughter of a shipwright, she subsequently became the first woman to write and publish on the Maghreb in English.

Elizabeth Marsh spent the late 1750s, and early and mid '60s, comparatively becalmed in London by marriage and childbirth, but watching her husband engage in trade with Western and Eastern Europe, Northern Africa, mainland North America and the Caribbean, and parts of South America and Asia. She also plotted with him to emigrate to Florida. Instead, bankruptcy drove him to flee to India; and in 1771 Elizabeth Marsh would join him there, sailing to the subcontinent by way of visits to Rio de Janeiro and the Cape, on the only ship then to have circumnavigated the world twice over. She did not stay in their new house at Dhaka for long, however. After dispatching her young son briefly to Persia, and her daughter back to England, Marsh set out by sea for Madras in December 1774.

She would devote much of the next eighteen months to visiting and exploring settlements, towns and temples in eastern and southern India, composing in the process one of the strangest and most emotive accounts of an overland journey in the subcontinent to be written at this time by anyone, male or female. Her closest companion on this Asiatic progress was an unmarried man; and although Elizabeth Marsh rejoined her husband in Dhaka in mid-1776, it was again not for long. From late 1777 to mid-1780 she was once more on the move, sailing first from Calcutta to England, and then, after more than a year's intrigue, and a further twelve thousand miles at least in sea distance, returning to the subcontinent. She embarked on these last circuitous voyages in defiance of French and Spanish warships and privateers that were now fighting in support of the new-minted United States, and because some of the long-distance repercussions of the American Revolutionary War were undermining her husband's business and existence in Asia, and threatening her children and herself.

As this suggests, while Elizabeth Marsh can seem an almost impossibly picaresque figure, viewing her thus would miss what was most arresting about her life, and all that lay behind it. To an almost eerie degree, Marsh was repeatedly caught fast in geographically wide-ranging events and pressures. This was true even of what should have been her intimate rites of passage. The circumstances of her birth (like the meeting and marriage of her parents), the nature of her upbringing, the sabotage of her first engagement, the making of her marriage, and the stages of its unravelling, her response to the advent of middle age, and the manner in which her two children were eventually provided for – all of these, and not just her travels and her writings, were influenced by transcontinental developments. For Elizabeth Marsh, there was scarcely ever a secure divide between her personal life on the one hand, and the wider world and its accelerating changes on the other. This was the nature of her ordeal. The degree to which she was exposed to it throughout the half-century of her existence was due in large part to circumstances beyond her control. It was due to the occupations of her male relations, and to the fact that she herself was a dependent woman without paid employment, and therefore vulnerable. It was due to her own, and her extended family's, connections with Britain and its tentacular, contested empire. And, crucially, it was due to the global circumstances of her times. But the intensity and relentlessness of Elizabeth Marsh's ordeal were also a product of the sort of person she was and of the choices she made.

Her Family

Elizabeth Marsh's father, *his* father and grandfather, and multiple cousins, were shipbuilders, mariners, and makers of charts and maps. Through these men, she was linked all her life to the Royal Navy, one of the few organizations at this time possessed of something genuinely approaching global reach, and to the sea: 'the great high road of communication to the different nations of the world', as Adam Smith styled it.[1] Marsh's uncle and younger brother were administrators and assemblers of information on behalf of the British state, men employing pen and paper in order to manage distance. Her husband, James Crisp, was a merchant, engaged in both legal and illicit long-distance trade. His dealings encompassed ports and manufacturing centres in the world's two largest maritime empires, those of Spain and Britain, and some of the commodities most in international demand: salt, sugar, cotton textiles, fish and tea. And he was associated with the British East India Company, the most important transnational trading corporation in existence, as subsequently were Marsh's son, her son-in-law, yet more 'cousins', and ultimately her half-Indian grandson.

Her husband was also involved in colonial land speculation and migration schemes, as was she. Her elder brother and still more 'cousins' were army officers, servicing empire and its wars; while the agency that was responsible for driving by far the largest numbers of human beings across oceans and between continents at this time, the transatlantic trade in West African slaves, may have given rise to the woman who became Elizabeth Marsh's mother. Marsh's husband certainly was implicated in this slave trade, though it was two other systems of slavery and slave-taking, in Northern Africa and in Asia, in which she herself became directly involved, both as an intended victim and as an owner.

By way of her extended family, then, Elizabeth Marsh was brought into contact with some of the main forces of global change of her time: enhanced maritime reach, transoceanic and transcontinental commerce, a more deliberate mobilization of knowledge and written information in the service of the state, the quickening tempo of imperial aggression and colonization, emigration, war, slavery and the slave trade. Many millions of people were caught up in one or more of these. Elizabeth Marsh was affected and swept into movement by all of them. This owed something to her gender and uncertain status. As a woman who was usually economically dependent, she was often dragged along in the wake of various menfolk. Consequently, *their* occupations, and *their* migrations, and *their* exposure to other societies frequently also entangled her.

In this and other respects, the near contemporary whom Elizabeth Marsh most closely resembles is Olaudah Equiano (c.1745–97), the one-time slave of African descent who, by way of his writings and travels, made himself a 'citizen of the world', as well as an African and a Briton.[2] It is telling that both Elizabeth and Olaudah were connected with the Royal Navy, with the slave trade, and with print; and they were alike too in their urge repeatedly to re-invent themselves. Their different, but essentially similar, lives also unfolded across great spaces and in a range of diverse cultural settings because of something else they had in common. Elizabeth Marsh, like Olaudah Equiano, chose to move, and was compelled to move. Avid travellers by instinct, they were each in addition forced into journeying as a result of their subordination to others: Equiano because for part of his life he was a slave, Marsh because she was a woman without independent financial resources.

It is significant, too, that these two self-made travellers and writers overlapped so closely in point of time, and that both of them were connected – though never exclusively – with Britain and its empire.

Her Worlds

Throughout Europe and in parts of the Americas – but also beyond them – the era in which Elizabeth Marsh lived, the middle and later decades of the eighteenth century, witnessed a growing awareness of the connectedness between the world's different regions and peoples. More informed and classically educated men and women were aware of course that accelerated bursts of what would now be styled globalization had occurred in earlier periods of history. 'Previously the doings of the world had been, as one might say, dispersed,' the ancient Greek historian Polybius wrote in regard to the third century BC. But, as a result of the conquests of imperial Rome, he continued, 'history has come to acquire an organic unity, and the doings of Italy and Libya [i.e. Africa] are woven together with those of Asia and Greece, and the outcome of them all tends toward one end'.[3] Historians since have identified other such 'global moments': how, by the end of the thirteenth century, trade was able for a time to link merchants in parts of India and China, the Levant, the Persian Gulf, and various European ports and city states, for instance, and how Spain's conquest of Manila in 1571 inaugurated new systems of commerce, migration and bullion-exchange between Asia, South-East Asia, the Americas and Europe.[4] Nonetheless, the rate at which different sorts of global connections evolved during and after the second quarter of the eighteenth century was perceived by observers in the West, but also outside it, as something new. 'Everything has changed, and must change again,' insisted Abbé Raynal in his *History of the Two Indies* (1770), this era's most influential discussion and denunciation of Europe's contacts with Asia, Africa and the Americas. Or, as Edmund Burke famously pronounced in 1777: 'the great map of mankind is unrolled at once'. It was potentially 'at the same instant under our view'.[5]

This sense that the world was becoming visibly more compact and connected was pronounced within Britain itself, and for reasons that shaped much of Elizabeth Marsh's life. The sea was the prime vehicle and emblem of connectivity, 'a mighty rendez-vous', as one writer expressed it in 1760; and – as she had ample cause to know – it was Britain that possessed both the most powerful navy and the biggest merchant marine. During Marsh's lifetime, these maritime advantages allowed Britain, along with France and Russia, increasingly to explore and invade the Pacific, an ocean that occupies a third of the globe's surface, and of which Europeans had previously possessed only limited routine acquaint-ance.[6] Before, throughout, and after Marsh's life, Britain was also involved in a succession of wars with France that expanded relent-lessly in geographical scale. As a result, London was able to lay claim to the world's largest and most widely dispersed empire. By 1775, as the German geographer Johann Christoph Gatterer remarked, Britain had become the only power to have intruded decisively, though not always securely or very deeply, into every continent of the globe.[7]

In addition, Britain's ambitious commerce, the terrible volume of its slave trading, the growing overseas migration of its own peoples, and its prolific print industry and consumerism – all of which impinged on Elizabeth Marsh's own experience – encour-aged a more vivid consciousness of the world's expanse and the range of human diversity, which extended well beyond the political class. Had she been more consistently prosperous during her resi-dence in London in the 1760s, Elizabeth might have purchased a

The world opened: a pocket globe made in London in 1776 and showing
James Cook's recent 'discoveries'.

pocket globe, an increasingly fashionable accessory at this time, or
invested in one of an array of new atlases, encyclopedias, gazettes
and children's books, all promising to unpack the 'world in miniature'.[8] In more senses than one, the proliferation of such artifacts
suggested a more graspable world: one that might even be pocketed.

However, there was more to Elizabeth Marsh's experiences and
shifting identity than this British imperial connection; just as there
was always more to the growing interrelationship between continents and peoples and oceans at this time than the exertions and
ambitions of Britain and other Western powers. That Marsh was

born at all was owing, indirectly, and possibly directly, to the enforced migration of millions of West Africans across the Atlantic; and that she was born in England, and not in Jamaica, was due to rebellion on the part of just some of these people. Her career was shaped throughout by the enhanced capacity on the part of British ships, soldiers and merchants to be present globally. But her life was also vitally changed by a Moroccan ruler's schemes to construct his own world system that would link together sub-Saharan Africa, the Maghreb, the Ottoman Empire and merchants in Western and Eastern Europe, Asia, and ultimately the United States. And if London, Barcelona and Livorno supply backdrops to her story, as centres of transcontinental trade, so also do Basra, and Boston, and Dhaka, and Manila. That Elizabeth Marsh's life was one of continuous transition was due in part then to a succession of influences and interventions issuing from *outside* Europe, and to actors who saw the world from different vantage points. Her ordeal was also due to her, to the sort of person she was.

Herself

I first came across Elizabeth Marsh while writing my previous book, *Captives*. To begin with, I was aware only of the Mediterranean portion of her life; and it was not until I began investigating the background to this that I gradually uncovered the other geographies of her story. I learnt that a Californian library possessed an Indian travel journal in her hand, and an early manuscript version of her book on Morocco. Then I came across archives revealing her links with Jamaica and East Florida. Further searches turned up connections between her and her family and locations in Spain, Italy, the Shetlands, Central America, coastal China, New South Wales, Java, Persia, the Philippines, and more.

That this international paper chase proved possible and profitable was itself, I gradually came to realize, a further indication of some of the changes through which this woman had lived. Elizabeth Marsh was socially obscure, sometimes impoverished, and elusively mobile. In the ancient, medieval and early modern world, such individuals, especially if they were female, rarely left any extensive mark on the archives unless they had the misfortune to be caught up in some particular catastrophic event: a trial for murder or heresy, say, or a major rebellion, or a massacre, or a conspiracy, or a slaver's voyage. That Elizabeth Marsh and her connections, by contrast, can be tracked in libraries and archives, not just at interludes and in times of crisis, but for most of her life, is due in part to some of the transitions that accompanied it. During her lifetime, states and empires, with their proliferating arrays of consuls, administrators, clerks, diplomats, ships' captains, interpreters, cartographers, missionaries and spies, together with transcontinental organizations such as the East India Company, became more eager, and more able, to monitor and record the lives of 'small' people – even, sometimes, female people – wherever they went.

Recovering the life-parts and body-parts of Elizabeth Marsh has been rendered possible also by the explosion in global communications that is occurring now, in our own lifetimes. The coming of the worldwide web means that historians (and anyone else) can investigate manuscript and library catalogues, online documents and genealogical websites from different parts of the world to an extent that would have been unthinkable even a decade ago. At present, this revolution – like so much else – is still biased in favour of the more affluent regions of the world. Even so, it is far easier than it used to be to track down a life of this sort, which repeatedly crossed over different geographical and political boundaries. The ongoing impact of this information explosion on the envisaging of history, and on the nature of biography, will only expand in the future.[9]

To say that Elizabeth Marsh's life and ordeal are recoverable, and that this in itself is eloquent about closer global connections in her time and in ours, is not the same as saying that the sources about her are abundant or easily yielding. To be sure, this was a woman who was addicted to writing. Even when (perhaps particularly when) she was confined to the lower decks of a store ship on the Indian Ocean, or in a Moroccan prison, she is known to have busied herself writing letters. Neither these, nor any other letters by her survive. Nor do any personal letters by her husband or parents survive, or any that might compensate for the lack of a portrait of her, by closely detailing her appearance. The colour of Elizabeth Marsh's eyes and hair, like her height and the timbre of her voice, and the way she moved, remains, at least at present, beyond knowing. So does how she and others perceived exactly the colour of her skin.

This absence of some of the basic information which biographers can normally take for granted is partly why I have chosen to refer to Elizabeth Marsh often by her whole name, and sometimes only by her surname. Mainly for the sake of clarity, but also because of how she lived, I also refer to her only by her unmarried name. So in these pages she is always Elizabeth Marsh, never Elizabeth Crisp. The practice of always referring to female characters in biographies by their first names can have an infantilizing effect. It also suggests a degree of cosy familiarity that – as far as this woman is concerned – would be more than usually spurious. Certain aspects of her life and mind, as of her appearance, are unlikely ever to be properly known; though the impact she was able at intervals to make on others is abundantly clear.

What has survived to convey her quality and her actions over time are a striking set of journals, scrapbooks and sagas, compiled by her and by some members of her family. There are Elizabeth Marsh's own Moroccan and Indian writings. Her younger brother, John Marsh, produced a memoir of his career. Her uncle, George Marsh, assembled a remarkable two-hundred-page book about himself and his relations and two commonplace books, and devoted journals to the more significant episodes in his life. Ostensibly concerned with personal and family happenings, achievements and disasters, these miscellaneous chronicles can be read also as allegories of much wider changes. Even some of the maps drawn by Elizabeth Marsh's father contain more than their obvious levels of meaning. I have drawn repeatedly on these various family texts in order to decipher this half-hidden woman's shifting ideas, emotions and ambitions.

Attempting this is essential because, although she undoubtedly viewed certain phases of her life as an ordeal, Marsh rarely presented herself straightforwardly as a victim. It was her own actions and plans, and not just the vulnerabilities attaching to her marginal status, the occupations and mishaps of her male relations, the chronology of her life, and the country and empire to which she was formally attached, that rendered her at intervals so mobile, and exposed her so ruthlessly to events. In particular, without attending closely to these private and family writings, it would be hard to make sense of five occasions – in 1756, in 1769, in 1770–71, in 1774–76, and again after 1777 – on which, to differing degrees, Elizabeth Marsh broke away from conventional ties of family and female duty, only to become still more vividly entangled in processes and politics spanning continents and oceans.

History and Her Story

So this is a book that ranges between biography, family history, British and imperial history, and global histories in the plural. Because of the tendencies of our own times, historians have become increasingly concerned to attempt seeing the world as a whole. This has encouraged an understandable curiosity about very large-scale phenomena: the influence of shifting weather systems on world history, ecological change over time, patterns of forced and voluntary migration, the movement of capital, or commodities, or disease over continents, the transmission of ideas and print, the workings of vast overland and oceanic networks of trade, the impact of conflicting imperial systems, and so on.[10] These, and other such grand transcontinental forces, were and are massively important. Yet they have never just been simply and inhumanly there. They have impacted on people, who have understood them (or not), and adapted to them (or not), but who have invariably interpreted them in very many different ways. Writings on world and global history (to which I stand enormously indebted) sometimes seem as aggressively impersonal as globalization can itself.

In this book, by contrast, I am concerned to explore how the lives of a group of individuals, and especially the existence of one particular unsophisticated but not unperceptive woman, were informed and tormented by changes that were viewed at the time as transnational, and transcontinental, and even as pan-global, to an unprecedented degree. I seek to tack between the individual and world histories 'in such a way as to bring them into simul- taneous view'.[11] Writing some fifty years ago, the American sociol- ogist C. Wright Mills suggested that at no other era had 'so many men been so totally exposed at so fast a pace to such earthquakes of change'. The 'earthquakes' happening in the 1950s were due, he thought, to the collapse of old colonial empires and to the emer- gence of new, less blatant forms of imperialism, to the horrific implications of atomic warfare, to politicians' surging capacity to deploy power over individual lives, to runaway modernization, and to inordinate pressure on marriage and the family. It was vital, Mills suggested, to try to understand the relationship between these 'most impersonal and remote transformations' and 'the most intimate features of the human self'. Not least because those living through such earthquakes were often unable themselves to see this relationship clearly and make sense of it:

> Seldom aware of the intricate connection between the patterns of their own lives and the course of world history, ordinary men [sic] do not usually know what the connection means for the kinds of men they are becoming and for the kinds of history-making in which they might take part.

> They do not possess the quality of mind essential to grasp the interplay of man and society, of biography and history, of self and world.

Instead, he suggested, men and women whose fate it was to 'cope with the larger worlds with which they are so suddenly confronted' often simply felt 'possessed by a sense of trap'.[12]

As far as Elizabeth Marsh is concerned, Mills' characterization of the responses of those who live through 'earthquakes' of global change is both right and wrong. As will become clear, at times, and for good reason, she was indeed 'possessed by a sense of trap'. But, like other members of her family, she tried to make sense of the changes transcending seas and continents that she and they were so markedly living through and acting out. The extent and quality of Elizabeth Marsh's global earthquake in the mid-eighteenth century was substantially different from that perceived by Mills in the 1950s, though the flux of empire, enhanced state power, runaway military violence, modernization, and strains on the family and marriage were part of her experience too. Elizabeth Marsh's earthquake was also very different from our own at the start of the twenty-first century. But the nature of her ordeal, her precocious and concentrated exposure to so many forces of transcontinental change, and her sense in the face of these 'impersonal and remote transformations' both of shock and wonder, entrapment and new opportunities, remain eloquent and recognizable. This is her story.

1

Out of the Caribbean

THE BEGINNING prefigured much of the rest. She came to life against the odds, in a place of rampant death, and in the midst of forces that were already transforming large stretches of the globe.

The man who became her father, Milbourne Marsh, first set foot on Jamaica on 20 July 1732, which was when his ship, the *Kingston*, anchored off Port Royal.[1] The *Kingston* was one of a squadron of Royal Navy vessels ordered to the Caribbean that spring with instructions to deter smuggling in the region and attacks on British merchant shipping by Spanish armed coast-guards, and to suppress any slave rebellions within Jamaica itself. Since wresting it from the Spanish in 1655, retaining this island had become increasingly important to the English, and subsequently to the British state, initially because of its location and size. Ninety miles south of Cuba, Jamaica was ideally situated for legal and illicit trade with Spain's settlements in the Americas, and for staging attacks on them and on Spanish treasure ships, bearing gold and silver from New World mines back to Seville. At some 140 miles from east to west, Jamaica was also ten times larger than the rest of Britain's Caribbean islands combined. Tropical, fertile and well-watered, it offered – for all its steep, mountainous interior and steamy forests – sufficient arable land, or so at first it seemed, to accommodate large numbers of incoming white small-holders. When Milbourne Marsh arrived, individuals of very modest means, indentured servants, shopkeepers, skilled labourers, cooks, peddlers, retired or runaway sailors, itinerants, pen-keepers

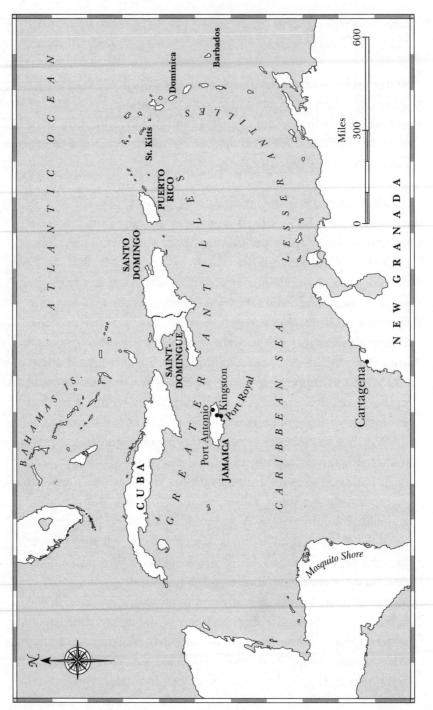

The Caribbean

(cow-farmers), garrison troops and the like still made up between a half and a third of Jamaica's white population. But the island's smallholders were in retreat before the rise of much larger landed estates and a single crop. Jamaica's sugar industry did not reach the height of its profitability until the last third of the eighteenth century. Even so, by the 1730s, with over four hundred sugar mills, the island had comfortably overtaken Barbados as the biggest sugar-producer in Britain's Empire.[2]

Although much of the technology employed on sugar plantations remained unchanged for centuries, these were still brutally innovative places. The unending work of planting, harvesting and cutting the sugar cane, milling it, boiling and striking the sugar syrup, transporting the finished products, rum, molasses, and the various sugars to the dockside, and loading them aboard ship, fostered task specialization, the synchronization of very large quantities of labour, and the imposition of shift systems and a ruthless time discipline.[3] Establishing the necessary mills, boiling houses and other fixed plant required large-scale capital investment; and plantation owners were acutely dependent on long-distance oceanic trade and communications to sell their products – and to recruit and import their workforces. As the historian David Eltis writes:

> The slave trade was possibly the most international activity of the pre-industrial era. It required the assembling of goods from at least two continents [Asia and Europe] ... the transporting of those goods to a third [Africa], and their exchange for forced labour that would be carried to yet another continent [the Americas].

Between a third and a half of the more than 1.2 million men, women and children purchased by British traders and carried in British ships from West Africa between 1700 and 1760 were probably landed in Jamaica. When Milbourne Marsh arrived here, the island contained almost eighty thousand black slaves, most of them recent arrivals from the Gold Coast, the Bight of Biafra and the Bight of Benin.[4]

There were other ways, too, in which Jamaica functioned as a laboratory for new ways of living and new types of people. Port Royal, Milbourne Marsh's landfall on the island's south-eastern coast, was an extreme case in point. The English had found its deep offshore waters, and its position at the end of a nine-mile spit separating Kingston harbour from the Caribbean, ideally suited for the loading and unloading of merchantmen from Europe and North America. Port Royal was also useful, they soon discovered, for piracy and for conducting contraband trade with, and raids against, Cuba, Hispaniola and mainland Spanish America. In 1688, 213 ships are known to have docked at Port Royal, almost as many as the total number calling that year at all of New England's ports. With its almost seven thousand slaves, shopkeepers, merchants, sailors, book-keepers, lawyers, sea captains, craftsmen, wives, children, smugglers and 'crue of vile strumpets and common prostratures', the town was also more populous at this stage than its main competitor in British America, Boston, Massachusetts. And since its two thousand houses, many of them brick and some of them four prosperous storeys high, clustered together on barely fifty acres of gravel and sand, Port Royal was probably the most crowded and expensive English-speaking urban settlement outside London.[5]

Then came the earthquake. It happened at 11.43 a.m. on 7 June 1692. In ten minutes, two-thirds of Port Royal and two thousand of its citizens disappeared beneath the sea. A further three thousand died of injuries and disease in the days after:

> The sky, which was clear and serene, grew obscured and red throughout the whole extent of Jamaica. A rumbling noise was heard under ground, spreading from the mountains to the plain; the rocks were split; hills came close together; infectious lakes appeared on the spots where whole mountains had been swallowed up; immense forests were removed several miles from the place where they stood; the edifices disappeared . . . This terrible phenomenon should

have taught the Europeans not to trust to the possessions of a world that trembles under their feet, and seems to slip out of their rapacious hands.

In so describing its destruction, Abbé Raynal and his collaborators were adding an anti-colonialist twist to a tradition of moralizing disapproval of Port Royal that was in existence well before the earthquake.[6] Yet this lost town, a kind of maritime Pompeii, had been a dynamic and creative as well as a corrupt, exploitative place, and after the earthquake there were repeated attempts to rebuild it. They were aborted by a major fire in 1704 and a succession of hurricanes; and when Milbourne Marsh arrived, little remained of Port Royal except 'three handsome streets, several cross lanes, and a fine church', the nearby garrison, Fort Charles, and a small naval dockyard where ships from Britain's Jamaica fleet were repaired and victualled. The town's main commercial and slaving businesses had moved to nearby Kingston, which was more sheltered from the elements, and there were barely five hundred white inhabitants remaining in Port Royal, most of the men amongst them employed by the Royal Navy or as soldiers in Fort Charles.[7]

Port Royal's most material legacy was arguably Jamaica's developing sugar monoculture, since both the town's gentile merchants and their Jewish counterparts had been important sources of credit for planters wanting to purchase land and slaves.[8] As this suggests, Jamaica was at once brutally divided by racial difference and violence, and in some respects also a cosmopolitan, even tolerant environment. The cosmopolitanism expressed itself in flamboyant consumerism. A taste for imported Chinese ceramics, for instance, seems to have been more prevalent in households in Port Royal before 1692, and in other Jamaican settlements, than in either British or mainland colonial American homes. At another level, British Jamaica resembled 'a curious terrestrial space-station' full of 'fragments of various races, torn from the worlds of their ancestors'.[9] Most white incomers, like Milbourne Marsh himself, were young, single, male Protestants from southern England; but there were also Scots, Protestant and Catholic Irish, Portuguese-speaking Sephardic Jews from Brazil and Surinam, Huguenots, Dutchmen, occasional French and Spanish spies, smugglers and traders from nearby St Domingue and Cuba, and mainland American colonists, principally from Boston, New York and Philadelphia. There were about 8300 of these miscellaneous whites by the early 1730s, and the island's ethnically and culturally diverse black population outnumbered them by more than ten to one.[10]

Many Africans caught up in the slave trade perished long before they arrived at Jamaica. They were killed resisting capture, or they died of shipborne diseases, or they committed suicide in order to escape the pain and humiliation of servitude, or out of a belief that death would restore their spirits to their homelands. Of those who reached the island and stayed there, as distinct from being re-exported to Spanish America or the Dutch West Indies, perhaps half died in the first two or three years, that apprentice phase of slavery which local whites termed 'the seasoning'. And few Jamaicans, black or white, slave or free, survived on the island for longer than fifteen years.[11]

Milbourne Marsh and the other men on the *Kingston* saw their first 'guineaman come in with slaves' to Port Royal harbour shortly after their own arrival. Captain Thomas Trevor was so struck by the sight, and by the sounds coming from those on board the slave-ship, that he made a special note of the event in his logbook.[12] It was an act that marked him out as a newcomer to the Caribbean; and neither he nor most of his fellow seamen on the *Kingston* were in a position to understand that slave ships might be lethal even to those who were not imprisoned on board. Jamaica's heavy rains and malarial swamps killed easily enough, and new arrivals were particularly vulnerable. They were still more so if they made landfall – as the crew of the *Kingston* did – during the rainy summer months:

> New-come buckra,
> He get sick,
> He tak fever,
> He be die
> He be die.[13]

Slave ships transported in still further risks. They often carried smallpox, and in their water casks and cisterns they also brought in the West African mosquitoes that spread yellow fever. Once in port, the insects would seek out fresh human hosts, and places in which to breed. New immigrants with no immunity were easy targets, and so were men crowded together in damp wooden ships equipped with their own water barrels.

The 327 seamen aboard the *Kingston* had remained healthy on the three-month voyage out from Portsmouth, but this changed once they were exposed to Jamaica's infection, climate, and the appalling sanitation of Port Royal and Kingston. Two weeks after its arrival, the ship was already 'growing bad' and losing men. The mortality rate lessened once it started patrolling the Caribbean, only to increase when it moored off Jamaica's other naval base, Port Antonio, on the north-eastern coast of the island, a place at this time of 'prodigious rains ... insomuch that sometimes for several months together, there is hardly one fair or dry day in a week between'. For some weeks in early 1733, the *Kingston* was unable to put out to sea. Many of the original crewmen had died, and some of the survivors were too weak for the heavy manual labour and agility demanded by a wooden ship of war.[14] And this was when the man called Milbourne Marsh began to show his quality.

He had come to Jamaica knowing something of the risks. Six years before the *Kingston*'s voyage, in 1726, Rear-Admiral Francis Hosier had led a naval squadron of 4750 men out of Portsmouth to intercept Spanish treasure ships in the West Indies. Yellow fever killed him in Jamaica within a year, along with four thousand of his men.[15] British newspapers, folk tales and ballads ensured that this disaster was widely known, especially in Milbourne's home town of Portsmouth, so joining a ship bound for the Caribbean was a calculated gamble on his part. In 1732 he was twenty-two and single, with no formal education or means of support except his own skills. The *Kingston*, with its sixty guns, was the flagship of Commodore Richard Lestock, who would soon be replaced by Admiral Sir Chaloner Ogle. Joining it as a carpenter's mate gave Milbourne more wages and status than were available on voyages and in shipyards nearer home, a chance of attracting the attention of influential patrons in the navy, and passage to a frontier society where poor whites could sometimes encounter greater opportunities, if they survived.

That Milbourne Marsh did so, and lived to father Elizabeth Marsh, was a function not simply of luck, but also of his persistent intelligence and confidence, and his specific skills. A carpenter aboard a Royal Navy warship was a warrant sea officer. Like his fellow warrant officers, the gunner and the boatswain, he was not regarded – as fighting sea officers usually were – as a gentleman. Ships' carpenters were not granted a formal navy uniform until the end of the eighteenth century, and they did not expect to dine at the captain's table or in the wardroom. They were specialist craftsmen with a distinctive role aboard ship, and a recognized status. Even a carpenter's mate was treated as roughly on a par with a midshipman, the apprentice rank for commissioned officers. 'The carpenter', declared the navy's printed regulations at this time:

> is to take upon himself the care and preservation of the ship's hull, masts, yards, bulkheads, and cabins, etc and to receive into his charge the sea stores committed to him by indenture from the Surveyor of the Navy. At sea, he is to visit daily all the parts of the ship, and see if the ports are well secured, and decks and sides be well caulked, and whether any thing gives way; and if the pumps are in good order; and from time to time to inspect into the condition of the masts and yards, and to make a report of every thing to the Captain.[16]

The ability to carry out these duties efficiently was especially valued in the Caribbean. Even after hulls began to be sheathed in copper, wooden ships rarely lasted in these warm, stormy, worm-ridden waters for more than three years, and constant maintenance was required to keep them seaworthy even for this long. Consequently, Milbourne Marsh's skills assured him a particular status here, and he seems consciously to have exploited this in order to advance and stay alive. In January 1733 he abandoned the fever-stricken *Kingston* to replace a dead man as ship's carpenter on the *Deal Castle*. The move increased his workload, since this new vessel was a modest twenty-four-gun frigate with a smaller crew to share the tasks of maintenance and sailing, but it gained him promotion, higher wages, and for a while a healthier working environment. In August, when crewmen were being taken off the *Deal Castle* to join an expedition against rebel slaves, Milbourne promptly switched ships again, moving this time to be carpenter of the *Rupert*, a veteran 930-ton warship with a crew of 350.[17]

Unlike most men at sea, a ship's carpenter was not woken up every four hours at night to stand watch. Nor did he usually have to snap to attention when 'All hands on deck' was piped. So although his was an arduous, often dangerous job, frequently carried out in the rigging fifty to seventy feet above deck, Milbourne Marsh experienced a better working life off Jamaica than many of his comrades. He was more rested and less stressed, and he would have been buoyed up by a consciousness of his modest indispensability. Once on the *Rupert*, he spent most of the next nineteen months at sea, and therefore less at risk of disease, but never straying out of the Caribbean, and returning at regular intervals to Port Royal, something that had begun to be important.

The name she went by was Elizabeth Evans, and he claimed later that she was about one year younger than himself. She had been an Elizabeth Bouchier, and living as a single woman in Port Royal, when she met and married James Evans in 1728.[18] Evans was another migrant, possibly Pennsylvanian by origin, and worked part-time as a shipwright on the Royal Navy vessels anchoring off the port. Milbourne Marsh and Elizabeth Evans appear to have known each other well before August 1734, because it was in this month that Evans made his will. For a man of his sort, this was an atypical act. Since death snatched Jamaicans so quickly, most died intestate; and white craftsmen and artisans only occasionally went to the expense of setting out their final dispensations and opinions in legal script. Evans, though, whose signature on the will, and the 'few old books' he left behind, reveal a certain level of literacy, chose to have this final say, this last exercise of power. Mindful of the 'peril & dangers of the sea and other uncertainties of this transitory life', he declared, he wanted to make his wishes known 'for the sake of avoiding controversies after my decease'.[19] As well as these formulaic pieties, he also had something substantial to leave; and someone, and perhaps two people, to accuse.

James Evans had prospered in Jamaica. He had obtained a licence 'to sell and retail wine, beer, ale or other strong liquor' in the house he rented in Port Royal.[20] Judging by the inventory, this drink shop was a modest establishment, with six old tables, each equipped with a candlestick, seating for eighteen, a spittoon, a close stool, and little else in its interior except a chest and a corner cupboard, and some beds (the establishment may have doubled as a brothel). But, together with the wherry he owned and rented out to the Royal Navy, the business had allowed Evans and his wife to live in modest style. They owned 'a new feather bed & pillows', pewter-ware, supplies of fine linen – and at least nine adult slaves. As was customary in slaveholding systems throughout the world, these people had been given new names so as to erase their pre-slave selves and re-inscribe them as property. For his female slaves, Evans had selected mock-classical names that bear witness again to his literacy, and to its limits. There was 'Cresia' and her two 'pickaninnys', and 'Palla' (Pallas?) and her child, and Venus and Silvia, who all worked in one capacity or another in the drink shop. Since Evans used his male slaves to crew his wherry, and rented them out to the navy as dock labourers and caulkers, they were named in more practical, masculine style. As with his women slaves, however, Evans gave them single names, not multiple names like white people. He called them 'Plymouth', or 'Gosport', or 'Bristol', or after other British ports, as if they were horses or pet animals, not human beings.[21]

By Jamaican standards, this level of slave-ownership on the part of a skilled craftsman was not unusual. The 157 inhabitants of Port Royal who were registered as slave-owners in 1738 laid claim on average to nine slaves apiece.[22] But to Milbourne Marsh, an English incomer with no property beyond the contents of his sea-chest, the sight of this level of affluence in a fellow shipwright must have been startling, and it is unlikely that it was merely physical and emotional attraction that drew him initially to James Evans' wife.

Evans took his meagre revenge, as he would have seen it, in his will. His still 'beloved wife Elizabeth Evans', he stipulated, was to inherit all of his estate, including 'all negroes', but with a single exception. One of the household's male slaves was to be given up, and shipped off in perpetuity to an Evans family member in Philadelphia. The slave who was to be sent away, James Evans specified, was 'one negro man named *Marsh*'. No individual of that name is included in the inventory of Evans' estate, which lists all of his slaves. He seems to have inserted this provision about a 'negro man named Marsh' in his will as a calculated, posthumous insult to an interloping Englishman named Milbourne Marsh, and perhaps also as a glancing verbal slight aimed against his own wife. By the end of the year, for whatever reason, James Evans was dead, leaving behind goods and human chattels valued in his inventory at more than £625. On 12 December 1734, the day after Elizabeth Evans was formally granted permission 'to take into her possession and to administer' all of her late husband's property, she married

Milbourne in Kingston's Anglican church.[23] By January 1735, she was pregnant.

Who was she, this woman Milbourne Marsh took to wife? And how had she come to be in Port Royal before marrying her first husband in 1728? The name 'Elizabeth Bouchier' does not appear in lists of indentured servants and convicts from Britain coming to Jamaica around this time, though this does not prove she was not amongst them.[24] Nor can she be conclusively identified from the surviving Jamaican parish registers – but then, these too are incomplete documents. No record of baptisms for Port Royal seems to have survived, for instance, earlier than 1722. More unusually, the Family Book that was compiled much later by Milbourne Marsh's younger brother, George Marsh, yields no information about this woman. It was George Marsh's custom, after introducing individual family members in the Book, to allocate a brief sentence to their spouses, especially if this could illustrate his clan's respectability and upward mobility. Thus, while he set down his cousin Warren's wife as 'a very bad woman', he was much more concerned to record how his own father had married 'the best of women', and how his niece Margaret Duval's husband was a 'most worthy sensible good man', and so forth. In the paragraphs of the Family Book he devoted to Milbourne Marsh, however, the relevant sentences where a judgement on his elder brother's spouse might have been expected have been inked out.[25] The Marsh family's surviving correspondence also reveals nothing about this woman, and only very occasionally acknowledges her existence. Virtually the only extant formal record of the Elizabeth Bouchier who became first Elizabeth Evans and then Elizabeth Marsh, after her brief appearance in Kingston's marriage register, is her (now removed) memorial tablet in a church in Chatham, Kent. 'She was', Milbourne Marsh had engraved there, 'a good Christian wife and mother.' But after this careful testimonial, he supplied no details of her parentage or place of origin.[26]

She remains a question mark in this story, therefore, but there are at least two possible answers. A widow called Margaret *Boucher* is listed in the Port Royal vestry minutes as living in a rented house in the town in the late 1730s, and as in receipt of occasional charity. Given the casualness with which surnames, especially those of the poor, were recorded at this time, Milbourne Marsh's new wife may have been this woman's daughter. If so, she was white or passed for such, since Margaret Boucher's name is included in 'A List of the white inhabitants of this parish' compiled in Port Royal in 1738.[27] If this particular 'Margaret Boucher' was her widowed mother, the woman who had once gone under the name of Elizabeth Bouchier clearly left her behind in Jamaica when she escaped to England in 1735, and she made no effort to perpetuate Margaret Boucher's first name when she came to christen her own daughter.

There is however another possibility. There were Bourchiers – and not just Bouchers – resident in Jamaica at this time. The former, whose surname was also spelt in various ways and who seem to have arrived on the island in the 1660s, were planters. If she did possess some blood relationship with this family, the woman who went on to become Elizabeth Marsh's mother is unlikely to have been a legitimate child. Daughters of Caribbean planters born in wedlock did not customarily go on to marry shipwrights. She might conceivably have been a mulatto, the mixed-race, possibly christened child of a white landowner – perhaps Charles Bourchier, who died in 1726 – and an African slave mother.[28] Or there may have been no blood relationship, just a plantation past at some point. Manumitted slaves in Jamaica sometimes took and kept the surnames of their former owners.

It was widely believed that incoming mariners established easier, more equal relations with members of Jamaica's black and mulatto population than most of the island's white residents were willing or able to do. 'Sailors and negroes are ever on the most amicable terms,' a one-time resident in Jamaica wrote later:

This is evidenced in their dealings, and in the mutual confidence and familiarity that never subsist between the slaves
and the resident whites. There is a feeling of independence
in their intercourse with the sailor, that is otherwise bound
up in the consciousness of a bitter restraint ... In the
presence of the sailor, the Negro feels as a man.[29]

This was an overly sentimental verdict. At least one of the reasons
for incoming British sailors cultivating members of Jamaica's black
population was crudely exploitative: the number of single white
women in the island's port towns who were of artisan or servant
status, and therefore potentially available as seamen's companions,
was very limited.

Nonetheless, this kind of socializing rested on more than sex,
money and loneliness. Visiting sailors and blacks tended to come
together on this and other Caribbean islands because they shared
a consciousness of difference. If blacks and mulattos were divided
from Creole settlers by their skin colour, culture of origin, belief
systems and, usually, their un-freedom, sailors too were a people
apart, 'a generation differing from all the world'.[30] Tanned, often
with long pigtails and amateurish 'tattoos' made with ink or
gunpowder, markedly agile, and frequently mutilated in some
way, sailors looked very different from men who spent all their
lives on land. They walked, moved and dressed differently. They
possessed, like Jamaica's black population, their own distinct voca-
bularies, songs and magical beliefs; and crucially they were transi-
ents, men who had left home, family and country, or been torn
away from them by press gangs. That they should sometimes have
gravitated towards men and women who had also been snatched,
even more brutally, from their homelands, was scarcely surprising.
In Kingston parish, where Milbourne Marsh married Elizabeth
Evans in December 1734, two graveyards 'to the westward and
leeward of the town' were reserved for 'free people of colour' on
the one hand, and for 'soldiers, seamen, and transient people of
every description' on the other.[31] Even in death, mariners, mulattos

and blacks might be set apart from everyone else, and placed together.

They also came together at sea. Rather like Jamaica itself, the Royal Navy was at once violent, dangerous, cosmopolitan and innovating: 'a new kind of power, which must change the face of the globe'.[32] Some of the most complex and expensive machines of their age, the navy's ships were relatively tolerant and – to a controlled degree – even meritocratic spaces. The skills involved in maintaining and sailing these vessels were so specialized, and in such high demand, that possessing them could sometimes trump a man's skin colour, just as it often trumped social class.[33] Like most navy men, Milbourne Marsh was accustomed to working alongside sailors who were free blacks. Such men enjoyed the same rights and earned the same wages as their white counterparts. In the Caribbean, the navy also employed black slave seamen, who did the same job as equivalent whites and free blacks, and worked and lived alongside them, but whose wages were paid to their owners. This was the case with a close comrade of Milbourne's, John Cudjoe. He worked as one of the two servants allowed Milbourne in his capacity as ship's carpenter: 'servant' in this context meaning an apprentice under training. Both servants earned the same wage, just under £14 per annum on top of their keep, but in Cudjoe's case the money went to his owner, a Jamaican settler. Both men shared quarters with Milbourne and worked with him on a daily basis; and when the latter moved from the *Deal Castle* to the *Rupert* in August 1733, John Cudjoe went with him.[34]

So while, in his choice of a wife, Milbourne Marsh was evidently willing to profit from slave-ownership, he also took daily, comradely contact across racial lines for granted. Whether he also knowingly crossed racial lines in marrying Elizabeth Evans, and whether this contributed to the Marsh family's subsequent documentary reticence about this woman, will probably never be known. Biography, it has been said, is like a net that catches and brings to the surface an individual life. But a net is only a set of holes tied together by string, so some things slip through. There are always life-parts, and body-parts, that get lost, and the birth identity of Elizabeth Marsh's mother is one of these.[35] As far as she herself is concerned, attempting to establish her precise ethnic origins may be more than usually inappropriate. In 1733, Jamaica's governing assembly passed a law stipulating that 'no one shall be deemed a mulatto after the third generation . . . but . . . shall have all the privileges and immunities of His Majesty's white subjects of this island provided they are brought up in the Christian religion', a belated recognition of the extent of miscegenation, and of its muddled human consequences.[36]

So, even if she was mixed race in terms of her origins, the one-time Elizabeth Bouchier may have seen herself, even before her two marriages, as a person undergoing change and flux, beyond easy categorization. 'The fiction of the census', Benedict Anderson has written of present-day attempts to fix a person's identity, 'is that everyone is in it, and that everyone has one – and only one – extremely clear place. No fractions.'[37] Elizabeth Marsh, brand-new wife of Milbourne Marsh, may have been a person of fractions. For a variety of reasons, her daughter, another Elizabeth Marsh, also seems at times to have viewed herself in these terms; and in her case, the fact that one of these fractions *may* have been linked in some manner with slavery will need at intervals to be borne in mind.

In 1735, Milbourne Marsh, his new bride and their unborn child had first to survive. Jamaica's parish registers suggest that a quarter to a third of white children born on the island at this time perished before their first birthday. James and Elizabeth Evans appear themselves to have buried a child in Port Royal in 1730, a daughter who can have been at most barely one year old. But Jamaican parish documents severely understated the volume of infant mortality. Vicars charged money to register baptisms, and parents often held off from making the monetary and emotional investment until a child had survived for several months. Many died earlier than this, and were buried unchristened and unrecorded. Among the children of black slaves, death in the early weeks and months of life was common, and on some plantations may have been the norm. Even if a child survived until its third decade, it was unlikely that both parents would see it do so. Jamaican marriages lasted on average less than nine years before being broken by the death of one or both partners. For a child to reach full maturity, and for its mother and father still to be around to witness this, was exceptional even among the very wealthy.[38] What prospects then – for all his newly acquired property – could there be for Milbourne Marsh, a working sailor at risk from the sea as well as from Jamaica? And what prospects could there be for his new wife, Elizabeth, who had already lost a child?

Their private fears of death, which determined so much on Jamaica, were sharpened by mounting racial unrest. Running away and forming armed communities in the island's rugged mountains was one of the oldest forms of slave resistance. By the early 1730s, these maroons – as the runaways were termed – had become so numerous, and sufficiently organized, for its continuance as a colony to seem at risk. Jamaica was some thousand miles distant from Britain's other Caribbean islands, but dangerously close to Spanish Cuba and French St Domingue. This was one reason why the *Kingston* and the *Rupert*, and by 1735 nineteen other Royal Navy warships, were patrolling the Caribbean. But the navy exercised limited power over Jamaica's interior, and – as was nearly always the case – the number of British soldiers available was painfully small. The island's governing assembly and plantocracy had therefore dual reasons for alarm. 'The terror of them spreads itself every where,' Jamaica's Governor, Council and Assembly reported to London of the maroons in February 1734. Their military successes had exerted 'such influence on our other slaves, that they are continually deserting'. 'Hopes of freedom' were even shaking 'the fidelity of our most trusty slaves'.[39] If this level of slave flight were to persist, and if slave anger mutated into large-scale violent resistance, the sugar industry might falter and white settlers might be tempted to abandon the island. In that event, the French or the Spanish, or both, might invade.

Milbourne Marsh experienced some of the consequences of growing panic among Jamaica's whites at first hand. Several of his former shipmates on the *Kingston* and the *Deal Castle* were swept into fighting the maroons on shore, and on 10 October 1734 John Cudjoe was taken off the *Rupert* at his owner's request. Slave escapes had reached such levels by now that Cudjoe's owner may have wanted him under her surveillance, or she may simply have been desperate for his labour. The fact that Milbourne's former servant shared his Akan surname, which means 'male born on Monday', with one of the most prominent maroon chieftains, Cudjoe, who would force the British to a treaty in 1739, may also have provoked superstitious unease and hostility aboard the *Rupert* itself.[40] During this same month, October 1734, martial law was declared on Jamaica. Six hundred additional men were raised from its parishes to serve as militia, and London shipped out six new military companies to aid them. By now, Milbourne was closely involved with Elizabeth Evans. Their marriage that December, the certainty by February 1735 that a child was on the way, and mounting fears among Jamaica's whites that 'We cannot say we are sure of a other day,' made them determined to get out.[41]

Milbourne Marsh acted with his customary efficiency. On 7 March the *Kingston* arrived at Port Royal and began lengthy preparations for its voyage back to England. By 10 March, Milbourne had signed on again with his old ship, where he retained friends and patrons. He seems to have sold, or given over his rights in, the drink shop at Port Royal and the wherry to a naval official there. It is possible, though not proven, that he sold the slaves, Palla, Cresia, Silvia, Gosport and the rest, to the Royal Navy, which employed both male and female slaves in its Jamaican dock-yards. This indeed may have been how he funded his new wife's passage to England.[42] Certainly, her escape from the island was aided by Milbourne's own specialized skills. On paper, Royal Navy warships were exclusively masculine spaces, but women who posed no obvious sexual temptation were sometimes permitted to sail on them, especially if their responsible male possessed leverage of some kind. When the *Kingston* left Jamaica that June, Elizabeth Marsh senior was six months pregnant, and she was the wife of one of the ship's most indispensable craftsmen. Twice married to a mariner, she also understood what was expected of her. She seems to have made private arrangements for her food with the *Kingston*'s purser so as to keep clear of the ship's formal accounting system, and she would probably have spent the days of the voyage resting her growing bulk on the orlop deck, the quietest, darkest and most secluded space aboard.[43] It was on 20 August 1735 that they sailed into Portsmouth harbour, barely a month before the birth of their daughter.

Such time as this new Elizabeth Marsh spent on dry land during her first nineteen years was mainly lived here, at Portsmouth. The family found lodgings in the New Buildings, a recent development of austere workingmen's houses in what was then the northern end of Portsea Island. It was only a short walk from here to St Thomas, the medieval church on Portsmouth's High Street where Elizabeth Marsh was christened on 3 October 1735.[44]

The New Buildings gave Milbourne Marsh easy access to his work. The development had been constructed with public money just outside the walls of Portsmouth's naval dockyard, so that shipwrights and other workers could arrive punctually for their thirteen-hour day. Although he worked sometimes in the dockyard, and sometimes at sea, Milbourne organized his life so as to spend as much time as possible with his family. He deployed his customary tactic of using his specialized skills to lever himself into a new job whenever the current one became inconvenient. In September 1735, the month he became a father, he abandoned the *Kingston* and, armed with a recommendation from Admiral Sir Chaloner Ogle, moved back as a ship's carpenter on the *Deal Castle*. The latter was classed only as a sixth-rate warship, and therefore unlikely to be sent into the thick of battle in the event of war. Small vessels like this could still however be dispatched on missions in foreign waters; and when the *Deal Castle* was ordered to South Carolina in 1739, Milbourne jumped ship again. He took himself off to the *Cambridge*, an eighty-gun warship undergoing conveniently lengthy repairs in Portsmouth harbour.[45]

Partly as a result of her father's ingenuity, these early years in Portsmouth were the most stable of Elizabeth Marsh's life. Yet, for all that this was a far more secure and healthy environment, Portsmouth shared certain important characteristics with Jamaica. It was vitally involved in empire and organized violence; it was a place of pioneering industrialization; and it was markedly cosmo-politan, and caught up in intercontinental trade and migration. Not for nothing was Portsmouth sometimes described – and sometimes condemned – as England's equivalent to Port Royal before the earthquake: 'If that was Sodom, this is Gomorrah.'[46]

At first sight, the town appeared an ancient, walled place of some six hundred houses, occupying part of the island of Portsea, and linked to the mainland by a system of gates and bridges. But the gates and bridges were closely guarded, because Portsmouth was Britain's premier military town, and the Royal Navy's main operational base and dockyard. There were six naval dockyards in England at this time, all of them situated along its southern coast. On the Thames there were Deptford and Woolwich, both small dockyards. At the mouth of the Medway in Kent there was Sheerness, and twelve miles up the river the much bigger yard of Chatham. Then there were the so-called western dockyards, Plymouth and Portsmouth. By the 1730s, the latter had overtaken Chatham as the most important.[47] Hidden behind high walls, inconspicuous to casual travellers arriving by road, Portsmouth looked utterly different when approached from the sea:

> A spacious harbour, and the great ships lying at their moorings for three or four miles up, and the harbour for a mile at least on each side covered with buildings and thronged with people; the water covered with boats passing and repassing like as on the Thames . . . The prospect from the middle of the harbour gives you the idea of a great city.[48]

The dockyard's specialized warehouses and rope-, mast- and rigging-houses were some of the biggest, most expensive constructions of the time dedicated to secular purposes. Almost 2200 skilled workmen were employed here in 1735, who were divided into twenty-three different categories, and tolled into work at morning and out at night by bells. A further 259 men were attached to the dockyard's ropeyard. In what was still a primarily agricultural economy, this represented an extraordinary concentration of labour. Even a hundred years after this, it was still rare for industrial establishments anywhere in the world to employ more than five hundred men.[49]

Surrounded by sea, but always short of fresh water, wreathed in coal smoke from the dockyard's many forges, and full of the noise of metal on wood, Portsmouth, then, was a prime site of state power and imperial projection. But, as indicated by the pair of seven-foot-high dragon-headed pagodas from China erected by its dockyard in the 1740s, and by the mixture of coins and languages in use in its streets, the town was also a magnet for outsiders and alien influences. Portsmouth was where most foreign diplomats made landfall in Britain before taking the London road to present their credentials at court. It was the main British depot outside of London of the East India Company. Ships from Calcutta, Madras, Bombay and Canton unloaded textiles, spices and ceramics in Portsmouth, as well as passengers and occasional Asian seamen. This was also a garrison town, and companies of soldiers marched through it en route for, or returning from, overseas expeditions;

'The West Prospect of Portsmouth, in Hamp-Shire'. Engraving by Samuel and Nathaniel Buck, 1749. Note, on the right, the black cabin-boy, and the steeple of St Thomas church, where Elizabeth Marsh was christened in 1735.

and Portsmouth was a commercial port as well as a naval base. There were Arab traders arriving from the Levant, seamen and fish-dealers from Hudson's Bay and New England, Baltic suppliers catering to the Royal Navy's ceaseless appetite for timber, so-called 'Port Jews' eschewing the distinctive life of their people in order to trade and lend money, and smugglers from nowhere in particular.[50]

Elizabeth Marsh's early exposure in Portsmouth to the sights and sounds of difference and diversity, and simultaneously to the Royal Navy and to the force of the British state, has to be factored in if we are to understand how she came to be the person she was,

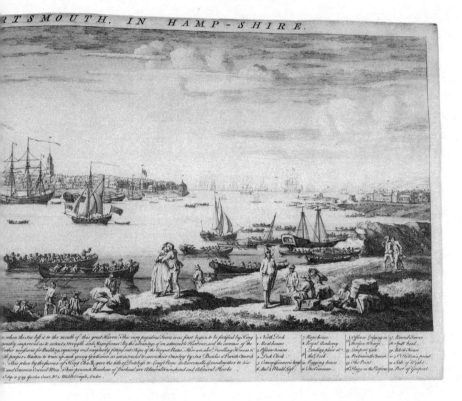

and to lead the life that she did. But she was also shaped of course by her family. 'I was the daughter of a gentleman,' she once wrote.[51] The truth was more interesting.

While almost everything about her mother remains unclear, her father's background is remarkably well documented. Milbourne Marsh had been christened in St Thomas church in Portsmouth in October 1709. *His* father, George Marsh (b.1683), was also a ship's carpenter with the Royal Navy, which was typical enough, since shipbuilding was a closely guarded trade, customarily passed on through the males of a family over generations. Milbourne's mother, who was born Elizabeth Milbourne in 1687, possessed her own link to the maritime, though a significantly different one. Her father, John Milbourne, 'an excellent pen man', was employed after

1713 as clerk to Sir Isaac Townsend, the Resident Commissioner at Portsmouth naval dockyard.[52]

This blood connection with someone who worked with pen and paper was important, and the careful perpetuation of his mother's surname in Milbourne Marsh's own first name shows that his family was well aware of this. Both of Milbourne's parents were literate, and both took pleasure in using words. As would be true of Elizabeth Marsh, they were compulsive storytellers. From his father, George Marsh, Milbourne heard tales about his grandfather, yet another mariner, called Francis Marsh. On a voyage from Lisbon back to Southampton in the early 1690s, this particular Marsh was wrecked off the Isle of Wight. 'The ship and everything in it but himself were lost,' but Francis Marsh – or so Milbourne and his siblings were told – plunged into the sea with his banknotes and valuable papers wrapped up in an 'oil skin bag', together with 'a small family bible, not above 7 inches long, 4 or 5 inches broad and about 1 inch and a half thick', and was 'miraculously saved on shore on the beach'. Milbourne's mother's favourite tales were of her grandfather, a Northumberland-based dealer in Scottish cattle called John Milbourne. In May 1650, she claimed, he had risked his life hiding the Scottish royalist hero James Graham, 1st Marquess of Montrose, when he was on the run from the Scottish Covenanters who were allies of Parliament. Only when Montrose left this plain man's sanctuary, and went seeking help from a nearby landowner, was he betrayed and handed over to his enemies and execution.

Tokens of these and other past family dramas were carefully preserved. George Marsh senior and his wife kept a print of the Marquess of Montrose on a wall in every lodging house they occupied. As for Francis Marsh's providential Bible and prayer book, what passes for this volume still exists today, its battered pages bearing annotations by one of George Marsh senior's sons. The content of these family legends, and the tenacity with which they were held, suggest the eagerness of Marsh family members to

The sea, mobility and Providence: page from the Marsh family Bible
detailing Francis Marsh's escape from drowning *c.*1694.

view themselves as something more than mere skilled artisans.
Milbourne Marsh and his siblings were brought up on 'a slender
income by good management and prudence', but the stories he
and they listened to, and that he passed on in turn to his own
daughter, Elizabeth Marsh, evoked a rather different status. God,
these family romances proclaimed, had intervened to preserve one
of their ancestors by a 'wonderful deliverance'. Yet another ancestor
had performed an act of signal service to the cause of Britain's
monarchy. Moreover, as Milbourne Marsh's mother told her children by way of other stories, they should rightfully have been rich.
Her father John Milbourne, she insisted, 'a fine handsome person,

a good scholar and of great abilities', had once owned a colliery in Northumberland and was 'highly esteemed by the nobility and gentry of the county'. But he lost some of his money to a nobleman (worthless aristocrats are a recurring motif in Marsh family sagas), and his housekeeper subsequently cheated her way into his bed, faked his will, and 'got possession of the whole fortune'.[53]

The moral that family members were encouraged to draw from these stories – and Elizabeth Marsh certainly grew up believing this – was that they were marked out in some fashion, and deserving of more than their immediate, circumscribed surroundings and conditions of life. The stories also reveal something else about how she grew up. Contrary to what is sometimes assumed, long-distance migration was not an aspect of the coming of modernity. Frequently, it was a practice that was learnt and adopted by a family's members over successive generations, and that often increased in scale and duration in the process. Elizabeth Marsh's restlessness, it is clear, was in part an inherited trait. Her father Milbourne Marsh took ship to the Caribbean, but his forebears were also sailors and migrants. His father and grandfather were mariners familiar with European waters. His mother's family moved between northern England and Scotland, and then down to southern England. And whether Elizabeth's own mother's roots lay in West Africa or in England, she too must have been of voluntary or involuntary migrant stock, before sailing herself across the Atlantic to England in 1735.

From Milbourne Marsh's family – and perhaps from her mother's – Elizabeth Marsh also inherited good looks and physical toughness. Milbourne's father, George Marsh senior, was described as a 'remarkable fine person', 'upwards of six feet high . . . very upright and well proportioned, [and] amazingly strong and healthy'. Although the Navy Board awarded him a pension in the mid-1740s, he seems to have continued working part-time as a shipwright, and was seventy when he was killed in an industrial accident in 1753.[54] Married in 1707, he and Elizabeth Milbourne produced nine children and, unusually for their time and social level, eight of them reached adulthood. What were then untreatable diseases, and maritime accidents, killed off five of these Marsh progeny before they reached the age of forty, but the life spans of the remaining three confirm a family tendency towards physical vigour and good health. Milbourne Marsh (b.1709) lived to be almost seventy; George Marsh the younger (b.1722) made seventy-eight; while their sister Mary Marsh (b.1712) reached her eighties. It is striking too how, in different ways, and in conformity with the family's stock of stories, all three of these longer-lived Marsh siblings constructed for themselves richer, more varied existences than their parents. Even Mary Marsh's life, hampered by her gender, illustrates this. Once in her teens, she went to London to find work, and married a French Huguenot, Jean Duval. He worked as a baker in Spitalfields, a once semi-rural suburb in the east of London that has always attracted a disproportionate number of refugees and immigrants. This alliance with a family of French origins, attached to another form of Protestantism, made more than Mary's own life more diverse. Visits to aunt Mary and uncle Duval in London in the 1740s and early '50s seem to have allowed Elizabeth Marsh to learn to speak and read French, one of the prime accomplishments that normally connoted gentility.[55]

The 'industrious revolution', as the marked changes in family aspirations at this time have been called, a rising level, throughout Europe and North America and possibly beyond, of individual and clan desire, expectations, and household expenditure, also affected Milbourne Marsh, and to a more spectacular degree his brother, George Marsh the younger.[56] The temperaments and changing fortunes of these two men, Elizabeth Marsh's father and her uncle, are important because both men played crucial roles in her development, influencing what she came to be, and what she came to do.

Like most mariners in the age of sail, Milbourne Marsh had gone to sea very early. He recalled in middle age how, when just eleven years old and already sailing the Mediterranean, he was regularly handling explosives. He would be sent on shore from whatever vessel he was on at the time, and ordered to blow up rocks into small stones so as to provide ballast for the ship's hold.[57] Yet to view him simply as a manual labourer would be quite wrong. Thomas Rowlandson's sensitive study of a ship's carpenter was made more than a decade after Milbourne's death, but the tools the artist gives his figure – an adze in one hand and a drawing instrument in the other – accurately convey the occupation's composite quality. As suggested by the adze (an axe with a curved blade), it involved hard physical effort. Timber had to be cut to size, a ship's rotten wood and any cannon shot embedded in it cut out and made good. As indicated by the drawing instrument, however, this was only part of the job. Milbourne was fully literate, and he had to be. A ship's carpenter was expected to write 'an exact and particular account' of his vessel's condition and propose solutions to any defects. He needed to know basic accounting so as to estimate the cost of repairs, and keep check of his stocks of timber and other stores. And he required mathematical and geometrical skills: enough to draw plans, calculate the height of a mast from the deck, and estimate the weight of anchors and what thickness of timber was required to support them.[58]

Looked at this way, it becomes easier to understand why the foremost English shipwright of the late seventeenth century, Anthony Deane (c.1638–1720), was knighted and made a Fellow of the Royal Society. Because of increased transoceanic trade, expanding empire, the growth of European and of some non-European fighting navies, and recurrent warfare, skills of the sort that Milbourne Marsh commanded were in urgent national and international demand. Not for nothing do we refer today to 'navigating' and 'surfing' the web. Rather like cyberspace now, the sea in Milbourne Marsh's time was the vital gateway to a more interconnected world. Consequently, those in possession of the more specialist maritime skills were in a position to rise economically, and often socially as well. 'The Ship-Carpenter . . . to become master of his business must learn the theory as well as practice,' Britain's most widely read trade directory insisted in 1747: 'it is a business that one seldom wants bread in, either at home or abroad.'[59]

The nature of her father's occupation was of central importance in Elizabeth Marsh's life. At one level, and along with her many other seafaring relations, Milbourne Marsh gave her access to one of the few eighteenth-century organizations genuinely possessed of something approaching global reach: the Royal Navy. This proved vital to her ability to travel. Long-distance oceanic journeying was expensive, but over the years Elizabeth's family connections repeatedly secured her free or cheap passage on various navy vessels. She also gained, by way of these maritime menfolk, a network of contacts that stretched across oceans: in effect two extended families, her own, and the navy itself. 'A visit from Mr. Panton, the 1st Lieutenant of the *Salisbury*,' she would record while sailing off the eastern coast of the Indian subcontinent in 1775: 'he seemed well acquainted with most of my family.'[60]

But her father's occupation also impacted on her in less enabling ways. It is conceivable that she grew up aware that her mother was different in some manner, or looked at askance by her relations. She certainly seems to have been perpetually insecure about her own and her family's social position. Milbourne Marsh was from a self-regarding maritime dynasty that encouraged ambition, and he was a master craftsman in a global trade; but his was still an interstitial, sometimes vulnerable existence, lived out between the land and the sea, and between the labouring masses on the one hand, and the officer class on the other. Some of the tensions that could ensue can be seen in two crises that threatened for a while to engulf them all.

In April 1741, six of Milbourne's workmen in Portsmouth dockyard sent a letter to its Commissioner accusing the carpenter of embezzlement. He had kept back new beds and bedding intended for his current ship, the *Cambridge*, his accusers claimed, and arranged for them to be smuggled out of the yard at midday, 'when all the people belonging thereto are absent'. He had used naval timber to make window shutters, chimneypieces, and even palisades. Milbourne's joiner reported that he had seen 'the outlines of the head of one [a palisade] drew with a black lead pencil on a small piece of board' on his desk, 'which he verily believes was intended for a pattern or mould'. Another of Milbourne's accusers told of being ordered to chop up good oak for firewood, and how he had carried the sticks out of the dockyard to the Marsh family's lodgings in the New Buildings, where the carpenter 'was in company the whole time'.[61]

Charges of embezzlement, if proved, normally brought instant dismissal from a navy dockyard. Milbourne Marsh retained his post and livelihood not because his excuses convinced (they were judged 'indifferent'), but because his superiors recognized his ability ('the carpenter bears the character of a good officer'). It is the private man and the family's lifestyle, though, which emerge most sharply from this incident. The workmen's resentment at Milbourne's efforts to add some distinction and ornament to his family's stark lodgings (and perhaps also to make extra money from selling illicitly-constructed window shutters, etc.), like their scorn for his small attempts at a social life ('in company the whole time'), and their determination to inform against him in the first place are suggestive. These things point to a man and a family visibly getting above themselves and their surroundings, experiencing industrious revolution, and consequently arousing envy. Milbourne's shuddering answer to his workmen's accusations confirms this, while also showing how entangled he necessarily still was in deference:

> Honourable Sir the whole being a premeditated thing to do me prejudice, for my using of them ill (as they term it) in making them do their duty. Hope you look on it as such, as will appear by my former behaviour and time to come.[62]

He was literate enough to know how to use the word 'premeditated', but his syntax was not, could not be, that of a formally educated man, and he was naturally terrified of dismissal. Even more revealing is his explanation of why exactly he had defied regulations and commandeered the navy's bedding:

> My wife having been sick on board [the *Cambridge*] for five weeks, and no probability of getting her ashore, [I] thought it not fit to lie on my bed till I had got it washed & well cleaned, so got the above bedding to lie on till my own was fit.[63]

So it was not just Milbourne Marsh who was amphibious, dividing his time between the sea and the land. His wife, and therefore presumably their five-year-old daughter also, were caught up in this way of living too. Already, Elizabeth Marsh was travelling.

Milbourne's wife and child – soon children – were also caught up in fears for his survival, and therefore for their own. He fought in only one sea battle during his career, but it was a major one. In 1742 he was sent to the Mediterranean. Based first on the *Marlborough* and then on the *Namur*, a ninety-gun second rate and the flagship of Admiral Thomas Mathews, Milbourne Marsh also worked on the thirty-odd other warships in Britain's Mediterranean fleet, dealing with day-to-day repairs as they waited for the combined Franco-Spanish fleet to emerge from Toulon, France's premier naval base, and fight.[64] It is not clear whether any of his family accompanied him, or if they waited throughout in Portsmouth, or London, or with his parents who were now in Chatham, Kent. What *is* known, because Milbourne Marsh later gave evidence to a naval court martial, is that on 11 February 1744, for the first and only time in his life, he saw action.

'I can tell you, exactly to a minute, the time we fired the first gun,' he would tell the court, for '. . . I immediately whip'd my watch out of my pocket, and it was then 10 minutes after one o'clock to a moment.' The enemy vessel that the 780-man crew of the *Namur* engaged was the *Real*, the 114-gun Spanish flagship and part of a twenty-seven-ship Franco-Spanish fleet. Initially, Milbourne the specialist was allowed to experience the battle below deck. Once the *Namur* started sustaining damage, however, his skills drove him above: 'The Admiral sent for me up, and ordered me to see what was the matter with the mizzen topmast' – that is, the mast nearest the ship's stern. He had to climb it, and then the main mast, under fire throughout, for the *Real* was only 'a pistol-shot' away from them. Milbourne's breathless account of what happened next is misted by nautical phraseology, but conveys something of what it was like to clamber across the rigging of a sailing ship under fire, and how difficult it was to make sense of a sea battle as it was happening:

> At the same time I acquainted the Admiral of the main top mast, I was told, but by whom I can't tell, that the starboard main yard arm was shot. I looked up, and saw it, from the quarter deck; I went to go up the starboard shrouds to view it; I found several of the shrouds were shot, which made me quit that side, and I went up on the larboard side, and went across the main yard in the slings, out to the yard arm, and I found just within the lift block on the under side, a shot had grazed a slant ... when I went down, I did not immediately acquaint the Admiral with that, for by that time I had got upon the gangway, I was told that the bowsprit was shot, and immediately that the fore top mast was shot.[65]

In strategic and naval terms, the Battle of Toulon proved an embarrassment for the British. For reasons that provoked furious controversy at the time and are still debated now, many of the Royal Navy ships present did not engage. The damage to the *Namur*'s masts and rigging, which Milbourne tried so desperately to monitor, persuaded Admiral Mathews to withdraw early from the fighting on 11 February, and he retreated to Italy two days later. The Franco-Spanish fleet was forced back to Toulon, but emerged from the encounter substantially intact. Milbourne Marsh's own account

'A Draught of the *Marlborough* as she appear'd in the late engagement in the Mediterranean'. Etching, 1744.

of the battle underlines again some of the paradoxes of his work. His testimony makes clear that he was obliged to possess a pocket watch, still a rare accessory at this time among men who worked with their hands. It is also striking how confidently this skilled artisan communicated with the Admiral of Britain's Mediterranean fleet. Indeed, when Mathews was court martialled for failing at Toulon, he asked Milbourne to testify on his behalf. Yet what happened in the battle also confirms the precariousness of the carpenter's existence, and therefore of his family's existence.

At one stage, the *Namur*'s withdrawal left the *Marlborough*, Milbourne Marsh's former ship on which many of his friends were still serving, alone to face enemy fire. He watched, from relative safety, as the sails of the *Marlborough* caught fire, and as its main mast, battered by shot, crashed onto its decks. The ship stayed afloat, but its captain and about eighty of its crew were killed outright, and 120 more of its men were wounded. The battle also killed the *Namur*'s Post-Captain, John Russel, who had been one of Milbourne's own patrons, along with at least twenty-five more of the ship's crew. As for the Spanish, a British fireship had smashed into some of their warships, resulting, it was reported at the time, in 'the immediate dissolution of 1350 souls'. Witnessing death on this scale, experiencing battle, persuaded Milbourne to change course. He was not a coward: one of his private discoveries at Toulon was that, at the time, he 'did not think of the danger'.[66] But he was now in his thirties, married, a father, and his parents' oldest surviving son, whereas most seamen were under twenty-five and single. So in 1744 Milbourne Marsh left the sea. For the next ten years he repaired ships at Portsmouth and Chatham dockyards. On land, at what passed for home.

For his daughter, Elizabeth Marsh, this decision led to a more stationary, and seemingly more ordinary, life. To be sure, there were certain respects in which her experiences in the 1740s and early '50s already made her distinctive. Moving between Portsmouth, London and Chatham, and between various ships at sea and the land, allowed her in some respects an ironic counterfeit of genteel female education, but also more. In addition to the fluent French she acquired from aunt Mary and uncle Duval, she learnt arithmetic and basic accounting from her father, and she acquired a relish for some of the more innocuous pastimes common among sailors, reading, music and singing. She learnt too how to operate without embarrassment in overwhelmingly masculine environments, and how to tolerate physical hardship; and she also learnt, through living close to it, and through sailing on it from infancy, how not to fear the sea, or to regard it as extraordinary, but rather to take travelling on it for granted. She also learnt restlessness and insecurity, and – from watching her mother – a certain female self-reliance.

Mariners' wives had to be capable of a more than usual measure of independence and responsibility, because their husbands were so often away. During Milbourne's absences at sea, Elizabeth Marsh senior ran their household in the New Buildings and its finances by herself.[67] She also had to cope at intervals with the harshness and enforced intimacies of living aboard ship. Both of their sons, Francis Milbourne Marsh and John Marsh, the latter Elizabeth Marsh's favourite and confidant, seem to have been born at sea. Giving birth to the elder, Francis, may indeed have been what confined Elizabeth Marsh senior to the *Cambridge* in Portsmouth harbour – that is, several miles from shore – for several weeks in 1741, and what tempted Milbourne to 'borrow' supplies of navy bedding 'till my own was fit'.[68]

In the normal course of events, none of these mixed influences on their daughter Elizabeth Marsh would have mattered very much. When her father left the sea in 1744 after the Battle of Toulon, his and the family's prospects were modest, and would have appeared predictable. One of the attractions of working in naval dockyards, as distinct from a commercial shipyard that paid higher wages, was that they allowed skilled employees a job for life. Once he came ashore in 1744, Milbourne's income declined slightly, from £50 per annum to around £40, a sum that placed the family at the bottom of England's middling sort at this time, 'the upper station of low life', as Daniel Defoe styled it.[69] But at least there was security. It seemed likely that Milbourne would build and repair a succession of warships until he was pensioned off, that his two sons would in due course become shipwrights in their turn, and that ultimately his only daughter would marry a man of the same trade. But this was to reckon without changes that crossed continents, and the second influential man in Elizabeth Marsh's life: her uncle George Marsh.

Born in January 1723, George Marsh was the eighth and

penultimate child of George Marsh senior and Elizabeth Milbourne. This position in a large artisanal family may have made him slighter in physique, and more susceptible to illness – he seems to have suffered sporadically from epilepsy – but he was as driven as any eldest child. Initially sent to sea in 1735, because his father was not 'able to purchase me a clerkship', he soon moved to an apprenticeship to a petty officer in Chatham dockyard, and by 1744 was working as a clerk for the Commissioner of Deptford's naval dockyard.[70] His next break came almost immediately. In October 1745 the House of Commons demanded a detailed report on how naval expenditure in the previous five years, when Britain had been at war with Spain, compared with that in the first five years of the War of Spanish Succession (1702–07). As he was 'acquainted with the business of the dockyards, and no clerk of the Navy Office was', George Marsh was 'chosen . . . to perform that great work'. Labouring at the Navy Office in London 'from 5 or 6 o'clock in the morning till 8 or 9 o'clock at night from October to the end of January', mining a vast, unsorted store of records for the requisite figures, and organizing and writing up the usable data, exacerbated his epilepsy. He suffered intermittent attacks of near-blindness and dizziness, and 'fell several times in the street', he recorded much later, 'and therefore found it necessary to carry constantly in my pocket a memorandum who I was and where I lodged'. He nonetheless produced the report 'in a few months'.[71]

This episode suggests some of George Marsh's qualities: his ferocious capacity for industry, strong ambition, and utter belief in paperwork. It also suggests how – through him – Elizabeth Marsh was connected to yet another aspect of modernity and change. The circumstances of her birth and upbringing had already linked her with slavery, migration, empire, economic and industrious revolutions, the navy and the sea. But it was primarily through her uncle George Marsh that she connected with the expanding power of the British state at this time, and with an ever more conscious mobilization of knowledge and paperwork in order to expand that

Detail from a pastel portrait of George Marsh by J.G. Huck, *c.*1790.

power. To paraphrase the economist J.R. McCulloch's later verdict on the East India Company, Elizabeth's father, Milbourne Marsh, was caught up with the power of the sword, Britain's fighting navy; but it was her uncle, George Marsh, who exemplified the power of the pen and the ledger.[72]

And he was unstoppable. He rose early every morning, drank only water, confined himself to two meals a day, took regular exercise, spent little on himself, and worked very hard. In 1750 he moved from the provinces to the tall pedimented brick building that Christopher Wren had designed for the Navy Office in Crutched Friars by the Tower of London. From 1751 to 1763, George Marsh was the Clerk in charge of seamen's wages. He then spent almost ten years as Commissioner of Victualling, before becoming Clerk of the Acts in 1773. This was the position that Samuel Pepys had occupied after 1660, and used as a power base from which to transform the administration of the Royal Navy. Pepys, however, had been able to draw on aristocratic relations and on high, creative intelligence. George Marsh possessed neither advantage, yet he retained the Clerkship of the Acts for over twenty years, and ended his career as a Commissioner of the Navy. At his death in 1800, this shipwright's son was worth by his own estimate £34,575, over £3 million in present-day values.[73]

The contrast between his remarkable career and his evident personal limitations reduced some who worked and competed with him to uncomprehending fury. George Marsh, complained his own Chief Clerk in 1782, was

> totally unfit for the employment as he can neither read, spell, nor write. This office has in my memory been filled with ability and dignity ... but the present Clerk of the Acts has neither, and we should do ten times better without him, for he only perplexes matters.[74]

Yet, as this denunciation suggests, some of the criticism George Marsh attracted at different stages in his career was rooted in snobbery, and he was always able to exploit people's tendency to underestimate him. In reality, he wrote all the time, privately, and not just in his public capacity. His papers also confirm that he read widely and that, like his parents and his niece Elizabeth Marsh, he enjoyed constructing stories. More than any other member of his immediate family, perhaps because he spent virtually all of his life in a single country, George Marsh seems to have been conscious of the scale of the transformations through which he was living, and he sought out different ways to make sense of them. He was the one who stayed behind. He was the spectator, the recorder, the collector of memories and eloquent, emblematic mementoes. Most of all, George Marsh was someone who relished facts and information, and knew how to deploy them: 'I am sensible my abilities fall far short of some other men's,' he wrote towards the end of his life, 'but [I] am very certain no one knows the whole business of the civil department of the Navy better or perhaps so well as I do.'[75] This massive, cumulative knowledge gave him an element of power, as did his acute understanding of how patronage worked.

As his correspondence with successive aristocratic First Lords of the Admiralty reveals, he was both unctuously deferential in his dealings with his official and social superiors, and capable sometimes of hoodwinking them. In private, and like his parents, George Marsh tended to be critical of members of the aristocracy, writing regularly about the superiority of 'the middle station of life', and of those (like himself) who had to work seriously hard for a living. But he was adept at the patronage game, which necessarily involved him paying court at times to 'the indolent unhappy nobility', and he was interested in securing advancement and favours for more than just himself. He 'always had a very great pleasure', he wrote, in 'doing my utmost to make all those happy, by every friendly act, who I have known to be worthy'.[76] Chief among these worthy beneficiaries were the members of his own family. It was George Marsh's willingness and ability to use his power and connections to promote his family that transformed Elizabeth Marsh's expectations, and that separated her forever from the life-trajectory that might have been anticipated for a shipwright's daughter. Having as her uncle someone with access to influence over several decades was one of the factors that made her life extraordinary. By way of George Marsh, she was able at times to have contact with some of the most powerful men in the British state, while also being helped to travel far beyond it.

His first substantial intervention in his niece's life was indirect, but it changed everything. In January 1755, using his connections at the Navy Board, George Marsh secured for Milbourne Marsh the position of Naval Officer at Port Mahón in Menorca.[77] A 'Naval Officer' in eighteenth-century British parlance was not a fighting sea officer. The post was a clerical and administrative one, in an overseas dockyard, and for a ship's carpenter it represented a distinctly unusual career break. To begin with, it tripled the family's income. In the late 1740s and early '50s, Milbourne had rarely earned more than £12 a quarter, whereas this new post brought with it an annual salary of £150, and the opportunity to make more.

The rise in income was only part of the alteration in the family's status and outlook. As a carpenter aboard ship, Milbourne had been an uneasy amalgam of specialist craftsman, resident expert and manual labourer. This now changed. Nothing would ever take him completely from the sea, or from his delight in the construction of wooden ships and in drawing plans, but from now on he ceased to work with his hands for much of the time. The announcements of his promotion in the London press referred to him as 'Milbourne Marsh Esq.', thereby conceding to him the suffix that was the minimum requirement for being accounted a gentleman.[78]

But the most dramatic change involved in his promotion to Naval Officer was one that affected his whole family, his wife, their sons, and – as it turned out – the nineteen-year-old Elizabeth Marsh most of all. In March 1755, the family left Portsmouth forever and sailed to the Mediterranean and Menorca. She was on her way.

2

Taken to Africa, Encountering Islam

MOVING TO MENORCA meant an immediate change of land-scape, climate and cultural and religious milieu, and a conspicuous change of scale. Accustomed, when on land, to crowded ports in the world's foremost Protestant power, Elizabeth Marsh now found herself on a rocky, sparsely cultivated, ten-mile-long Mediterranean island of twenty-eight thousand souls, where a sprinkling of Jews and Greek Orthodox Christians were overwhelmingly outnumbered by Catholics, and where the dominant language was a form of Catalan. Most of the four-thousand-odd Britons on Menorca were soldiers or sailors. The officers among them, and the few civilian professionals and merchants, generally held aloof from the local Catholics (who tended to cold-shoulder them in turn), organizing for themselves a cosy, desperately restricted simulacrum of social life back home.[1] In her case, the claustrophobia scarcely had time to register. What did was a rise in status marked out by shifts in behaviour and consumerism. She seems to have learnt how to ride and to have acquired a riding costume. Her father could now afford a music teacher, and she began reading sheet music, as distinct from simply memorizing tunes. And, in place of shared lodgings, she moved with her family into a substantial freestone house on Hospital Island, a twelve-acre offshore islet in Mahón harbour. She was 'happily situated', she wrote later, abruptly promoted to minor membership of a colonial elite, and refashioning herself in a setting where young, single Protestant women who might conceivably pass as ladies were flatteringly sparse.[2]

Milbourne Marsh's new life was also substantially different. No longer a full-time manual worker, he was now a 'pen and ink' man, without a uniform or a sword, and therefore on a different and lower level than the senior military and sea officers who ran the colony, yet indispensable and multi-tasked. Part of his job as the island's Naval Officer was to act as Clerk of the Cheque: that is, as senior financial officer of Menorca's naval dockyard. The naval stores lining the wharves of Mahón's huge harbour, which extends inland for some six thousand yards, were his responsibility. So was paying the Britons and Menorcans who worked in the dockyard as shipwrights, sail-makers and carpenters, and in the navy's victualling office, bakehouse, windmills and magazines. In addition, Milbourne acted as Clerk of the Survey, drafting maps and drawing up plans for new buildings and defences. At intervals he was Master Shipwright too, overseeing the repair and careening of incoming British warships and transports, and keeping an eye on the merchant ships arriving with provisions and bullion to pay the troops. In his limited leisure time he joined his wife, sons and newly accomplished daughter on Hospital Island, with its 'rocks and precipices . . . intermixed with scattering houses', where the navy's local commander, surgeon and any visiting admirals were also accommodated.[3] But Milbourne's daylight hours were spent in the undistinguished row of low-storeyed sheds that made up the naval dockyard, or rowing the small boat that came with his office from ship to ship in the harbour, seeking out information from their captains, or mustering men and resolving disagreements, or surveying the island's innumerable coves, inlets and bays.

For Menorca was not a place of refuge and colonial ease. The British had seized it from Spain in 1708 for essentially the same reason that had led the Phoenicians, Greeks, Carthaginians, Romans, Arabs and Catalans to invade it before them, and for much the same reason too as would cause the United States Navy to maintain a base of operations there in the nineteenth century. Menorca offered an advantageous location from which to monitor and to seek to dominate the western Mediterranean. In the words of a British writer in 1756:

> All ships sailing up the straits of Gibraltar, and bound to any part of Africa, east of Algiers, to any part of Italy, or to any part of Turkey, either in Asia or Europe, and all ships from any of those places, and bound to any port without the straits-mouth, must and usually do pass between this island and the coast of Africa.[4]

Some of the main sea routes to and from Genoa, Livorno, Nice, Sicily, Marseilles, Lisbon, Tetuan and Tripoli lay within easy reach of Menorca. So did ships setting out from Spain's Mediterranean ports, and from its naval bases, Cartagena and Cádiz. Possessed of Menorca and sufficient force, Britain could intervene in the commercial and naval activities of three of its imperial competitors: France, Spain, and the Ottoman Empire with its provinces in Northern Africa. Toulon, the prime French naval base, was 220 miles away from Menorca, within striking distance of a British fleet using the island as a base. Of course, the converse also applied. Ringed and replete with commercial, strategic and warlike possibilities, Menorca was itself a natural target. It was a 'frontier garrison', one politician had remarked in the 1720s, where discipline and watchfulness were mandatory 'as if it were always in a state of war'.[5]

The members of the Marsh family were introduced to the risks attendant on the island's location and strategic role almost as soon as they arrived in 1755. The aftershocks they experienced that November from the Lisbon earthquake, which killed over 100,000 people in the Iberian peninsula and Morocco, and caused tremors in France, Italy, Switzerland and Finland, and tsunamis as far apart as Galway, Ireland, and Barbados, were accompanied by other far-reaching convulsions, engineered by human actors. France and Britain were at war again. This time, by contrast with their previous conflicts, the fighting did not begin in Europe. The initial battles

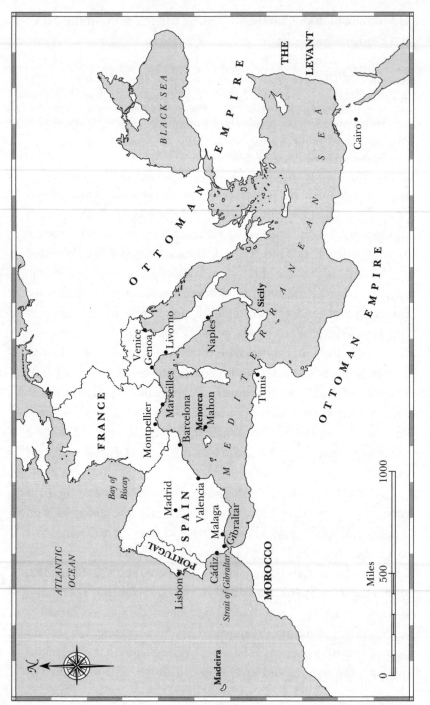

The Mediterranean world of Elizabeth Marsh and James Crisp

of what Americans generally term the French and Indian War, and Europeans call the Seven Years War, took place in parts of Asia and the Caribbean, and above all in North America; and both the onset of the war, and its unprecedented geographical extent, impacted directly on Menorca – and on Elizabeth Marsh.[6]

Although Menorca was tiny, its complex coastline, 'indented with long bays and promontories', and its disgruntled Catholic population were too extensive to be adequately guarded in wartime by the resident British garrison. Retaining the island in these circumstances required reinforcements on land, and also a significant naval presence. This time, such reinforcements were not easily available. Before the 1740s, it was rare for large numbers of Royal Navy ships to be stationed for any length of time in Asian or American waters. Now that war was spilling over into different continents, the resulting dispersal of Britain's naval resources left traditional European frontier sites like Menorca more exposed and potentially vulnerable. As a later Admiralty report argued:

> If our possessions and commerce increase, our cares and our difficulties are increased likewise; that commerce and those possessions being extended all over the world must be defended by sea having no other defence ... [Yet] it is impossible to keep at all of them, perhaps at any one, a strength equal to what the enemy can send thither.[7]

In late 1755, when rumours were already circulating of a French invasion force assembling in Toulon and Marseilles, there were just three British ships of the line in the Mediterranean, as against fifteen patrolling off the coasts of Bengal and North America. By early 1756, when 150 ships and 100,000 troops were in readiness along France's Mediterranean coast, the situation for the British was only marginally better. More than one hundred Royal Navy vessels were under repair or guarding Britain's own coasts, and an additional fifty were in service in extra-European waters, but only thirteen warships were available for other locations.[8]

As a result, in 1756 those on Menorca were left substantially to fend for themselves. For Milbourne Marsh, in his capacity as Naval Officer, this meant locating and purchasing obsolete vessels from various Mediterranean ports, and then converting them into fireships that could be sailed against any invading French fleet. He also supervised the splicing together of surplus masts and cables to fashion a 250-yard-long barrier that could be floated across the narrow entrance to Mahón harbour. In early April, Menorca's military out-stations and outlying wells were destroyed to keep them from falling into French hands. Most of the island's Catholics were disarmed, and soldiers and their families, along with the island's pro-British Jewish and Greek inhabitants, began assembling, with hundreds of live cattle and other supplies, behind the walls of Fort St Philip at the entrance to Mahón harbour.[9]

Had Elizabeth Marsh and her family belonged unquestionably to the lower ranks, this would have been their refuge too. As almost four hundred other women did, she would have spent the next two and a half months under siege in Fort St Philip's web of subterranean stone passages, 'the garrison knocked about her ears every minute, and some of her acquaintances killed or wounded every day'. Conversely, had the family's social status been more assured, she might have been dispatched – like many of the officers' womenfolk – to Majorca, the neighbouring Balearic island ruled by still-neutral Spain.[10] As it was, her fate was determined once again by the distinctive, indispensable nature of her father's skills. On Saturday, 17 April, Milbourne Marsh was summoned to the island's naval commander:

> Upon the French being landed on the island of Menorca, Commodore Edgcumbe gave him an order . . . to proceed from thence in His Majesty's ship the Princess Louisa to Gibraltar, and there to take upon him the duty of Master Shipwright.[11]

By now there were five Royal Navy ships off Mahón, 'moored head and stern in line across the harbour's mouth', but still manifestly too few to engage the 120 French warships and transports assembling off the coast of Ciutadella, to the west of the island, or to slow for very long the troops that these vessels were disgorging. Two of these British warships left on 21 April, which was when Milbourne Marsh carefully finished up and signed his remaining official paperwork, and 'the same day the enemy appeared on this side of Mahón'. The following day, a Thursday, the forty-gun *Princess Louisa* with the Marsh family on board, together with the *Dolphin* and the *Portland*, slipped away to Gibraltar.[12] She was rescued, but not saved.

☙❧

For it is now that Elizabeth Marsh begins to struggle out of the meshes of family plots and transcontinental forces and events, and seeks to take charge of her own life. She arrives in Gibraltar on 30 April 1756. Within two months, she has determined to sail to England by way of Lisbon. Although by this stage Britain and France are formally at war, and the Mediterranean is criss-crossed by French and British warships under orders to 'take, sink, burn or otherwise destroy' each other's naval and merchant vessels, she insists on setting sail, initially in defiance of her parents' wishes, and as a lone female traveller among men.

She has her private reasons for acting this way, but she can also make a prudential case for her decision. After just three days in Gibraltar, Milbourne Marsh has been able to compile a report on its naval facilities and defences. The British have long neglected the fortress for reasons of economy, and his assessment is uncompromising and discouraging:

> The capstans, partners and frames [are] entirely decayed, the mast house, boat house, pitch house, smiths shop and cable shed all decayed, and tumbling down; the yard launch

wants a thorough repair, and in case there may be a necessity to careen or caulk any of His Majesty's ships, there is neither floating stages for that service, or boat for the officers to attend their respective duties; the shed within the new mole gates that was used for repairing sails in, likewise the shed for the use of the artificers are both decayed and tumbling down.

This, and more, is what he proceeds to tell Admiral John Byng, who is also newly arrived at Gibraltar, under instructions to sail with ten warships to relieve the besieged British garrison on Menorca. Even before Byng sets out, Milbourne's damning report has therefore encouraged him to begin contemplating failure. 'If I should fail in the relief of Port Mahón,' he informs his superiors in London on 4 May, 'I shall look upon the security and protection of Gibraltar as my next object.'[13]

Subsequently, these words will be interpreted by the senior officers at Byng's court martial as evidence of a lack of determined resolution and aggressiveness on his part. Yet this is not altogether fair. Gibraltar, a three-mile-long rocky promontory off southern Andalusia in Spain with no source of fresh water at this time except for the rain, is like 'a great man of war at anchor'.[14] It is formidable, a natural fortress, but with weaknesses corresponding to its strengths. The Rock gives its British occupiers a strategically key position from which to monitor the straits between the Mediterranean and Atlantic. If it is closely besieged from the sea, however, there is nowhere for its inhabitants to retreat except into Spain. Reports from diplomats and spies have been circulating since March 1756 that if Menorca falls (as it does at the end of June), France will move on to attack Gibraltar, and then offer both of these territories back to Spain in return for the loan of its naval fleet in the war against Britain.[15] If the French do attack Gibraltar – and if Spain turns hostile – how can the fortress defend itself without adequate stores, or the dockyard facilities necessary to keep a fighting navy at sea and in action?

Because he is thinking along these lines, Byng will decide to retreat after his fleet's inconclusive encounter with the marquis de la Galissonière's French squadron on 20 May 1756. He will hurry back to defend Gibraltar, leaving Menorca's garrison to its fate, and so ultimately condemn himself to a naval firing squad. For the men of the Marsh family, however, Byng's anxieties about the poor state of Gibraltar's naval dockyard and defences have substantial compensations. 'It requiring a proper person to inspect into and manage these affairs,' Byng informs London, 'I have taken upon me to give Mr. Milbourne Marsh . . . an order to act as Master Shipwright . . . and have given him orders to use his best endeavours to put the wharf etc. in the best condition he can, for very soon they will be wanted.'[16] The added responsibility boosts Milbourne's annual salary from £150 to £200, and this is in addition to the accommodation and food the navy allows him. By July, John Marsh is also in naval employ, working as clerk to his father, who no longer has the time to write his own letters. Elizabeth Marsh's situation is necessarily different. For her, there can be no job. If a Franco-Spanish force lays siege to Gibraltar, there may be no easy means of escape this time, especially for a single, twenty-year-old woman who is associated with the British. Moreover, now that the war has reached Europe, Gibraltar itself is filling up with troops and is increasingly crowded and unhealthy. There are over a thousand men confined in its naval hospital, and every day some of them die.[17]

All this enables Elizabeth Marsh to rationalize her decision to leave and to persuade her parents to agree, but she is also influenced – indeed misled – by her past. She is used to sailing in large, well-crewed, well-disciplined warships that are designed to take punishment as well as give it, and accordingly she has no fear of the sea. But the *Ann*, on which she embarks on the afternoon of 27 July, is a battered, unarmed 150-ton merchantman, loaded with casks of brandy, and with only ten crewmen. The man in overall charge is James Crisp, a nominally British merchant based in

Barcelona who is already known to the Marsh family; and there are two other passengers, an Irish trader called Joseph Popham who is in his late forties, and his adolescent son William.[18] Since it is wartime, the *Ann* sails in convoy with fourteen other merchant vessels bound for Lisbon and under the protection of the forty-four-gun *Gosport*. This too misleads Elizabeth, for naturally she trusts the Royal Navy. Unfortunately, and like most sea officers, Captain Richard Edwards dislikes convoy duty, and he is also peculiarly bad at it. On the *Gosport*'s previous voyage, from Plymouth to Gibraltar, he has more than once lost sight of all thirty-four vessels entrusted to his care. In the case of this new Lisbon convoy, the fog that is so common in this stretch of the Mediterranean puts a further strain on his abilities. Although there is 'moderate and fair weather to begin with', one day out from Gibraltar the mist is so thick that he can no longer see any of the fifteen merchantmen sailing with him. Edwards orders the *Gosport*'s rowing boats to be hoisted aboard so as to make up speed, and fires its guns to signal his location.[19] Those on the *Ann* hear the shots, and on the morning of 30 July catch a last glimpse of the *Gosport*, seven miles away. The *Ann*'s Master desperately carries 'all the sail he could, in order to keep up with the man of war, even to endangering our lives, for there was six feet [of] water in the hold, before any one knew of it'. Used to the sea, but not to the limitations of small merchantmen, Elizabeth Marsh, by her own admission, was 'entirely ignorant of the danger we had been in until it was over'.[20]

But by now they are all lost: the other merchant ships, the *Gosport* that takes ten days to reach Lisbon, and the *Ann* that finally emerges from drifting in deep fog at 2 p.m. on 8 August to see 'a sail to windward giving us chase and at half past seven came within pistol shot of us'. It is not – as they first think – a French warship. It is a twenty-gun Moroccan cruiser with more than 130 armed men on board. With flight now out of the question, Crisp and the Pophams agree to row over to the Moroccan vessel, thinking that it is simply a matter of showing their Mediterranean pass and establishing their identity, for Morocco and Britain are formally at peace. Elizabeth Marsh meanwhile was 'tolerably easy, until night drew on, when fear seized my spirits, at their not returning at the time appointed. I continued in that state, until the morning . . . [when] instead of seeing the gentlemen, boats, crowded with Moors, came to our ship, in exchange for whom our sailors were sent on board theirs.' She remains on the *Ann* four more days, as do the Moroccan boarders. Then, on 12 August, she is rowed over to their ship, terrified by 'the waves looking like mountains', because she is no longer observing them from the secure upper decks of a warship, and because – like most seafarers at this time – she is unable to swim. Once all are on board the corsair ship, there is a brutal social but not yet a gender divide. The ordinary sailors from the *Ann* are left roped together on deck. But James Crisp, Joseph Popham and his son, and Elizabeth are pushed into a cabin 'so small as not to admit our standing upright. In this miserable place four people were to live.'[21]

During the three days she is confined here – and still more afterwards – what become significant are the things that she takes note of and is careful to remember, and the aspects of her ordeal and changing surroundings that she either refuses to acknowledge, or is in no position to understand. She is used to living at intervals at sea among hundreds of men, and so copes well with the utter lack of privacy, the discomfort, the smells, the stray glimpses of the others' nudity, the glances they snatch of her own. 'Miss Marsh', Joseph Popham concedes later, '. . . has supported herself under her misfortunes beyond what may be expected from her tender sex.'[22] It is not so much the embarrassments and hardships of being mewed up in a stinking cabin with three males that begin to undermine her, or even the shock of violent capture, so much as a sense of being torn from all moorings. She has grown up in tight, usually well-disciplined communities, the cherished only daughter of a respected master craftsman. Socially marginal in

A Moroccan corsair ship and some captives. Engraving by A.H. Stibold, *c.*1779.

terms of British society in general, she has nonetheless been sure of
her place in her own maritime sphere. As this strange, nightmarish
ordeal progresses, her sense of personal anchorage loosens, and she
feels marked out by her gender in new and dangerous ways.

She has already spent several days on the *Ann* surrounded by curious, occasionally ribald Moroccan seamen, with – or so she later records – only the ship's elderly steward standing between her and them. Now, imprisoned on the corsair ship, William Popham tries to relieve his own fears by telling her 'stories of the cruelties of the Moors, and the dangers my sex was exposed to in Barbary'. When they finally disembark at the port of Sla (Salé) on Morocco's Atlantic coast on 15 August, and Elizabeth Marsh rides the mule they give her for two miles over rough tracks into its old town, she is greeted by 'a confused noise of women's voices from the top of the houses, which surprised me much, until I was informed it was a testimony of joy on the arrival of a female captive'. There are more reminders of her difference. As she, the Pophams and James Crisp wait in the half-ruined house allocated them, confined again to a single room, some local European merchants bribe their way in and undertake to smuggle out letters. The captives wait until night 'lest the guards should suspect what we were upon', and then they write.[23] Joseph Popham writes to a patron, Sir Henry Cavendish in Dublin, urging him to get his brother the Duke of Devonshire, a former Lord Lieutenant of Ireland, to intervene on the captives' behalf. James Crisp writes to the new Governor of Gibraltar, James O'Hara, Baron Tyrawley, and to Sir Edward Hawke, who has replaced Byng as Commander-in-Chief of the British fleet in the Mediterranean. Both Popham and Crisp pass on personal messages in postscripts to their letters, but their first instinct is to make contact with public figures who are possessed of influence. When Milbourne Marsh finally learns of his daughter's real plight (the newspapers initially report that the *Ann* has been seized or sunk by the French), he reacts in a similar fashion. He immediately, and with characteristic confidence, appeals for aid to the First Lord of the Admiralty, Lord Anson. Elizabeth Marsh by contrast has no contacts with powerful males at this stage of her life, and so writes only to her parents. Consequently her letters, unlike most of the others, do not survive.[24]

Those who now have power over her also remind her of the vulnerabilities of her position. When the captives are taken for questioning before a high-ranking Moroccan official at Sla, James Crisp is able to converse with him in Spanish, the language that Maghrebi elite males and incoming Europeans often employ to communicate with each other. But Elizabeth, who knows little Spanish, is conducted into the official's harem, 'the apartment of his ladies', and brought for the first time into the company of a Moroccan woman, whose name she never learns. With no interpreter available, they see each other – or so she claims later in print – only in terms of mutual strangeness:

> She was surprisingly tall and stout, with a broad, flat face, very dark complexion, and long black hair. She wore a dress resembling a clergyman's gown, made of muslin, and buttoned at the neck, like the collar of a shirt, which reached her feet. She had bracelets on her arms and legs; and was extremely inquisitive, curious in examining my dress and person, and was highly entertained at the appearance I made.

Whatever her own ancestry, Elizabeth Marsh will later stress for her readers this Moroccan woman's 'very dark' skin. More significantly, she will parade her own Christian, Anglican faith by evoking a vicar's surplice in her description of the Moroccan's *djellaba*.[25] Yet, at the time, it is the possible resemblances between her plight and the situation of the other woman – not what divides them – that nag at her most. Both of them are confined in different ways; but what if, in the future, she herself comes to be immured in Morocco in a similar fashion to that of the other woman? It is someone who has access to both local Muslim and Christian societies, a slave called Pedro Umbert, who first puts this possibility into words. A Menorcan by birth, captured by corsairs and now the property of Morocco's acting Sultan, Sidi Muhammad, Umbert has been ordered to Sla to negotiate with members of its European merchant community.[26] He is drawn to the captives because both

Elizabeth Marsh and James Crisp can speak some Catalan, his cradle tongue, and having established their story, he urges them to replace one deception with another.

Since their capture, Crisp has been posing as Elizabeth's brother 'in order to be some little protection to me'. Now, Umbert warns them:

> I should be in less danger of an injury, at Morocco, by his [Crisp] passing for my husband than my brother. My friend replied, he imagined I should be entirely safe, by his appearing in the character he then did; and, as he had been examined by the principal people of [Sla] concerning the truth of it, it was then too late to alter that scheme. The conversation then dropped, and he left us; but his advice, and the manner in which he had given it, greatly alarmed me.[27]

Her unease at masquerading as James Crisp's wife, which she finally agrees to do, sets her even more apart from her male companions. With the terrors and discomfort of their capture at sea receding, and epistolary contacts with home restored, they are feeling moderately complacent. Even when the order arrives for them to be escorted to Marrakech, where Sidi Muhammad has his court, Joseph Popham for instance remains phlegmatic. He feels sorry for 'poor Miss Marsh', he writes in one of a series of smuggled-out letters, faced with the prospect of a three-hundred-mile ride across mountains and desert, but 'not under the least apprehension . . . nor was not from the beginning'. Perhaps, he adds, Milbourne Marsh might be contacted in Gibraltar and encouraged to ship over some practical comforts for his daughter: 'a small firkin of good butter, some cheese, tea and sugar . . . a little mace, cinnamon and nutmegs, two bottles of Turlington drops for fear of illness, [and] half a pound of best sealing wax'.[28] Basic groceries, herbs and condiments to offset the unfamiliar, almond sweetness of Moroccan food, a laudanum-based medicine that is widely used on both sides of the Atlantic for everything from bruises and coughs to headaches, and wax to seal up their incessant correspondence: these are the only precautions and palliatives that occur to Popham at this stage. Nor does he worry that sealing their letters with wax may prove an insufficient safeguard. Like Elizabeth Marsh, he does not yet fully understand.

※

In part, Joseph Popham's confidence reflected the transformations that had occurred in Britain's relations with Morocco and other Maghrebi powers since the seventeenth century. At that time, corsairs operating out of Morocco, and from Tunis, Tripoli, Algiers and other Ottoman ports, had posed a major threat to Christian shipping in the western Mediterranean and parts of the Atlantic, and also and intermittently to some western European coastlines.[29] Before 1660 – though not after – there may have been as many European sailors, fishermen, traders, male and female passengers, and coastal villagers seized and enslaved in this manner in Morocco and throughout the Ottoman Empire as there were West Africans traded into Atlantic slavery by Europeans. Perhaps 1.25 million Europeans were captured and initially enslaved in this fashion between the late 1500s and the end of the eighteenth century; and many more were taken overland by Ottoman armies, in eastern Europe and Russia, and in occasional forays into western Europe. The Ottoman assault on Vienna in 1683 alone is said to have resulted in over eighty thousand men, women and children being carried into slavery.[30]

As far as the Mediterranean was concerned, these modes of violence and enslavement were never one-sided. There were abundant, nominally Christian, corsairs and pirates also active in the eastern and western portions of the sea in the late medieval and early modern eras. Many were sponsored by France, or Spain, or various Italian states, or by the Knights of St John on Malta; and – as was true of their Islamic counterparts – many of these Christian sea-raiders were motivated more by greed for potential ransoms than by religious zeal or antipathy. But so long as Ottoman and Maghrebi corsairing and slave-taking persisted, they could pose considerable dangers to vulnerable individuals and regions, and the fears they aroused were far more widespread. Even in the 1750s, ships belonging to some of the weaker European states, such as Genoa, and small villages situated around the rim of the Mediterranean, remained exposed to Maghrebi sea-raiders. Sailing past coastal Spain in transit to Menorca and Gibraltar, the members of the Marsh family would have noticed how rare it was to see inhabited villages close to the shorelines, and how small fishing and trading communities tended to cluster instead on hillsides at a prudent distance from any beach. As a Royal Navy officer remarked in 1756:

> The reason of their houses being thus situated is the fear of the Moors, who would, if their houses were accessible, land and carry whole villages into slavery, which is frequently done notwithstanding all their caution, much more so in that part of Spain that lies on the coast of the Mediterranean.[31]

For the British, the threat from Maghrebi corsairs was normally minimal by this time. The Royal Navy's power and Mediterranean bases deterred most corsairs from attacking British merchant shipping. So too did a certain community of interests. Since the early 1700s the British had come to rely on Morocco, and to a lesser degree on Algiers and Tunis, for supplies of provisions, horses and mules for their garrisons in Menorca and Gibraltar; and they paid for these not only with cash and luxury re-exports like tea and fine textiles, but also with guns, cannon and ammunition. Set apart by religion, culture, mutual prejudice and different levels of power and wealth, imperial Britain and imperial Morocco were to this extent interdependent and usually tolerant of each other in practice.[32] This was why Joseph Popham and the other male captives from the *Ann* initially allowed themselves to feel relaxed about their predicament in 1756. They assumed that once the British authorities learned of it, an appropriate ransom would be paid, a warship would be dispatched to rescue them, and that would be the end of it. The politicians and navy officials in London, Dublin and Gibraltar who received their written requests for assistance took a more serious and more accurate view of the *Ann*'s capture, though they too failed to appreciate all the forces that were involved.

Since the death of the 'Alawi dynasty's most famous Sultan, Moulay Ismail, in 1727, Morocco's wealth and importance had been undermined by epidemics, earthquakes, recurrent periods of drought and repeated civil wars. The right to the throne of Moulay Abdallah, the nominal Sultan in 1756, had been violently contested on five different occasions. By this stage, real authority had definitively and by his own wish slipped away from him to his son, Sidi Muhammad, who was a very different ruler in both calibre and ideas. Sidi Muhammad was 'too fierce to be tamed without some chastisement', the British Governor of Gibraltar had predicted some months before the *Ann*'s capture, though this was neither true nor to the point.[33] But the new acting Sultan was ruthless and adroit enough to play on Christian preconceptions about arbitrary and barbaric Muslim rulers. In 1755, the captains of some Royal Navy vessels had cut deals with some independent warlords on Morocco's northern coast, supplying them with armaments in exchange for fresh provisions for their crews. Sidi Muhammad's response was swift. He launched a punitive strike against the European merchant communities in Sla:

> His Highness made prisoners of all the Christian merchants and friars; but Mr. Mounteney being English, he put a large chain on his neck, and bolts upon his legs, and gave him so many bastinados that he was left for dead, although he afterwards died in his own house, for understanding that the Prince intended him a lingering death because he was an Englishman, and having lost his senses, he hanged himself.

This was not merely one more stock European horror story of Barbary cruelties. Jaime Arvona, yet another Menorcan-born slave who was fluent in French, Spanish and Arabic, and who acted as treasurer, secretary and royal confidant in the acting Sultan's court in Marrakech, sent this account of Mounteney's miserable fate to a British diplomat in September 1755 on Sidi Muhammad's explicit instructions.[34] The British might have recognized in this communication a violent opening bid. They might have remembered that European traders and Christian clerics were normally free to operate in Moroccan cities, just as low-grade Christian slaves, as well as privileged individuals like Arvona, were routinely given days off to celebrate the main Christian holidays and freedom of worship every Sunday. But they focused more on Sidi Muhammad's threat as transmitted by Arvona:

> I dispatch this express to give you advice that His Highness intends to place his Governors all along the coast as far as Tangier and Tetuan . . . the first Englishman that puts foot in his country he will make him a slave.[35]

'My ships and galliots at sea shall look out for you,' Sidi Muhammad himself had warned a British sea officer in the summer of 1756, 'and take you wherever they meet you.' This deterioration in Anglo–Moroccan relations in late 1755 and early 1756 formed part of the background to the corsair attack on the *Ann*. When the Danish Consul in Morocco, Georg Höst, learnt of the incident, his sense of the captives' plight was therefore initially unambiguous. 'The passengers (some merchants and a woman)', he noted in his diary, had been 'detained as slaves'.[36]

Riding out of Sla under guard with the rest of the captives on 30 August, Elizabeth Marsh knows little of this. She is both caught up in violent public events that she is in no position fully to understand, and preoccupied with the personal. She is intent, to begin with, on her physical comforts, on the fact that a Spanish merchant from Rabat has lent her a tent for the journey and improvised a sidesaddle for her mule that soon proves both painful and insecure. As the caravan moves southwards through plains and deserts towards Marrakech, she struggles more seriously with agoraphobia. For the first time in her life, she has moved out of sight of the sea, and she can no longer make out either any signs of permanent human settlement: 'there was no appearance of a house or a tree but a large tract of country, abounding with high mountains, affording little worthy of notice, though I made as many observations as I could in my confined situation, without any books'.[37] Without books or maps, or personal access to Arabic, or Spanish, or any Berber language, and with no sequence of built towns by which to measure distance and progress, only a succession of *douars* or encampments, she is robbed of formal geography. She cannot give names to the stages of her journey. Since the caravan travels in the cool of the nights, and stops for short intervals of sleep during the hottest parts of the day, she is also deprived of a confident sense of clock and calendar time. She is dehydrated and malnourished, surviving for the most part on eggs and milk, and is now persistently reminded of her exposed female status. The makeshift sidesaddle has had to be abandoned for 'such a machine as the Moorish women make use of'. This is placed across her mule 'over a pack, and held a small mattress; the Moorish women lie on it, as it may be covered close; but I sat with my feet on one side [of] the mule's neck, and found it very proper to screen me from the Arabs'. The device also increases her isolation, while further advertising that she is the lone female member of the caravan. When some passing Bedouin tribesmen are 'inclined to be rude', her guard shouts out – or so she is told – that 'I was going as a present to Sidi Muhammad'.[38]

The Moroccan admiral in charge of the caravan, Rais al-Hadj al-Arbi Mistari, seems to have taken it along a customary route for slaves and captives disembarked at Sla. Over the course of six or seven days (there is no sure way of telling, for the captives lose

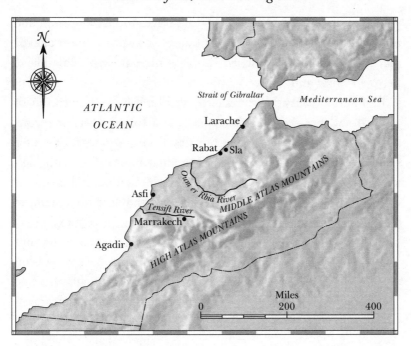

Elizabeth Marsh's Morocco

track of dates), they move south from Rabat, skirt the Middle Atlas mountains, cross the Oum er Rbia river, where she almost drowns, and finally the Tensift river just north of Marrakech. Elizabeth Marsh is not the first woman claiming Britain as her home to be forced to make this journey, nor will she be the last. She is, however, the first to record her experiences; indeed she is the first woman in history to write at length about Morocco in the English language. But the mental notes she stores up at the time are only occasionally those of a conventional travel-writer. Unlike many other eighteenth-century female travellers, she does not for example commit to memory anecdotes illustrative of her unusual pluckiness (though her physical hardiness in making this journey on mule-back and at a rapid pace is clear). Nor, with some exceptions – like her first sight of mountains 'which reached above the clouds' – is she much concerned with a landscape that for the most part she can see only as empty.[39] She travels under coercion, and under growing mental as well as physical stress, and as a result the journey she comes to describe is partly internal, an exploration of her own mind and fears.

Eight miles outside Marrakech, the caravan halts, her tent is pitched and her sea-chest is opened, and through an interpreter Mistari orders her to change her dress 'in order to make some figure at going into Morocco'. For the first time since leaving Sla, she puts on fresh clothes, wrapping a nightcap around her head for protection from the sun, 'as I was told they did not intend to let me wear my hat'. Once 'ornamented, as they imagined', she is placed, not on her own mule, but in front of James Crisp on his:

> At the same time, one of the guards pulled off his hat, and carried it away with him; which treatment amazed us extremely: But our astonishment increased, when our fellow-sufferers were made to dismount, and walk, two and two, bare-headed, the sun being much hotter than I had ever felt it, and the road so heavy, that the mules were knee-deep in the same.[40]

So, as Elizabeth Marsh and James Crisp finally ride into Sidi Muhammad's city and power base, they are cut off from the thousands crowding to see them, not just by fear and fatigue, but also by different systems of signs. The watching Moroccans *may* have interpreted their comparatively affluent Western clothes as a welcome demonstration that higher-grade captives than usual had been won, and could be ransomed accordingly. They would undoubtedly have noticed that all of the prisoners had been deprived of their hats, and therefore stripped after a fashion of their identity. Hats at this time were the most obvious sartorial markers of people who were European. But for Crisp – and even more for Elizabeth Marsh – being made to ride together on a broken-down mount amidst noisy and abusive crowds is likely to have had a different set of connotations. Apart from the obvious humiliation and discomfort, the ordeal would have been reminiscent to them of the crude *charivari* or rough music processions still sometimes inflicted by vengeful villagers and townsfolk in Britain, and in other Western European societies, on conspicuously adulterous or disorderly couples. Placing victims on a donkey, parading them through the streets 'amidst raucous, ear-shattering noise, unpitying laughter, and the mimicry of obscenities': this is what is customarily involved in rough music rituals. And this is what the 'shouts and hallooings' of the Marrakech crowd, the cuts inflicted on Crisp's legs by the horsemen who hurtle past them, and the crude gestures made at Elizabeth herself would have reminded them of now.[41] Already deeply conscious of masquerading as husband and wife, they enter Marrakech the red, with its landscape of scattered, quadrangular minarets, in a manner reminiscent (to them) of shame and sexual misbehaviour.

Their self-consciousness increases when they are made to dismount, separated from the other captives, and confined for most of the afternoon alone in the upstairs room of an ancient castle three miles' distance from Sidi Muhammad's palace. Unconcerned by now with polite Western conventions, Crisp and Elizabeth Marsh allow themselves to sit on the floor, 'lamenting our miserable fate'. As a result, when they are finally let out, brought outside the palace gates and, after more hours of standing, at last see the acting Sultan, it is through a haze not simply of exhaustion and European preconceptions, but also of more personal preoccupations. Elizabeth does register some things with conspicuous accuracy. She takes note of the acting Sultan's concern with dignity and ritual: 'He was mounted on a beautiful horse with slaves on each side fanning off the flies, and guarded by a party of the black regiment,' that is by members of the *'Abīd al-Bukhārī*, forcibly recruited dark-skinned *Haratin* and black slave soldiers. She reports, correctly, that this encounter occurs in the open air. Unlike their fellow Sunni Muslims, the Ottoman Sultans, Moroccan rulers do not traditionally receive envoys, petitioners and supplicants in

A view of Marrakech. Danish engraving of 1779.

rich interiors. Nor do Moroccan Sultans customarily issue their pronouncements at audiences in writing by way of scribes, but – as on this occasion – personally and through the spoken word. She notes too how the 'Moorish admiral and his crew' fall on their knees before their ruler, kiss the ground 'and, as they arose, did the same to his feet'. As a Moroccan envoy later records, it is a 'custom with our Sultan, when we are close to him, we kiss the soil, which is considered as a prostration of gratitude [to God]'.[42] All these things Elizabeth Marsh sees and later writes down. But what does Sidi Muhammad see in this meeting?

In 1756 he is in his mid-thirties, very tall by contemporary standards at five foot ten, and in the words of one of his British slaves at this time, 'well made, of a majestic deportment, of a dark chestnut colour, squints with his right eye, but still an agreeable aspect'.[43] Indeed, Elizabeth Marsh judges him, wrongly, to be about twenty-five. Sidi Muhammad is determined to restore and expand the Sultan's authority over his divided, partly tribal society, and he can be ruthless in response to foreign and domestic enemies. As more percipient European envoys are increasingly willing to acknowledge, however, the new acting Sultan is also conspicuously charitable, highly organized and hard-working, sharply intelligent, and possessed of wide interests. Robbed in his youth of a conventional, princely education by Morocco's civil wars and the need to fight, he now operates according to a fixed and demanding schedule. His custom is to get up very early every morning, ride out to inspect his city and the work of his outdoor slaves, breakfast alone sitting in his gardens, and then combine governance with intellectual and religious study. He has set up a small council with which he can discuss works of Islamic literature and history, and he meets daily with the scholars who are attached to his court.[44] As this suggests, Sidi Muhammad is devout, and deeply attached to a kind of pan-Islamic world-view. All too aware of the growing wealth and aggression of the major European powers, he is eager to consolidate defensive alliances with other Muslim rulers, especially with the Ottoman Sultan in Istanbul, the world capital of Islam. During his formal reign as Sultan of Morocco (1757–90), Sidi Muhammad will dispatch three embassies to Istanbul, in each case to advance pacts of mutual support against the 'infidels'.[45] His desire for a close rapport with the Ottoman Sultan, and his concern to support his fellow Maghrebi rulers in Tunis and Algiers against European predators, also rest on deep religious conviction.

Like Christianity, Islam is a monotheistic religion with universalistic aspirations. Wherever in the world they live, Muslims are linked by Arabic, Islam's sacred language, by the injunction to carry out the *hajj*, the pilgrimage to Mecca, and by the concept of the *dar-al-islam*, the land of Islam, which allows them to 'imagine and experience the local as part of a larger Islamic universal whole'. These tenets of belief inform Sidi Muhammad's own brand of internationalism, though they do not account for all of it. Unlike his father and predecessor as Sultan, Moulay Abdallah, he has gone on the *hajj*, and is an attentive visitor to other pilgrimage sites.[46] The evidence suggests that he may even have aspired to be recognized as Caliph of the Muslim west: that is, as a politico-religious sovereign acting as a twin pole, along with the Ottoman Sultan in the east, in upholding the entire Islamic world. In other words, the ruler whom Elizabeth Marsh and her fellow bedraggled captives confront this early September 1756, outside the gates of his Marrakech palace, is a clever, determined and reflective individual who possesses horizons that are far wider than Morocco itself. Sidi Muhammad makes this clear even in what he announces to them, through his interpreters, although the captives are scarcely in a position to appreciate the full significance of his words. They are not after all to be enslaved, he tells Elizabeth, James Crisp and the others. Instead, they will be detained as hostages until Britain agrees to establish a proper Consul in Morocco.[47]

For Consul, read commerce. Sidi Muhammad has perceived that, in order to consolidate his own authority and to restore Morocco's viability as a stable and prosperous polity, any suspicion of the non-Muslim world must be balanced by more normalized relations and positive engagement based on trade. He may conceivably aspire to be Caliph of the West, and he certainly wants to forge closer alliances with fellow Muslim rulers. But he also wishes to foster connections with other parts of the world in order to develop his country's commerce and thereby increase his own revenue. He has already, in 1753, negotiated three trade treaties with Denmark. Over the course of his reign, the Sultan will go on to sign some forty agreements with other major European states and entrepôts, with Britain, France, Portugal, Spain, the Netherlands, Prussia, Sweden, Venice, Hamburg, and with Dubrovnik, an important commercial player in the Adriatic.[48] 'The present Emperor is so very circumspect in all his affairs,' Joseph Popham will write in 1764, by which time Elizabeth's one-time fellow captive has been transmuted into British Consul to Morocco, 'that he concerns himself in the most trifling transactions relative to European matters.' And Sidi Muhammad looks to the west beyond Europe. He will become the first Muslim ruler in the world to acknowledge American independence. In 1784, he will also order his corsairs to capture a US merchant ship, the *Betsey*. Once they are taken hostage, the Sultan uses the members of the *Betsey*'s crew as bargaining tools, and in 1786 the US Congress agrees to a treaty establishing full diplomatic relations with Morocco.[49]

There are clear and significant parallels between what happens to the *Betsey* in the wake of the American Revolutionary War, and the fate of the *Ann* at the start of the Seven Years War. In both cases, Sidi Muhammad has resort to a traditional mode of maritime violence for novel and constructive purposes. He is not in the business of making holy war on Christian seafarers, nor is he straightforwardly in search of ransoms, though to his victims it can seem like that. This is not *jihad*, as it is conventionally and narrowly imagined in the West, but something very different. These particular acts of Moroccan corsairing are designed not to punish or distance non-Muslims, but to force Western powers into closer dialogue and into negotiation. Sidi Muhammad wants the West's attention and respect. Most of all, he wants and needs increased access to and influence over Western commerce. The essential reason for this lies in that same semi-desert emptiness of much of Morocco that has perplexed and disoriented Elizabeth Marsh.

Like the rest of the Arab world, Morocco at this time was severely underpopulated. As late as 1800, there may have been only seventeen million people scattered throughout Arabia, North Africa, the Western Sahara, Sudan and Greater Syria. By contrast, the Indian subcontinent and China, both geographically smaller territories, contained respectively some two hundred and over three hundred million inhabitants at this time. In contrast too with India and China, the Arab world – with the exception of Egypt – was not populated overwhelmingly by productive peasant farmers, but substantially by semi-autonomous tribespeople. Outside its great cities, many of Morocco's inhabitants were what Elizabeth Marsh chose to style as 'wild Arabs', peoples who were often nomadic and beyond the ruling Sultan's easy control.[50] All this influences Sidi Muhammad's determination to build up Morocco's overseas commercial connections, while at the same time exercising some authority over them. His country is too arid, and too sparsely cultivated, to provide for a highly productive agricultural economy, and there is consequently no large, docile peasantry that can easily be fleeced by way of royal taxation. His best hope of enhancing royal revenue and reach, therefore, is by expanding and supervising Morocco's trade. To be sure, trans-Saharan trade still remains important; and, in addition, there are and there have long been plenty of European merchants active in Morocco's ports and cities. In the three months she is a hostage here, Elizabeth Marsh will record meetings with traders from England, Ireland, Sweden, France, Spain, Denmark, Greece and the Dutch Republic. But in earlier reigns it has proved easy for such European intruders to get Morocco's overseas trade substantially into their own hands, and cream off some of the profits. Sidi Muhammad's aim is therefore both to make his country even more wide open than before to European commerce and commercial players, and to monitor such trade more closely and effectively so that he is able to tax it. This is why, as one French diplomat puts it, 'the emperor . . . became a merchant himself'.[51]

In the process, Sidi Muhammad also became an actor in what in retrospect can be viewed as this period's proto-globalization, a man preoccupied both with extending his influence in the Islamic world, of which he and Morocco were a part, and with developing and exploiting connections with widely different regions of the Christian West. Sidi Muhammad's reign is a vivid reminder that, in the words of one historian: 'proto-globalization was, in effect, a multi-centred phenomenon, strengthened by the active partici-pation of Muslim elements'. As European and American diplo-mats will become increasingly aware, the Sultan is at one and the same time devoutly Muslim and interested in traditional scholarship, and in some respects a cosmopolitan, commercially driven and consciously innovative figure. 'A man of great quickness of parts and discernment,' the British Ambassador conceded in 1783, '. . . beloved much by his subjects.' However, added this same writer, the Sultan possessed another marked characteristic: 'his excess in women, in which he confines himself within no bounds'.[52]

And so Elizabeth Marsh re-enters the story. After hearing the interpreter translate Sidi Muhammad's formal declaration, she and the other weary hostages are dismissed and taken to a house in the *mellah*, the Jewish quarter of Marrakech, just to the east of the royal palace. Normally this is walled in on all sides, a segregated place with a single gate guarded by the Sultan's soldiers. But the Lisbon earthquake and its aftershocks, which recur throughout her time in Morocco, and remind her with their noise of 'a carriage going speedily over a rough pavement', have reduced sections of the *mellah* and its walls to rubble. Although Jews in Morocco are generally allowed freedom of worship, and some play important commercial roles, and act as intermediaries in diplomatic encounters with European Christians, they are still marginal people, subject to mistreatment and punitive taxation. The largest in Morocco, the Marrakech *mellah* is essentially a ghetto for the disadvantaged, the home not just of the city's Jewish population, but also of many of its European slaves.[53]

Elizabeth takes in the dismal, half-ruined one-storey square building that is to be their prison, 'its walls . . . covered with bugs, and as black as soot', and chooses to have her tent pitched outside in its open courtyard. But there is no time to rest. Jaime Arvona, the acting Sultan's high-level Menorcan slave and favourite, arrives with an order that she, but not the other hostages, is to be escorted to the palace. She goes with him through a succession of gates and gardens, and past a series of guards. As she draws nearer to the centre of the palace complex, she is instructed to take off her shoes because she is entering the domain of a prince of the blood, a descendant of the Prophet. Once inside, there are more rooms, and more guards, until finally there is 'the apartment wherein His Imperial Highness was'.[54]

Until now, Elizabeth Marsh's ordeal in Morocco has been shared with others. Progressively more isolated in her own mind, she has in fact hardly ever been alone. Accordingly, a number of different individuals have been able to observe and report on her. Some of the other captives and several European merchants and envoys have written about her time in Sla and the journey to Marrakech. She has featured in official and private correspond-ence between British sea officers, politicians, diplomats and col-onial officials. And she and the others have been the subject of formal diplomatic missives and proclamations by Sidi Muhammad himself, as well as detailed accounts by slaves and interpreters attached to his court. Individuals of no political weight or wealth, Elizabeth and her companions nevertheless leave an extensive and unusually diverse imprint on the archives. But once she enters barefoot through the gates of Sidi Muhammad's palace, she becomes the sole chronicler of what happens there, a solitary voice. And her story will only be written down much later, when she is in another country, and subject to different influences and new pressures.[55]

As she describes it, this first palace encounter is brief, an occasion at which she is carefully appraised perhaps, but unable to register much herself except the cool, richly clad individuals gazing curi-ously at her. Sidi Muhammad sits at his ease alongside four of his women, 'who seemed as well pleased as he was himself at seeing me. Not that my appearance could prejudice them much in my favour.' Elizabeth is self-conscious as well as frightened, aware of her sun-scorched face (or is this a deliberate assertion for her reading public that she is indeed pale-skinned?) and of her crumpled riding-dress, marked with sweat and sand from her journey. One of the women offers her, through an interpreter, some fresh Moroccan clothes. When Elizabeth declines, she takes 'her bracelets off her arms; and put them on mine, declaring I would wear them for her sake'. Without much experience of jewellery, Elizabeth's immediate, dazed reaction to these open-sided silver bangles is that they look like horseshoes. The rituals of hospitality over, she is dismissed:

> But my conductor, instead of taking me to our lodgings, introduced me into another apartment, where I was soon followed by the Prince, who, having seated himself on a cushion, inquired concerning the reality of my marriage with my friend. This enquiry was entirely unexpected; but, though I positively affirmed, that I was really married, I could perceive he much doubted it . . . He likewise observed, that it was customary for the English wives to wear a wedding ring; which the slave [interpreter] informed me of, and I answered, that it was packed up, as I did not choose to travel with it.[56]

At last the acting Sultan allows her to leave, giving her 'assurances of his esteem and protection'. She is escorted back to the dim, mosquito-infested house in the *mellah*, but over the next two days her situation changes. As at Sla, the hostages are visited by some members of the European merchant community, who come to offer assistance. There is John Court, an intelligent and cultivated London-born merchant based at Agadir, who has travelled widely in sub-Saharan Africa, and has been summoned to Marrakech by Sidi Muhammad to act as an intermediary. His companion is an Irish trader called Andrews, from Asfi on Morocco's Atlantic coast. Naïvely, Elizabeth Marsh confides to these two men both that her 'marriage' to James Crisp is only a pretence, and tells them something of her encounter in the palace.[57]

Naïvely, because she is now doubly at risk. As Andrews warns her, there is a danger that some of Sidi Muhammad's spies and slaves will hear gossip, or find evidence in her papers, that she has lied and is not in fact a married woman. She is also increasingly at risk among her own people. It has been over a month since their capture, and by now the other passengers from the *Ann*, Joseph Popham and his son, are noticeably going their own way: 'We seldom had the pleasure to see our fellow-captives, as they found much more amusement in the company of the ship's crew, than with my friend and myself.'[58] Even thirteen years after the event, when she wrote these words, Elizabeth Marsh was unwilling to admit that it might not have been a search for amusement that kept the Pophams away from her and James Crisp, but disapproval and/or embarrassment. At the time of her Moroccan ordeal – for all her recent gloss of ladylike accomplishments – she was still firmly artisan in background, and used to the compromises of shipboard life. She may thus not fully have appreciated that her conduct had gone well beyond what conventional middle-class males like the Pophams would have seen as acceptable in a young unmarried woman. She had chosen to travel without a female chaperone. She had been obliged to sleep (or not sleep) in rooms alongside three men to whom she was not related. She had pretended to be first the sister, and subsequently the wife, of James Crisp. And now she had been escorted, without the others, to the palace of a Muslim prince. Whatever happened in the future, and however involuntary some of these actions had been, her reputation was under pressure.

It becomes still more so when Jaime Arvona returns with 'a basket of fruit . . . [and] a variety of flowers', and an order that she accompany him once more to the palace. She dresses herself, she will write, 'in a suit of clothes, and my hair was done up in the *Spanish* fashion'.[59] True or no, this is a wholly exceptional detail. Nowhere else in any of her writings does Elizabeth Marsh comment on her appearance, except to note its deterioration. During the various journeys and emergencies that make up her life, she may record that her hair is becoming brittle, or that her complexion is burnt, or that she is eating too much, or that she is sick, but the only gesture of physical vanity she admits to is before this second meeting with Morocco's thirty-five-year-old acting ruler. As before, her errand takes her through gardens and buildings that are aesthetically mixed. Now that Morocco and Denmark are in commercial alliance, the acting Sultan has secured a succession of royal Danish gardeners who are busy redesigning three of the gardens in his palace complex, creating walkways of trees, intricate mazes and flowerbeds. The interior of Sidi Muhammad's stone and marble palace is also, seemingly, a study in hybridity. There is traditional mosaic work and glazed tiles in geometric designs, but there is also a smattering of Western consumer goods: 'several fine European pier glasses with very handsome hangings' in the royal apartments, for instance, and 'in each room is a fine gilt branch for wax candles'.[60] This is not a straightforward act of emulation of Western tastes, however. In Islamic tradition, light possesses a divine quality as the visible manifestation of God's presence and reason. As he consistently tries to do, Sidi Muhammad has borrowed from the West with premeditation, for his own purposes and in his own way.

The man himself is

> tall, finely shaped, of a good complexion ... Dressed in a loose robe of fine muslin, with a train of at least two yards on the floor; and under that was a pink satin vest, buttoned with diamonds. He had a small cap of the same satin as his vest, with a diamond button. He wore bracelets on his legs, and slippers wrought with gold. His figure, altogether, was rather agreeable, and his address polite and easy.

As this suggests, it is primarily in terms of surfaces and commodities, and their seductive power, that Elizabeth Marsh describes this second palace encounter. She is offered not traditional coffee, but tea, a re-export from Asia. It arrives in 'cups and saucers which were as light as tin, and curiously japanned with green and gold. These I was told were presents from the Dutch.' This is one of

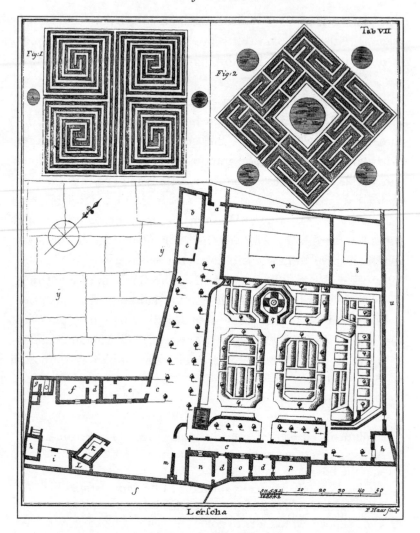

A plan of the Danish gardens outside Sidi Muhammad's palace.

the details that confirm that she did indeed witness the royal apartments of Sidi Muhammad's palace. Earlier in 1756, the Dutch government and the VOC, the Dutch East India Company, had sent the acting Sultan a series of presents in the hope of securing a commercial treaty with Morocco: luxury textiles, a coach, ornamented pistols, and these cups and saucers that were probably, like the tea, imported from China and Batavia (today's downtown Jakarta). It is with yet more international commodities that the acting Sultan makes his proposition:

> A slave brought a great collection of rarities, which were the produce of different nations, and shewed them to me. I greatly admired everything I saw, which pleased the Prince exceedingly; and he told me, by means of the interpreter, that he did not doubt of my preferring, in time, the palace to the confined way of life I was then in; that I might always depend on his favour and protection; and that the curiosities I had seen should be my own property.

Elizabeth Marsh rejects his suggestion. She reiterates through the interpreter that she is married to James Crisp, and that she does not 'wish to change my situation in that respect, and whenever it was agreeable to him, I would take my leave'.[61]

Instead, she is passed on to one of Sidi Muhammad's women, seated at the opposite end of the room. Elizabeth Marsh describes her, too, in terms of surfaces and commodities. But while the acting Sultan, who aspires to be a merchant of sorts, is surrounded by the products of transoceanic trade, this lesser, female being is mainly, though almost certainly not entirely, Moroccan in ornament:

> She had a large piece of muslin, edged with silver, round her head and raised high at the top; her ear-rings were extremely large, and the part which went through the ears was made hollow, for lightness. She wore a loose dress . . . of the finest muslin, her slippers were made of blue satin worked with silver.

Dressed in fine Indian textiles, which have perhaps also been presented by the Dutch, or which may have been shipped across the Indian Ocean by Arab or Asian traders, this woman converses with Elizabeth, using as her interpreter a French boy-slave who is young enough to be allowed in the company of the acting Sultan's harem.[62]

It is at this point that the narrative changes in quality and tone.

Given the quantity and quality of detail she supplies, much of it unavailable in any other English-language source at this time, there can be no doubt that Elizabeth Marsh did have at least one close encounter with Morocco's acting ruler in the inner rooms of his Marrakech palace. It is probable too that he sought to retain her there for sexual purposes. But what kernel of accuracy there is in Elizabeth's scarcely believable account of what happens now, when she is in the company of the acting Sultan's woman, is simply unknowable. As she tells it, the French boy assures her that the Moroccan woman alongside her is merely uttering routine pleas-antries. Since the woman appears friendly and waves her hands as if making gestures of encouragement, Elizabeth risks repeating some of her words. What she inadvertently says, or attempts to say, is as follows: '*Lā ilāha illā Allāh wa-Muhammad rasūl Allāh*'. This is of course the primal statement of Muslim commitment: the affirmation that there is no god but God, and that Muhammad is God's prophet.

Unsurprisingly, on her speaking these words, 'the palace was immediately in the utmost confusion, and there was every sign of joy in all faces'. Sidi Muhammad orders silence, and Elizabeth Marsh is taken swiftly out of the public rooms into a large, secluded apartment 'much longer than broad, and crowded with women, but mostly blacks', that is part of the seraglio. (There may be a small ring of truth here. An English slave at Sidi Muhammad's court reported in the 1750s that it was the acting Sultan's custom to have a black, that is a sub-Saharan, female slave bring his chosen women to his bed.)[63] Elizabeth waits there, both frightened and intensely curious, refusing offers of refreshments in case the food and drink are drugged. Then she is summoned to attend Sidi Muhammad once more, this time in a different, private apartment. He is

> seated under a canopy of crimson velvet, richly embellished with gold. The room was large, finely decorated, and sup-ported by pillars of mosaic work; and there was, at the other

end, a range of cushions, with gold tassels, and a Persian carpet on the floor.

They converse again through an interpreter:

'Will you become a Muslim? Will you properly consider the advantages resulting from doing as I desire?'

'It is impossible for me to change my sentiments in religious matters, but I will ever retain the highest sense of the honour you have done me, and hope for the continuance of Your Highness's protection.'

'You have this morning renounced the Christian faith and turned Muslim. And a capital punishment, namely, burning, is by our laws inflicted on all who convert and then recant.'

'If I am an apostate, it entirely proceeds from the fallacy of the French boy, and not from my own inclination. But if my death will give you any satisfaction, I no longer desire to avoid this last remedy to all my misfortunes. Living on the terms you propose would only add an accent to my misery.'

He seems perplexed, but continues to importune her. On her knees, she replies:

'I implore your compassion, and – as a proof of the esteem you have given me reason to expect – I beseech you to permit me to leave you forever.'

He covers his face with his hands and waves her away. The slave interpreter grabs her by the hand, and:

Having hurried, as far as possible to the gates, found it no easy matter to pass a great crowd which had assembled there. My worthy friend [James Crisp] was on the other side, with his hair all loose, and a distracted countenance, demanding me as his wife; but the inhuman guards beat him down for striving to get in, and the *black* women, holding me and hallooing out – No Christian, but a Moor – tore all the plaits out of my clothes, and my hair hung down about my ears. After a number of arguments, my friend prevailed; and, having forced me from the women, took me in his arms, and, with all possible expedition, got out of their sight.[64]

❀

Rewritten and converted into dialogue, Elizabeth Marsh's retrospective published account of the climax of this, her last interview with Sidi Muhammad, reads like an extract from a contemporary play or novel. This is scarcely surprising since she certainly drew some inspiration from the latter form of literature, and possibly also from the former. Nor is the drama, even melodrama, of this part of her story at all surprising. She wrote it in 1769, in the midst of another and different phase of her ordeal, when she was under acute pressure. Yet for all the naïve literary artifice, and a clear element of invention (it was Western European states, for instance, not Maghrebi societies, that traditionally burnt religious apostates), authentic bewilderment and terror still seep through her words. This was not surprising either. Her danger in Morocco had been real, and her temptations had been real.

Because women rarely worked as sailors or traders, and travelled far less frequently than men, they formed over the centuries only a minority of the Europeans who were captured at sea by Muslim corsairs. But European women who were captured in this fashion were far more likely than their male counterparts to be retained for life for sexual or other services in Maghrebi and Ottoman households. This was particularly the case if they were young, single, poor, or in some other way unprotected. In the 1720s, Moroccan corsairs are known to have taken at least three British women at sea. Two of these were the wives of prosperous Jewish merchants who were captured alongside them, and in due course all of these individuals were ransomed and handed over to the Royal Navy. The remaining woman, Margaret Shea, was young and single when she was captured travelling on her own from Ireland in 1720, and she was treated very differently. Impregnated after being brought to Morocco, passed between several owners, and converting or forced to convert to Islam, she seems never to have got home.[65] Such incidents also occurred in the second half of the eighteenth century. After his formal accession to the Sultanate in November 1757, Sidi Muhammad committed himself to reducing corsairing and slave-taking as part of his wider policy of improving commercial relations with the West. Nonetheless, he is known to have retained attractive and vulnerable Christian female captives. In about 1764, a very young Genoese woman was shipwrecked on Morocco's Mediterranean coastline. Like Elizabeth Marsh, she was brought to Sidi Muhammad's palace at Marrakech, but unlike Marsh she converted to Islam, submitted to entering the harem first as a concubine, then as one of his wives, learnt to read and write Arabic, and was renamed Lalla Dawia.[66]

As a Genoan, this woman hailed from a modest republic possessed of only a small navy and limited diplomatic leverage. Yet although Elizabeth Marsh and her fellow hostages came by contrast from the world's foremost Protestant power, this did not automatically guarantee their safety or her own virtue. When Lalla Dawia told her story in the 1780s to an English doctor, William Lempriere, who had been allowed into the Sultan's harem in order to treat her, she made no mention of actual acts of coercion, as distinct from threats, being used against her when she first arrived at Sidi Muhammad's palace in 1764. With no immediate prospects of escape or rescue, and cut off from her family, her resistance had simply been worn down over time in the face of the Sultan's blandishments. This could easily have been Elizabeth's fate too. In 1756 Britain was engaged in a transcontinental war, and needed Moroccan supplies for its only remaining Mediterranean base,

Gibraltar. Its politicians were in no position to dispatch an expeditionary force against Sidi Muhammad to rescue a handful of low-grade hostages, and in any case, acting in that fashion was never at any time standard British policy. Britons who were captured at sea and brought to Morocco in this period customarily spent at least a year, and usually more, in confinement or engaged in hard labour there, until the Sultan of the day allowed negotiations to get under way for their release. So the *Ann*'s crew and passengers could well have found themselves in Marrakech for many months, if not years, and Elizabeth Marsh, a twenty-year-old woman with 'nobody near me that I knew', could have been exposed to many more palace encounters.[67] She could also of course have been forced into sexual submission.

The romantic, salacious and imperial legends that have clustered around female slavery in Islamic societies – and the considerable ignorance and archival silences that still surround these women – can obscure what this would have meant. Female slaves in Moroccan and Ottoman households normally enjoyed safer, easier lives than slave soldiers in these regions, or than most Africans sold into slavery on Caribbean and American plantations. Female slaves might, if they were very lucky, and if they were purchased by affluent men, be beautifully adorned and elegantly accommodated, as Sidi Muhammad's favourites evidently were. Their owners might even come to love and cherish them. But even the most cosseted female slave was still property. She had no right of refusal to sexual congress with her master. Coerced into intimacy, she was always vulnerable to physical indignities and violence. A slave soldier was at least mobile; and, if he survived, he might even win some kind of advancement through his exploits. But, unless she was taken as a wife, or produced a child for her master, once her physical attractions faded, a slave woman could easily become neglected, or be married off to another slave, or to a free person of her owner's choice.[68] As Elizabeth Marsh perceived retrospectively, giving in to Sidi Muhammad's gift-laden seductions would have reduced her to 'passive obedience, and non-resistance'.[69] Her own resistance, such as it was, may have helped to save her from this. Rather more important though, for a devout and personally charitable Muslim ruler like Sidi Muhammad, is likely to have been her claim that she was married.

The surviving evidence suggests that he was not convinced of the truth of this claim, but also that he did not feel able simply to disregard it. Elizabeth Marsh's precise marital status really did become the salient point. A possible proof of this lies in the official correspondence of Jaime Arvona, Sidi Muhammad's Menorcan slave-secretary and confidant. In the letters Arvona wrote on his master's instructions to various British officials at this time, he habitually refers to James Crisp and the Pophams by their surnames. But he calls Elizabeth Marsh just 'the Lady'. Arvona may have described her thus simply in accordance with the protocol of Islamic societies. According to this, one did not, politely, refer directly to females by their names and thus expose them to a public knowing, except in legal processes where formal nomenclature had to be a matter of record. Thus, when Lady Mary Wortley Montagu made her famous visit to Istanbul in the early eighteenth century alongside her Ambassador husband, her Ottoman hosts invariably and out of courtesy referred to her as 'leydi/lady' or 'Madam', never by her name.[70] But in Elizabeth Marsh's case, Arvona may have exploited this particular piece of etiquette in order to help a stranded female and a fellow European in distress. Whatever the reason, he did not call her 'Mrs. Crisp' in his letters, since the acting Sultan refused anyway to believe that this was really her title. But neither did Arvona refer to her as 'Miss Marsh', even though he knew very well that this was who she was in fact. His fellow Menorcan slave, Pedro Umbert, who had talked to Crisp and Marsh during their time at Sla, had earlier informed him of the subterfuge they were intending. Instead, Arvona habitually referred to Elizabeth Marsh simply as 'the Lady', a title that conceded nothing, but also gave nothing away.[71] It was the only time in her life that she seems routinely to have been accorded on paper a status that she always coveted.

Since her story held, and since Sidi Muhammad had much greater priorities, negotiations to do with sex were quickly overtaken by more conventional, exclusively masculine politics. The day after his final interview with Elizabeth, the acting Sultan summoned James Crisp, the Pophams, the Master and crew of the *Ann* – but not her – to the palace. At his order, they attached their signatures to a letter to the British Governor of Gibraltar, Baron Tyrawley. In it, the acting Sultan complained again of the 'ill treatment' he had met with from the British, but declared that 'he would set them an example of moderation, as well as justice'. The hostages were free to leave. Or, more precisely, they were free to be fetched. The British would not and could not invade Morocco. Effectively, this letter gave formal notice that the Royal Navy would now be permitted to retrieve the hostages from its shores.[72]

Once the letter reached Gibraltar, the wheels began to turn. On 7 October 1756, the *Portland*, the same fifty-gun warship that had helped to escort Elizabeth Marsh and her family away from Menorca the previous April, was dispatched by Admiral Sir Edward Hawke to rescue her again.[73] A week later, the ship reached Larache, a trading and corsairing centre on the southern embankment of Morocco's Loukos estuary, and by 21 October it was in sight of 'the towers of Salleè' (Sla). Anchored in Sla road the following day, Jervis Maplesden, the *Portland*'s captain, took note of what little was left of the *Ann*, 'laying on her beam ends on the shore'. Most of its usable timber was missing, he reported, having been cannibalized by the corsairs in order to repair their own ships. The *Ann*'s cargo had also vanished, as the locals had promptly unloaded James Crisp's casks of brandy and sold them to some local Dutch merchants.[74]

The *Portland*'s arrival at Sla, and subsequent mooring off Asfi, were followed by an extended game of epistolary diplomacy, hard bargaining and naval posturing. 'I am come in peace and humility,'

Captain Maplesden assured the acting Sultan in his first letter, and he maintained this conciliatory tone throughout. But, while flying a flag of truce from the *Portland*'s masthead, he also took care to exercise his ship's 'great guns and small arms' on a daily basis and within sight of those on shore. 'His Imperial Highness took a great deal of pleasure of the contents and style of your letter,' was Arvona's response to Maplesden's first communication. It showed, he went on smoothly, that Britain did, after all, possess some public servants who were both 'capable and civil'.[75] By early November, Sidi Muhammad had formally agreed that 'Mr. Crisp, the Lady, Mr. Popham and his son', and the crew of the *Ann* would be allowed to board the *Portland* and 'proceed on their voyage'. Naturally, he told Maplesden through Arvona, there would need to be some return. By March 1757 he expected Britain to appoint a full-time consul in Morocco to facilitate trading relations between the two countries. He also expected presents – which meant naval stores. Otherwise, Gibraltar would be starved of Moroccan supplies, and he would declare war on Britain's merchant shipping, which was already under pressure from French warships and privateers:

> Thank God, all the empire [Morocco] is in peace, and . . .
> [obeys] one Head, that knows everything that passes in
> Europe, and knows how to distinguish what is convenient
> to his dominions.

All the mutual compliments, bluffs, counter-bluffs and barely concealed threats ended at 10 a.m. on 17 November, when Elizabeth Marsh and the men who had travelled with her on the *Ann* were finally rowed out to the *Portland*.[76] Captain Maplesden gave up his cabin in the forecastle for her private use. It was the first time in over three months that she had slept in a room on her own.

Elizabeth Marsh's last weeks in Morocco seem to have been deeply troubled. She was physically unwell, probably from a mixture of malnutrition and heat stroke, but suffering too from a 'dejection of spirits'. John Court, the Barbary merchant who had helped the hostages in Marrakech and subsequently accompanied them to Asfi, commented later on how she had 'lost so great a share' of her usual liveliness and stamina during this final phase of captivity. She was understandably nervous that something might go wrong, that Maplesden's negotiations would misfire, and that she would never be allowed to leave. Even when being rowed out from Asfi to the *Portland*, she remained 'in extreme dread, until we reached the man of war, fearing a signal from the shore to order our return'.[77] The confrontation with Sidi Muhammad, and having to pass 'for what I really was not', also preyed on her mind. Not least because what she 'really was' seemed now far less clear than before. She had lost sight of her family, and been taken away from the sea. She had been brought against her will to another continent, and into a physical, cultural and human landscape that she barely understood. She had masqueraded first as James Crisp's sister and then as his wife; and in Sidi Muhammad's palace she had come close to losing her religion, name, language, country, mode of dress, virginity and moral moorings; had perhaps even been tempted at some level to abandon these things. She had wanted travel, but found instead, as she put it, varieties of 'cruel restraint'.[78]

This sense of restraint had only increased at the end of September 1756, when they were allowed to leave Marrakech. With the immediate danger and excitement receding, she became almost paranoid that spies working for Sidi Muhammad might uncover evidence of her unmarried status in her papers. She persuaded James Crisp to purchase a gold ring from a Swedish merchant, and hid it in her clothes chest in case her belongings were searched. She was torn between desperately longing for letters from her parents (and hence reassurance that they still acknowledged her) and fear of 'their being intercepted, as they would have discovered my real name'.[79] Although her last weeks in Morocco were spent in relative comfort, in a house in Asfi owned by Andrews, the Irish merchant, and his Greek trading partner Demetrio Colety, she seems to have been unable to rest or relax. For a while, John Court remained with them, entertaining her with 'new and improving' tales of his travels in Africa. But in general this period of waiting was 'irksome' to her. Even dressing was 'a pain', she admitted later in print, 'any farther than what decency required'; and for several reasons she was weary of enforced male company, 'solitude being the principal object I desired'. Beneath her agitation and despondency lay not just physical and mental exhaustion, uncertainty and fright, but also ambivalence about the prospect of return. She worried about being forcibly retained in Morocco. She was also afraid of returning to what she knew, and to those who knew her, in case 'the ill-disposed part of the world would unmercifully, though unjustly censure my conduct'.[80] At the heart of these fears was a specific, legitimate concern.

What this was emerges indirectly from an account she wrote of a wedding procession in Asfi. She observed it through the narrow windows of Andrews' house during this final period of waiting, when she was feeling 'extremely melancholy':

> The Bride was invisible, it being the fashion of the country to conceal such persons from public view; the vehicle wherein she was enclosed resembled a garland, not unlike that our milk-maids carry on a May-day, decorated with flowers and other ornaments. In a little time after this, the Bridegroom followed, on a mule richly caparisoned, with a Moor on each side, fanning him to keep off the flies; they went a slow pace, with a band of music before them; and the lady, as I heard, was not above twelve years of age, and, in all probability, had never seen the man she was married to, until that very day.[81]

There is an obvious way in which this passage might be interpreted. Western observers at this time regularly employed the treatment of women as a prism through which to examine and judge other societies. Then, as now, dwelling on the real and reputed restrictions faced by Muslim women could be a way of criticizing Islam and Islamic societies' perceived limits on political and personal liberty far more broadly. Yet in this case such a conventional reading would be inadequate. Too much of Elizabeth Marsh's account of this Asfi wedding procession evokes joy and celebration, and is suggestive more of envy than of censure. As she describes them, the Moroccan couple go to their wedding amid music, ornament, richly decorated mules, and so many flowers that it reminds her of May Day. Most of all, the couple marries in the customary manner, ceremoniously, watched by 'a great crowd', and with all the proper ritual. By contrast, what sort of wedding – and what sort of marriage – could *she* expect, once her masquerade as a wife and her near-disappearance into a harem became more widely known? The best she could hope for, given conventional expectations of unsullied female virtue, must have become increasingly clear to her during these final weeks in Asfi. Rather as she imagined the young Moroccan bride she observed there, Elizabeth Marsh could no longer expect much real choice over whom she was to marry.

The *Portland* and its passengers reached Gibraltar on 27 November. Some time between early December 1756 and 7 January 1757, in a private ceremony there, she became in law, and not merely in counterfeit name, Mrs James Crisp.

3

Trading from London, Looking to America

WHEN JAMES CRISP proposed to Elizabeth Marsh at Gibraltar in December 1756, she 'was not much surprised at this declaration'. Nor was she immediately won over, but his 'general good character, the gratitude I owed him, and my father's desire over-balanced every other consideration; and . . . we were married'. This, at least, was the version of events that she subsequently published for anyone to read. But what it left out is as suggestive as what she chose to emphasize. She admitted feeling grateful for Crisp's aid and protection in Morocco. She stressed that her father, Milbourne Marsh, had pressed the match. She was careful to allude, for all sorts of reasons, to Crisp's 'general good character'; and she described how he had worked hard to persuade her 'of his love for me, and the unhappiness he was under at the thought of parting'.[1] Neither in her accounts of her Moroccan ordeal and its aftermath, nor in any other writings that survive, however, does she use the word 'love' in connection with her own feelings for the man who became her husband.

She claimed indeed that there had been 'many difficulties to surmount' before she could resign herself to marrying him, and that the struggle 'caused me many tears'. The account of the making of this marriage supplied by her uncle, George Marsh, is more comprehensive but still slanted. In his Family Book he records, as she never did, that James Crisp had first 'paid his advances' to Elizabeth Marsh in 1755, when both of them were living in Menorca. These initial approaches were rejected, he claimed, because Crisp 'was not thought a suitable match for her, though a fine, handsome man and rich'. Instead, the Marsh family at this point had another candidate in view. Before being captured at sea and taken to Morocco, George Marsh asserts, Elizabeth 'was contracted to Captain Towry of the Navy', information that she half-corroborates in her own writings.[2] Who was this individual? At the time that Elizabeth was briefly engaged to him, Captain Henry John Phillips was not yet a Towry. He was the nephew and heir of a Captain John Towry, who was the navy's Commissioner at Mahón, Menorca, and he inherited the latter's surname along with the bulk of his estate when Towry died in 1757. The worldly attractions of Elizabeth Marsh's first fiancé went beyond this, however. The Towrys were a Scottish naval dynasty well represented in the higher echelons of the Royal Navy's administration and among fighting sea officers. A later Towry fought alongside Horatio Nelson at the Battle of Cape St Vincent in 1797. Commissioner John Towry was also closely connected by marriage to another originally Scottish naval clan, the Clevlands, and from 1751 to 1763 John Clevland was Secretary to the Admiralty.[3]

Some of the reasons why Henry John Phillips, the future Captain Henry Towry, was judged preferable as a likely husband for Elizabeth Marsh are therefore obvious enough. As she later wistfully recalled, this was an 'alliance . . . such as I had no reason to expect'.[4] It would have offered her social as well as economic advancement, a definitive remove from her own distinctly mixed origins to within touching distance of Britain's governing class. Given the paramountcy of kinship links, her marriage to a future Towry would also have been potentially transformative for her ambitious, striving father and uncle. It would have given both men a direct line to the Admiralty and more, since John Clevland was also a Member of Parliament. From such a connection, the men of the Marsh family could plausibly have anticipated enhanced access to the powerful, and swifter promotion. All this they might have hoped for; and all this was lost when Moroccan corsairs intercepted the *Ann*, and Elizabeth Marsh's reputation was compromised. Milbourne Marsh promptly received a letter from the soon-to-be Henry Towry withdrawing his suit, and 'importing that his cousin, Mr. Clevland . . . insisted upon his marrying a lady he had provided for him'.[5] As for James Crisp, whose reactions no one took the trouble to record, he was abruptly promoted from rejected suitor to the one possible candidate for Elizabeth's hand, the only man who, in the light of events in the Mediterranean and Morocco, could reaffirm her respectability to the world through the act of offering her marriage.

Hence at least some of Elizabeth Marsh's ambivalence in the face of Crisp's renewed proposal, and her parents' urgings this time that she accept it. How much she felt for the soon-to-be Henry Towry is unclear. She claimed later that it was in order to join him that she had embarked on her disastrous voyage on the *Ann*; and certainly she understood something of the future she was losing along with their engagement. She also recognized that, in the wake of her North African ordeal, marriage to James Crisp was now imperative.[6] It was a union that reinforced the distinctive, revealing trajectory of her life. Becoming Mrs Henry Towry would not, in the event, have provided for prolonged happiness, since the by-now Captain Towry died in battle in 1762. But the Clevland connection, and the Towry family's wealth, would have guaranteed her a more than satisfactory widow's pension. Like many other prosperous naval widows, an Elizabeth Marsh-turned Elizabeth Towry might have retired to Bath, with its genteel society, spa, and constantly replenished supply of possible second husbands. She would probably have spent the rest of her life in England, and there would have been no further dramatic links between her private story and more extensive histories. As it was, she married James Crisp, and was caught up again in the flux of transcontinental events and contacts. Slavery, the sea, empire, war and the ambitions of contending states had brought her into being and shaped her experiences across three continents. Now it would be the turn of international trade, and the lure of transatlantic projects.

Arriving at a fair and comprehensive view of the man responsible for this shift in Elizabeth Marsh's experience is difficult, in part because she and other members of her family distorted the record. In his wife's retrospective writings, and in those of her uncle, George Marsh, James Crisp features from the outset as the eager, already slightly suspect suitor, while she is the reluctant, put-upon bride. In reality, Crisp too may have felt under constraint in 1756. Given what was expected of a gentleman, there were few decent alternatives available to him in the wake of events in Morocco except to renew his proposal to Elizabeth. But whereas her doubts and struggles and subsequent escapes are preserved in intermittent, always intense autobiographical writings, most of Crisp's personal papers, like all of his account books, disappeared in the successive crises of his life. Such business correspondence of his that does survive gives little away about his inner life. Establishing *his* perspectives and actions, which in the 1760s and early '70s substantially determined Elizabeth's own life, thus requires a different kind of narrative and analysis. In his case, personal information has to be garnered and inferred from a mass of seemingly impersonal sources. Most of all, Crisp's intricate commercial existence has to be tracked across at least three oceans, and four continents.

꩜

James Crisp (it was sometimes spelt Crispe) was a member of one of early modern Britain's most consistently extrovert commercial dynasties. His most famous ancestor, Nicholas Crisp (c.1599–1666), had started out as a Mediterranean trader, but then moved into the East Indies and Africa. He was a leading figure first in the Guinea Company, the earliest joint-stock enterprise in England to trade with Africa, and then in the Company of Merchants trading to Guinea which was established by Charles I in 1631. Both companies focused on Sierra Leone and the Gold Coast, and on gold, ivory, redwood, sugar and, over time, slaves. The English had been voyaging to West Africa to buy and sell since the sixteenth century, but Nicholas Crisp helped to alter the quality of this trading connection. He and his brothers took on Dutch and Portuguese competitors more aggressively than their predecessors and, by way of an agent, established English factories and forts at Kormantin in Abanze in present-day Ghana, and at Komenda, Anomabu and elsewhere on the Gold Coast. Kormantin remained the headquarters of England's dealings in goods and ultimately human traffic in West Africa until it was superseded by Cape Coast in 1665, by which time Nicholas Crisp was a baronet and had imported by his own estimate half a million pounds in African gold. He also established a manufactory for glass and ceramic beads on his landed estate in Hammersmith, to the west of London. Together with the cloves, indigo, ivory, silks, calico and shells he imported from the East Indies, these brilliantly patterned beads supplied him with the wherewithal for barter in the trade in West African cloth and slaves. 'There was scarcely a branch of English overseas trade in which he had no interest,' one historian has written of Nicholas Crisp, 'so that he was justly termed "the most general trader of the time".'[7]

Even during Sir Nicholas's lifetime there were many branches of this Crisp dynasty, not all of them enterprising or successful. Yet over the generations the family exhibited certain recurring characteristics. There was a predilection amongst its males for particular names: Nicholas, Samuel, Rowland, Ellis and James. One of Sir Nicholas's distant cousins was a James Crisp, a London-based embroiderer.[8] As in this case, there was a persistent and unsurprising family association with the City and port of London. There was an intermittent family connection with the production and sale of salt, one of the prime commodities in transcontinental trade; and there was an intermittent connection too with the slave trade. There was also a marked, sometimes disastrous proclivity for participating in conspicuously long-distance enterprises, and for taking risks. In 1670, Ellis Crisp, a descendant of Nicholas Crisp and a factor with the East India Company, became the first English merchant to voyage to Taiwan. He won an audience with its acting ruler, Cheng Ching (1642–81), who was determined to make Taiwan 'a place of great trade', and wrote an account of the 'soile, customes, habitation & healthfulness for merchants to live in that country, as also . . . the merchandise desireable to bee imported and of merchandise propper for us to exporte'. The following year, 1671, Ellis Crisp embarked for Taiwan again, intending to establish a permanent factory there. He disappeared at sea along with his ship, the *Bantam Merchant*.[9] Other branches of the family remained active in West Africa and India; still others crossed the Atlantic and settled in North America and the West Indies. By the early 1700s there were members of this Crisp dynasty in St Kitts, Barbados and South Carolina, some of them substantial plantation- and slave-owners.

The man who courted and married Elizabeth Marsh came from a minor, and mainly Eurocentric, branch of the family. As was true of Sir Nicholas Crisp, James Crisp's initial area of concentration was the Mediterranean. His father *seems* to have been a Harvey Crisp who obtained his Lieutenant's certificate with the Royal Navy in 1711, but subsequently went into the merchant marine and trade with Spain. Harvey Crisp married a Dorothy Burrish in 1722, and James and his brother Samuel were *probably* born in the Iberian peninsula or on one of the Balearic Islands in the late 1720s or early '30s.[10] 'Seems' and 'probably' because, like many actors in this story, like Elizabeth Marsh herself, James Crisp was a transient, one of the many 'problematically hybrid people' being created at this time by expanding geographies of trade and rising levels of migration.[11] Accordingly, he evaded some of the routine documentation that accumulated around more settled lives: but two things are clear. Socially, James Crisp's background was superior to that of the Marsh family, and in marrying Elizabeth Marsh he made a substantial economic sacrifice.

For any overseas merchant, and especially for one who was just starting out, marrying well was a vital part of business strategy. A well-dowried bride provided a nest egg of capital, and eased any difficulties a young trader might experience in obtaining credit. Elizabeth Marsh could not offer these advantages.[12] By the 1760s, Milbourne Marsh's naval posts at Gibraltar and Menorca had enabled him to begin accumulating savings, as well as consumer goods appropriate to his rising status, including plate, table linen and fine glassware. When Elizabeth's younger brother, John Marsh, got into financial difficulties during the 1770s, Milbourne was able to lend him £1000 at a derisory rate of interest without any difficulty or need for retrenchment on his own part. As for her uncle George Marsh, the Seven Years War catapulted him decisively into the ranks of the substantial professional class. In 1762 alone he made £1500 from acting as an agent dealing in captured French ships, in addition to his government salary.[13] Back in 1756, however, the brothers were still climbing slowly into respectability. They could give James Crisp advantages in kind, namely useful Navy contacts, but not a large cash sum. That he still offered Elizabeth marriage shows kindness and a sense of honour on his part, or deep affection, or infatuation, or possibly all of these things. The fact that the new couple chose to return to England from Gibraltar in February 1757 on a merchantman called the *Elizabeth* may suggest a degree of romance on Crisp's part, and perhaps at the time also on hers.[14]

James Crisp felt able to take the risk of marrying an under-portioned woman because his elder brother Samuel was already well established in the family business, Crisp Brothers, and because he himself at this stage was moderately affluent. Like many overseas traders, James Crisp had started out working as a ship's master and supercargo for more senior merchants, sailing regularly between Spain, Portugal and the main Italian ports with cargo and ballast while still in his teens.[15] Then family connections gained him the captaincy of one of the packet boats operated by the

British Post Office: an eighty-ton ship called the *Lovel* operating between Mahón in Menorca and the two most thriving ports in the Mediterranean, Marseilles and Livorno (Leghorn). Seemingly mundane, this appointment was actually a significant coup. In the 1750s, Post Office packet boats carried more official than private mail; in the case of the *Lovel*, not just communications between British Consuls and agents in France, Italy, Spain and Menorca, but also secret correspondence to and from ships in the Royal Navy's Mediterranean fleet. In return for their usefulness to the state, packet-boat captains were allowed considerable slack. They wore elaborate uniforms of their own devising, and they could make substantial profits from carrying passengers, bullion and freight, and from private trade. They were also able to engage in some mild smuggling, since British customs officials were under instructions to look the other way as far as packet-boat officers were concerned.[16]

From the outset, then, James Crisp enters this story as an agent of communication between different countries and ports, and as someone traversing the legal boundaries established by states and politicians. It was his extra income from captaining the *Lovel* that enabled him to propose to a woman lacking capital, as well as a secure reputation. Before Menorca came under French threat in 1756, the packet boat was probably bringing Crisp in some £1000 a year. It seemed enough to gamble on; enough for him to retire from active sea-going and become a land-based merchant; enough for marrying Elizabeth Marsh and setting up house with her in London.

For all the growth of Britain's outports, London was still the undisputed hub of the country's overseas trade, shipping and retail industries, as well as its political, cultural and financial centre. Well before James Crisp made the city his prime base, he and his brother were paying rent on vaults and a warehouse in Mark Lane, near the Thames.[17] From London, James Crisp looked outwards to five other prime commercial locations. There was Barcelona, where his brother Samuel Crisp and another partner, a Swiss merchant called Jacob Emery, presided over a counting house; Emery, in turn, linked the company with a woman partner, Cathalina Lavalée, who operated out of Montpellier. A major port for Mediterranean and Atlantic trade and a mart for Catalonia's important salt trade, Barcelona was a site of Spain's emerging industrial revolution, a place of tobacco-processing plants, textile manufacturers and calico printers.[18] The second side of James Crisp's trading web was made up of a cluster of ports on Italy's western coast, especially Genoa and Livorno, both of which had close commercial links with Spain, and with North Africa and the Levant.[19] Then there was Hamburg. This was a markedly cosmopolitan free port of ninety thousand inhabitants, where foreigners enjoyed religious freedom and the right to trade on equal terms with the local burghers. Blessed by its situation on the River Elbe, which was ice-free except in the coldest winters, Hamburg was another big importer of Spanish wines and colonial produce, and a leading exporter of linen, grain and timber.[20]

By comparison with these great cities and entrepôts, James Crisp's two other favoured business locations within Europe might appear minor, even eccentric choices. They were not. The Shetlands, a group of sparsely inhabited islands about a hundred miles off northern Scotland, where Crisp and his brother began purchasing and salting cod in 1759, four thousand quintals every year (a quintal equaled 112 pounds), was 'at the centre of the European fishing world'. With little arable land available, most adult men on the Shetlands worked in fishing and whaling, sometimes venturing as far north as Greenland; and their fresh and salted fish was always in high demand, especially in Catholic countries for fast days, and for victualling ships bound on long-distance voyages.[21] The commercial significance of the Isle of Man, James Crisp's final site of concentration within Europe, was also out of all proportion to its size. Barely thirty miles long and a dozen miles wide, the island was held from the British Crown by the Dukes of Atholl. This quasi-autonomous status allowed it to function as a busy, unsupervised warehouse for large quantities of imported goods from a wide variety of destinations. Rather like the American colonies, the Isle of Man accepted the authority of the British monarch, but did not recognize the fiscal control of the Westminster Parliament. Ships arriving at or leaving the island, and the cargoes they carried, were exempt from the attentions of English, Scottish and Irish customs and revenue officers; and the Dukes of Atholl themselves charged no export duties except on the island's own products, and only token import duties. As a result, the Isle of Man was a haven for comparatively free trade. It was also, as Edmund Burke remarked, 'the very citadel of smuggling', a well-known stopping-off place for anyone wanting to ship goods into Britain, Ireland and beyond, duty-free.[22]

These different locations – London, Barcelona, Hamburg, Livorno and Genoa, the Shetlands and the Isle of Man – provided James Crisp and his partners with a closely interconnected trading network. Fish caught and salted by Crisp employees in the Shetlands would be shipped to London. Once there, the ship might also take on grain from Mark Lane's famous Corn Exchange. Crisp's ship's masters might sail with these cargoes to Barcelona, since Spain was Europe's biggest market for salted fish, or to Livorno, another fish-hungry market, or to Genoa, a city with a poor agricultural hinterland that was always in need of external supplies of foodstuffs. Once in port in Spain or Italy, Crisp's ships would take on wine, brandy, silk or other textiles and – from Barcelona – salt. They might unload these goods in Hamburg, lading in return linen for Barcelona's textile factories, or yet more grain for Genoa. Or they might return to London, where the salt would promptly be shipped onwards to the Crisps' fishing venture in the Shetlands. Or they might offload their cargo at the Isle of Man, in which case some of the Crisps' wine, brandy and textiles would be reloaded onto large wherries moored off the island, many of them crewed by Irishmen, and sailed into secluded coves and

ORIGINS

The making of the Crisp family fortune. Some of the fifteen varieties of beads known to have been manufactured on Nicholas Crisp's Hammersmith estate before 1640 for his trade in gold and slaves in West Africa.

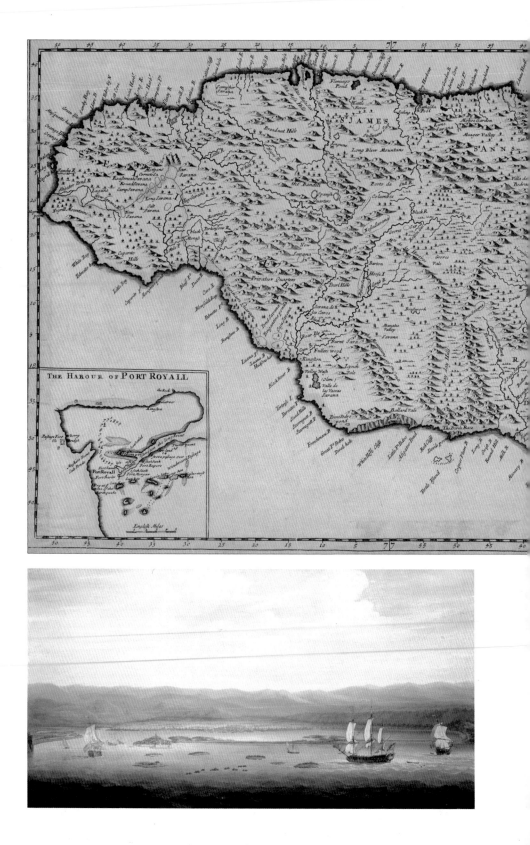

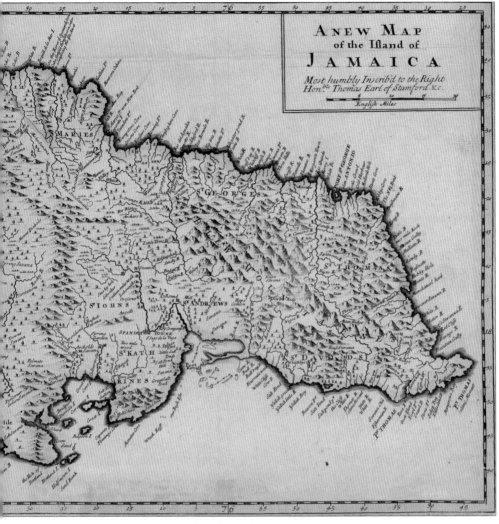

A NEW MAP
of the Island of
JAMAICA

*Most humbly Inscrib'd to the Right
Hon.ble Thomas Earl of Stamford &c.*

English Miles

KINGSTON HARBOUR in JAMAICA

Above 'A New Map of the Island of Jamaica', by John Senex, 1719. The place of residence, but not perhaps the place of birth, of Elizabeth Bouchier, Elizabeth Marsh's mother.

Far left 'View of Port Royal', by Richard Paton, *c.*1758, Milbourne Marsh's first landfall in Jamaica in 1732, and where Elizabeth Marsh was probably conceived.

Left Kingston harbour. A major slaving and sugar port, from which Milbourne Marsh and his pregnant wife set sail for Portsmouth in 1735.

THE SEA, THE SEA

'Ship's Carpenter', etching by
Thomas Rowlandson, 1799.
The occupation of Elizabeth
Marsh's father and paternal
grandfather. The tools and
instruments reflect the trade's
mix of manual and highly
specialized labour.

George Marsh, a painting
by Benjamin Wilson.
Elizabeth Marsh's powerful
uncle, and the chronicler of the
family's fortunes across
continents.

The Navy Office in Broad Street.

'The Navy Office in Broad Street', engraving by Benjamin Cole, *c.* 1756.
The Royal Navy's administrative headquarters in London, and where George Marsh
intrigued to get his brother Milbourne Marsh appointed Naval Officer in Menorca.

Saffron Island, Menorca, showing some of the naval installations designed by Milbourne Marsh.

'Chatham Dockyard', by Joseph Farington, *c.*1788-94.
A painting which conveys something of the scale and intricacy of the Royal Navy's dockyards.
It was in the victualling yard here that Elizabeth Marsh wrote *The Female Captive* in 1769.

PATRONS

An illuminated letter from Sidi Muhammad, the Moroccan ruler who was responsible for Elizabeth Marsh's capture and release in 1756, and indirectly for her marriage. In keeping with his interest in transcontinental and cross-cultural exchanges, the Sultan sought in this message to George III in 1766 to recruit engineers from Britain.

bays off western Scotland. In 1764, a Scottish customs official
described what usually happened then:

> The farmers, their servants, and the lower sort of people in
> general are adventurers or abettors of the smugglers, and on
> the particular parts of the coast at which any wherries or
> boats are expected to arrive a great number of people with
> horses do assemble, and as fast as the goods are landed they
> are put upon horses . . . and in this manner, escorted by a
> number of the principal smugglers, they proceed up this
> country, and into the north of England through moors
> and unfrequented roads, and then dispose of the goods to
> shopkeepers, carriers, and other persons.[23]

This sort of commercial circuit, with goods and vessels moving
between separate but connected sites of business, was common
even among perfectly law-abiding merchants, because it made for
an efficient use of ships' holds. The idea was for some cargo to be
transported at every leg of a merchantman's voyage, with no expensive ship time and space being wasted simply carrying ballast. Yet
while James Crisp's commercial web was designed to operate
in this way, it was never self-contained. At each of its main
nodes, Crisp Brothers and their agents branched out in search of
additional business. Thus, their Barcelona office also traded with
Cádiz, Valencia and Madrid, with Palma on Majorca, and Lisbon
in Portugal.[24] Moreover, at no stage was the Crisps' trading web
exclusively European. In commercial terms, as increasingly in other
respects, Europe, Asia, the Americas and parts of Africa were not
distinct or separable entities; and the way of life that James Crisp
and his new wife constructed for themselves in London in the late
1750s and early '60s was funded in part by the profitable exchange
of goods between all of these continents.

Each of the main nodes of Crisp's commercial web allowed him
to reach beyond Western Europe. This was manifestly true of
London, then the world's busiest port, an imperial metropolis
and the Crisp family's traditional power base. It seems likely, for

instance, that James Crisp had an interest in the *Countess of Effingham*, a two-hundred-ton ship commanded by his kinsman Rowland Crisp, that sailed regularly in the 1750s and '60s with cargoes of wine between London, Madeira, Boston and Jamaica, returning loaded with sugar, rum and ginger.[25] James Crisp also made his own forays into the Caribbean. The 1764 issue of *Lloyd's Register* lists four ships for which he was the managing owner (one indicator of his considerable success at this stage). Three of these ships, the *Favourite*, the *Maria* and the *Union*, left London that year declared to be bound respectively for Italy, Spain and the Shetlands. The fourth, the *Maria Burrish* (named after a relation of Crisp's mother), was carrying cargo to Dominica, a former Spanish colony seized by Britain in 1761.[26] James Crisp did not confine himself to a single imperial system. Some of the salted fish he exported to Barcelona from the Shetlands, and on occasions from Boston, ended up on Spanish domestic dining tables. But imported salt fish, *bacalao*, also went to victual the royal fleets sent out at intervals to Spain's colonies in South America. And Crisp Brothers traded to Spanish America directly, and in their own right. In 1761 the company's Barcelona office took delivery of 379 casks of olive oil from 'San Juan in the New World', in other words from Puerto Rico. Notarial documents make clear that the two brothers worked hard to maintain these links with Spain and its imperial markets even in 1762–63, when Madrid and London went to war over trade and colonies.[27]

By the same token, Hamburg offered the Crisps not only a ready market for colonial re-exports (perhaps from Jamaica, or Boston, or Dominica, or Spanish America), but also access to trade with the Baltic, and to a network of fairs and exchanges in its hinterland that extended as far as Archangel in Russia. From Livorno, a port that was open to ships from every state and to merchants of all religions, and firmly neutral in wartime, James Crisp gained access to business in the Levant and North Africa. In 1764, for instance, his company was exporting Spanish textiles and wine to Tunis, an outpost of the Ottoman Empire, and taking on foodstuffs for Italian markets in return.[28] A disproportionate number of the traders and bankers Crisp dealt with in Tunis and Livorno were Jewish. 'There are Turks, Levantines, some few French, Venetians, Genoese, Corsicans, Greeks, Armeneans, Neapolitans,' wrote the British ambassador of Livorno's merchant community in the 1760s, but prefaced this by remarking that 'the Jews are more numerous than any'. An important site for Hebrew publishing, Livorno contained Europe's biggest concentration of Sephardic Jews after Amsterdam, and the financiers and merchants among them controlled a third of the city's commercial houses. Livorno's Sephardi community was especially prominent in the city's jewel trade, dealing in Indian diamonds, mainly from Goa, and coral, 'which is fished for about Corsica by the Neapolitans and others, is totally in the hands of the Jews ... and is a very lucrative trade; the greatest part of it is sent to England and from thence to the East-Indies'.[29]

James Crisp is known to have possessed family associations with the international trade in precious stones. At least three of his kinsmen, Nicholas Crisp, Thomas Crisp and Edward Crisp, worked (among other things) as jewellers in London. It seems likely that an occasional aspect of James Crisp's business activity in the early 1760s was shipping in coral, and possibly diamonds, from Livorno for these jewel-making and jewel-trading kin, and facilitating the export of their finished products to the Indian subcontinent and elsewhere.[30]

Yet it was the smallest point of his commercial web, the Isle of Man, which allowed Elizabeth Marsh's husband the widest access to the world. His contacts here were long-standing. Already, in 1752, ships owned by the island's merchant-cum-smuggler-in-chief, George Moore, were carrying New England fish to the Crisps in Barcelona, and lading wine and brandy in return.[31] James Crisp's connection with Moore, and with another important Manx merchant, John Taubman, proved invaluable when Britain went to war

'A New Map of the Isle of Man' by Thomas Kitchin, 1764.

with France after 1756, and with Spain in 1762–63, and trade between these countries was officially suspended. Manxmen took scarcely more notice of London's wars than they did of its taxes, and the island's neutrality protected it from attack or invasion. So, throughout the Seven Years War, some of Crisp's Spanish wares, like those that his agents persisted in obtaining from Marseilles, Montpellier and other French ports, went on being unloaded on the Isle of Man, and were ferried discreetly over to Britain and Ireland by way of wherries operating out of its two main ports, Douglas and Peel.

Apart from brandy and other spirits and wines, the contraband goods that James Crisp and his brother increasingly concentrated on were Barcelona silk handkerchiefs. These were large, four to five palms in width, made of soft Spanish twilled silk, variously coloured, and favoured as luxury fashion accessories by both sexes. They were also perfect articles for smuggling, being light, easy to transport in large numbers, and yielding a very good price. The Crisps shipped out tens of thousands of them from Barcelona to the Isle of Man over the years: plain black handkerchiefs for purchase by men and women in deep mourning, handkerchiefs in 'black with red cross bars' for use in light mourning, and 'assorted in lively colours' for everyday display. The brothers shipped them in boxes marked only with letters of the alphabet, and fudged names on the bills of lading. They supplied their sea captains with 'fictitious papers' in case their vessels were stopped and searched; and during wartime they were careful to employ only Danish or other neutral ships. In the process, they made a great deal of money. Between January and June 1765 alone, John Taubman purchased over £7000-worth of smuggled goods from Crisp Brothers (the equivalent now of over half a million pounds), mainly in the form of silk handkerchiefs and brandy.[32] As in Tunis and Livorno, the brothers' business transactions here involved Jewish agents. The Isle of Man had 'no restrictions ... against any sect of religion'. 'Equity and justice to the trading part of the isle' were the only criteria for being allowed the freedom to operate. So when Abraham Vianna, Solomon Da Costa and Jacob Osorio applied to the Duke of Atholl for naturalization on the Isle of Man in 1760, James Crisp in London and his brother Samuel in Barcelona were able cheerfully to act as their referees, along with traders in Amsterdam, Cork, Gothenburg, Lisbon, Cádiz, Venice and Leeds.[33]

Relative openness to dealers from different nations and religions, minimal import and export duties, and resolute neutrality were only part of the Isle of Man's attractions. Rather like Livorno, the island produced few exports of its own, but it offered invaluable storage for outside goods that were then shipped lucratively elsewhere. Not all of James Crisp's contraband wine, brandy and silk handkerchiefs transported by way of Manx wherries into Scotland ended up moving southwards into England. Some went to Glasgow, to be re-exported to the American colonies. Some of his other imports into the island (especially the textiles) may even have reached West Africa, since slave ships operating out of Liverpool, Whitehaven and Lancaster routinely stopped at the Isle of Man to pick up any goods that might serve as barter in the trade for slaves.[34] As far as Crisp himself was concerned, the island was also one of several points of access to Asian commodities. French, Danish, Dutch and Swedish merchantmen regularly brought in cargoes of East Indian goods. By law, such commodities could only enter Britain through London and under licence from the East India Company; but Crisp Brothers ships unloading cargoes in the Isle of Man could take on East Indian goods in return. John Taubman, for instance, was in a position to supply them with occasional cargoes of tea from Canton shipped into the island, virtually duty-free, by Dutch traders.[35]

It was in part these highly flexible, essentially cosmopolitan business practices – this commercial international – that caused George Marsh, a loyal employee of the British state, to view his nephew-in-law as lax, duplicitous and, as time went on, wicked. James Crisp, he wrote at one point, appeared 'to have no good principles'.[36] Yet there were important respects in which Crisp's behaviour was not aberrant at all. Over the course of the mid-eighteenth century, British merchants became notably more aggressive and successful in exploring extra-European markets, and Crisp's progress, from a concentration on Mediterranean commerce to involvement in ever more distant seas, perfectly exemplified this trend. Nor was it unusual, at this or at any other time, for traders to seek out ways of evading government regulations restricting the free flow of goods. To the extent that Elizabeth Marsh's new husband *was* at all unusual, it was in being for a while so successful, so quickly.

The prominence of some of his early business associates is one indication of his calibre. In Livorno, James Crisp dealt with James Clegg, who made a fortune from salted fish, Francis Jermy, a Norfolk-born banker whose profits allowed him to build a lavish and beautiful villa outside the city, and Peter Langlois, a member of its best-known Huguenot trading dynasty.[37] He also worked closely with George Moore and John Taubman, who were probably the chief Manx merchants of their time, and with the Català family in Barcelona, who were among the city's main calico printers. The Crisp family's name and pre-existing networks may have smoothed his way to such contacts, but – for all the suspicions he aroused among some members of the Marsh family – James Crisp seems also to have possessed unusual energy, enterprise, and a personal capacity to impress. He was 'a merchant of so much eminence', wrote a British aristocrat and former cabinet minister who knew him socially as well as a businessman, 'and so large dealings'.[38]

The life that the Crisps constructed for themselves in London also bore witness to James's skills as a merchant – and to Elizabeth Marsh's own ambition. The couple seem to have moved from one rented address to another, but by late 1765 they were living in Camomile Street, in Bishopsgate ward. This area had remained untouched by the Great Fire of 1666, and was still full of narrow, crowded streets and wooden tenements and courtyards. Markedly ancient as a place of habitation (Roman remains were periodically

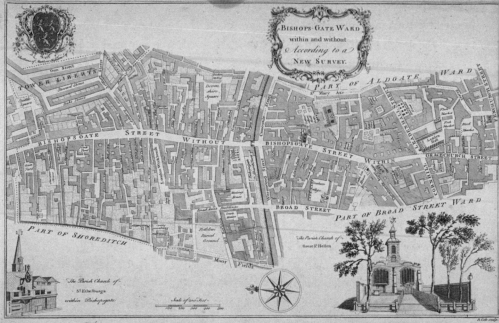

'Map of Bishopsgate Ward' by Thomas Bowen, engraved by
Thomas Bowles, 1767.

unearthed in Camomile Street throughout this period), the neighbourhood was conspicuously mixed and dynamic. The local rate
books reveal a markedly high proportion of Huguenot, Dutch and
Sephardic Jewish names even by London standards – van Neck,
de Aguilla, Benjamin, Israel, Salvador, Modigliani – and a rapid
turnover of tenants, businesses and warehouse lessees.[39] Dirty,
crowded and polluted, the location's advantages for James Crisp
emerge most clearly from glancing at a map. Camomile Street
intersected with Bishopsgate Street, one of the main coach roads
to the north of England, which was convenient for when business
took him to Scotland or the Isle of Man. Devonshire Square,
where merchants involved in Britain's Levant trade concentrated,
was only two streets away; and East India House in Leadenhall
Street, the headquarters of the East India Company, was at most

five minutes' walk from the Crisp residence. This was probably on the south side of Camomile Street, where the house plots included space for warehousing. James Crisp had only to walk southwards for fifteen to twenty minutes in order to reach the Thames, the customs house, Billingsgate fish market and his firm's vaults in Mark Lane.

When he did so, he would have passed down Gracechurch Street. This is where Jane Austen pointedly situates Elizabeth Bennet's aunt and uncle Gardiner in *Pride and Prejudice*. Pointedly because, as Austen makes clear in the novel, Gracechurch Street, like most of Bishopsgate, was not a fashionable or smart neighbourhood during the eighteenth and early nineteenth centuries. The Bingley sisters, who gravitate conventionally towards landed society for all their own background in trade, despise the address. But, as Austen suggests, by making the Gardiners affluent and cultivated as well as virtuous, Bishopsgate, with its warehouses, insurance and shipping offices, its many coaching inns and its mushroom businesses, was a recognized site for the making of mercantile fortunes, a place for people to move up. One of Elizabeth Marsh's woman friends in Camomile Street, for instance, was a Mrs Jewson.[40] Her husband, Charles Jewson, subsequently became Chief Cashier of the Bank of England.

As far as James Crisp and Elizabeth Marsh were concerned, the evidence suggests that even in the very early 1760s they were living more than comfortably. In 1762 only thirteen other households and businesses in All Hallows Bread Street, the parish where the Crisps were living at that time, were assessed at a higher rate than they were for payments 'towards the necessary relief of the poor of the said parish'.[41] In the view of Elizabeth's uncle George Marsh, however, it was not what the couple paid in taxes, but their level of expenditure that merited comment. He viewed them as extravagant, and he was right. Husband and wife were both already highly experienced travellers, but neither had spent much time in London before 1757, and both were young, divided, self-inventing individuals with something to prove. As a result, they clutched eagerly at the capital's pleasures and possibilities. When their first child, Burrish Crisp, was born on 27 April 1762, and again at their daughter Elizabeth Maria's birth two years later, James Crisp seems to have gone out of his way to seek out not just expert but highly fashionable assistance for his wife. He called in a well-known man-midwife, Dr David Orme of Threadneedle Street, a pioneer in the improved use of forceps.[42]

Such expensive behaviour (which in this case also suggests Crisp's attentiveness as a husband) infuriated George Marsh. It was a perennial complaint among social commentators and satirists that upwardly mobile London tradesmen and merchants, egged on by their over-ambitious womenfolk, lived beyond their means. The economic dislocations that followed the Seven Years War amplified the stridency of this kind of critique. 'How many packs of cards were sold in the year 1716, and how many in 1766?' thundered a London journalist in 1767:

> How many coaches, chariots, chaises, horses and footmen were kept in 1716, and how many in 1766? . . . How many tradesmen wore laced waistcoats in 1716, and how many in 1766? How many bankrupts were there in 1716, and how many in 1766?[43]

George Marsh, who enjoyed pasting improving and admonitory extracts of this sort into his commonplace book, would have agreed both with the sentiments and the implicit *schadenfreude*. Physically plain, fond of sober (though not inexpensive) dress, and almost immoderately temperate out of choice and because of his epilepsy, he disapproved of his niece and her glittering, indulgent husband not simply because they were extravagant, but because they were different, and to begin with successful. When this ceased to be the case, he felt thoroughly vindicated, and he converted what had happened to the couple into a morality tale of the perils of waywardness and improvidence. He also saw the Crisps, with more acuity, as exemplars of wider, international changes:

One of the worst effects of that great wealth, which flourishing manufactures and an extensive commerce bring into a country, is the prevalence of extravagance. Luxury is but another word for a rapid consumption, and as the Prince's revenue in all modern states depends on that consumption, monarchs are in general ready enough to encourage it. Courts are the great scenes of it. Capitals are full of it ... [The] frugal and modest become in the vortex of a great city, like the surrounding particles which whirl them about.

James Crisp and Elizabeth Marsh, he wrote, had been 'too much inclined to ape the fashion and expense of people of very great fortune, in all kinds of entertainments and ruinous follies'.[44] The vortex, and their undue enjoyment of it, had whirled them to destruction.

This was an insufficient explanation of events, but George Marsh's perspective on the Crisps' London life, and on his niece Elizabeth herself, is still valuable. He saw more of them at this stage than any other member of the family, since his work at the Navy Office in Crutched Friars and at the Victualling Office at Tower Hill brought him into close proximity with Bishopsgate. Normally he devoted little curiosity to women. Although he was careful to allot sentences to his female relations in his Family Book, he rarely enquired into their lives deeply. A 'very nice affectionate woman' is, for instance, virtually the sum total of his description of his own wife, Ann Marsh.[45] But, even more than her husband, Elizabeth Marsh challenged and troubled his understanding, and he devoted several pages to describing her. She had been, he conceded towards the end of his life, and looking back on these years in London, 'a handsome and very engaging woman with great abilities' – though even now he could not resist remarking that she had eaten too much, evidence to his mind not simply of the sin of gluttony, but of undue sensuousness and a lack of discipline. By this time he was anyway even more convinced that great abilities were dispensable:

Every day's experience ought more and more to convince the world that happiness in human life depends more on small virtues than on splendid qualities . . . Splendid qualities are of little use in the common transactions of the day. Let mankind then who would wish their children happy, rather than great, give them ideas and habits which will befriend them in the common transactions of the day. Of those none are more valuable than economy.[46]

Yet, as was often the case in Elizabeth Marsh's experience, things were far more than they seemed, and far more than the personal. The tensions between James Crisp and members of her family stemmed from more than a clash of temperaments and lifestyles, just as what happened to her and her husband now was due to far more than their mutual delight in spending money.

At the root of these troubled family politics lay substantially different interactions with, and perspectives on, the world. George Marsh only journeyed outside Britain once in his life, but in his own modest fashion, he possessed a global perspective. As a member of the navy's Victualling Board after 1763, he oversaw the supplying of ships in all of the world's oceans, including those that sailed with James Cook into the Pacific. But for him, engaging with the world meant following the flag. In this he was typical of his family. By the 1760s a growing number of Marsh family males were using the British state and empire to secure and advance their own personal mobility. Milbourne Marsh, Elizabeth's father, kept his position at Gibraltar until 1763, and then returned to being Naval Officer at Menorca, which the British regained at the end of the Seven Years War. Her elder brother Francis Milbourne Marsh was by now a captain in the British Army, and was stationed for part of this and the following decade in Ireland and the West Indies; while in 1768 her younger brother, John Marsh, was appointed British Consul at Málaga in Spain. Then there was

Milbourne Warren, a son of Milbourne Marsh's maternal aunt, who worked for the East India Company as a master shipbuilder in Madras, and who also took part in the brief British occupation of Manila in 1762–63. Marguerite Duval, the daughter of Elizabeth's aunt Mary Duval, was married to a James Morrison who later climbed steadily up the ranks in the Mint, the agency responsible for designing and manufacturing Britain's copper, silver and gold coins, as well, increasingly, as the coinage used in its colonies. Linked through their employments to the British state, these men were naturally predisposed to view the world through the lenses of the British nation, state and empire.

Almost certainly born outside Britain, James Crisp, by contrast, was hybrid in culture and, like many merchants, conspicuously polyglot. He was fluent in Castilian and Catalan, and seems to have been able to make himself understood (though not to write) in Portuguese, Italian and French.[47] He was used to working in mixed, highly urban neighbourhoods, employed and dealt with men (and women) of several different nationalities, and relished doing business in neutral, free ports like Livorno, Hamburg or Douglas on the Isle of Man, places operating outside – and sometimes in defiance of – the jurisdiction of major states. Although he traded with British colonies in mainland America and the Caribbean, James Crisp also did business with parts of Spain's rival empire; and he corresponded and dealt indiscriminately with Jews, Catholics and Muslims in a fashion that could appear strange and even unscrupulous to those who were not overseas traders. Elizabeth Marsh had been shocked to see the casualness with which European merchants in Morocco (and their Muslim counterparts) shrugged aside religious barriers for the sake of mutual commercial benefit. 'The difficulties a Christian was exposed to in that country,' she wrote wonderingly of an encounter with a Dutch merchant who was planning to settle in Marrakech, 'were overlooked by him as matters of no importance or consideration.'[48] Like George Marsh, then, and more consciously, James Crisp thought and acted in transcontinental terms, his business interests extending across northern and southern Europe, and into Africa, Asia, and British and Spanish America. But unlike the males of Elizabeth Marsh's family, Crisp's contacts with and perception of the world before 1767 were not overwhelmingly determined by British state and imperial imperatives. His livelihood – and now hers – depended rather on the free movement of commodities, information and capital across state, imperial and maritime boundaries, and across ethnic, cultural and religious boundaries.

Like all major conflicts, the Seven Years War caused immediate disruptions to this kind of free economic movement. It also contributed to attitudinal shifts that were not always compatible with the kind of busy, protean adaptiveness that James Crisp exemplified and relied on. 'A merchant,' Adam Smith would write in *The Wealth of Nations* (1776),

> . . . is not necessarily the citizen of any particular country.
> It is in a great measure indifferent to him from what place
> he carries on his trade; and a very trifling disgust will make
> him remove his capital, and together with it all the industry
> which it supports, from one country to another.[49]

As Smith's more than usually austere tone suggests, ancient arguments over the degree to which commerce was a national and social benefit or liability were rehearsed in the middle decades of the eighteenth century with greater political edge and precision. On the one hand, patriotic Britons were proud of their expanding commerce, while many merchants profited from the consequences of Britain's military and imperial aggression at this time. On the other hand, intensifying national and imperial rivalries and violence also meant that individuals and groupings who were accustomed to trading and moving easily across political, religious and ethnic boundaries could sometimes find themselves obstructed or coming under greater suspicion, while the growing geographical range of warfare undermined some commercial projects and actors, even as it benefited others.[50]

Some of the qualities that made James Crisp a successful merchant – his cultural mix, his enthusiasm for new contacts, and his impatience with state controls and fixed boundaries; his entrepreneurship, in short – possessed the potential then to cause him problems at a time of massive warfare, and in the more nationalistic, imperially conscious British state that was so evidently emerging by 1763. The size and range of Crisp Brothers' commercial web, spun so rapidly, and out of limited reserves of capital, were a more practical source of vulnerability. 'Serve all nations,' was Abbé Raynal's advice to overseas merchants in *The History of the Two Indies*, 'but whatever advantage may be offered to you from speculation, give it up, if it should be injurious to your own country.' And Raynal added a more practical caveat: 'Do not embrace too many objects at once.'[51]

To begin with, the geographical diversity and partial illegality of James Crisp's trading interests proved advantageous. They helped him flourish despite the disruptions to trade brought about by the Seven Years War. Even though Spain's entry into the conflict in 1762 almost halved the level of southern European imports into London that year, Crisp Brothers, with their well-established Barcelona office, cosmopolitan staff and covert Isle of Man networks, seem initially to have held on to much of their Iberian and Spanish colonial business. It was the last stages of the war, and some of its repercussions, that began fraying, one after another, the threads of the brothers' commercial web.

Their Hamburg links probably suffered first, and as a direct result of the scale and intensity of the war. In 1763, the appetite of Frederick the Great of Prussia for wartime loans, and his limited capacity to repay them, provoked a major banking crisis in Amsterdam. This in turn put pressure on banks and merchants in Stockholm, London, Berlin and even the American colonies, but above all in Hamburg. For a while that autumn, trade in Hamburg, and its supplies of linen, grain and timber, ground to a halt, and the dislocations lasted until 1764 at least.[52] Then, Britain's own need for extra revenue to offset its huge wartime debts led to a spate of new fiscal regulations. The most notorious of these were the succession of new taxes aimed at Britain's American colonies: the Sugar Acts of 1764 and '66, the Stamp Act of 1765, and the Townshend Revenue Act of 1767. But it was a connected fiscal measure, aimed however at a very different part of the world, that most affected James Crisp.

As Edmund Burke remarked, Parliament's Revestment Act of May 1765, which returned sovereignty over the Isle of Man to the British Crown, and consequently made the island liable to customs duties established by the Westminster Parliament, was 'to the same purpose' as post-war British efforts to tax America. In both cases, the official intention was at once to increase revenue, to attack smuggling, and to assert London's imperial control. In 1764, British customs officials calculated that during the 1750s Manx smuggling had cost the British Treasury £100,000 per annum in lost revenue. The Spanish, Dutch, Swedish, Danish, French, Caribbean and British-based traders who continued shipping goods into and out of the island, they further estimated, were now depriving the Treasury of three times that amount every year in customs and excise duties.[53] The Revestment Act put an end to this by placing Manx commercial life under stringent new regulations. British customs and excise officers were given the power to search vessels arriving at or leaving the Isle of Man, and to confiscate illicit cargoes. As a result, the island's capacity to foster cheap trade between Asia, Africa, the Americas and Europe came to an end. The imposition of parliamentary control also put an end to the Isle of Man's capacity to adopt a neutral stance in time of war. The opportunities it had allowed Crisp Brothers and other traders to continue transporting Continental goods and re-exports into Britain, even when Europe's competing states were at war, were now, as James Crisp wrote, 'infallibly ruined'.[54]

Nonetheless, he went on, in what might have been the motto of his life: 'There are not wanting many profitable ways for a man to employ his capital.' The substantial closing down of Manx smuggling also put out of work the wherries, and their mainly Irish crews, that had previously ferried contraband goods from the island into Britain. By late 1765 Crisp and a new partner, Francis Warren, had purchased some of these wherries and persuaded their crews to move to the Shetlands to expand his fishing business there. The Inspector General of Scottish Customs reported dourly on this new Crisp initiative in July 1766. 'A separate fishery' had been initiated, he informed his Treasury masters,

> by the employing [of] eight Irish wherries of about twenty five tons burthen, each manned with eight men, inhabitants of Ireland . . . by which boats one thousand and fifty-six quintals of fish were caught at an earlier than usual season of the year, and at a greater distance from the shore, owing to the size of the boats, and expertness of the fishers employed; in the curing of which fish, about forty men and fifty or sixty women and children, natives of Shetland, were employed, and the same were afterwards exported in the name and on account of the said Messrs. Crisp and Warren.[55]

It was an admirable act of resilient entrepreneurship. Irish sailors and fishermen, recently put out of work on the Isle of Man, had been found new jobs. Their skills and boats extended Shetland's fishing season and catch. This in turn increased the island's job opportunities, and James Crisp's export business. The scheme's only weakness was typical of its originator. It paid scant regard to the pretensions of state and nation. The Scottish landowners and merchant land-masters who still dominated Shetland's fisheries heartily disapproved of Crisp's Irish interlopers, not least because, as he naïvely informed the authorities, 'the hardiness, diligence, and superior judgment of the Irish in fishing is very well known'. It was not just Scottish grandees and their Edinburgh-based lawyers who began putting pressure on the new venture, but offi-cialdom in London too. To the extent that he thought about it all,

Crisp viewed his Irish fishermen as British: 'The subjects of Ireland being by the 13th and 14th of Charles II . . . and the subsequent acts accounted British', he informed the Treasury confidently and carelessly.[56] Imperial British trade was not yet that simple. In terms of fishing rights, as in so much else, the inhabitants of Ireland were not in fact 'accounted British'. The Treaty of Union with Scotland in 1707, and subsequent legislation, had made clear that no one was to 'catch, cure, or land fish on any part of Britain but the subjects [and] inhabitants thereof, in all which cases the Irish are expressly considered as foreigners'.[57]

James Crisp tried hard to legitimize his new Shetlands initiative by reference to patriotic arguments that did not come naturally to him. 'The granting of this indulgence,' he pleaded, '. . . would be a means of your memorialist carrying on this great and valuable branch of trade to the kingdoms, in a more extensive manner than it has been,' but the Treasury in London and various Scottish dynasts were unmoved. Nor were they impressed by Crisp's proposal that he should be allowed to 'ship thirty-five thousand gallons of British spirits duty free' every year into the Shetlands, 'for the use of about one thousand five hundred fishermen'. As Crisp pointed out, it was common knowledge that Shetlanders smuggled in large quantities of spirits from Continental Europe, since how else could they withstand the bitter winters, short days and long, dark nights that geography inflicted on them for much of the year, and the iciness of their coastal waters. But as far as his official critics were concerned, fiscal principles were at stake, and ultimately the authority of the state. Allowing Crisp to ship British spirits into the Shetlands duty-free might establish 'a dangerous precedent', wrote one bureaucrat. 'In its nature' such an enterprise was 'not subject' to adequate state control.[58]

The saga of James Crisp's first economic ruin is much less, then, a morality tale of the penalties of personal extravagance, as George Marsh contended, than a more representative fable of how individual enterprise and transnational and transoceanic trade and con-

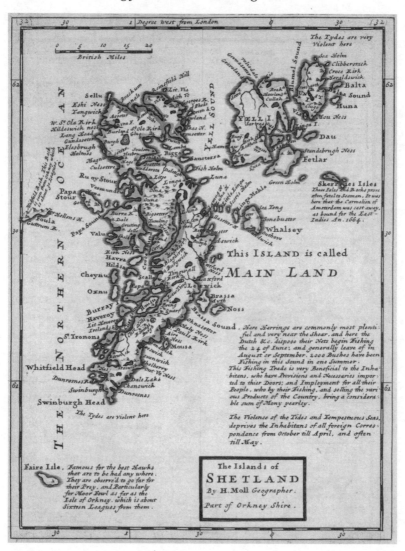

'Map of the Islands of Shetland' by Herman Moll, 1745.

tacts could come under extreme pressure from state interference, national rivalries, war and imperial adventures. This was not the entire story, however. Crisp would probably have survived the combined effects on his business of Anglo–Spanish warfare in

1762–63, the temporary collapse of Hamburg's trade, and the assaults on his Isle of Man outlet and his Shetland ventures, had his wider Mediterranean trading world remained intact. But after 1764, this part of his commercial web also began to unravel.

On 16 April 1764, three Crisp Brothers ships arrived at Genoa loaded with flour and wheat, the *Peggy*, the *Kitty* and the *Young Lady Maria*, the latter possibly named in celebration or anticipation of the Crisps' new daughter, Elizabeth Maria, whom her parents always referred to as 'The Young Lady'.[59] The ships' captains were under orders to take on more goods at Genoa, and then to sail quickly on to Livorno and Naples so as to take advantage of the rocketing prices in those ports caused by a local grain shortage. Instead, Genoa's Senate, anxious about the republic's own acute dearth of grain, impounded the three ships and their cargoes. Such flour as the Crisps were able eventually to recover was (they claimed) substantially spoilt, while for the grain and flour retained for Genoan use, Crisp Brothers were allowed only a 20 per cent profit on the purchasing price. This, they insisted, was 'so far out of proportion to the then actual price . . . [at] Leghorn and Naples markets, that it makes a difference to your memorialists of about two thousand pounds sterling'.

This represented a hideously large sum for a still-young firm with limited capital. Although James Crisp had insured his ships and cargoes with a London broker, marine insurance at this time rarely covered these kinds of losses; and the campaign the brothers initiated to recover the money they believed Genoa owed them, plus damages, made things worse, because it went on for almost two years, soaking up legal fees and their own time, optimism and enterprise. The dispute lasted for so long because it hinged on something far more momentous than a few petty cargoes belonging to a small merchant house, which was why both Genoa's Senate and magistrates and senior British politicians became involved, the latter for once weighing in on Crisp's side. Once again, this was in essence a clash between mercantile appetite for unhampered long-distance trade on the one hand, and local loyalties and state priorities on the other. It was vital, the Genoa authorities insisted in a lengthy written defence of their actions, 'that every nation should be supplied with such commodities as are wanting in their own country at a reasonable price'. Nations were 'reckoned among themselves to be in a state of nature', and a ruler's authority and his inhabitants' needs outweighed the interests of any private traders or companies. Certainly, they conceded, Crisp Brothers had lost money on their original grain speculation, and been deprived for a while of their own property, but this was nothing by comparison with the risk of allowing merchants and the market unmitigated freedom: 'For should the proprietors be invested with such power . . . the Prince would be deprived of the supreme right in him invested, of fixing just and equitable prices on grain, a step so highly necessary for the preservation of his own subjects' lives.'[60]

Against this position, the British Board of Trade deployed diplomatic pressure, and ultimately a counter-manifesto signed by thirty-four of 'the most able and respected merchants in London'. Temporary food shortages, these men and James Crisp countered, were no justification for a state to bypass the free market. This would be shifting off 'that calamity upon a foreigner, which the hand of God had laid upon the state itself'. If Genoa's Senate wanted Crisp's wheat and flour to feed its citizens, it should have paid for these cargoes 'according to the price at the market to which they were destined'. Issues of fairness or human need had nothing to do with it. James Crisp himself was adamant:

> Nothing (the proprietors desire to repeat and insist upon it) can give any Prince or State a power to lay any kind of restraint upon a foreign subject in the disposal of his property . . . To talk of what is equitable and reasonable independent of circumstances, is to talk at random. The reasonable because the real price of everything is what it will sell for.[61]

The reasonable because the real price of everything is what it will sell for. It was a thoroughly stark and modern position, and James

Crisp's insistence on it shows again how, behind the sentimentality that made him name his ships after female relations, lay an uncompromising conviction of the overwhelming importance of unfettered trade, and an impatience with anything restricting it – distance, corporate monopolies, national and imperial boundaries and *diktats*, and even human need and ancient notions of a just price for grain. Yet, for all his grand certainties and ambitions, Crisp and his partners were still small-time merchants with very limited leverage. Not until February 1766, and then only under sustained British diplomatic pressure, did Genoa's Senate finally agree in principle to settle the dispute, and it is unlikely that Crisp Brothers ever received their compensation, for by then the damage had long since been done.[62]

As was true of all merchants, the glue of James Crisp's commercial web was credit. Crisp Brothers' continuing success depended on his own and his firm's reputation for reliability and fair dealing, and on bills of exchange. These were documents roughly comparable to today's travellers' cheques: not simply promises to pay, but orders to pay in a foreign place, in a foreign currency, at some future time. By way of networks of agents and bankers, merchants used bills of exchange to arrange credit with each other across large geographical distances, to raise loans, and to take advantage of favourable exchange rates in different locations. In the process, however, they quickly became caught up in a string of reciprocal legal and financial obligations that could tighten around them if things went wrong. As the geographical range of trade widened in the eighteenth century, as credit networks expanded, and as ever more transactions and locations had to be dovetailed together, so the possibilities of things going wrong multiplied, not least because in some respects overseas commerce remained a dangerously primitive business.[63]

For all that James Crisp's enterprises extended into Africa, Asia, the Americas and Western and Eastern Europe, his goods still could not travel faster than a sailing ship or a horse could carry them.

For much of the time he dealt with people he had never seen, who were located in places even he had never visited. For information on these individuals and places he relied mainly on a stream of business letters, which again could only travel as fast as a sailing ship or a horse. The regular invocations of Providence in James Crisp's surviving business correspondence, like the phrase 'by the Grace of God, in good order' included in the manifests drawn up by his ships' captains, show the degree to which commerce remained at the mercy of natural and man-made contingencies, and was fraught with risk.[64] Genoa had been impounding incoming grain ships for some weeks before Crisp's vessels were seized in April 1764, but this was insufficient time for a written warning of what was happening in the republic to reach him or his brother in London and Barcelona. Even if, by some lucky chance, such a message had reached them in time, there would of course have been no speedy way for them to communicate this information to their three ships as they sailed confidently towards Genoa and the trap.

The slow haemorrhage of their firm's credit in the wake of this Genoa episode, and other setbacks, can be measured by the succession of failed bills of exchange crossing the desk of Sebastià Prats, the brothers' Barcelona notary. By late 1765 Crisp Brothers was desperately presenting bills of exchange to those traders in different countries who still owed them money. Since some of the latter were also in difficulties from post-war economic dislocations, many of these debts were never paid.[65] Earlier, the Crisp brothers' own credit reputation had been good. 'We are well persuaded of your punctuality at maturity,' the Livorno fish merchant James Clegg had assured James Crisp in 1764, but over the next two years the brothers began repeatedly to default. By early March 1767, Samuel Crisp was renouncing shares in ships' cargoes arriving in Barcelona that the company had previously purchased on credit, because there was no money available to honour the bills. Some weeks later it was left to Juan Francisco Fontannaz, the Crisps' chief assistant in Barcelona, to turn away the ships' captains coming eagerly to the door of their counting house in search of future cargoes, for by now Samuel Crisp and Jacob Emery had slipped out of the city and away from their creditors.[66] That same month, March 1767, the London newspapers published the formal announcement that James Crisp was bankrupt.[67]

Just before, he had written to his main banker in Scotland, William Hogg & Son of Edinburgh. He was in 'extreme anguish', he confided, shocked for once out of the customary impersonal style of business correspondence. Crisp Brothers was still owed, he claimed, 'between 15 & £16,000' – over £1.3 million in present-day terms – but he hoped that, out of 'extraordinary friendship', the banker would be content with confiscating the company's ships, buildings and fishing equipment in the Shetlands, for the brothers had no liquid capital left. 'Please to destroy this,' he scrawled at the end of the letter.[68]

※

James Crisp was not destroyed, but he was damaged. Bankruptcy was too much part of economic normalcy in London, especially in the 1760s, to be regarded as irrefutable proof of a trader's incompetence or improper dealings. Nonetheless, his freedom and independence were now far more limited, and his ambition of expanding a firm that had been mainly Mediterranean in scope into a business operating across different oceans and continents was in tatters. And, as always, bankruptcy was a personal as well as a monetary and commercial blow. It engulfed the victim's family, and easily poisoned relations and trust between husband and wife. A wife who purchased goods on credit was exempt by law from imprisonment for these debts. So, to the extent that Elizabeth Marsh herself had been extravagant during the couple's time in London – and George Marsh suggests that she was – any debts that she had accumulated continued to be James Crisp's responsibility, for all that he was now bankrupt.[69]

This may have embittered him, but Elizabeth was also given cause to feel bitter. In the spring of 1767 she, and not merely her husband, had to live with the humiliation of seeing repeated notices of his failure printed in the *London Gazette* and other newspapers, and with the knowledge that friends, relations and business rivals were reading these notices too. As was routinely the case with bankrupts, their home was searched so that Crisp's assets could be scrutinized and assessed. The law allowed 'doors, trunks, and chests' to be broken open if necessary. Any moveable property could be seized to pay the bankrupt's debts, except for 'the necessary apparel of himself, wife and children'; and the bankruptcy commissioners might 'examine on oath the bankrupt's wife'. Crisp was obliged to attend a series of creditors' meetings at London's Guildhall and at the Rainbow coffee house, Cornhill, a favourite resort of ship-owners and overseas traders. Like all bankrupts, he had to agree to the election of assignees, four of them in his case, who took responsibility for the valuation and sale of his estate.[70]

Only when the commissioners of bankruptcy were satisfied with a bankrupt's cooperation, and four-fifths of his creditors 'in number and value' had agreed to sign a special certificate, was he able securely to retain a percentage of assets, and win release from any remaining obligations and from the fear of being sued or arrested. It is unclear whether James Crisp ever succeeded in obtaining this essential document. Some London newspapers reported in late May 1767 that he had, but George Marsh, predictably, refused to the end of his life to believe it.[71]

One of the results of James Crisp's bankruptcy was indeed that the balance of power between himself and his in-laws swung markedly in their favour. For all their early ambivalence, the Marsh family had previously held him in some respect as their social superior, and as Elizabeth Marsh's rescuer. Now, however, while so many Marsh family members were rising in society and the state, James Crisp was in the shadows. This influenced how they all, including his wife, subsequently wrote about him; but it did not prevent members of the Marsh family from trying to help him, while simultaneously entangling him in imperial and national projects that were more their métier than his. In October 1765, when Crisp was still struggling to recover what was owed him at Genoa, Milbourne Marsh left Menorca for the position of Agent Victualler at the naval dockyard at Chatham, Kent, in order to be within easier reach of his daughter and son-in-law. George Marsh drew on his patronage powers at the Victualling Board to effect this transfer, and he did more. He introduced James Crisp to John Perceval, 2nd Earl of Egmont, and since 1763 the First Lord of the Admiralty, and thereby opened up to his niece and her husband the prospect of a fresh start and a new world.

❀

It is worth examining just how George Marsh, the son of a ship's carpenter, came to be able to make introductions to one of the most important figures in the British state, because it illumines why this deceptively ordinary, essentially second-rate man was so persistently successful, and why Elizabeth Marsh's own progress was punctuated by his interventions. In the mid-1740s George Marsh had gone out of his way to provide Perceval, at that stage heir to an Irish peerage and a Member of the Dublin Parliament, with some useful naval and legal information. Perceval responded by grandly extending the promise of future favours, but Marsh was too shrewd to take him up on the offer immediately. Perceval was still an opposition politician, a stray Irishman with a reputation as an intellectual and a visionary, scarcely an appropriate patron for an aspiring civil servant in London. On the evening of 10 October 1763, this changed. As George Marsh was reading his newspaper 'at my lodging in Peckham', he noticed that Egmont, as he now was, had been 'appointed First Lord of the Admiralty'. By 6 o'clock the following morning, he had composed his letter and dispatched it: 'If his Lordship thought I could be of any service to him, I

122

would do myself the honour of waiting upon him.' One week later, George Marsh had secured his meeting and one of the most crucial breaks in his career. Egmont 'desired to know if I would accept of being his private secretary, as he should stand in great need of my assistance in naval affairs'. Apart from its intrinsic significance, the position of private secretary to the First Lord traditionally carried with it promotion to the Victualling Board; and soon George Marsh was hiring 'a chariot by the month' (not for him the extravagance of purchasing a carriage) 'as I was obliged to go every day to the Admiralty'.[72]

George Marsh used a similar blend of patient, studious deference and shameless self-advancement to woo subsequent Lords of the Admiralty. When John Montagu, Earl of Sandwich, regained the position in 1771, Marsh not only bombarded him with sycophantic letters, but also lent him money, and even seems to have made room in his house for a relation of Sandwich's mistress, Martha Ray. Yet, at base, it was Marsh's industriousness, and his encyclopaedic knowledge of naval administration, that made him indispensable to successive patrician First Lords. These were the qualities that impressed Egmont, an intelligent, deeply serious man; it was rather different aspects of Egmont's character that drew him for a while into collaboration and even friendship with James Crisp.[73]

Egmont and Crisp were drawn together by their taste for enterprise and their broad, even romantic, geographical vision and imagination. As First Lord of the Admiralty, Egmont had been the leading sponsor of two important circumnavigations of the world, John Byron's in 1764–66, and that captained by Samuel Wallis in 1766–68. His interest in the extra-European world was dynastic and personal as well as official and imperial. In the 1730s, Egmont's father, the 1st Earl, had been one of the main sponsors of Georgia, at that point Britain's southernmost American colony. The 2nd Earl inherited these transatlantic interests, and his position at the Admiralty enabled him to take maximum advantage of the speculative boom in North American land that followed Britain's victory in the Seven Years War. Defeating the French and Spanish empires in North America had resulted in the transfer to Britain of some 1240 million acres there. This provoked a rash of Anglo-American land acquisition and development schemes during the 1760s. On the American side of the Atlantic, the decade saw the creation of the Mississippi Company, a syndicate of wealthy Virginia and Maryland colonists, including George Washington, who petitioned for a total of 2.5 million acres along the Ohio, Wabash and Tennessee rivers. Somewhat later, Benjamin Franklin and others formulated a scheme to found a new colony called Vandalia on the banks of the upper Ohio. The British government was opposed to further westward settlements of this sort, but it did favour expansionist schemes to the north and south of the original thirteen colonies, and these were the 2nd Earl of Egmont's own chosen directions for investment.[74]

Egmont eventually acquired over 120,000 acres in Nova Scotia (out of a total of 3.5 million acres of land granted away there in the 1760s), and 65,500 acres in Florida. He also encouraged some of his friends, dependants and navy employees to invest in colonial land, including his new secretary George Marsh. 'He was certain he should raise a considerable fortune' in America, Egmont told Marsh, 'and next to his own family, he wished most heartily success to me and mine'.[75] Marsh took him at his word. Late in 1763, he contemplated acquiring land for himself in Nova Scotia. He subsequently also seems to have encouraged James Crisp to apply to Egmont for fishing grounds off what later became Prince Edward Island.[76] These early schemes came to nothing, but in January and June 1766, at Egmont's prompting, the Privy Council issued orders allotting James Crisp first five thousand acres, and then a further fifteen thousand acres, in East Florida, 'to be surveyed in one contiguous tract in such part of the said province as the said James Crisp or his attorney shall choose'. This placed the Crisps potentially on a par as landowners in the new province with the likes of Charles Townshend, the British Chancellor of the Exchequer, the Duke of Buccleuch, one of Scotland's richest patricians, and General James Oglethorpe, founder of Georgia, each of whom also received twenty thousand acres of East Florida land.[77]

These Privy Council orders were not land grants, but warrants of survey. Recipients were expected either to journey to East Florida in person, or to appoint agents to go in their stead, to select a stretch of land equal in extent to the number of acres specified in the order, have it properly surveyed, and record the survey with the colony's Governor, Colonel James Grant, a Highland Scot, who would then, and only then, formally authorize the grant. After that, the new landowners were expected to recruit and transport out Protestant white settlers, one for every hundred acres of Florida land in their possession. If a third of an estate was not so settled within three years, all of it could be forfeit to the Crown.[78] As suggested by this lengthy process, and by the status of James Crisp's fellow would-be great landowners in East Florida, large-scale transatlantic land speculation usually demanded a substantial outlay of capital over many years. Yet Crisp was already in business difficulties when he received his allocation of East Florida land in 1766, and was declared bankrupt the following year. That he nonetheless embarked on this Florida speculation, devoting most of his energies to it during his last years in England, owed something to his appetite for risk (and his desperation at this point), and more to the fact that he and Egmont had been able to forge a close working relationship, and were alike in scheming in large, sometimes overreaching terms.

James Crisp embarked on this land speculation as part of a consortium, the 'Adventurers', as Egmont called them. These consisted of some of Crisp's own business associates, along with navy contacts of the Marsh family, plus Elizabeth Marsh's cousin by marriage, James Morrison, who received his own five thousand acres in East Florida. The idea was that the Adventurers' respective stretches of land in the province should lie adjacent to each other, a colony within a colony, as Egmont explained when he wrote to Governor Grant introducing the agent they had dispatched to East Florida, one Martin Jollie:

> This gentleman is employed by Mr. [Turner] Fortrey, Commissioner of the Victualling, [by] Messrs. [James] Crisp and [James] Anderson, merchants of eminence in London and of extensive dealings, by Messrs. [Edward] Wood and [James] Morrison and Mr. Porett of the Navy to wait upon you ... to view with your permission the province of East Florida, to fix upon the land and to take up the portions to which they are so entitled.

All of the Adventurers, Egmont assured Grant, were 'very able to exert themselves effectually in this undertaking, which is intended to be carried on by a common fund, and joint stock without any loss of time'. As for himself, he continued: 'I am requested not only to give my advice and to suggest a plan for their proceeding, but even to become an adventurer with them in the execution.'[79]

This severely over-modest assessment of his role pointed to another distinctive aspect of this land speculation – and to the reason why, for a while, James Crisp and Elizabeth Marsh could plausibly view Florida as a second chance. Egmont did join these strictly middle-class adventurers. As the months went by, he also 'took front place and all the troubles' in the project, as well as bearing of necessity most of the growing expenses. As far as James Crisp was concerned, Egmont made sure that 'his lands were long before his bankruptcy perfectly secured to me, so that his creditors have no claim upon them'. This was not because he wanted to absorb the Crisps' twenty thousand acres, or the land allocations of the other consortium members, into his own huge Florida estates. Rather, as Egmont wrote, 'I desire a great deal of land because I can then be able to give away a great deal.' The idea was that James Crisp and the other Adventurers would convey their Florida acreage to him, Egmont, and that he would bear most of the preliminary monetary and managerial burdens. Then, Egmont would 'execute reconveyances to each of them', and the Adventurers would take back their now up-and-running Florida estates.[80] James Crisp and Elizabeth Marsh had, apparently, found a way of becoming major American landowners at minimal cost to themselves.

Egmont wanted to develop East Florida in this way because he imagined the country (which he never saw) in quasi-feudal terms, and specifically in terms of Ireland. His family had previously given away over 160,000 of its Irish acres, partly to 'natives', but mainly to 'younger sons of gentlemen and tenants in England'. The result, Egmont believed, had been a 'bond of union' on his Cork estates, and a 'gentle', useful and appreciative spirit of subordination. He now intended to attempt a similar social and economic experiment across the Atlantic. He envisaged the 'conquered countries' of North America being 'cast into provinces (nearly the size of Ireland) of eighteen million of acres each'. As far as their settlement was concerned, he wanted to encourage 'the employment of small capitals' as a means of avoiding both the 'outrageous monopoly' characteristic of Caribbean plantation society, and the aimlessness that would leave 'the creation of the New World . . . to a fortuitous concourse of heterogeneous atoms'.[81] This vision of a systematic and paternalistic American empire shaped his treatment of the 'Adventurers', and the way in which he and James Crisp planned the twenty thousand acres allotted to Crisp in East Florida. There was, they decided, to be a 'Lordship of Lower Crisp' (or Crispe) on the north shore of Doctor's Lake, extending inland through the oak, hornbeam and magnolia trees for six miles from what is now Orange Point. This would contain a little (not an unseemly large) town, and at least two 'villages'. 'Upper Crisp', on the south side of the lake, was to include a 'manor house' or a 'castle' for James Crisp and his family, or their chosen prime tenant, and a village of sixteen log cabins with a one-acre garden, a cow and a pig apiece. There was to be another 'little town' where some chosen Native Americans were to be encouraged to settle in the 'English fashion', and would be treated with justice. While Egmont supplied most of the money, ethos and official sponsorship for this model community, James Crisp's role was to fill it with industrious tenants and workers – and with commercial enterprise. 'Mr. Crisp . . . really meant to embark himself largely upon the lands of his grant,' Egmont assured Governor Grant from London, '. . . and was prepared to engage not only many adventurers from hence, but many useful people for raising silk, wine etc. from Italy where he had a great correspondence.'[82]

As this suggests, while Egmont saw East Florida through a dream of Ireland, James Crisp seems to have yearned for it to be another, better Mediterranean world. In more than one way, he viewed the colony potentially as home. Spain had ceded it to the British in 1763, and although most of the former colonists had left, East Florida's buildings, the layout of its agricultural system and the ordering of its one substantial city, St Augustine, forty miles south of Doctor's Lake, were still recognizably Spanish. As far as James Crisp was concerned therefore, with his memories of more prosperous years in Barcelona, this new land was in anticipation not alien at all. He knew and had made money in Spain, and had traded with its empire. Now he would get to know and learn how to flourish in a one-time Spanish colony. East Florida's projected economy, too, seemed peculiarly well suited to his commercial strengths and mixed cultural background. Its coastline was conveniently situated for trade with Spain's Caribbean and South American colonies. He was used to trading in textiles, and East Florida was expected (legitimately) to offer fertile ground for the growing of indigo, one of the most valuable blue dyes for fabrics. The colony's rivers, claimed the author of *An Account of East Florida* (1766), contained 'rather more fish' than those in the rest of the American south, and Crisp understood the catching and salting of fish. Vines were expected to grow abundantly in East Florida, which was also judged 'better adapted to the silk-worm than any country in Europe', and Crisp had dealt in wine and silks. Most

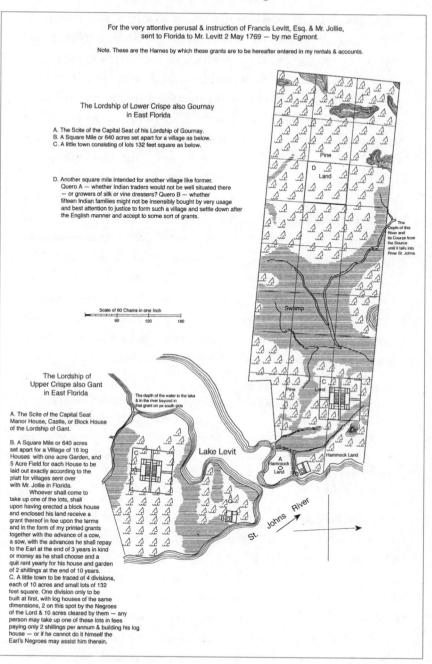

'Plan of the Lordship of Lower Crispe and the Lordship of Upper Crispe', a version drafted in 1769 of a plan made earlier by James Crisp and the Earl of Egmont.

of all, 'the fogs and dark and gloomy weather, so common in England, are unknown in this country'.[83] Elizabeth Marsh and James Crisp were in flight from darkness. East Florida was bright.

Exactly what Elizabeth thought of the scheme is not known, but she was certainly aware of the details of it, and not just from her husband. Her father, Milbourne Marsh, signed several of the legal documents to do with these Florida lands.[84] Her uncle, George Marsh, acted as link man between Egmont and Crisp, while James Morrison, her cousin by marriage, was also one of the 'Adventurers'. Members of her family became involved in this way because they were a cohesive clan, but also because 'Upper Crisp' and 'Lower Crisp' did appear a potential haven. They seemed to offer a sanctuary in which James Crisp might finally escape his creditors, and where he and his wife and children could rebuild their lives among other sympathetic souls, including Crisp's London partner, Francis Warren, who migrated to the province around 1768. Moreover, as substantial landowners, the Crisps could hope to possess assured status there, a manor house even:

> Since the great increase of expence in England, of every article of life, persons of liberal minds but narrow fortunes, feel immeasurable distresses. The impossibility of preserving rank without a fortune, and the mortification of finding our accustomed respect in life daily diminish, and our circumstances more and more confined, is a situation thoroughly miserable.

Yet, argued the author of this 'Exhortation to gentlemen of small fortune to settle in East Florida', published in London two months before James Crisp's bankruptcy, by crossing the Atlantic to this new land, 'a gentleman with only a thousand pounds, whether with or without a family', might be 'happy, independent, and in a few years rich'. 'There is neither mystery nor speculation in the case,' he concluded: 'it all turns upon a solid matter of fact.'[85]

Because so many early schemes woven around British East Florida were naïve, hyperbolic or dishonest, and because of what happened after the Declaration of Independence in 1776, historians have sometimes dismissed the province as doomed to failure from the start, a sort of eighteenth-century New Eden, a swamp relentlessly sucking up money and dreams. In reality, as more experienced land developers recognized, what settlers and investors in East Florida needed, even more than money, was time. Time to survey and mark out viable plantations and farms in a place for which, in 1763, there were not even any British maps available, or reliable descriptions in the English language; time to import a sufficient labour force; and time to establish crops that were appropriate for a subtropical climate and for land that was only a hundred feet above sea level. Those British investors who did have time to hang on had cause, by 1775, to believe that theirs had been a sensible investment, and that future prospects were good. By then the Earl of Egmont's East Florida lands were securing his heirs a modest profit. Even parts of New Smyrna, Andrew Turnbull's initially disastrous experiment of relocating Menorcan and other Mediterranean labouring families in East Florida (something that James Crisp had envisaged earlier), were beginning to be well cultivated and to make money.[86]

But James Crisp was a bankrupt, and therefore desperately short of time. He was able to keep afloat for a while, and even to cover some of his East Florida expenses, by handling navy victualling business for George Marsh, and by exploring some new and important contacts with the East India Company. Then, in September 1768, under pressure from both new and old debts, he 'suddenly failed' to such an extent that absconding became the only alternative to debtors' prison. East Florida could not be the bolt-hole of choice, because the Adventurers' agent there, Martin Jollie, had still not obtained all of the necessary official paperwork for Upper and Lower Crisp. It was only on the last day of December 1768 that a surveyor called George Rolfe dispatched the relevant papers to Gerard De Brahm, the brilliant Swiss cartographer who was responsible for mapping Britain's new North American lands and waterways. In keeping with the ownership of the estates now encircling it, Rolfe proposed that Doctor's Lake should in the future be renamed 'Lake Crisp'. Not just twenty thousand acres of land, but also a stretch of water, were to blazon the Crisp name on future maps of Florida.[87] Five days after this, on 5 January 1769, on the other side of the Atlantic, with no means of knowing that these documents were finally available, and that his land grant might therefore soon proceed, James Crisp signed a conveyance surrendering all rights in Upper and Lower Crisp to the Earl of Egmont.[88] Then, in order to avoid the bailiffs and utter ruin, he carried out a scheme that he had plotted some months before, in the event of Florida and his affairs failing. He set sail from London, without his wife and children, and not westwards for America, but rather to the eastern coast of the Indian subcontinent.

❀

And Elizabeth Marsh? These years in London were the longest time she spent living continuously on land and in one place. For much of this period hers was a conventional, and therefore largely invisible, and essentially dependent, middle-class female existence. She looked after a husband in a succession of rented houses. She gave birth to and brought up children; and she enjoyed for a while a degree of metropolitan style and socializing that she never subsequently forgot. Now, in early 1769, she was thirty-three years of age, with two children under the age of seven, no money, no house, and of course no paid employment. She was forced back on her parents' support, and she possessed no guarantee that even if James Crisp survived the voyage out to India, he would ever send for them all to join him there. 'I . . . may say, with too much truth,' she wrote bitterly at this time, 'that the misfortunes I met with in Barbary have been more than equalled by those I have since experienced, in this land of civil and religious liberty.'[89]

Beyond the obvious self-pity, this yoking together of her North

African ordeal and her experiences in London contained a funda-
mental truth and synchronicity that she did not wish however to
explore or even to acknowledge. In the mid-1750s, wide-ranging
warfare and the transnational ambitions of a Moroccan prince had
shattered her life, broken her engagement and forced her into a
different marriage. In the 1760s, James Crisp's enterprises and
reputation, which had been built on dealings with four continents,
had in turn foundered on events and forces in many different parts
of the world. To be sure, he had sometimes overreached himself,
just as she, in setting sail from Gibraltar in July 1756, had been
personally foolhardy. But in both cases, the root causes of their
respective disasters had been changes and conflicts over which
individuals could have little or no control. The world was both
widening and shrinking, and both of their lives had been twisted
out of customary moulds in the process. Elizabeth Marsh was not
much concerned, however, with the parallels between her husband's plight and her own. She was preoccupied with her own
despair, and with the need to redeem her reputation and finally to
assert herself. It was a commonplace that bankruptcy and a loss of
credit-worthiness dishonoured a man in much the same way as
loss of sexual virtue, or the imputation of it, dishonoured a woman.
Directly in Morocco, and now indirectly because of her husband's
far-flung business failures, she had been exposed to shame and
ruin twice over. Hers was 'a story of real distress': and she resolved
to tell it.[90]

4

Writing and Migrating

THE FEMALE CAPTIVE, Elizabeth Marsh's only venture into print, and ostensibly an account of her ordeal in Morocco, was published anonymously in London in August 1769. Like so much else that she did, it was a singular, thoroughly individual performance, and simultaneously an outcrop of much wider contemporary trends. Books which allowed men and women the illusion that, 'without stirring a foot', they could nonetheless 'compass the earth and seas, visit all countries, and converse with all nations' had always been a significant genre wherever printing presses operated, and the more sustained, violent and exploratory contacts occurring between diverse peoples by the mid-eighteenth century only increased the lure, volume and variety of travel writings.[1] In 1756, the year of Elizabeth's capture in the Mediterranean, Charles de Brosses published his *Histoire des navigations aux Terres Australes*. This was the first major compendium of voyages to the Pacific, and a version speedily appeared in English. Two years earlier, indigenous warriors in Pennsylvania had seized a Scottish indentured servant called Peter Williamson. He converted his real and imaginary adventures in their company into *French and Indian Cruelty exemplified in the Life ... of Peter Williamson* (1757), a more nuanced text than its title suggests, and one of the most frequently reissued and expanded volumes in Britain to be devoted to a vision of Native American society.[2]

The decade after the appearance of Elizabeth's own book saw the Scottish explorer James Bruce reaching the source of the Blue

Nile, Olaudah Equiano voyaging to the Antarctic, the publication of Louis de Bougainville's account of his circumnavigation and researches in the Pacific (1771), John Hawkesworth's version of James Cook's first voyage on the *Endeavour* (1773), Constantine John Phipps's *A Voyage towards the North Pole* (1774), and Cook's own *Voyage towards the South Pole and Round the World* (1777). By comparison with these polite and popular bestsellers and startling journeys, *The Female Captive* was a minor work by an under-educated woman who had been exposed to the Maghreb only very briefly. But it included previously unavailable ethnographic and political observations, and it was, among many other things, a travel book. Its publisher, Charles Bathurst of Fleet Street, who was also a printer and a bookseller, took care to market it as such. He insisted on a no-nonsense subtitle ('A Narrative of Facts which happened in Barbary'), and prefaced the work with a map of Morocco.

Elizabeth Marsh's book was a product of its time in a more specific respect. In the 1760s, more than twice as many new and reprinted works of fiction by women were issued in Britain as in the previous decade.[3] There was also a marked increase in women's non-fiction, including a sub-genre to which *The Female Captive* loosely belongs. By now, the number of British men holding official, imperial or commercial posts outside Europe was expanding conspicuously. Some of these individuals took their womenfolk along with them, and some of these women subsequently wrote and published. An early example of this new writing about the non-European world by attendant British females was Lady Mary Wortley Montagu's letters, which were published posthumously in three volumes in 1763, and included her experiences in Istanbul in 1717–18, when her husband had been Ambassador Extraordinary to the Ottoman court. Lady Mary had preserved (and invented) some of her letters home from Istanbul, Belgrade and Tunis, intending to work them up into a coherent travel book, but she was too patrician, and too much of her generation, to risk such sustained exposure in print in her lifetime. The belated appearance of what became known as her Turkish letters, a calculated mix of reportage, reflection and fiction, influenced passages in Elizabeth Marsh's book, and possibly also Charles Bathurst's willingness to publish it. 'I confess,' Lady Mary says in the preface to the Turkish letters,

> I am malicious enough to desire, that the world should see, to how much better purpose the LADIES travel than their LORDS; and that, whilst it is surfeited with *Male-Travels*, all in the same tone, and stuft with the same trifles; a lady has the skill to strike out a new path, and to embellish a worn-out subject.[4]

The women most likely to strike out and commit their travel writings to print remained, however, those not born to regard themselves securely as ladies. Janet Schaw, a Scot with aristocratic connections, compiled a long, vivid narrative of her voyages to the West Indies and North Carolina in 1774, accompanying a brother in transit to a government post in Jamaica. She was careful to leave it unpublished. Middle- and lower-class women travelling overseas with and for their menfolk could be less diffident. Frances Brooke was the wife of a British Army chaplain, and joined him in Quebec in 1763, just days before it was formally declared a British colony. She incorporated some of her husband's military experiences during the Seven Years War in Nova Scotia and New York, and her own observations of settlements of Huron peoples and French Catholic society in Quebec, in *The History of Emily Montague* (1769), the first novel in English to be devoted to Canada, and a highly successful, still readable work of faction. Jemima Kindersley, who published *Letters from the Island of Teneriffe, Brazil, the Cape of Good Hope and the East Indies* in 1777, was from a similar background, the widow of an army officer who took her to Bengal and Allahabad in the mid-1760s, and then died, leaving her in economic distress. Mary Ann Parker, a navy widow who had previously accompanied her husband to Botany Bay, prefaced her account of their journey, *A Voyage round the world* (1795), with a plea on behalf of her 'numerous family' of bereft children. Anna Maria Falconbridge was less impecunious, but still part of this same pattern of dependent but opinionated females writing in the last third of the eighteenth century about a more interconnected world. Falconbridge's social origins were modest and controversial. Her first husband, a slave-ship surgeon turned abolitionist, was dispatched in 1791 to re-establish a colony of free blacks in Sierra Leone. She made use of her experiences alongside him there to write her *Narrative of two voyages to the River Sierra Leone* (1794–95) so as to make money, communicate topographical and ethnographic information, and advance a cause – in her case support for slavery, but opposition to colonialism.[5]

Elizabeth Marsh had obvious points in common with these women. She too was socially marginal. The overland and overseas journeys that she described in *The Female Captive* had also occurred in the wake of her accompanying a male relation in British state employ abroad, in this case her father Milbourne Marsh. And, more even than was true of Brooke, Kindersley, Parker or Falconbridge, she wrote while in desperate need of funds.

Yet *The Female Captive* differs from most self-professed travel books, whether by female or male authors, the formally educated or the autodidactic. Strange, awkwardly written, and even shocking, it broke new ground in more than geographical and observational terms. Contemporaries dimly perceived this. Issued in two slim volumes priced at five shillings the set, and manifestly written by an amateur, the book sold out rapidly. About 750 copies were probably issued in 1769. There was no later edition, and by the early 1770s Marsh's book had become 'very scarce' and difficult to obtain. Several circulating libraries kept it in stock for decades, but only one copy now appears to survive.[6] This suggests that *The Female Captive* was swiftly bought up by the sort of private individuals whose libraries and other belongings were not preserved after their deaths, and/or that copies were scanned and thumbed so often, or lent out to others so much, that they simply fell to pieces. The book also received more critical attention than most published at this time. No review seems to have greeted the initial publication of Mary Wortley Montagu's Turkish letters, but *The Female Captive* provoked at least two long notices. Elizabeth's reviewers, though, were left bewildered and irritated. Her book contained 'no very interesting incidents', one complained, but then went on to quote from it for five pages.[7] The biggest challenge it posed for unwitting readers was that it was about less, but also far more, than its title promised.

Unlike many travel writers, Elizabeth Marsh possessed no detailed notes compiled at the time of her journey, and no conspicuous reserves of knowledge about the society she was describing, because her Moroccan progress had been involuntary and carried out under duress. And unlike Peter Williamson and other narrators of captivity, she was not writing in the immediate aftermath of escape. When she planned *The Female Captive*, events in the late 1760s were far more to the foreground of her mind than 'Facts which happened in Barbary' in 1756. As a result, the book became not just a version of her Mediterranean and Moroccan experiences, but a personal statement, and a meditation on a variety of restrictions and desires. This is why it still possesses the power to move. Travel writing, like the novel, focuses on 'the centrality of the self', and for Elizabeth Marsh this was a critical part of its attraction.[8] *The Female Captive* is a guide to her state of mind and her emotions in the wake of James Crisp's bankruptcy and flight. It is the closest she comes to sustained autobiography. It is also a work in which she gives more away than she probably intended. As the title page proclaimed, this was 'WRITTEN BY HERSELF'.[9]

Elizabeth Marsh wrote the book in her parents' house in Chatham, Kent, where she took refuge with her children, Burrish and Elizabeth Maria, after James Crisp left for India in early 1769, and no money remained to pay for lodgings in London. In returning to England in 1765, at the age of fifty-six, and accepting the post of Agent Victualler at Chatham, her father Milbourne Marsh had made both a professional and a creative sacrifice. Two years before, at the end of the war, he had resumed his old job as Naval Officer in Menorca. Given the brief to oversee essential repairs on the island in the aftermath of the French occupation, he had instead devised a scheme that transformed its dockyard into the most substantial and impressive overseas naval facility controlled anywhere by a European power.

Milbourne had tried his hand at such plans before. While in Gibraltar he had presented his superiors with a scheme to modify its defences, 'humbly proposed by Mr Marsh Master Shipwright'. He was now confident enough to attempt something far more ambitious. Early in 1764 he submitted a set of plans that provided for some of Menorca's dockyard amenities to be removed from the existing crowded and inadequate site near Mahón, and re-established on Saffron Island, a speck of ground just offshore from the north side of the harbour. 'And having proposed the doing thereof,' reported the Navy Board to the Admiralty in London excitedly,

> as also the levelling the island, and that wharfs, careening pits, sheds for stores and other like conveniences may then be erected, the whole expense whereof, he has estimated will amount . . . to the sum of £6348 exclusive of timber to be sent from England . . . And he having also acquainted us, that by performing the aforesaid works, the island will then have upon it six [in fact eight] wharfs, each of two hundred feet long and be capable of careening that number of ships at the same time.[10]

It was a measure of how seriously London took the Mediterranean in strategic, imperial and commercial terms – and of how seriously Milbourne Marsh was taken – that, at a time of anxious post-war retrenchment, this initial, far too conservative financial estimate was accepted, Saffron Island was purchased, and the scheme put in force. It was Milbourne who drew up most of the plans for the extensions to the dockyard and for Saffron Island's eight new careening wharves, based on observations and notes he had been assembling since his first visits to Menorca in the 1720s. He also designed the new dockyard buildings, many of which remain intact today. They are austere, clean-lined constructions, sheds, warehouses and dormitory wings for the dockyard workers and for visiting sailors and officers, with their only concession to ornament a handsome clock tower for the measuring out of time and work. Saffron Island, 'so necessary and noble an undertaking', as one senior navy officer later described it, was where Milbourne Marsh's deep knowledge of the practicalities of ship design and repair, his talent for technical drawing, and his compulsion wherever he was to build, finally came together in a significant way.[11] This was the project he had substantially to abandon in 1765 in order to return to England so as to be nearer to his only daughter and his failing son-in-law.

Superficially, his new posting seemed a promotion. Perfectly located for defending southern England and London, and with a large, naturally protected harbour, Chatham had been the site of a naval dockyard since at least the 1500s. Since then, its highly specialized buildings had grown in tandem with the navy itself, and when Milbourne took up his position in October 1765, Chatham's dockyard extended for over eighty acres. 'The buildings here are indeed like the ships themselves, surprisingly large, and in their several kinds, beautiful,' Daniel Defoe had written earlier in the century:

> The warehouses, or rather, streets of warehouses and store-houses for laying up naval treasure are the largest in dimension and the most in number, that are anywhere to be seen

in the world: the rope-walk for making cables and the forges for making anchors and other ironwork, bear a proportion to the rest; as also the wet-dock for keeping masts and yards of the greatest size, where they lie sunk in the water to preserve them, the boat-yard, the anchor yard; all like the whole, monstrously great and extensive . . . like a well-ordered city.[12]

But although Chatham's dockyard now looked even more 'monstrously great and extensive', it was in partial decline, the gradual silting up of the River Medway clogging its usefulness and range of functions. By the 1760s, deeper-bottomed vessels were taking over three months to sail along the river into Chatham's estuary, and the largest warships could only attempt the journey for a few days during the spring tides. No longer able to operate as a prime base for the fleet, Chatham dockyard was obliged to reinvent itself. Its labour force of 1400 men increasingly concentrated on repair work and ship construction (Horatio Nelson's flagship the *Victory* was built and later refitted here), while the dockyard's senior officers consoled themselves with their substantial, often elegant brick houses, a legacy of when this was Britain's most important naval site on land.[13]

Chatham's victualling yard was situated a little upstream of the main dockyard. Nothing remains of it today, but the surviving ground plan of the house that Milbourne Marsh occupied in his capacity as Agent Victualler shows that this dwelling was close to the street, and its dimensions – thirty-two by thirty feet – suggest at least eight or nine rooms arranged on three main storeys, in addition to attics and cellars. At the back of the house there were steps leading down to a seventy-five-foot-long walled garden, while across the yard Milbourne had access to a wash-house and stables, and his own office, maintained, one visitor recorded, 'in the completest order imaginable'.[14] Lord Tyrawley, an irascible, efficient man who was Governor of Gibraltar during Elizabeth Marsh's Moroccan ordeal, expressed a widely-held view when he complained that men of Milbourne's type and rank, 'paymasters, clerks, store-keepers, agent victuallers, naval officers and all this pen and ink branch', who were provided with tied houses of this sort, could end up 'better lodged than . . . persons of birth and quality and every way their superior'. This indeed was part of the allure of a senior job in naval administration, especially for those born ambitious and property-less.[15] But the spacious Queen Anne and Georgian residences made available at taxpayers' expense to senior employees at Chatham and the navy's other dockyards were more than perquisites. Like the dockyards as a whole, they demonstrated in brick and mortar and stone the growing power and wealth of the British state. They also signalled that 'pen and ink' men, administrators, accountants, makers of lists and archives and plans, were becoming increasingly important here, as in other states. The management and supervision of victualling, which preoccupied both Marsh brothers after 1765, was not the most heroic branch of the navy, but it was the most vital. Far more than improved ship design, or acts of individual heroism, it was the growing capacity to provision ships, which might remain out of reach of land for months on end, in such a way that sailors kept healthy and active, that most underpinned the Royal Navy's growing effectiveness and global reach at this time. As James Cook's three voyages to the Pacific in 1768–71, 1772–75 and 1776–80 demonstrated, more efficient naval victualling was also making possible increasingly ambitious voyages of maritime exploration. As one circumnavigator remarked in the 1760s: 'Discovering new worlds . . . depends on the men's health.'[16]

Elizabeth Marsh was never in a position to forget that her refuge in Chatham was also a vital site of industry. She was more spaciously accommodated than she had been in London. She had a room of her own in which to write, and a garden in which the children could play. Her mother was on hand to supervise them while she worked, and at intervals she could walk or ride to view the yellowing waters of the Medway. But, whatever she did, she was surrounded by activity and noise. From the windows at the front of the house she could see the coopers' shop, the place where wooden casks were made, and the pickle store, since pickling, along with drying, smoking and salting, were the only available means of preserving food for long voyages. The storehouses for meat and beer, and the bakehouse where they made ships' biscuits and the two-pound brown loaves 'commonly call'd by the sailors Negroe heads', were located a little further away. So were the slaughter-house and the cutting house, though this scarcely mattered. Almost every day, oxen, sheep, pigs and cows arrived on the hoof in the street outside the Agent Victualler's house, and were driven through the entrance of the yard into a pound where they were left to cool down for twenty-four hours. She would hear the sound of them. Their time elapsed, the animals would be 'examined by a master butcher, and by the officer of the cutting-house; and then if the master butcher and the officer of the cutting-house approve, they kill the beasts'. The carcasses were promptly hacked into quarters, weighed in special scales, and then hurried to the yard's boiling, salting and pickling houses, while the pound was swept and got ready for the next batch of short-term occupants.[17] The title Elizabeth selected for her book can possibly be understood as an allusion not simply to her time in Morocco, but also to her compulsory stay in Chatham for months on end, with no husband, only solicitous, anxious parents and bewildered children, and outside, scenes of incessant work and the cries of imprisoned animals.

The Female Captive was also explicitly an assertion of exceptionality. As with Henry Fielding's satire *The Female Husband* (1746), or the story of Hannah Snell's reputed actions in the ranks and in drag, *The Female Soldier*, a semi-fictional work that had been a runaway success in 1750, the title of Elizabeth's book announced that the experiences contained in its pages were unusual, even aberrant as far as a woman was concerned. This was a legitimate claim. Substantial numbers of European women, and far more women who were black, had of course been held captive over the centuries, in the Maghreb as in other regions of the world. But it was almost unknown for a woman who had been held against her will in an Islamic polity subsequently to admit to her experiences at length in print. As far as Morocco was concerned, the only precedent for *The Female Captive* was an account by a Dutch Catholic, Maria Ter Meetelen, of her twelve-year captivity there, which was published in Holland in 1748 and which Elizabeth Marsh can never have seen. Apart from being far more protracted, Meetelen's captivity had been significantly different in another respect. When Moroccan corsairs captured her ship in 1731, she was a twenty-seven-year-old matron, and her first husband was seized alongside her.[18]

By contrast, Elizabeth Marsh was only twenty and, as she told her readers, still unmarried when taken at sea in 1756 (and therefore, contemporaries would have understood, a virgin), with no male relation on hand to protect her. Revealing this in print was a remarkable act, a 'bold . . . attempt' as she described it. To be sure, in British North America there was a tradition by now of women who had been captured by Native Americans subsequently writing or dictating narratives of their experiences that were then published. But it was widely known and accepted that indigenous warriors in North America rarely raped their female prisoners.[19] In Morocco and the Ottoman world, the treatment of female captives was often very different, and was infinitely more so in European imaginings.

Even men seized by Muslim corsairs, and subsequently enslaved, were believed by some European commentators to be vulnerable to rape by their male captors and owners. As far as women captives were concerned, those who were subsequently sold as slaves *were* by law and custom at the sexual mercy of their purchasers. And that *all* females brought captive to Islamic societies were automatically liable to sexual assault, and/or to absorption into harems, was the stuff of a massive and still-expanding learned and popular literature:

All women, there, obey – because they must.
Silent, they sit, in passive rows, all day;
And musing, cross-legg'd, stitch strange thoughts away.
Provoking life! – Stew'd up like ponds of fish,
They feed, and fatten, for one glutton's dish.[20]

Elizabeth Marsh made some attempts in *The Female Captive* to protect her reputation and repel criticism. She was careful to stress that she had not been enslaved, and her theme throughout is resistance: how she overcame fear, hardship, physical danger, a hostile landscape, and attempted seduction by the most powerful man in Morocco. This was unlikely to compensate, however, for some of her other admissions: that she had determined to set sail, as a single woman, in a ship full of men; that she had masqueraded for months as the wife of someone she later married; that in Sidi Muhammad's palace she had twice been exposed to what one reviewer called 'the machinations of [this] Morisco lover'.[21] Nor could she rely on readers responding favourably to the evidence she supplied at intervals of her personal toughness, her proven capacity to endure extreme heat, long journeys on a mule, inadequate food, an absence of fresh clothes and of rudimentary privacy. 'It's very unnatural,' an English writer observed at this time in a magazine essay devoted to 'Woman',

> to love those who are neither of a tender or delicate disposition; but on the contrary are of a bold, impudent deportment. What a grovelling soul must he have who can mix his passions with any thing so odious! . . . Courage in that sex is to me as disgustful as effeminacy in men. I cannot bear to find even their sentiments of the male kind.

George Marsh was so struck by this extract that he pasted it into what he appropriately regarded as his commonplace book. Even though the scope of female writing and publishing was expanding, it was still the case that 'women of reputation almost never offered for publication accounts of their own lives except with heavy overlays of piety'.[22] Elizabeth Marsh made room in *The Female Captive* for 'overlays of piety', and at this stage she may have meant them, but she also wrote about her boldness, impudence and courage, and other deviations from customary female norms. Why did she embark on such a level of exposure?

At one level, the answer must be that she had little choice. As a now penniless woman whose husband was voyaging further away from her with every day that passed, and who was immured in Chatham with her children and under parental supervision, writing for the market on a subject likely to attract public attention was one of the very few ways available whereby she could hope to earn any money. Moreover, although she published anonymously, she had no choice but to reveal the fact of her writing to others. As a first-time, female author with no funds at her disposal, Elizabeth was in a weak negotiating position *vis à vis* her publisher and retailer Charles Bathurst. He was a well-established, experienced man in his fifties, who claimed to possess genteel connections, and had a reputation for publishing dead, stellar literary figures such as Jonathan Swift, and sheet music. It may have been the latter which brought him and his bookshop at 26 Fleet Street to Elizabeth's notice.[23] Or George Marsh may have known and recommended Bathurst on the strength of the printing work he sometimes carried out for Parliament. Either way, she had to offer the bookseller some economic incentive for undertaking the risk of publishing an unknown. She did so in a fashion that was traditional among writers operating under more than usual pressure: she sold her book by subscription. That is, friends, relations and anyone else she could persuade – eighty-three people in all – were got to commit to buying single or multiple copies of *The Female Captive* in advance of its publication, in return for their names being displayed on its opening pages. This lessened Bathurst's risk in publishing the work, and provided Elizabeth's acquaintances with a discreet means of extending charity to her in her emergency.[24]

Publishing in this fashion meant, of course, that she wrote with the certainty that everything she was confessing to – every thought, every action, every judgement she included about others – was likely to be read and become known by virtually everyone in her own circle. Stripped of privacy by others during her Moroccan ordeal, she now discarded it herself. Although she concealed certain dates in her book and replaced letters in names with dashes, she provided ample clues to the identity of her various characters. In addition to applying to scores of potential subscribers, she also discussed her book and its background with other, more distant acquaintances. These included Sir William Musgrave, a bibliophile, a trustee of the British Museum, and a Commissioner of the Customs, whose office near the Thames was only streets away from the Crisps' final London home in Camomile Street. As his copy of *The Female Captive* reveals, Musgrave found it a simple matter to fill in the names of virtually everyone referred to in it. He also jotted down on its pages personal details about Elizabeth Marsh herself, and his conviction that hers was 'a true story'.[25] So although she withheld her name from the title page, she did not strive to keep her authorship a secret, and this was not simply out of necessity. The opportunity to insert certain arguments and information in the public domain cancelled out for her the risks that she was running.

This tension between Elizabeth Marsh's desire to vindicate herself in the wake of yet another shameful disruption of her life, and seemingly an urge also to give herself away, shapes the book. At one level she was anxious to appear in print as a suffering innocent, and to offer up her hardships as conclusive proof of that innocence. Most members of the Marsh family read avidly, and purchased novels as well as non-fiction. A family copy of Samuel Richardson's evocation of the perfect moral gentleman, *The History of Sir Charles Grandison* (1753–54), still exists today in an Australian library.[26] In this, as in all of his highly profitable novels, Richardson makes his heroes, but more especially his heroines, undergo pitiful ordeals and scenes of distress, in order that their virtue may be exhibited and still further refined. In these, as in other novels of sentiment, 'sensibility, and therefore virtue, is most excited, and therefore most manifest, when threatened'. Suffering, especially on the part of women, becomes a proof of moral worth, and is expressed overwhelmingly through the body, by faintings, tears, sobs, shrieks, clutching hands and distraught facial expressions.[27]

Elizabeth Marsh drew on all of these conventions from the sentimental novels that she knew well when writing *The Female Captive*. In 1756 her fellow captives in Morocco had commented on her physical and mental resilience, 'beyond what may be expected from her tender sex'. But in print Elizabeth droops, melts, faints and near-faints at intervals, is 'shocked . . . beyond expression', is only able to 'answer with my tears', is sometimes prepared to rely 'on Divine Providence for support in all my afflictions', but on other occasions craves, like Richardson's most famous female victim, Clarissa Harlowe, 'to be taken from this world, as it afforded me no consolation'. She deliberately re-enacts at least part of her Mediterranean and Moroccan ordeal in the guise of a sentimental heroine, so that 'the Generous, the Tender, and the Compassionate' whom she appeals to in her preface, those whose minds are properly 'endowed with sensibility', will interpret her serial misfortunes, too, as evidence of unjustly abused virtue.[28]

Her descriptions of trauma were more than literary pastiche however. In the immediate aftermath of her time in Morocco, Elizabeth Marsh seems to have tried to exorcise any remaining shock and anger through a mixture of talk, humour, creativity and vanity. Even then, she had been busy converting what had happened into stories, but at this early, verbal stage, stressing and inventing elements of the ridiculous. Shortly after her return to England in 1757, for instance, she confided to George Marsh how she and James Crisp had made a point of addressing each other very loudly as 'husband' and 'wife', both in company and behind the doors of successive cells in Sla and Marrakech, in the hope that any nearby Anglophone Moroccans might overhear and believe them really married. And she told self-regarding tales of the obesity of some of Sidi Muhammad's silk-and-muslin-clad women ('a vast number, and so fat that they could hardly walk'), and of how the acting Sultan had remarked by contrast on her own comparative slenderness: that 'she was very pretty, and would be remarkably so, when she grew fatter'.[29] None of these early anecdotes appears in *The Female Captive*. Instead, Elizabeth created its mood of menace, misery and fear not just by emulating some of the novels that she knew, but also out of her own recent experiences. Some of the depression and bitter, near-suicidal despair she describes herself as feeling in Morocco in 1756 probably represents more accurately her emotions during and after James Crisp's bankruptcy and departure: 'tho' I was preserved, yet it was for still greater sorrows, and in *my own country*, than any I ever experienced, even in Barbary'.[30]

James Crisp himself appears repeatedly in the book, though never under his own name, or with any reference to his commercial exploits or misfortunes. Instead, he features as her 'faithful friend', her 'worthy friend'. He did 'all in his power to render my situation tolerable', she writes of their time together in Morocco, and said 'all he could to keep up my spirits'.[31] 'The most affectionate parent,' she claimed in a draft version, 'could not have been more tenderly careful of me.' He had behaved towards her as if 'to a sister'. In the aftermath of her husband's ruin and flight, she seems, and in part genuinely was, determined to assert his integrity and decency, not least so as to rebut the criticisms that were now being levelled against him by members of her own family. 'His behaviour would always bear the most accurate inspection,' she insists. His conduct 'must gain him the esteem of the honest and virtuous part of mankind', she has another character in her book remark. He is 'a man of honour and [her own italics] a *Christian*'.[32]

Bombarded with these tributes, it takes time to register that Elizabeth Marsh only ever mentions James Crisp in relation to herself, and that he is an almost inaudible, often helpless actor in her story. Her frequent likening of him to a brother, a friend or a father, a strategy that is transparently designed to make her own conduct in Morocco seem more acceptable, also has the effect of making Crisp appear almost sexless. None of this remotely conveyed his real role and behaviour in 1756, or probably her own attitude to him at that time. Rather, the passages devoted to Crisp in *The Female Captive* can be read as suggesting how Elizabeth Marsh was coming to view her husband by 1769, though at this stage only at intervals: as congenitally unlucky, as incapable of supporting her or the children, even as no longer effectively male. In the book's climax, it is she alone who confronts and eludes Sidi Muhammad. Just as, for all the periodic tears and faints she lays claim to, it is she who frequently takes the initiative: 'The heat of the sun, as the day advanced, was extremely great . . . I purchased some water-melons; and distributed part of them among the sailors.' Meanwhile, in the text, James Crisp struggles: 'my friend . . . was always ill-treated, and never able to succeed'.[33] He is a vague, emasculated creation in another sense. Other than his usefulness to her, she reveals little about his attributes, and nothing at all about his appearance.

This may have been decorum on her part, a disinclination to publish personal details about the man who had become her husband. Yet in regard to some of the other men she encountered in the Mediterranean world in 1756, she was not reticent. In some ways, indeed, *The Female Captive* is a book about Elizabeth Marsh and a quartet of males, of whom James Crisp is only one. She describes at the outset how, when driven out of Menorca, she had entertained 'pleasing hopes' of being reunited in Gibraltar with her then fiancé, the future Captain Henry Towry, and how 'greatly disappointed' she was on finding that he had already sailed for Britain. When discussing her time at Marrakech and Asfi, she refers to her pleasure in the 'agreeable company' of John Court, the Barbary merchant and traveller, with his 'amiable' manner and fine singing voice.[34] She describes in far more detail Court's delight in herself. At one level, the role she assigns him is to perceive and testify to her quality and purity, something that a sympathetic male character frequently does in regard to the heroines of sentimental novels. Thus she prints a letter that (she claims) Court sent her while she was still in Morocco, urging that:

> While you are obliged to remain in Barbary, endeavour to reconcile yourself to it; reflect, that it is a misfortune you have no way brought upon yourself, nor have it in your power to remedy; have a firm trust in Providence, and be assured Virtue and Innocence will ever be the peculiar care of that supreme Disposer of all Events, who is capable of extricating you from your present distresses.[35]

The inclusion of letters within her story was another device that Elizabeth Marsh borrowed from sentimental novels. But, as she quotes them, John Court's letters convey more than reassurance. 'You engross much of my thoughts,' he tells her. She has made a 'lasting impression' on him 'that I am not capable of shaking off', and their time together has been 'as a dream'. 'Those you were most intimate with in Europe,' he assures Elizabeth before she escapes, 'cannot be under greater anxiety for your deliverance than I am.'[36] Even when she is safely back in Gibraltar, he begs to be allowed to continue their correspondence, 'which I fear I am totally deprived of', assuring her that this request 'is no way contrary to the severest rules'; and he (or she) goes on to misquote from a poem by Alexander Pope: 'Though seas come 'tween us, and whole Oceans roll'. As educated readers at the time would have recognized, the line is adapted from 'Eloisa to Abelard' (1717), a lament on a great passion cruelly sundered:

> Rise Alps between us! And whole oceans roll!
> Ah, come not, write not, think not once of me,
> Nor share one pang of all I felt for thee.[37]

Some of this may have been self-regarding fantasy on Elizabeth's part, or her publisher's, but it is likely that John Court was a lonely man when she met him in Morocco, 'banished for some years, from every thing that is polite', as he told her, and that he did respond warmly to the unexpected company of a very young, attractive, intelligent and extremely vulnerable woman.[38] By 1769 Court was safely married, but he still subscribed that year to four copies of Elizabeth's book.[39] Recalling his attachment, and publishing or refurbishing extracts from his letters (which she must have kept), may have salved her pride at a time when, for all she or anyone else knew, James Crisp was gone forever.

Describing how the acting Sultan of Morocco had sought her out and sought her favours was obviously a far more dramatic assertion of her singularity and capacity to fascinate. Sidi Muhammad emerges from *The Female Captive* more vividly than any other character except Elizabeth herself. She describes his face and physique, the different clothes and jewels he wore, his voice, the objects that he touched, how he moved and sat, and the interiors surrounding him. And far more than in regard to James Crisp, or John Court, or her lost fiancé, she confesses to her own excitement in the acting Sultan's presence, though in so contorted a manner that the admission is easily missed. 'I was ever in dread,' she writes of her time in Asfi, 'that His Imperial Highness would again send for me, *having heard from undoubted authority, that I was not indifferent to him.*'[40] She was afraid of going back, not just because of his desires, but also because of her own.

This is such an extraordinary admission in an avowedly autobiographical book by a woman at this time that it is tempting to dismiss it as someone else's titillating insert. Charles Bathurst certainly did make some alterations to the text of *The Female Captive*. In manuscript, for instance, Elizabeth Marsh seems to have written straightforwardly of how she was allowed to kiss the hands of 'a young Prince and Princess', two of Sidi Muhammad's children, during her second visit to his Marrakech palace. In print, these young royal hands became 'tawny', an adjective that she herself never employed. In the case of her statement that she was 'not indifferent' to Morocco's acting Sultan, however, there was no editorial interference. These are her own words, printed unaltered from an original draft copy.[41]

There were other ways in which Elizabeth Marsh departed from convention, and more alert readers noticed this at the time. 'I have always imagined that nowhere do the arbitrary will and passion of the Prince bear so unlimited sway as in the states of Barbary,' wrote Thomas Shadwell to Elizabeth's younger brother, John Marsh, after reading *The Female Captive*, 'and I was really surprised to find in your sister's narrative such an instance of the Emperor of Morocco's command over his own passions as is therein related.' Shadwell was the secretary to the British Ambassador at Madrid. He and John Marsh, who was British Consul at Málaga by this stage, were both self-consciously self-improving men, who corresponded regularly about the latest books, pamphlets and literary reviews. Marsh had sent his friend a copy of *The Female Captive* out of fraternal pride, and because Shadwell possessed first-hand experience of an Islamic society. He was an intimate of Lady Mary Wortley Montagu's son, Edward Wortley Montagu, a strange, intelligent individual who claimed (among other things) to have converted to Islam. It was Wortley Montagu's 'great encomiums of the government of the country' that had encouraged Shadwell himself to travel in the Ottoman Empire 'to examine it with what judgement and capacity I was able', and he had lived in Istanbul for some time. He discovered there, he told Marsh: 'a purity of morals and simplicity of manners ... which I have not found amongst the inhabitants of any other country'. Nor did he think the heartland of the Ottoman Empire any 'worse administered' than the Christian polities he knew. Like many other Turkophiles, however, Shadwell drew the line at the Ottomans' North African provinces, and at Morocco. For him, this region was barbarous and peculiarly subject to capricious, oppressive rulers, and he took it for granted that tyranny within a state was naturally 'conjoined to the servitude of women'.[42] Political despotism by its very nature, Shadwell believed, in accordance with the writings of

Montesquieu and others, must also foster acts of male despotism against the weaker sex. The coercion and passivity that were believed to exist within the harem only mirrored a more profound absence of liberty outside its luxurious, imprisoning walls. Thomas Shadwell was consequently perplexed by Elizabeth Marsh's account of Sidi Muhammad's behaviour in *The Female Captive*. She herself had described him as 'an absolute Prince'.[43] What did it mean, then, that such a ruler, in such a place, had exhibited chivalry and restraint in the face of a young, helpless and desirable female?

Of course, Elizabeth Marsh was not versed in abstract political theories: she was just a reader of novels. She described Sidi Muhammad's sexual advances and his ultimate mercy as she did, partly out of a recognition that he had indeed been generous 'in permitting me to leave him, when it was in his power to detain me'. But her memory and interpretation of events are likely once again to have been influenced by Samuel Richardson, and especially by his most popular work, *Pamela* (1740–41). The young heroine of this novel is a servant, impoverished but deserving, possessed of 'qualifications above my degree' and 'always scribbling' (rather like Elizabeth Marsh). Pamela's parents have been financially ruined, caught up in the pernicious web of credit and bankruptcy (rather like James Crisp), but 'They are honest: They are good: it is no crime to be poor.' And Pamela is also a captive of sorts, confined to the secluded rural estate of her employer, the wealthy 'Mr B', who lusts after her and tries to seduce her with lavish gifts (just as Sidi Muhammad had tried to tempt Elizabeth). At the end of Richardson's novel, however, Mr B refrains from ravishing the eponymous heroine because he is overwhelmed by her innocence and her wholly exceptional qualities.[44] Elizabeth Marsh seems to have wanted to alert readers of *The Female Captive* to the parallels between her situation and that of the virtuous Pamela. In the process, she made Sidi Muhammad appear rather less an alien despot, and rather more a recognizable and sympathetic figure who was amenable to conscience and ultimately responsive to a woman in distress.

This may indeed have been deliberate on her part, because she seems to have censored the record in order to soften the Sultan's image. During her last visit to his palace, Elizabeth told her parents on one occasion, she had witnessed 'a young European slave' being abruptly decapitated for insolence. True or no, this incident was suppressed when she came to publish. So the impression she gives of Sidi Muhammad is in the end deeply fractured. There are instances of his 'despotic power', but these are mingled with evidence that he was actually 'a tender hearted man'.[45] There are other fractures. Elizabeth Marsh wanted to appear in print as virtuous, Christian and wronged. Yet she was also willing to admit to her ambivalent responses to attempted seduction, and eager to remind herself and to inform others of the existence of her lost fiancé, and of John Court's doting attachment in Morocco. And even as she sought to defend and champion her husband James Crisp, she also wanted – or so it seems – to belittle him. Like her desire to appear simultaneously as frail and as physically resilient, her treatment of these four men suggests not only uncertainty over how best to present herself, but also splits and divisions within her mind and her emotions.

These four male actors, Sidi Muhammad, Towry, Court and Crisp, serve another function in Elizabeth Marsh's book. At times when the world seems dangerously open, men and women often try to close and contain it through stories. Usually such stories are private, the stuff of imagination only. Occasionally, though, they are committed to paper. This was the deeper function of *The Female Captive*. As is often the case with individual and family sagas that are composed in periods of crisis or extreme change, the book is in part an allegory.[46] Telling a story of her encounters with four different men allowed Elizabeth to imagine other life-choices than the one she had been obliged to make in 1756 and was now beginning to resent. This plot line also translated the changing world she was conspicuously exposed to into a more human, more comprehensible form. A Royal Navy captain who is familiar with the world's oceans, a Muslim prince with international commercial and diplomatic ambitions, a Barbary trader who has also 'resided in the southern parts of Africa', and a merchant trading across the continents: these are the male characters who chiefly circle around Elizabeth Marsh as she tells her story. *The Female Captive* can thus be seen, along with so much else, as a book by which she sought to represent her world.

❦

Writing as she did was a cruel, even brutal act in regard to her absent husband, who was doing his best, as it turned out, to restore their fortunes in Bengal and Madras. Especially as copies of her book were bound to circulate among those relations, friends, neighbours and former business associates of Crisp who had subscribed to its publication. Exactly what it says about the state of their marriage and her own mind that Elizabeth Marsh was willing to commit these mixed messages about her husband to print, while also publishing compromising material about her relations with other men, is not clear. She undoubtedly felt angry and humiliated in the aftermath of Crisp's business failures and flight. She may conceivably also have felt something more.

The list of eighty-three subscribers at the front of *The Female Captive* provides an optic into the range of the couple's contacts by this stage. It includes some of her women friends about whom we otherwise know little: a Miss Franks, a Mrs Kettle, Mrs Batt, and Mrs Jewson, her former neighbour from Camomile Street. Then there are the London traders and professionals with whom the Crisps had done business in their early, prosperous days in the capital, and who were still prepared out of charity to subsidize Elizabeth's book: Walter Cope, James Crisp's insurance broker in Cornhill; Alexander Allan, a Scottish wine merchant in Mark

Lane, who may have purchased some of Crisp's Spanish brandy, or catered to the couple's joint and growing taste for alcohol; and Ralph Fresselicque, a Huguenot attorney who had acted for Crisp during his bankruptcy in 1767.[47] There is predictably a smattering of navy names, too, including some that reveal how the Crisps, in their London heyday, had been able and eager (as George Marsh grumbled) to forge contacts with people of a much higher social position. Knowing Captain Matthew Whitwell RN and his wife, who each subscribed to a copy of *The Female Captive*, evidently also won them the acquaintance of Whitwell's elder brother, John. The latter had changed his name on inheriting the great house and estate of Audley End near Saffron Walden in Essex.[48] Sir John Griffin Griffin, as John Whitwell had now become, and Lady Griffin both subscribed in 1769 so that Elizabeth Marsh could publish.

There is another prominent group among the book's subscribers. It includes Charles Pinfold, who had been Governor of Barbados since 1761, and William Rufane, a former Governor of Martinique. Then there is Ralph Payne, born on the tiny Caribbean island of St Kitts, and a future Captain General and Governor-in-Chief of the Leeward Islands. And there is Sir John Boyd, who owned plantations in the Windward Islands and Grenada, as well as a share of Bance Island, which is situated twenty miles upriver from modern-day Freetown in Sierra Leone and is now called Bunce Island. An English fort and factory had existed on Bance Island since the 1670s, for while it was very small – only fifteen acres – its location made it highly profitable. At the limits of navigability for early modern European ocean-going ships, Bance Island was a natural meeting place for incoming slave purchasers and African slave traders bringing their human wares with them on the river routes down from the interior. In the two decades before the publication of *The Female Captive*, ten thousand African slaves are known to have passed through and been exported from Bance Island by British traders.[49]

Members of the Crisp family had been involved in the trans-atlantic slave trade since the mid-seventeenth century; and like most substantial London merchants, James Crisp had relations and business contacts who had some connection with the slave trade and the Caribbean. A John Crisp, who was kin to James Crisp in some way, was active in London in the 1750s and '60s, recruiting indentured labourers to be sent out to the mainland American colonies and the Caribbean islands.[50] But while James Crisp dealt occasionally in plantation products in the 1750s and early '60s, for as long as his company, Crisp Brothers, continued to flourish, he appears to have remained aloof from the purchase, sale and enforced transport overseas of other human beings. Like so much else, this changed after his bankruptcy in 1767.

Becoming involved in the Earl of Egmont's colonizing projects in East Florida, in the hope of replenishing his fortunes, also brought James Crisp into direct contact with issues of forced labour and its supply. From the outset, James Grant, the British Governor of East Florida, had advised investors in the new colony that white voluntary immigrants alone were unlikely to be sufficient to cultivate it and make it pay, and that – as in neighbouring Georgia – importing unfree black and possibly Native American labour was going to be essential. By the time James Crisp and the other 'Adventurers' joined his East Florida project, this was also the Earl of Egmont's view. Egmont was eager to recruit cheap white labour and settlers from the Mediterranean, but he also urged each man in the consortium to provide ten black slaves for the land granted them in East Florida during the first year of their investment, ten more in the second year, and twenty more within six years.[51] Part of Crisp's attractiveness to Egmont as a business partner may indeed have been the combination he offered of a wide range of contacts in the Mediterranean, and long-established family links with the Caribbean and the slave trade. By the same token, one of Crisp's fellow middle-class 'Adventurers' in Egmont's East Florida schemes was James Anderson, a nephew of Richard Oswald, an immensely rich Scottish merchant who was by far the main share-owner on Bance Island.[52]

Richard Oswald is known to have sent slave families from here to his own East Florida plantations in the 1760s, just as the Earl of Egmont is known to have spent over £3700 purchasing and bringing over ninety-five black slaves to East Florida between 1767 and 1770. How many African slaves James Crisp himself was responsible for organizing through his London, Caribbean and shipping contacts, and ultimately laid claim to in East Florida, is not known, but there were certainly some. In December 1768, still hoping for a last-minute miracle that would retrieve his affairs, he had leased his estates of Upper and Lower Crisp in East Florida back to Egmont for a year. The legal documents involved describe these lands as coming complete with all their 'Negro houses' and 'Negro and other slaves of both sexes'.[53] The plethora of major Caribbean and slave-trade players included in Elizabeth Marsh's subscription list was thus a testimony to how, in the wake of bankruptcy, James Crisp had reverted to his family's ancestral links with West Africa and with the slave trade.

And Elizabeth Marsh herself? Like most people at this time, in all continents, she took the existence of slavery for granted; and for better reasons than most, because she knew about the phenomenon in diverse settings, and in diverse forms. She had listened to her parents' stories of how the maroon risings in Jamaica had led to their departure from the island in 1735, and to the fact that she had been born in England. She must have encountered free black sailors, and possibly also enslaved blacks, while sailing aboard Royal Navy ships. In Morocco she had come very close to enslavement herself, and had seen and conversed with black household and military slaves, and with white slaves. In the 1770s she would take advantage of the system whereby the very poor in Dhaka, then part of Bengal, sometimes out of necessity became slaves to the more prosperous, a system in existence before the British arrived there. About the transatlantic trade in slaves, however, her sentiments are unknown. By the early nineteenth century the Marsh family had connected itself by marriage and friendship to some leading abolitionist dynasties, such as the Roscoes of Liverpool; and George Marsh at least appears to have collected material on the slave trade, and to have gone out of his way in the 1780s to assist poor blacks in London.[54] So it is possible that, like others in Britain, Elizabeth Marsh was beginning by the 1760s to feel some scruples about the slave trade, even as she was obliged to seek out and accept charity from individuals who were vitally connected with it.

There is a further possibility that can only be touched on. If her mother was indeed a mulatto, a former slave herself, or a descendant of someone seized in West Africa and shipped to Jamaica, Elizabeth Marsh's reactions to her husband involving himself in the slave trade in order to keep the family solvent may have been disordered and confused. Those 'unacquainted' with Morocco, she wrote inaccurately but pointedly in *The Female Captive*, would find it strange that 'Mahometans' held their Christian slaves 'as sacred as the tombs of their saints, from the ill usage of any but their master, the Prince'.[55] The treatment of non-Christian slaves shipped out of West Africa, she would have known, was not like this. Some of the ambivalence and occasional cruelty she displays towards her husband in the book, which would become more pronounced in the future, may conceivably have been deepened by these tensions. By her knowledge that, for all her insistence in print that he was 'a man of honour and a *Christian*', James Crisp had also become entangled in the trade in slaves. For a married woman, publishing anonymously could be a declaration of independence, and not simply an act of modesty and decorum. Elizabeth Marsh's book is explicitly and only by 'HERSELF'. For whatever reason, she chose not to appear in print as Mrs Crisp.[56]

Yet in August 1770, the month before her thirty-fifth birthday, she left England with her daughter Elizabeth Maria and sailed to join James Crisp in Madras. 'Nature is turn'd upside down,' the novelist Laurence Sterne had written some years earlier in regard to another woman setting sail to the subcontinent in order to rejoin a less than satisfactory husband: 'for wives go to visit husbands, at greater perils, and take longer journeys to pay them this civility now-a-days out of ill-will than good ... How far are you going to see your helpmate – and at such hazards to your life.'[57] As Sterne knew full well, the options available to married women in this position were in reality very limited, especially if they were not affluent. Elizabeth Marsh might have chosen to remain with her parents in their large, subsidized house at Chatham. But this would have been to close down any prospect of a rapprochement with her husband, and would have left her in legal limbo; and while her attachment to her family of birth was immensely strong, so – judging by her actions – was her desire repeatedly to get away from it. This restlessness, as well as residual affection for Crisp and a wish that her children should have the prospect of growing up with their father, seems to have influenced her determination to set out. Sir William Musgrave noted down her public rationale for leaving: that 'on her husband's success in India she went thither to him', but this was hardly the case.[58] At this stage, neither James Crisp nor Elizabeth Marsh was in a position to have a confident expectation of prosperity in the subcontinent. She embarked for India because it seemed the right and the only thing to do, and because she felt most at home when in motion.

Her petition 'to proceed to her husband in the Company's military service at Bengal, [and] also to take her daughter Elizabeth with her' was approved by the Court of Directors of the East India Company in London in June 1770. Recognizing her poverty, the directors excused her from 'paying the customary sum for permission'.[59] No Company ships were available at this point, since East Indiamen normally only set out from England in the autumn and the spring. So she opted to travel on the *Dolphin*, an extremely fast, three-masted Royal Navy sloop, built in 1751 and with room for thirty-two guns. As Milbourne and George Marsh would have known, this was one of the first navy vessels to have its bottom sheathed with copper, a powerful barrier against the weeds and sea worms that accumulated on wooden-hulled ships and slowed them down. The *Dolphin*'s copper sheathing had been renewed in 1770, so it was a highly desirable vessel, sailing at a time when no other ships to India were available, and holding out the promise of a more rapid voyage than the usual six or seven months. If he accepted 'one third' of the civilians clamouring for a passage on the *Dolphin*, its captain, Digby Dent, complained that summer, 'he ought to have the command of a First Rate instead of a sloop'. In the event Dent turned down most of the would-be passengers petitioning for a berth, since 'there was not a single inch unoccupied'.[60] But he agreed to take Elizabeth Marsh and her daughter. Of course he did. Both her uncle and her father now played vital roles in navy victualling, and were therefore in a position to repay Captain Dent a favour. Moreover, Dent knew Milbourne Marsh from Gibraltar, and his father had served with him in Jamaica, while the *Dolphin*'s own ship's master was a Joseph Milbourne, one of Elizabeth's vast network of maritime 'cousins'.[61] It was a classic example of how her travels were facilitated by her family's multifarious naval contacts.

An individual's decision to migrate, John Berger has written, is often 'permeated by historical necessities of which neither he nor anybody he meets is aware', and to a degree this was true in Elizabeth Marsh's case.[62] She had her own distinctive reasons for leaving when and as she did, but she was also part of what has been called 'a world in motion': the appreciable rise after the Seven Years War in the number of people involved in long-distance overseas migration. As had been the case before the war, most of those migrating over extensive distances after 1763 were Africans sailing into slavery. More than 70 per cent of the slaves traded across the Atlantic by France during the entire course of the

Sketch of the *Dolphin* made by Captain Samuel Wallis on his voyage
around the world, 1766–68.

eighteenth century, for instance, were forced to make this passage
in the three decades after 1762. The scale and range of white
diaspora also mushroomed at this time. Between 1760 and 1775,
some 125,000 individuals left Britain and Ireland for different locations in North America, encouraged – as the Crisps had been in
regard to East Florida – by the availability of so much new conquered land there. Simultaneously, those European powers that
had lost rather than gained territory in the Seven Years War now
sought out new extra-European lands in compensation, and
migrants who might inhabit them. Between 1763 and 1765, over
thirteen thousand men, women and children set out from France
and the German states for 'Kourou', a new settlement in Guyana
designed on Enlightenment principles. This did not prevent most
of them speedily dying from disease and starvation.[63]

Overseas migration to the Indian subcontinent in the aftermath
of the Seven Years War is rarely considered in tandem with these
other long-distance movements of black and white human beings,
in part because the numbers involved were so much smaller. Unless
they were Crown or East India Company officials, Britons were
forbidden – at least in theory – to travel to India without a licence.
Because of this, and the dangers and huge distances involved, the

British male population in the subcontinent remained very sparse, and the total number of 'white' women was minute. When Elizabeth Marsh and her daughter arrived in Madras in 1771, only eighty-five women and children classified as European were listed as residing there.[64] Nonetheless, and as suggested by the Crisps' own progress from favouring East Florida to migrating to India, there were ways in which British voyagers to the East after 1763 resembled their counterparts who were voyaging westwards. Their numbers too expanded after the ending of the Seven Years War. Before 1756, it is unlikely that there were ever at any time more than a thousand nominal Britons in the subcontinent. By contrast, 6500 men who were originally from England, Wales, Scotland, Ireland, the Caribbean or mainland North America are *known* to have left Britain for India in the ten years after 1762, and the real total must have been higher. Those leaving Britain for India, like those departing for America, came disproportionately from the towns, and were mostly male and mostly young. The majority had either been born in very modest circumstances, like Elizabeth Marsh, or, like James Crisp, they had undergone some kind of economic crisis in adulthood. And whether they were setting out for North America or for the Indian subcontinent, most migrants were at some level 'lured . . . by their own ambitions', not simply acting out of desperation.[65] Elizabeth Marsh did not embark on the *Dolphin* with any firm expectation that she, her husband and her children would soon return prosperously to Britain. Some of James Crisp's creditors were still trying to recover their debts, so remaining overseas was his only real safety. But this did not mean that she – or he – migrated without hope or plans for the future.

There were other ways, and Elizabeth Marsh was conscious of some of them, in which this, her first journey to India, was freighted with a wider significance. As she had cause to know, the *Dolphin* was the only vessel at this time to have circumnavigated the world twice over. Between July 1764 and May 1766, the ship had sailed to the Pacific and back under the command of Commodore the Hon. John Byron in twenty-two months, and at the cost of only seven men's lives, a faster speed and a lower death rate than any of James Cook's three Pacific voyages achieved. During his own circumnavigation, Byron laid claim to the Falkland Islands for the British, an acquisition which the then First Lord of the Admiralty, the Earl of Egmont, viewed as key to 'the whole Pacific Ocean . . . the ports & trade of Chile, Peru, Panama, [and] Acapulco'. In 1766–68, Captain Samuel Wallis had taken the *Dolphin* to the Pacific again, under orders this time to locate 'a continent of great extent never yet explored or seen between the straits of Magellan and New Zealand'.[66] In the event, Wallis 'discovered' Tahiti and fourteen other islands, but not the great south land. Elizabeth Marsh knew a great deal about the *Dolphin*'s voyages of exploration and empire, because her uncle George Marsh had been involved in planning them while working for Egmont at the Admiralty. 'When Admiral Byron went the voyage round the world,' George Marsh later recorded, 'he asked me . . . if I could recommend any gentleman to go with him as his secretary.' Naturally, Elizabeth's uncle immediately located 'a very proper fit person' to sail alongside Byron and to compile a record of his circumnavigation, and 'recommended . . . him accordingly'.[67]

As was true of these earlier, more ambitious voyages, the *Dolphin*'s mission to the Indian subcontinent in 1770 was bound up with an increasingly confident sense of imperial entitlement on the part of the rulers of the British state. Living in London in the late 1750s and '60s, just streets away from East India House, with Parliament close by, and with the capital's newsprint at their disposal, James Crisp and Elizabeth Marsh had been well placed to keep abreast of how rapidly the East India Company's role was evolving. The couple were in London when the news arrived of the Battle of Plassey in 1757, and of the Company's defeat of Siraj-ud-Daulah, the Nawab of Bengal. They were there in 1765, when the Mughal Emperor was forced to grant the Company revenue-raising powers, the *diwani*, over the provinces of Bengal, Bihar and Orissa in northern India. And they were there in 1767, when Parliament embarked on its first full-scale inquiry into the Company's affairs in the subcontinent. The corruption, violence and incompetence revealed in this inquiry, and in a flood of pamphlets and books published at this time, deepened the conviction that the East India Company's affairs were now 'much too big for the management of a body of merchants'. For commercial, fiscal, humanitarian and imperial reasons, it was increasingly argued, the British state needed to assume a greater supervisory role over the Company, and over those sectors of the subcontinent it was seeking to rule.[68] This new voyage of the *Dolphin*, already a vessel with a reputation for extending British power over distance, was part of a range of official initiatives intended to achieve exactly this.

Along with Elizabeth Marsh and her daughter and its 150-man international crew, the ship was transporting to the subcontinent two sets of the insignia and ribbons of the Order of the Bath. The intended recipients were Sir John Lindsey, a Scottish naval officer, and an experienced Irish soldier, General Eyre Coote, who had been ordered to Bengal and Madras to monitor and report on the East India Company's performance there. The Order of the Bath is awarded only at the pleasure of the British monarch, and it was being shipped out to Lindsey and Coote in 1770 so as to underscore their role and authority as agents of the Crown. 'We fear the worst,' an East India Company official wrote on hearing the news of the *Dolphin*'s arrival in Madras in late February 1771: '. . . that the [British] Government are about to interfere with the Company in the management of affairs in India.'[69]

The ship's imperial and global portentousness affected even Elizabeth Marsh and her six-year-old daughter in their damp, crowded cabin. They and the crew of the *Dolphin* kept remarkably healthy during the early stages of the voyage, but the ship 'strained much in the weather we met with'; and in October 1770 it had to veer away from its planned route and schedule and moor off

'A View of the Town of Rio Janeiro'. Pencil drawing by Alexander Buchan, 1768.

Rio de Janeiro, then part of the Portuguese empire. Captain Dent hoped 'to have got the ship caulked' here, and to reprovision with the sugar, coffee, rum, tobacco, limes and cheap vegetables that the new capital of the Brazils famously afforded. This project, and Elizabeth Marsh's own plans to spend days exploring the city, were aborted when Rio's Viceroy refused to grant the *Dolphin* 'any assistance', and they were forced to set sail almost immediately. The *Dolphin* was all too evidently a ship redolent of transoceanic ambitions, and the Portuguese authorities were nervous that the British might be seeking to encroach on their own colonial space in South America.[70]

Because of the bad weather it had suffered, and of not being able to refit and reprovision at Rio de Janeiro, the *Dolphin*'s timbers and shipboard discipline both came under strain during the twenty-nine days it took Digby Dent to sail across the South Atlantic to the Cape of Good Hope. One sailor died, another fell overboard, and Elizabeth Marsh quarrelled with the ship's surgeon, a Mr Davis, because he 'behaved extremely disrespectful to the young lady and myself'. For whatever reason, she always bridled quickly if anyone treated her with condescension or discourtesy. By the time the *Dolphin* finally made landfall at the Cape on 18 November, the mixture of euphoria, inadequate diet and long-suppressed anger among the crew was so volatile that five seamen and two marines had been flogged, the latter for defying the ship's officers. For Elizabeth, however, who was not afraid of rough weather at sea, and was used to scant rations and witnessing navy floggings, these last phases of the journey were refreshing, and even restful. The ship moored off the Cape for four weeks, and she was able to pay visits to the settlement and meet its Dutch Governor when he came aboard for a ceremonial visit. They set sail again on 18 December, and because the *Dolphin* was fast, saw the coastline of Ceylon on 17 February 1771, reaching Madras road three days later.[71] Her real challenges and revelations began then, when she disembarked from familiar naval space, and left her chosen medium, the sea.

In one respect, James Crisp – and therefore indirectly Elizabeth Marsh – entered this new terrain and phase of their lives possessed of a distinct advantage. The Crisp family's commercial connections with South and South-East Asia went back to the early seventeenth century. Sir Nicholas Crisp, his father and his wife had all invested in the East India Company; in the early 1700s, various members of the extended Crisp clan were among regular purchasers of goods from Asia at the Company's London auctions; and by now there were also Crisps active in parts of the subcontinent. In the 1740s, for instance, a Phesaunt Crisp was working as a merchant in Bombay.[72] James Crisp's own point of contact with the subcontinent was more than simply commercial and familial. In his childhood he 'had been a playfellow of Eyre Coote', and the two men had renewed their friendship in Menorca in 1753 when Coote 'was a subaltern officer there, and he [Crisp] was Captain of the pacquet'. As with his association with the Earl of Egmont, this capacity to attract and hold the attention of Eyre Coote, a notoriously difficult and haughty man, suggests charm on James Crisp's part and an ability to impress. It may also suggest that he had Irish links somewhere in his immediate family background, for while the Percevals, Earls of Egmont, hailed from County Cork, Eyre Coote was from Limerick. Coote had developed into a very powerful friend. He had been second in command to Robert Clive at the Battle of Plassey, and had subsequently won significant victories against French-led armies at Wandiwash (Vandavasi) and Pondicherry in southern India.[73]

In the wake of his bankruptcy, James Crisp had made contact with Eyre Coote again, who was by then back in London. It may have been Coote's support that helped Crisp to secure the East India Company's permission to leave for the subcontinent and reside there as a private individual, trading 'in the seafaring way', concessions that were by no means easily obtained.[74] Coote and his wife also subscribed generously to the publication of *The Female Captive* in 1769. That same year, Coote returned to India as Commander-in-Chief of the Company's armed forces in Madras. So, in the immediate aftermath of his own migration, James Crisp possessed an extremely powerful patron in the subcontinent, who is known to have recommended him to senior Company officials and to useful commercial contacts. Even before he set out, Crisp's intention was to break into private trade in Asia, focusing on some of the commodities he knew best, textiles, salt and precious stones. 'My sufferings *thank God* seem to be coming to a happy conclusion,' he had written to a friend in November 1768, and he was 'actually preparing for the voyage full of hopes that (if please God) in a few years I shall be able to . . . [make] a provision for my family'. Once arrived, it took time for him to build up the necessary networks and indigenous auxiliaries, so in the interim Coote secured him a cadetship (the bottom level of the commissioned ranks) in the East India Company's army as a means of ensuring him a guaranteed salary and some minimum status.[75]

Again, this was a considerable favour, since cadetships normally had to be purchased and were expensive, but James Crisp was out of his element. Quintessentially a commercial man, and now probably in his mid- to late thirties, he had to adapt to a uniform and an alien discipline. And initially he and his newly-arrived, culture-shocked and semi-estranged wife and daughter were under economic pressure. Eyre Coote had arranged for Crisp to hold his cadetship in Bengal, where the opportunities for military officers to engage in private trade were extensive. But the Company sent him by mistake to Madras, where the risks of active military service were greater, commercial prospects less, and the pay for junior officers 'too contemptible to afford the common necessaries of life'. In 1771, some Company cadets in Madras were reportedly living on five pagodas a month (equivalent to less than £2), and 'unless they are assisted . . . [or given] advances out of the Company's cash they must be reduced to very great distress'.[76]

The extent of the Crisps' difficulties at this stage emerges from the fact that for a while the couple were forced to give up both of their children. Elizabeth Maria, who was seven years old in 1771, was quickly shipped back on her own to England, in the hope that she might become 'well educated and accomplished' in the care of Milbourne Marsh and his wife at Chatham. By contrast, Burrish Crisp, who had been left behind there, was summoned to join his parents in Madras. Milbourne gave the captain of an East Indiaman over £80 to take the boy on the eastwards passage, and when the ship's chief mate ran off with the money, paid out a further £50. He even gave the ship's steward presents in a pitiful attempt to secure some kindness for a nine-year-old child making the six-month voyage to India on his own. As it was, Burrish, 'a manly beautiful boy', seems to have been neglected and abused on the voyage. When the ship docked in Madras in 1772, his parents found him in the hold 'almost destroyed with vermin and filth'. Nor were they able to keep him with them for very long:

> In about a year after his arrival, a Persian merchant who had concerns with his father was so struck with the boy, that he begged he might go with him to Persia and learn the language which he argued would be the means of his making his fortune upon his return.

'With much persuasion', the Crisps gave Burrish over to this merchant, who may have been British, or Dutch, or Armenian, or Bengali, or Persian. Whoever he was, he took the boy into Persia (Iran) for 'a considerable time', and whatever else happened to him there, Burrish Crisp did indeed learn Persian.[77] By the time he was twelve, he spoke and wrote the language perfectly.

This episode makes clear how hard-pressed the Crisps were in the early 1770s, and helps to explain why Burrish Crisp grew up both personally awkward and withdrawn, and intellectually fascinated with the diversity of Asiatic cultures and languages. Being introduced to the interior of Persia, as he seems to have been, was a very rare experience for a Westerner at this time. Since an Afghan invasion in 1720 the country had suffered from political instability, and most European visitors never penetrated further than the coastal towns and ports of the Persian Gulf.[78] Having to migrate twice over so early seems however to have inflicted psychological damage on Burrish, and he may have been damaged sexually as well.

Yet in bringing their son first to Madras, and then letting him go into Persia with only a near stranger for company, his parents demonstrated family ambition and political alertness as well as the extent of their poverty. Already, it seems, they were ceasing to regard themselves as migrants, and thinking seriously of an Asian future. Persian was the language of Mughal scholarship, politics, law and administration; and it remained the official language of the East India Company until the 1830s. Now that the Company was in practical terms the ruler of Bengal, and an encroaching diplomatic and military presence in other parts of the subcontinent, a command of Persian and other indigenous languages was becoming ever more advantageous for access to, and advancement in, its civil and commercial ranks. As Sir William Jones argued pointedly in his *Grammar of the Persian Language* (1771), it was important for the British to study the 'languages of Asia with uncommon ardour', so that 'the limits of our knowledge will be no less extended than the bounds of our empire'.[79] Consigning their only son to Persia was therefore a way – among other things – of giving Burrish the skills he would need for future advancement. His parents had no money to give him. Eyre Coote's favour might not last. The boy's only hope for a secure future in India had to lie in his own wits, and in his being able to offer something special in the way of attainments. Elizabeth Marsh's father Milbourne Marsh, his father, George Marsh senior, and James Crisp himself had all, as very young children, been obliged to leave home and parents, to travel long distances, and to learn to survive on their own. Such lonely, perilous apprenticeships were often the only career training open to boys without means. Looked at this way, Burrish Crisp's lonely voyage to Madras and his subsequent Persian ordeal were particularly stark and transcontinental variations of a customary young male rite of passage.

And, in career terms, the enormous gamble that the Crisps took with their son's life paid off. In March 1774 Bengal's Governor, Warren Hastings, and his Council in Calcutta informed the East India Company's directors in London that, while they had 'hitherto been extremely cautious in troubling you with any recommendations', they felt obliged to make an exception in the case of Burrish Crisp:

> He is a youth of about 15 [he was in fact twelve] and educated to accounts, of a very promising genius and has already made so remarkable a progress in learning the Persian, Bengal and Moors languages and acquiring a know-

ledge of the business and customs of the country that we really think he will be a credit to the Hon'ble Company's employ and therefore take the liberty to recommend him.

They included with this letter 'a specimen of his [Burrish's] writing in Persian'.[80] That so much trouble was taken on the boy's behalf probably owed something to his father's known connection with Eyre Coote. It also reflected the fact that by 1774 the Crisps themselves were in a stronger position. That year, six provincial councils were established throughout Bengal as part of a campaign to make the Company's administration at once more entrenched and less corrupt. Each of these provincial councils consisted of five senior Company officials, plus a secretary, a Persian translator, an accountant and three assistants; and, as a friend of James Crisp reported, 'the revenue, the internal police, and civil judicature were all under their control'. 'An appointment under either [sic] of these boards,' he went on, 'was considered a certain promotion.' This was what Crisp now secured. He was appointed one of the salt agents working for the provincial council of Dhaka, helping to administer the Company's monopoly on the sale of salt there. The move took him back into the civilian sphere where he belonged, and out of penury in Madras to an annual salary in Bengal at the Company's pleasure of £450.[81] It also brought him and Elizabeth Marsh once again into contact with one of the main sites of an increasingly global economy.

The city of Dhaka stretches along the northern shore of a tributary of the Ganges, and is close to the Meghna River, which itself runs into the mighty Brahmaputra.[82] Every summer, when the monsoon arrives, parts of the surrounding countryside are flooded; when the Crisps lived here, it was common for the water level in the region to rise between May and August by as much as fourteen feet. For about seventy miles around Dhaka, towns and villages became for a while 'so many small islands', which could only communicate with each other by boat. The ubiquity of water was one reason why salt production flourished. The region's rivers

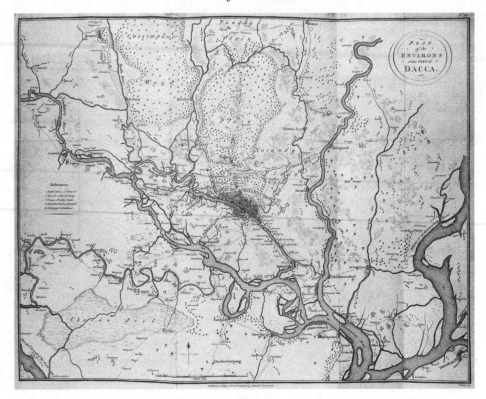

Waterland: 'A plan of the Environs of the City of Dacca' by James
Rennell, *c.*1781.

flowed into and mingled with the waters of the Bay of Bengal.
Every spring, seawater would be collected and processed in clay-
bottomed salt ponds. The resulting lye was then boiled into salt
in earthen pots, using wood from the dense local forests as fuel.
Omnipresent water also made for fertility and abundance.[83] The
four miles over which the city of Dhaka straggled, and its outlying
regions, produced quantities of fine-quality rice, and the city's
traders also exported betel leaf and nuts, sugar, cumin seed, fish
and wooden furniture. And virtually every substantial resident
established a garden, taking advantage of the climate to grow fruit
and vegetables as well as vivid plants. For all its natural beauty,

and its 'bridges, decayed porticos, and columns, some of them of no mean architecture', Dhaka could strike newly arrived and uninformed Westerners as a place in decline. Yet there was an important sense in which, as other, more percipient Europeans acknowledged, this was 'one of the richest [cities] in the world'.[84]

The reason was cotton, another outcrop of the ubiquity of water. The superiority of the cotton grown on lands around Dhaka, wrote an East India Company official later, could be attributed to

> their vicinity to the sea, the water of which mixing, as the tide rolls it in, with the other water of the Meghna, which overflows that part of the country, during three months of the year, deposits as it subsides, sand, and saline particles, which very considerably improve and fertilise the soil.[85]

Cotton is the only natural textile plant that is not grown in Europe, and it has the supreme advantage of being able to be made into a fabric suitable for all climates. In locations where the weather is very hot, it can serve to make up an entire wardrobe. In colder regions it is perfect for layers or underclothes, because it is easy to launder and dry. It also holds colours well. Even in the Crisps' lifetime, when only vegetable dyes were available, cotton could be intricately patterned in brilliant or subtle shades, while still remaining colourfast. And it was cheap – much cheaper than wool or linen, the standard fabrics produced in Britain and Ireland.

For much of the seventeenth and eighteenth centuries the cotton grown and woven in the Indian subcontinent offered these practical advantages, and much more besides. India offered a deep reservoir of particular skills that were passed down over the generations, and labour costs were very low. This was vital, given that the work of planting cotton seeds every autumn, of picking the grown cotton in the spring, and then of cleaning, spinning, weaving and embroidering all demanded a very large number of hands.[86] According to one estimate, of the roughly 450,000 people living in the Dhaka region in the 1770s, 147,000 were involved in some aspect of the manufacture of cotton. There were over twenty-five thousand weavers, all men. In addition, thirty thousand women worked as cotton spinners and cleaners. A further five thousand, it was claimed, were employed embroidering the most luxurious and expensive fabrics, especially Dhaka's muslins, which were so fine and delicate that a length of this fabric could, it was said, pass easily through a woman's ring.[87]

This burgeoning indigenous economy influenced how James Crisp perceived and interacted with his new environment. Most white civilian incomers to the subcontinent settled in Calcutta, or Madras, or Bombay, places where Europeans had played a major role since the seventeenth century, and which they could therefore choose to view as substantially their creations. But while stray Europeans had been coming to Dhaka for centuries to trade, it was still visibly a Mughal city, full of splendid buildings, and with an affluence and an international significance that considerably predated the East India Company's *coup d'état* in Bengal. In 1610, the then Mughal viceroy of Bengal had made Dhaka his capital and headquarters, and this had transformed its size and building stock. The city lost its high political status in the early eighteenth century, but its cotton and its commerce had continued to attract Armenian, Arabian, Persian, Pathan and Bengali traders, and a medley of Europeans, Dutch, French, Portuguese, as well as British merchants. When the Crisps arrived in Dhaka in 1774, most of the textiles produced there and in the rest of Bengal were still consumed locally, or traded elsewhere in the subcontinent. Nonetheless, Indian cotton had already become 'the only textile that can be said to have been integral to the global trading system'.[88]

Asian traders had long been exporting cotton textiles to West, Central and South-East Asia, and to East Africa; Indian cotton had also traditionally penetrated the Ottoman Empire by way of Cairo; and a growing amount went to Europe, and from there on to other continents. In 1665 the East India Company had exported seven thousand pieces of cloth from Bengal to Britain. By the time James Crisp arrived in Dhaka, 650,000 pieces were being shipped from Bengal to London every year. Some of this fabric was subsequently re-exported to North America and the Caribbean. Indian cotton was also traded to Spanish-controlled Manila, and passed from there into Latin America. And Indian textiles were an integral part of the transatlantic slave trade. As far as British slave traders were concerned, textiles from the subcontinent seem to have made up at least a third of the barter they offered in return for slaves on the West African coast during the eighteenth century, so some of these cotton goods also passed inexorably into the interior of Africa.[89]

By the early nineteenth century, most – not all – incoming Westerners had come to view India as entangled in all sorts of ways in an archaic past, and consequently in need of advancement and modernization from without. By contrast, James Crisp was able to view Dhaka, with its abundant, high-quality cotton industry, almost as a traditional site of economic modernity. As another recently-arrived Briton wrote in 1776:

> The consumption of foreign commodities by the natives of
> Bengal is very inconsiderable . . . But the productions of
> Bengal have been in request, in almost every part of the
> world . . . [If] selling be the essential property of commerce,
> Bengal was a commercial nation of the first order.[90]

To a degree, indeed, Crisp could view his new surroundings in Dhaka, over-confidently, less as a breach with his previous existence than as a continuation of it. He was used to international cities engaged in transcontinental trade. Now, after Barcelona, and London, and Hamburg, and Livorno, and the rest, he was in yet another dynamic centre of this sort, which just happened to be located in the subcontinent. In his European ventures he had been involved in the salt trade. Now, in Dhaka, part – though only part – of his business was once again dealing in salt. He was already familiar with Indian textiles from working as a merchant in Britain and Spain. Now the move to Dhaka placed him, a supremely entrepreneurial man who was accustomed to dealing with different cultures and languages, in one of the great centres of the textile industry, in daily reach of a commodity that was in growing demand across the world. Dhaka's high-grade cotton would be the means, then, of rebuilding his reputation and restoring his family's fortunes.

And, as even George Marsh was prepared to concede, once settled in Dhaka, James Crisp 'flourished in trade there very fast'.[91] Just how fast is suggested by an inventory, compiled in 1780, of the house in which he and Elizabeth Marsh intermittently lived. It helped that living stylishly in Dhaka was relatively cheap. The difference in outlay for a European resident between there and Calcutta, one visitor calculated in 1765, bore the 'same proportion as between country and city in England'. Maintaining a suitably fashionable house in Calcutta could cost a merchant up to £1000 *every year*. But the substantial house that the Crisps acquired in Dhaka, together with its compound, was valued at 9010 rupees, the equivalent at the time of about £900.[92] With less need to sink money into accommodation, the Crisps were able to invest more in consumer goods. The inventory suggests that they lived for a while in a higher style than most Europeans were able to do in the subcontinent. It also suggests that, as in London, the couple indulged themselves, and seized upon objects as a means of redefining themselves in a new environment.

Less than half of the tiny European civilian population in Madras at this time, for instance, seem to have been able to afford their own household palanquin. But the Crisps made a point of owning one, complete with 'bamboo tassels', presumably also paying the four to eight bearers who were needed to carry it. The couple adopted other artifacts and emblems that were traditionally associated with the Mughal elite. A *morchal*, a flywhisk or fan made of peacock feathers, was an Indo-Persian symbol of power. The Crisps acquired four of them. They genuflected to their new environment, too, by adopting a more minimalist style of décor than they would have been accustomed to in Europe. Their Dhaka house seems to have possessed no curtains or carpets, though they may have covered its floors with locally produced or Chinese rattan mats. Their couches, beds and chairs were made of blackwood, an indigenous hardwood much used by native carpenters; while their lacquered card tables and two 'japanned' (painted and gilded) cabinets were probably East India Company imports from Canton. James Crisp also introduced cross-cultural borrowings into his own wardrobe. He continued to wear his wig for formal meetings with other Europeans (just as Elizabeth continued to use curling irons on her fraying hair). And Crisp owned four European-style suits, albeit made of buff, black and blue Indian silk. But in his own house, and when travelling Dhaka's interminable waterways, he wore 'Banyan' coats and shirts, loose, Indian-style cotton garments; and by now he had acquired at least twenty-five 'pairs of short drawers' and fifty-nine pairs of cotton stockings.[93] The extreme heat, and abundant indigenous servants to do laundry, meant that like other Europeans in Asia, he was much cleaner than was customary in his home continent.

Historians disagree about the deeper significance of these kinds of cultural and material borrowings by invading Britons in India. For some, they are evidence of the fact that for much of the eighteenth century there was a greater willingness than would exist later to forge connections and understandings of different kinds across religious and racial lines. For others, it is axiomatic that 'the appropriation of Indian habits or the use of Indian objects did not affect the identity of the British in India', and that everyday contact with difference only amplified the intruders' self-consciousness.[94] Yet this sort of polarized position-taking is not the best way to unpick the complexities and inconsistencies of past individual lives and mentalities. Elizabeth Marsh and her husband had come to India out of desperation and for selfish reasons, and they were attached to and ultimately dependent on – though crucially not *of* – a paramilitary trading company that had usurped fiscal, commercial and legal authority in Bengal. Part of the story from now on must be concerned with establishing how far each of them was corrupted by all of this. But it was intrinsically unlikely that the already mongrel identities of Elizabeth Marsh and James Crisp would remain unaffected by this further violent migration, and by exposure to a very different life in Dhaka.

This was not simply because the city's landscape, climate, wildlife, bodily practices and cuisine were so unfamiliar, but also because coming to South Asia, and living where they did, stripped the couple of all formal contact with their religion, still the bedrock of most people's identity at this time. In London the Crisps seem to have attended Church of England worship regularly, and naturally they had their two children christened. But at Dhaka, no Protestant place of worship of any kind was available to offer an alternative to the region's more than 230 mosques and fifty-two Hindu temples. The Crisps did keep a Bible in their Dhaka house, but its position in the inventory seems eloquent of the diminished role that religion, any religion, now played in the couple's lives. 'One Bible,' wrote the inventory's compiler, 'and 12 packs of cards.'[95] Elizabeth Marsh had referred to God regularly in *The Female Captive*. After she arrives in the subcontinent, she writes of God no more. The Crisps' capacity to use their birth language, or any other European language, and to be easily understood by those around them, was now anyway inevitably very circumscribed. According to a 'List of Europeans in this province' compiled by the East India Company in 1778, there were just forty-eight white males of any description living in Dhaka that year, including James Crisp and, by now, Burrish Crisp. Thirty of these men were formally attached to the Company as civil or military servants, while the rest were either private merchants, like James Crisp, or individuals 'with no visible means of livelihood'.[96]

No woman was included in this list, because European females exercised no formal public function in the subcontinent in the Company's eyes, and there were anyway very few of them. In 1785 there were just three married women in Dhaka who were accounted white. 'They live all very retired,' reported one resident at that time, 'and though the ladies seem very good friends they meet very seldom.'[97] For Elizabeth Marsh, who was at least nominally white, there was therefore little to do, and few of what passed for her own kind to socialize or converse with. For ambitious, energetic and greedy white males, Dhaka could be a rich, demanding place, a frontier environment, replete with opportunities. It catered to those in search of another chance like James Crisp. It provided for men who were well-born but with inadequate incomes, like the Honourable Robert Lindsay, the son of a Scottish peer with eleven children, and only £1000 per annum to raise them on, who arrived in Dhaka on the make in 1776 and who knew the Crisps. It suited the politically driven, since partisan rivalries among the tiny British community were fierce and bitter. And Dhaka's relative cheapness and isolation made it a haven for male loners and eccentrics of various kinds.

Even though they could not assemble at Protestant worship, ways existed for the few British men living here to express their solidarity. There was already a Masonic lodge in Dhaka in which they, and other European males, could observe the newer rituals of the Enlightenment. As for the 'unmarried gentlemen', it was their custom to go together 'every Friday at about 20 miles from the town, to hunt wild boars and deer, where we remain to the Monday in tents. There we ride morning & evening on horseback or upon elephants which are here in plenty; almost every gentleman here keeps one or two of these large animals.'[98] Whether married or unmarried, all European males in Dhaka, as elsewhere in the subcontinent, could also seek out and forge relationships with indigenous women, learning in the process more about local cultures, while still carefully vaunting their superiority if they chose to do so. But these options and occupations were not available to Elizabeth Marsh.

She benefited of course from the material luxuries of her position, while participating in some of the risks, living as a highly privileged intruder in a waterworld where there were half a million indigenous inhabitants and scarcely more than fifty white civilians. Not for nothing did she and James Crisp equip their Dhaka household with guns and bows and arrows. But, with one child in Persia, and the other in Chatham, and with her husband absent on his salt and textile business for much of the time, she had very little to do. She could easily have escaped to Calcutta, the Company's power centre and the showpiece of British society in India, and sought distraction in its theatres, music societies and abundant bazaars, its stuccoed classical buildings and steepled churches, and its deliberately ornate and time-consuming social life. It was a mark of Elizabeth Marsh's quality and distinctiveness, though also of her perversity, that she went instead a great deal further, and looked for other things.

5

An Asiatic Progress

SHE WAS SICK, 'very ill indeed'. 'In a very languid state', she complained, and experiencing 'much pain in my side'. As in Gibraltar in
1756, pressures that were to some degree real – the risk of invasion
then, illness now – became a rationalization for abrupt departure
and extensive movement: 'My extreme ill health *obliged* me to
undertake a journey to the coast.' She left Dhaka for Calcutta on
13 December 1774, and from there took ship for Madras (Chennai).
A century later, incomers to the subcontinent who were unwell
and sufficiently moneyed normally sought refuge in one of the hill
stations, Almora, or Simla, or Darjeeling in the east, or Ooty in
the south, convalescing in their cooler climates, and in the secure,
well-regimented society of other Britons. But in Elizabeth Marsh's
lifetime, more than usually ailing Europeans in northern India who
were unable or unwilling to voyage home had few options but to
sail southwards in the hope that fresher coastal breezes might effect
a recovery. One of her fellow passengers for part of the voyage to
Madras was John Shore, at this time a twenty-four-year-old Writer
(a junior civil servant) with the East India Company, and a future
Governor General of India. 'Troubled with a severe disorder', he
too was setting out 'to try the sea air', just as, ostensibly, she was.[1]
Invalids rarely stayed away from their families or their posts out of
choice, however, for as long as Elizabeth Marsh. Nor did they
usually employ their time like her: for while she followed custom
in sailing to Madras, she did not stay there. Instead, she spent over
a year moving between different settlements in what are now Tamil

Nadu and Andhra Pradesh, ultimately exploring some of their most significant religious, urban and economic sites. When she finally returned to Dhaka in July 1776, by way of an arduous overland route along the subcontinent's eastern coastline and through Orissa, she had been away and often in motion for over eighteen months.

By all accounts this was an extraordinary progress. Although the frequency with which individuals from outside the subcontinent travelled within it had been increasing exponentially since the fifteenth century, it was still unusual for white civilian males – and exceptional for women of any kind – to undertake protracted overland journeys here, unless they were driven to do so by religion, commerce, or in order to accompany a spouse.[2] James Crisp seems never to have ventured southwards out of Bengal after 1774. Nor, at a very different level of the East India Company food chain, did Philip Francis, for instance, after taking up his position on Calcutta's Supreme Council that same year. The pressure of business, fear of disease, intense heat and saturating monsoons were all powerful disincentives to non-essential long-distance travel. So were the practical challenges of journeying inland. Europeans remained largely ignorant of such indigenous maps as existed; and although the Company possessed good surveys of Indian coastlines, it was only in 1767 that James Rennell was appointed as its Surveyor General to oversee the internal mapping of parts of the subcontinent. Even where moderately accurate surveys were available, overland travel was often slow and physically arduous. 'The roads are at best, little better than paths,' claimed Rennell:

> and whenever deep rivers (which in that country are frequent, and without bridges) morasses, chains of mountains, or other obstacles, oppose themselves to the line of direction of the road, it is carried round, so as to effect the easiest passage; and for this reason the roads there, have a degree of

crookedness, much beyond what we meet with in European countries.

Since tracks were rough and circuitous, 'an ordinary traveller' in India, he suggested, was unlikely to cover more than twenty-two miles in a day.[3]

By no means an ordinary traveller, Elizabeth Marsh carried out her own protracted Asiatic journey in the company mainly of indigenous soldiers, guides and servants, but in the absence of James Crisp. In this respect, too, the circumstances of this journey mirrored her behaviour in 1756. Then she had set out from Gibraltar leaving her parents and brothers behind. Now she embarked on her progress without her husband or son; and, as in 1756, she travelled in close companionship with an unmarried man. The individual concerned on this occasion was a Captain George Smith, whom Elizabeth referred to as her 'cousin'. Smith and she were in daily contact from their joint departure from Dhaka in December 1774 to her return to the borders of Bengal in June 1776. This, but also much more, sets her apart from other early foreign female travellers in the subcontinent, such as Jemima Kindersley, who visited Madras and northern India in the 1760s, or Sophia Plowden, who travelled from Calcutta to Lucknow in 1777–78, or Eliza Fay, who wrote about her adventures in southern India in the 1780s.[4] These women travelled overwhelmingly by water, in a *budgerow* (a sort of keel-less river barge), or along the coast. When they did venture overland, it was usually in order to accompany their spouses. And in writing about their travels, Kindersley, Plowden, and even Fay were careful to stress how bound up they remained in structures of family and social obligation. Kindersley, for instance, begins her *Letters from the Island of Teneriffe, Brazil, the Cape of Good Hope, and the East Indies* (1777) with an allusion to a possibly fictional friend in England, and to 'the promise I made, of giving you a particular account'.[5]

Elizabeth Marsh's description of her Asiatic progress was very

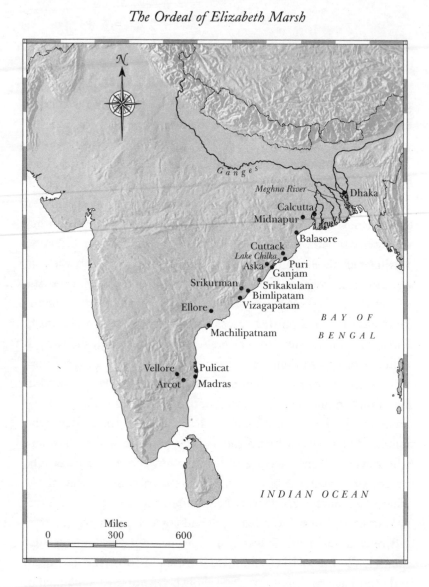

Elizabeth Marsh's Indian journey

different. She had not been able to make notes during her Mediterranean and Moroccan experiences in 1756, and had bitterly regretted having to rely only on memory when drafting *The Female Captive* thirteen years later. It may have been in part so as to leave open the possibility of publishing some version of this new journey that she embarked on a diary now. The snippets of sometimes overconfident information she includes ('a *coss* is two English miles and half') suggest that she had a future audience in mind; but she also had more immediate reasons for writing. The experience of serious illness, or fear of it, can often prompt a resort to some kind of autobiographical testimony.[6] So can the consciousness that middle or old age has irremediably set in. When she embarked on this Indian journey, Elizabeth Marsh was less than a year away from her fortieth birthday, and she had already struggled through the two monsoons that were all that many incomers to the sub-continent could hope to survive. The diary was a way of taking stock of what she had become, and of how far she still possessed opportunities to change. As the months went by, it also became a chronicle of exhilaration and perplexity in the face of multiple discoveries.

This was no purely introspective document, however. Nor was hers simply a private progress. She could not have travelled within the subcontinent as ambitiously as she did without the East India Company's much increased and unevenly expanding military and political reach. It was this epochal shift in imperial and transcontinental history that made up the background to her progress and the stuff of much of her journal. In retrospect, the Company's takeover of Bengal by way of the *diwani* in 1765 represented the first of a succession of European conquests of substantial Asian territories, a coup that ultimately provided 'a platform – of men, money and matériel – for the subjugation of the entire region from the eastern Mediterranean to the South China Sea', and consequently for the temporary emergence of a more Western-dominated world.[7] Like most of her contemporaries, Elizabeth Marsh had only a glimmer of foreknowledge of this. But she did observe and describe some of the alterations in power taking place about her, as well as the limits of these changes, and signs of resistance to them. That she should have set out on, and

A page from Elizabeth Marsh's Indian Journal.

documented, by far the most exploratory journey in the subcontinent known to have been attempted by a woman in the aftermath of the *diwani* seems in keeping with her strange, recurrent role as a kind of female Candide. Once again she blundered into the path of momentous events and transitions, coming in contact with individuals who were infinitely more powerful than herself. Once again she brought to bear on these encounters an uninformed, not unperceptive gaze.

❧

To begin with, perhaps because she is ill and afraid, she scans the physical and social landscape less with curiosity about what is new and difficult, than for scenes she can choose to view as familiar in some way. Jotting down notes almost every day that she and George Smith are in motion is itself a way of seeking reassurance, a ritual that supplies a modicum of continuity. Whenever they are stationary and she feels more secure, staying in a fort, or a Company cantonment or house, or a *choultry* (a travellers' resting place), she indicatively stops writing. But otherwise she scribbles impressions and encounters as they go along in her clear, spiky hand, conveying the movement she is involved in by employing dashes in place of full stops.

Having completed the trip from Dhaka to Calcutta, 380 miles as the river systems in the Ganges delta run at this time, and said farewell to those whom she still describes as 'my dear Crisp and sweet boy', Elizabeth Marsh and George Smith embark on a storeship. This is the *Goodwill*, commanded by a Captain Burford, 'a good, plain character', she quickly decides, 'but by no means an entertaining one'. The *Goodwill* is a privately owned 'large stout ship in good condition, well manned with European seamen and lascars with guns and ammunition for defence', regularly leased out, as on this occasion, to the Royal Navy, but even this does not immediately reassure her.[8] She spends much of the day after they set sail from Calcutta not conversing with Smith or any of the other passengers, but standing on deck, staring at the passing Garden Houses to the south of the city, the one- and two-storey buildings to which its more affluent residents escape during the hottest summer months. From her viewpoint, these seem as elegant as 'the most noble houses in any of the large squares in England', by which she means, she immediately clarifies, London. As they sail on, she takes note of 'a Point called Melancholy, so named on account of the first English lady that ever came to Bengal being buried there'. And when the *Goodwill* has passed Baj Baj, Phalta and Kulpi, and is lying 'off the dreary island of Sagar', seventy miles downriver from Calcutta, she observes 'on the other side, a flat country, where many of my poor countrymen are deposited, as numbers of sailors and soldiers are there buried'.[9]

As well as suggesting the scale of her despondency at this time, these are some of the most forthright statements she supplies about certain strands of her identity. Elizabeth Marsh aspired, though not invariably, to be viewed as an English lady. She was also minded to regard men wearing British military uniform, and especially Royal Navy uniform, as her countrymen, as 'us'. And she still missed London, the elegant squares that she had walked through but never lived in, and the social opportunities and style the city had briefly given her. All of these ties of nation, place and culture, which she was sometimes anxious to acknowledge, emerge from her description of the *Goodwill*'s encounter with the Royal Navy's East Indian squadron in the Bay of Bengal in late January 1775. She watched from on deck as Captain Burford's crew loaded fresh stores onto the *Salisbury*, the flagship of the squadron's Commodore, Sir Edward Hughes, and recorded, at the end, a significant passage: 'The men of war saluted, and then all the ships were in motion, the Commodore bound to Madras, Sir John Clerke to the China Seas, the Swallow sloop, Captain Pigot, for Ganjam.' Clerke's ship, that same *Dolphin* which had brought her to India, was now engaged in transporting eight hundred chests of opium to the free port of Balambangan in easternmost Java. As for Hughes' ship, the *Salisbury*, while en route for the Indian Ocean in 1772 it had anchored in Table Bay off the Cape of Good Hope next to the *Adventure* and to James Cook's ship, the

Resolution.[10] These two latter vessels were in transit for the Antarctic and the Pacific, in Cook's second circumnavigation of the world. Being acted out in the Bay of Bengal, as Elizabeth Marsh partly understood, was a scene of the Royal Navy's increased presence in Asian waters, and also an illustration of its growing capacity to connect different sites of empire, commercial effort and exploration across the globe.

For her, though, this nautical encounter chiefly signified an opportunity to rehearse again some of the modes of politeness she had grown used to in London. As long as the *Goodwill* remained moored close to the East Indian squadron, she made a point of dressing for dinner. She unearthed her tea caddy and teaware from her 'very comfortable, excellent' cabin, and made tea on one occasion for 'a large company' of navy officers; and she received other visits. Sir John Clerke was rowed over from the *Dolphin* to pay his respects. Sir Edward Hughes' son-in-law and his secretary also called on her. The Commodore himself did not visit, but he sent her 'a polite note' and 'a number of refreshments', she recorded proudly, including three dozen bottles of English spa water, warm and stale in its glass.[11]

However physically reduced she was, Elizabeth Marsh always seems to have behaved like a woman who knows herself to be attractive and winning. Yet, as she acknowledged in the diary, it was not just her residual allure that prompted these flattering attentions, or even the simple absence of alternative female company on offer in the Bay of Bengal. The men who visited the *Goodwill* and bestowed courtesies on her were also 'well acquainted with most of my family'. Sir Edward Hughes' secretary, Arthur Cuthbert, for instance, was a close friend and business associate of her uncle George Marsh; and, in addition to the Royal Navy networks she was always able to exploit, there was another connection of her family who was bound to secure her official notice and attention within the East India Company's sphere of authority.[12]

Richard Smith (1734–1803), a Londoner 'of very obscure origin' but 'great ambition to command', had started out as a purser's mate in the Company's fleet. As proved possible for a minority of men, he had used the physical mobility afforded by ships and the sea, and the opportunities on offer from war and empire, as a springboard to power, wealth and vertiginous social mobility. Soon switching to the Company's army, and fighting its battles, Smith rose swiftly through the ranks, and in 1767 was appointed Commander-in-Chief in Bengal. In the process he also made a fortune, in part by lending money at exorbitant rates of interest to Muhammad Ali Khan Walajah, the Nawab of the British-'protected' province of Arcot, near Madras. On his return to Britain in 1770, Smith claimed to be worth £200,000–£300,000, which in present-day values meant that he was a millionaire more than twenty times over. In Samuel Foote's highly successful play *The Nabob*, which opened in London's Haymarket Theatre in 1772, General Richard Smith, as he now was, appeared in the guise of 'Sir Matthew Mite', as the archetypal East India Company capitalist-cum-military adventurer, whose complexion had 'been tinged by the East', who had 'risen to uncontrolled power abroad', and who had returned to Britain, 'thundering amongst us, and profusely scattering the spoils of ruined [Asian] provinces'.[13] In reality, Richard Smith was not without perceptiveness, or a capacity to criticize some of the military and commercial projects in which he acted, which was why he subsequently became a political ally of Edmund Burke in his parliamentary campaigns to reform the East India Company. It was contrary to common sense, Smith himself would tell Parliament in 1781 in regard to the Company's takeover of Bengal, 'that 5000 men should force a system upon ten millions', especially as those intruding themselves amongst the indigenous peoples of 'that vast territory' were 'but men like themselves, or very little better'.[14]

The links between this sharply intelligent, aggressive and corrupt man and the Marsh family were intricate. At least one male 'cousin' of Milbourne Marsh seems to have married a Smith in the early

1700s; and in his will Richard Smith would claim to be the real father of the woman to whom George Marsh later married his eldest son (netting in the process a dowry of £40,000).[15] As far as Elizabeth Marsh was concerned, it was the existence of her family's links with Smith, not their precise nature, that mattered. Men and women who migrate over extensive distances, especially those with limited resources, tend to make the most of any kin or contacts who can ease their progress in a new land; and it is clear that Elizabeth capitalized on her relationship with Richard Smith as greedily and as purposefully as James Crisp sought out help from his boyhood friend, Eyre Coote. She seems to have dined with Smith, Captain Digby Dent and the Company's historiographer, Robert Orme, shortly before embarking on the *Dolphin* and sailing to Madras in 1770. Once established in Bengal, the closest friend she went on to cultivate in Calcutta was a wealthy widow named Johanna Ross, who was also the aunt of Richard Smith's wife. Johanna Ross subsequently became one of James Crisp's most valuable business creditors.[16]

It was Elizabeth Marsh's known relationship to Richard Smith, a former commander-in-chief of the East India Company's legions, and still a powerful figure in its affairs, to which she owed some of the attentions she received from the likes of Sir John Clerke and Sir Edward Hughes; but the more significant benefits of her connection with him only became apparent once she made landfall.

The further south the *Goodwill* sailed, the harder she initially found it to banish strangeness simply by a resort to dress, or manners, or food, or language. Resorting to stock phrases in her diary like 'the country charming – and weather delightful' scarcely comprehended all that she was now seeing every day from the decks of the *Goodwill*. It was predictably the sea and a ship that drove this point home to her. When, on 14 February 1775, they finally moored off Madras, which possessed no natural harbour, the state *mussoola* was sent to convey her ashore: 'formed of a particular construction, being sewed together, with packthread, and not any iron work about it, extremely high at the sides, and very roomy'. Deliberately without the fixed beams or metal fastenings Elizabeth Marsh was used to in Royal Navy vessels, a *mussoola* was designed to bend and adjust in response to the fierce surf off Madras, 'which made so horrible an appearance, that the idea of going through it was dreadful'. Unable, once she was in the boat, to see far above its sides, and feeling its wood and skins rippling around her, she was 'almost sick, and frightened to death'. 'Supped in heaven,' she records, quite atypically, that evening, 'being on shore.'[17]

For a while, Madras allowed her a cocoon in which to retire and pretend again. Although this was emphatically an Asian city, a sprawling composite of agricultural and fishing villages, of the so-called 'Black Town', which contained Portuguese and Armenian merchants as well as indigenous residents, and of the Company's own heavily fortified settlement, Madras could still appear in parts, to those who wished to view it in such terms, as quasi-English, even classically European. Laid out in streets and squares, with an Anglican church, St Mary's, the Company sector of the city held some 'neat and pretty' houses, equipped with chaste verandas, and its few public buildings gleamed with a kind of white plaster, *chunam*, that was made out of crushed seashells.[18] Elizabeth Marsh's first serious venture beyond the city's boundaries in early April seems to have brought on panic ('my disorder seemed to increase'), and it was not until 16 June 1775 that she finally made the break with counterfeit familiarity and began the second phase of her journey. This was when being able to lay claim to family ties with General Richard Smith, and having as her companion Captain George Smith (who may also have been related to him), became vital.[19]

When the artist William Hodges subsequently travelled through parts of the subcontinent between 1780 and 1784, seeking out scenes and buildings to paint and engrave, he was only able to secure a substantial military escort to protect and guide him along the way because his patron happened to be Warren Hastings, the Governor General, who made sure he was provided with the necessary armed followers.[20] Elizabeth Marsh was a mere woman, with no officially recognized purpose for travelling, the absentee wife of a private merchant and minor official who was not even a covenanted servant of the East India Company. Yet, by way of Richard Smith and George Smith, she gained access to a substantial militarized retinue, without which she could never have ventured as far, or as riskily, as she ultimately did.

Until April 1776 she was usually accompanied on her various excursions by European as well as indigenous troops. Even after she finally left the boundaries of the Madras Presidency, the region the British laid claim to on the subcontinent's eastern, Coromandel coast, and started moving northwards again, her travelling party included at its smallest 'about 40 coolees . . . with peons, debashes etc', and eight sepoys and a havildar, native infantry of the Company. She herself travelled for much of the time, though not all of the time, in considerable style. While she was in Madras, the Company's Commander-in-Chief allotted her one of his own houses close to the fort; and when she finally committed herself to leaving the city, she did so reclining in a state palanquin, a box-litter with a pole projecting before and behind, carried along in her case by four bearers. The vehicle 'was greatly admired', she recorded complacently, 'being extremely high finished'.[21]

Here was one of the paradoxes of Elizabeth Marsh's progress. That she was at once ill, of no social or political significance, and sporadically very frightened, and, simultaneously, profoundly privileged. An outsider in multiple respects, she travelled none-theless with some of the perquisites normally attached to wealth, status and power.

Over the next eleven months Elizabeth Marsh spends time in various settlements in the Madras Presidency, most of them places where Company troops are stationed: in Vellore, Ellore, Pulicat, an important cloth-producing centre that was still controlled by the Dutch, and in Machilipatnam, Ganjam, Aska and more. At first glance, the strictly selective account of these excursions she commits to her diary suggests only a continued, solipsistic clinging to European conventions and European people. Yet even a superficial reading makes clear the startling resurgence of her energy and confidence over this period. Whatever had been the source of her ill health in Dhaka, acute depression, or – since she was now forty – an early menopause, or, as some of her symptoms suggest, an attack of gallstones, she now cast it off, or made herself disregard it. Most of the Company officers she mentions encountering at this stage were younger than she, yet several of these men died during or shortly after her progress, not from war, but from heat or disease. Captain John Candler, for instance, whom she meets at Ichapur, and Captain Francis Bandinel, her host at Aska, will both be dead by the end of 1776.[22] Elizabeth Marsh, however, for the rest of a journey in which she is rarely in a bed – or trying to sleep in a palanquin or a tent – before 2 a.m., and in which she is alternately drenched by rain and sunburnt, appears to suffer nothing worse than occasional colds, and bouts of indigestion brought on by the oysters and Madeira she consumes at every opportunity.

She invests some of this renewed energy in hectic socializing that signifies much more than that. Like her contemporary James Boswell, an infinitely more distinguished diarist who, as a Scot in London, was also an outsider of sorts, Marsh seems to have accepted the possibility of being 'in some degree whatever character we choose'.[23] The self was malleable, and could be acted out and written up in multiple versions. As a recent migrant to the subcontinent, and as a woman who was travelling in extraordinary circumstances, Elizabeth Marsh was at one level obliged to try out new roles. But she seems always to have felt the need to do this; and what preoccupied her for much of this middle part of her journey, to a degree that seems, and sometimes was, intensely self-indulgent, was this persistent enterprise of refashioning herself, and of striving to secure respect and attention. 'However low rated in England,' an Englishwoman in Calcutta remarks in Phebe Gibbes' novel *Hartly House* (1789), 'I am a sovereign princess here.' This character is referring to the indigenous servants, colonial airs and conspicuous consumption that living in Bengal allows her, and which she has never known at home. Elizabeth Marsh would have understood the desire to become someone different, and to clutch hold of something better in India. In her case, though, this appears to have involved less extracting deference from its native inhabitants than securing respect from the British themselves, specifically Britons of a certain sort. More than anything else, she seems to have been searching in this middle, Madras segment of her progress for 'a society' that would accord her some recognition, one that 'studied to make me happy'.[24]

So she lingers in her diary over every courteous gesture and sign of approval, especially from influential males. Virtually her only comment about her stay in the city of Madras is that she 'saw much company', just as her sole farewell comment on Dhaka had been how 'the company of the settlement . . . parted with me in the most friendly manner possible'. Arriving on her second visit to Machilipatnam, she records glowingly how 'My company [was] daily solicited . . . my tea table was the resort of all the sensible and polite, and crowded every evening.' In Ichapur, she reports being able to dine 'with a very large company all cheerful and well-bred', and that the conversation was 'lively yet delicate'. And then there is the music, as at Aska, where she is requested to sing 'many songs with the head violin-player'. Above all, there is the dancing. In Ganjam, the local Company chief gives a ball 'in compliment to me: I opened it with a minuet': that is, with a dance in which by convention the leading couple performed initially alone on the dance floor, being watched by everyone else in the room. A week later, Robert Maunsell ('second in Council') arranges a supper party where she finds 'all the company ready for me to open the Ball, which I did'.[25]

This rather poignant litany of minor social successes underlines of course how cliquish prosperous and would-be prosperous Britons in India could be even at this early stage. How much polite rituals and conventions from home like tea-making ceremonies, calling and playing cards, the formalities of the minuet, and the habit of Company army officers like George Smith of buttoning their woollen uniform jackets close to the throat whatever the heat, were drawn on in order to display and cement together a tiny minority whose authority in the subcontinent was still very patchy and at times uncertain. Such rituals could also weld together rich and moderately affluent whites from different parts of Europe, not just British and Irish servants of the Company and their women-folk, but also stray Portuguese, Danish, Dutch, Swiss and German players in India (though only occasionally individuals who were French, and therefore still deemed to be threatening). As a former Company official wrote in 1780:

> On account of the small number of European ladies in India, a constant intercourse between families is more encouraged there than in any other part of the world ... The Europeans all mutually receive and pay visits; and from this practice they all become personally acquainted.[26]

But the politics of Elizabeth Marsh's own socializing were more complicated than this. The people whom she conversed and danced with, sang to and played at cards with while journeying around the Madras region were certainly European in many of their cultural practices, but by no means all of them were European in terms of their place of origin or upbringing. At this time, a proportion of the East India Company's army officers were – as she may have been herself – of mixed racial descent. Because white women were so sparse, some of the wives of Company civilian and military officers were also of necessity, as well as for reasons of desire, what was termed 'country born'. And those Company army officers who had been born in India of British parents might well – as seems to have been the case with George Smith – never themselves have spent any time in Britain at all.[27] It was the actual heterogeneity of the 'British' presence in India at this time, and not just its self-consciousness, which lay behind the feverish succession of balls, card parties, ornate suppers and decorous picnics of the sort in which Elizabeth Marsh rapturously took part. Such 'elegant' socializing did not provide for racial equality (a phrase and a concept which would anyway have meant very little at this time) in the subcontinent, any more than similar rituals made for social equality within Britain itself. But, in India as in Britain, these performances of politeness could provide for 'access of different kinds of people to the same places and allowed interaction among different groups on the basis of a shared set of manners'. Learning to dance the minuet could be a way of deftly concealing and counterfeiting one's origins, as distinct from simply displaying and celebrating them.[28]

This may well have been one reason why Elizabeth Marsh found this interlude in her life so exhilarating. In the Madras region, where the British were far less powerfully entrenched than in Bengal, and less hidebound than they were in the most affluent neighbourhoods of Calcutta, her uncertain origins, her riven past and her only moderate sophistication simply did not matter so much. Her bankrupted husband was far away in Dhaka. Her childhood in a Portsmouth tenement was not known. And if she retained any self-consciousness on account of what her mother was or was not, this too could be overlaid with displays of her own hard-won accomplishments – just as participation in an agreed set of social rituals, in certain forms of dress, and speech, and behaviour, successfully overlaid the mixed backgrounds and origins of some of her companions. There was a degree to which, at this stage of her Asiatic progress, Elizabeth Marsh was able to become a Cinderella allowed metaphorically, and not just in reality, to go to the ball. Although Captain George Smith seems only to have joined the Company's military in 1765, the death rate amongst its officers in this region was such that he was often the most senior commissioned man present in the various settlements and assemblies the couple visited. In which case he – and therefore she – would make their entrance amidst 'all the customary compliments . . . all the drums and fifes . . . and every honor which possibly could be shown us', 'every mark of attention, and real hospitality'.[29] For the daughter of a shipwright, who was compromised in different ways by her past, these were ravishingly flattering experiences, and the portions of her diary devoted to them are dizzy with exultation.

Since she travelled through two late Indian springs and summers, there was often intense heat that split her hair, and made her sometimes cry with fatigue, because she 'could only sleep upon a fine mat, which was constantly wetted, and dried up as fast, and was too hot to admit of my lying down'. But she did not slow down. She was 'gasping for air', she writes, 'yet in spirits'. 'I,' she boasts on another occasion – unnecessarily – 'was amongst the number of restless beings.' A British visitor to eastern India at this time remarked wryly how dancing in such temperatures, as Elizabeth Marsh regularly did when staying in Company settlements into the early hours of the morning, converted makeshift ballrooms into something closer to swimming baths, saturated not only with the dancers' sweat (and their stench), but also with water that had regularly to be poured on the floor in order to keep feet bearably cool and the wood from cracking.[30] She, though, was too euphoric by now to acknowledge such inconveniences, 'for when the weather was so hot as to oblige the floors to be kept continually wet, yet at times we could not resist dancing'. And when, on the hottest days, the thermometer climbed above 115 degrees, there was always 'delightful night':

The tablecloth spread as usual on the grass, cold fowl and
oysters were our repast – sung some songs, danced a reel,
and again seated ourselves in our palanquins – the moon
was clear, and the gentlemen preferred walking some miles
at the side of my palanquin – We chatted the night away.[31]

Reading such passages, one has to remind oneself not only that
she was supposed to be ill, but also that Elizabeth Marsh was by
law Elizabeth Crisp.

In this respect too, more was happening than her diary made
explicit. Although she moved on occasions between different villages, army camps and ports in the Madras region, for much of
the time between late June 1775 and February 1776 she was based
at Ellore, a military settlement three hundred miles from Madras,
where about a thousand of the Company's sepoys and seven
hundred European troops were stationed. She did not live there
on her own. Captain Smith commanded a regiment at Ellore, and
she stayed with him in his house at the settlement, 'that most
agreeable spot'.[32]

This is the second obvious paradox of her Asiatic progress: that,
for all the stress in portions of her diary on modes of politeness and
social conventions, there were crucial respects in which Elizabeth
Marsh was living and travelling in defiance of both.

Who was George Smith? He was possibly the individual of
that name who was born in Madras of English parents in 1746,
and probably the George Smith who became an ensign in the
East India Company's army there in 1765 and a lieutenant a year
later, and who was promoted captain in 1772. This particular Captain Smith, who may also have been related to General Richard
Smith, did indeed command a regiment at Ellore.[33] But since
'George Smith' was one of the most common pairings of names
in English, it is just possible that Elizabeth Marsh employed it in

An officer of the Madras army, possibly by Tilly Kettle, *c.*1770.

her journal as a pseudonym for another man, of whom we know nothing.

Certainly, she severely rationed what she wrote in her diary about George Smith, whoever he was. She does not reveal how exactly he was connected to her other than by calling him a 'cousin', a term that in the eighteenth century was used to signify kinship of some kind, but did not necessarily imply a blood relationship.

She says nothing about the man's appearance, or about any of their conversations during the journey, though it is sometimes possible to infer the content of what they said to each other. And she only touches in any detail on their joint sleeping arrangements once, near the end. She and Smith had been travelling back to Bengal through Orissa slowly and in torrential monsoon rain, and by the time they found a river low enough to cross, it was night:

> Our people again lost their way, therefore [I] was obliged to remain up on the beach till day-break, and though that part of the country was greatly infested with tigers, sleep overcame all considerations, and I never enjoyed a sweeter rest – My cousin kept his palanquin near mine.

Immediately, she corrects herself. There were, she adds, 'besides all our servants'.[34]

Her family also tampered with the record of this part of her life, as with much of the rest. Her Indian travel journal, which may once have been part of a longer diary, only survived because in 1788 her daughter, Elizabeth Maria, gave the volume to John Marsh, Elizabeth Marsh's younger and always doting brother. He had it bound together with a draft account of her Moroccan travels in red and gold-tooled leather, with marbled endpapers. He also prefaced the volume with his own bookplate, bearing the bogus coat of arms and motto that the more successful males of the family had adopted by this point. Posthumously, the record of Elizabeth Marsh's Asiatic progress was absorbed into the family archive, decently bound and contained, apparently rendered respectable. One of its pages seems to have been razored out. Two more pages are stuck together.[35]

Yet the censorship (if that is what it was) that she imposed on her own references to George Smith, and what seems to have been a weeding of her papers by her descendants, are in a vital sense beside the point. By abandoning her husband and her son for over eighteen months, by travelling in constant companionship with a younger man who was not a member of her immediate family, and by living in his house for more than half a year, Elizabeth Marsh had incontestably passed outside the conventions of proper female behaviour that pertained in her lifetime and after. And, for all her caution, she still writes enough to show how she was able to exert emotional power over George Smith, and to reveal her own pleasure at this. Thus, on one occasion when they were staying together in Ganjam, she records how Smith left her one evening to dine with the settlement's Company chief, and underlines in her diary that this was '*by my desire*'. To be sure, the impression that her relationship with Smith may have been more than cousinly is deepened, and conceivably distorted, by the lack of any surviving letters between Elizabeth and her husband. But if she did manage to maintain a correspondence with James Crisp throughout the course of her progress, her diary makes no mention of this. After 23 January 1775, when she records him dispatching her a boat 'with a fresh supply of necessaries' at the start of her voyage to Madras, there is no further allusion, until the very end of her progress and the last surviving page, to the man she refers to only as 'my dear Crisp'.[36]

This seems in keeping with the occasional dismissiveness, even cruelty, towards her husband that Elizabeth Marsh displayed when writing *The Female Captive* in 1769. Her behaviour was also influenced, however, by the changes in her circumstances that had occurred since then. Newspapers, satirical verses and novels at this time frequently accused middle- and upper-class European women in India of displaying 'vacuous idleness', extravagance and, sometimes, sexual immodesty:

> . . . And yet, dear Girl! This place has charms,
> Such as my sprightly bosom warms!
> No place, where at a bolder rate,
> We females bear our sovereign state.
> Beauty ne'er points its arms in vain,
> Each glance subdues some melting swain.[37]

These sorts of (male-written) caricatures and condemnations, like the perduring argument that developed later that British women in India were more racially prejudiced than their menfolk, were partly a way of shifting the blame for moral turpitude among the white community as a whole onto its more marginal female members. But accusations that British females in the subcontinent were more libidinous and self-indulgent than at home were also an acknowledgement that, in this new environment, incoming women could indeed sometimes venture far outside conservative notions of their proper role. As one novelist wrote of the British expatriate community in the 1780s: 'Control is not an article of matrimonial rule at Calcutta.'[38]

The root cause of this was that white females, and females who passed for white, were so extremely sparse. There were probably fewer than two hundred white women in the whole of Bengal when Elizabeth Marsh arrived there, as against four thousand British troops, 250 East India Company civilian officials, and an unknown but much larger number of private merchants, tradesmen, miscellaneous servants and mariners.[39] Their rarity, and the availability of large numbers of indigenous servants and slaves to take care of domestic chores and child raising, allowed some female immigrants to seize hold of levels of opportunity only occasionally available to women in Europe and colonial America. To be sure, female incomers were also very sparse at this time in some of the newer, more westerly regions of the American colonies. But in the latter case the hard manual labour that was involved in a settler existence, the unending work of cultivating the soil, planting, harvesting, building barns and outhouses, cooking, laundry, and making clothes, preserves and soap, tended to reinforce traditional gender roles, and encouraged immigrant families to stay together in order to survive.[40] By contrast, in the Indian subcontinent, incomers from Europe were not allowed to settle land. Here, female immigrants were not just extremely sparse; those who were possessed of any means at all were likely also to command abundant leisure.

As a result of this, and because of the availability of long-established, indigenous commercial and cultural networks, some incoming women, far from being merely complicit in empire, were able at this time conspicuously to profit from it. Marian Hastings, the German-born second wife of Warren Hastings, who was first Governor, then Governor General, of Bengal between 1771 and 1785, had accumulated over £100,000 from her contacts in the subcontinent by the 1790s.[41] Few other women possessed her opportunities for graft, but many widows and spinsters seem to have engaged directly in Asian commerce, like Mary Cross of Bombay, who in the 1770s was trading regularly with Persia. Other women, like Elizabeth Marsh's friend and patron in Calcutta, Johanna Ross, made money by lending capital through their *sarkars* – personal Indian bankers – to British and sometimes to indigenous merchants. And some women worked for their husbands. Eliza Draper, whom Elizabeth encountered during her progress in Machilipatnam in 1775, had in earlier years carried out much of the official and commercial paperwork of her husband, a Company servant and factory chief outside Bombay. As Eliza Draper wrote: 'I'm necessitated to pass the greatest part of my time in his office.' Even when not doing his work, or choosing to 'bathe in the sea, read volumes – and fill reams of paper with my scribble', she frequently had to deal with 'a full house of shipping gentry, that resort to us for traffic and intelligence from all parts of India, China and Asia'.[42]

Other privileged women in India seized the chance to engage in modes of study that were often denied them in Britain. The wife of Robert Clive, victor of the Battle of Plassey in 1757 and the first British Governor of Bengal, reportedly enjoyed 'lectures on astronomy, [the] solar system and the use of globes' and mathematics. The latter subject, which was traditionally of great importance in Indo-Persian and Hindu culture, seems to have become something of a cult among elite white females in the subcontinent. Margaret Clive passed on her interest in mathematics to Margaret Fowke, daughter of a leading diamond merchant in Calcutta.

Fowke in turn went on to study Euclid and Newton, and left behind at her death five volumes of mathematical deductions and two volumes of algebraic exercises (all of which her family seem to have destroyed). 'She had moreover,' wrote her son in his memoir of her, 'a great love of liberty, and dislike to the idea of restraint upon her freedom of will.'[43] It is clear, too, that some women participated in the developing interest among senior Company officials at this time in Indo-Persian and subsequently Hindu science and culture. Hester Johnston, wife of Samuel Johnston, whom Elizabeth Marsh met at Visakhapatnam, employed 'the most distinguished of the Brahmins in the neighbourhood to collect for her information on Hindu knowledge of mathematics and astronomy'. Again, one notes how the study of mathematics and female high rank – Hester Johnston was the daughter of a Scottish aristocrat – tended to go together in India at this time. When Colin Mackenzie, a fellow Scot, arrived in Madras in 1783, Hester Johnston introduced him to her circle of indigenous scholars, thereby contributing to Mackenzie's ultimately very important collection of south Indian learned manuscripts and antiquities.[44]

How far European women in India at this time wanted and were able to enjoy greater sexual freedoms and unconventionality is less clear. Custom, the constant surveillance of indigenous servants who placed a high value on female modesty and seclusion, together with laws passed in Britain, ensured that white females only rarely formed relationships with indigenous men. After 1730, 'every child born abroad, whose *father* was a natural born Protestant subject of Great Britain', could in law be accounted a natural-born subject also; and in 1772 this privilege was extended to the grandchildren born abroad of such 'natural born [male] subjects'. Many East India Company officials, fathering children on Asian wives or concubines, sought to take full advantage of these laws. However, no such provisions existed for British women. Indeed, it is indicative of contemporary expectations that, before 1791, Parliament declined to legislate about what should happen if a

British woman abroad gave birth to a child by an 'alien' of any kind.[45]

Yet there is more evidence in the correspondence and wills of European women at this time of friendship with, and on occasions of physical awareness of, Asian men than has been acknowledged. 'In the evening,' wrote the young Margaret Fowke in Calcutta in 1783,

> Bahauder . . . came with a most jockey-like air, and a smart pair of boots. His turban was of a fine geranium. I declare he had chosen the most beautiful colour in the rainbow. Lady Day and I admired it extremely. His cummerbund was of a light yellow. After he dismounted, he stood playing with his whip with the most careless and satisfied air imaginable.[46]

There is evidence, too, that even conspicuous illicit sexual liaisons between Europeans did not *necessarily* damage a married woman's reputation in the subcontinent to the same degree as obtained at home. In 1773, Eliza Draper abandoned Bombay and her indolent, abusive husband to run off with Sir John Clerke, the same man whom Elizabeth Marsh encountered on the *Dolphin* in the Bay of Bengal two years later. Subsequently in 1775, Elizabeth also met Eliza Draper herself at Machilipatnam. By now, the latter was no longer living under Clerke's 'protection'. But, as Elizabeth records, Eliza Draper was still able to preside, alongside her uncle, who was the Company chief at Machilipatnam at this time, and apparently involved himself in a passionate homosexual relationship, at a 'very polite reception . . . [and] continual parties and engagements'.[47] It is unlikely that a runaway wife who was known to have been recently involved in scandal could have won acceptance as a hostess in this manner in contemporary European or colonial American polite society.

In much the same way, Elizabeth Marsh's capacity to absent herself from her husband and child for over a year, and to travel and share a house with an unmarried man, while still being abundantly fêted by what passed for genteel white society throughout the Madras Presidency, illustrates how at this time women – as well as men – associated with the British in India were able, on occasions, to chart a more erratic, independent course.

Marsh's behaviour during her progress illustrates something else. During the eighteenth century, as now, extensive kinship networks could ease the experience of long-distance migration. Being able to make claims of family obligation on General Richard Smith, and on George Smith, whoever he was, considerably smoothed Elizabeth Marsh's passage through eastern and southern India. But while elaborate kinship ties of this sort could facilitate an individual's extreme physical mobility, the latter inevitably placed strains on, and sometimes shattered, nuclear family and marital solidarities. It is inappropriate therefore to view Elizabeth Marsh's actions at this stage of her life only in terms of her personal waywardness and desires. The fissures in her marriage with James Crisp – like the making of their union in the first place – were also due to the way in which she and he were repeatedly driven and chose to travel very large distances on land and sea. At least some of the stresses that were increasingly evident in their relationship were part of the price that each of them paid for being so markedly itinerant.

By this time, members of the extended Marsh clan were already well familiar with how moving across oceans and continents could put pressure on an individual's marriage and morals. Milbourne Marsh's own passage to Jamaica in the 1730s, and his courtship there of the woman who had once been Elizabeth Bouchier, or Boucher, or Bourchier, had, after all, been at the cost of the peace, and perhaps the life, of her first husband, James Evans. Then there was Elizabeth Marsh's eldest brother, Francis Milbourne Marsh. While on military service overseas in the early 1770s, he seems to have fathered a child on the wife of his sergeant, Isaac Myers. George Marsh was obliged to pay off Myers with a comfortable post in Chatham's naval dockyard in order to avoid any scandal.[48]

Until now, however, it had been Milbourne Warren, a first cousin of Milbourne Marsh, who best exemplified to the family the emotional and sexual disruptions that could ensue when individuals ventured too much across great distances.

Yet another mariner, Milbourne Warren, had clandestinely married a Mary Brown 'in the liberty of the Fleet prison London' in the early 1750s, and then sailed without her to Madras, intending to work there as a shipwright and make their fortune. In 1762 Warren was swept into the combined navy and East India Company invasion of Manila in the Philippines, sailing on Admiral Samuel Cornish's seventy-four-gun flagship the *Norfolk*, the first time that a member of the Marsh family is known to have reached South-East Asia.[49] Since Spain had colonized the islands in the sixteenth century, Manila had developed into one of the most vital conduits between eastern and western sectors of the world for trade, bullion and people. Silver from Spain's colonies in South America passed regularly through Manila en route to Asia in payment for commodities from China and the Indian subcontinent; and from the early 1600s onwards, thousands of Asians migrated every year by way of Manila into Mexico. The settlement itself attracted Spanish, Chinese, Japanese and Mexican immigrants, who lived moderately peaceably alongside its indigenous population. The British occupation of Manila, which lasted from 1762 to 1764, added further strands to its tapestry of multiple cultures. Six hundred Indian sepoys arrived with the British invasion force, and some of these men chose to stay on in Manila and raised families there.[50]

Milbourne Warren, though, sailed back to Madras on the *Norfolk* in 1763, having invested all of his earnings from private trade in the subcontinent in purchasing precious commodities and booty in Manila. His plan was to dispose of some of these luxury and exotic goods in Madras, and then to carry the remainder back with him to London and sell them at a high profit so as to provide himself and his wife, Mary, with security. All of this cargo, and all of these dreams, were lost at sea when the *Norfolk* was caught in a storm on the return voyage to Madras. When Milbourne Warren finally left the subcontinent and arrived back in London in 1765, it was in an almost penniless state, and to find that Mary – left on her own for seven years – had been unfaithful. The family's fixer, George Marsh, patched things up by having Warren replace Milbourne Marsh as Naval Officer in Menorca, and this time made sure that he took his wife with him.

The story of the next phase of the Warren marriage, its next fracture through distance, was read aloud in the Court of Arches in London, the ecclesiastical court that dealt with petitions for divorce. The Warrens had 'cohabited together at Port Mahon' in Menorca until 1768. Then:

> She, the said Mary Warren, being unmindful of her conjugal vow and not having the fear of God before her eyes, but being instigated and seduced by the devil did frequent the company of William Madox Richardson Esq., Captain in the third regiment of foot then stationed at Port Mahon aforesaid, and had the carnal use and knowledge of his body.

Richardson and Mary Warren, the court was told, would 'retire to a bed-chamber' in the smart new naval officer's house in Mahon whenever Milbourne Warren was absent at his duties on the island. When Warren discovered what was going on, he sued for divorce 'from bed and board and mutual cohabitation'.[51] Thus, in 1769, when the Marsh clan was coping with the backwash of James Crisp's bankruptcy and flight to India, and with Elizabeth Marsh's revelations in *The Female Captive*, it also had to contend with Milbourne Warren's protracted and graphic divorce proceedings. It had, in other words, to deal simultaneously with three unhappy family stories that together involved events and individuals in North and West Africa, the Mediterranean, Florida, and parts of the Indian subcontinent and South-East Asia.

In Elizabeth Marsh's own case, experiencing distance and exten-sive mobility once more, with all their potential for loosening established ties, seems to have acted as a source of renewal and redirection, and not just in emotional and possibly sexual terms. In early February 1776, George Smith's regiment was ordered to leave Ellore for Madras. She and he lingered behind in the settlement 'some days after' most of the soldiers had departed, on the grounds that Smith was needed to escort 'the remaining troops, who were either sick, or in confinement'; and it was not until 22 February that the couple made themselves leave the house which they had shared together, 'with tears, and infinite regret, having passed there many, many pleasing hours'.[52] She was already substantially altered by her journey, but moving on again precipitated a different kind of looking.

For a week it was easy: 'the life was new and by no means unpleasant'. She and George Smith were able to follow in a carriage, as the troops marched on to Machilipatnam. It was there that a change in her priorities began. Their host and the new acting chief at Machilipatnam was a Scot named Quintin Craufurd (1743–1819). Elizabeth Marsh had been 'particularly recommended to him' because he had been in Manila for some of the same time as Milbourne Warren, and 'an intimacy . . . had long subsisted' between Craufurd and George Smith. Unlike most East India Company officials she had encountered up to this point, Craufurd was a scholarly, though quirkish and greedy, man, multilingual, well read in the classics, and interested in the study of comparative mythology and religions. 'To hate or despise any people, because they do not profess the same faith with ourselves,' he wrote some years later, 'to judge them illiberally, and arrogantly to condemn them, is, perhaps, in fact, to arraign the wisdom and goodness of the Almighty.' It was necessary and important, Craufurd believed, that Islam, Hinduism and Christianity be studied in conjunction, since these religions together attracted 'by far the greatest portion of the inhabitants of the globe' – though, like many other Company intellectuals, he himself was increasingly drawn to concentrate on Hinduism and its adherents. He wanted, Craufurd wrote in a book published in London in 1790, to distract 'the attention of the public, for a moment, from the exploits of Mahomedans and Europeans, and direct it to the original inhabitants' of the subcontinent.[53]

Craufurd's intellectual sophistication and application were far beyond Elizabeth Marsh's own reach. But conversing with him over the five weeks she remained at Machilipatnam seems to have contributed to making her intensely curious to see some religious sites and buildings for herself. When, in early April, George Smith was ordered to go to Aska to supervise some court martial proceedings there, she seized her opportunity. As the road system worked, Aska was about forty *coss* (eighty miles) inland from Ganjam, in the northernmost part of the Madras Presidency. Her plan initially had been to wait in Machilipatnam for a ship that would take her back to Calcutta. Now, with Smith heading northwards overland, she decided 'it would be a fine opportunity for me to proceed to Bengal by that route'. It would delay her return to Dhaka and allow her to remain longer in Smith's company, while providing opportunities to observe and explore as they went along.[54]

Elizabeth Marsh's willingness to begin looking outwards was clearly belated; and to readers now, this is likely to seem the most glaring paradox of her progress. She had been in motion since December 1774. Yet, on the evidence of her diary, it was only in the spring of 1776 that the cultures and the indigenous peoples of the subcontinent began to attract her sustained gaze and interest. Earlier, she had been obsessed with her own ill-health, and subsequently with other priorities. But of course these were not the only reasons why she behaved and reacted as she did.

South Asians naturally populated the entirety of her progress, just as at one level they populate the entirety of her diary. She mentions in passing how swiftly she is carried along once she leaves the city of Madras, far faster than James Rennell had judged feasible: 'the palanquin boys run at the rate of 28 miles in less than six hours – only eight men, four to relieve four'. She makes regular references to her 'three slave girls', who looked after her clothes, organized her frequent baths in tank water and guarded her precious stock of tea, and who followed her for some of the time on bullocks, and sometimes in a *doli*, 'which is a sort of palanquin but made in a more humble style'. She mentions the men who fetch fresh milk at intervals so as 'to make butter for our journey', and the man whose task it is to hold a *chatta*, an umbrella or parasol, over her palanquin when the heat is fiercest. And there are umpteen other individuals who make brief appearances in her diary when putting up and dismantling her tents, or cooking her meals, or taking her messages, or acting as porters. In this sense, indigenous individuals (particularly males) are omnipresent. But, to borrow a famous analogy, they appear mostly as servants in a country house traditionally do: as at once indispensable to the running of things, and firmly in the margins and in the background. And at no time does Elizabeth Marsh refer to any of these people in her diary by his or her own Indian name.[55]

This in itself does not signify all that much. On the few occasions that she and James Crisp refer in writing to such servants as they were able to afford in London, they do not name these people either.[56] Servants, anywhere, of whatever origin, were not accorded the same courtesies that their self-regarding social superiors owed to each other. Even the fact that Elizabeth Marsh *was* now a slave-owner does not tell us as much about her attitudes to the peoples among whom she was now travelling as it might seem. In the Dhaka region where the Crisps settled, as elsewhere in the subcontinent, slave-ownership was widespread among the prosperous, whether they were Asian or European incomers:

> The custom with respect to slaves in this country is this:
> Any one who is without a father, mother, or any other
> relation ... who is destitute of the necessaries of life &

A box palanquin, with four bearers and a parasol holder.
Anonymous watercolour in the Benares style.

should propose selling himself . . . becomes a slave, and any person possessing such slave or slaves and are in want of the necessaries of life may sell him, her, or them, to whomsoever they please & the purchaser, from that time is considered as the master of the slave or slaves. The children, grand children & so on to many generations become the slaves of their parent masters & they must do whatever is ordered, whether to cultivate, build, or any sort of drudgery.

That Elizabeth Marsh was accompanied on her progress by at least three female slaves (two of whom she seems to have renamed 'Phillis' and 'Mary') reveals more about her pretensions to some affluence and status at this stage than it does, necessarily, about her attitudes to Indians and to race.[57]

More suggestive in this regard is the way in which she omits to name the few elite male Indians that she encountered during her progress. Whenever Elizabeth met a high-ranking white male official of the East India Company, she carefully recorded his name. But when, for instance, she describes how, en route for Aska in April 1776, 'a severe land wind' obliged them 'to take shelter in a new built house, belonging to a black man of note', this is all the detail she provides.[58] Her not attempting to name this man suggests that in some way, and perhaps subconsciously, she chose not to view him as powerful. Instead, she treated this man on paper in the same way that she did virtually all of the white wives, stray white children, white private soldiers and white servants who briefly crossed her path during her travels: she noted the fact of his existence in passing, but withheld any acknowledgement of his individual identity or significance.

As this suggests, it would be quite wrong to romanticize Elizabeth Marsh's attitudes to human difference. It would also be wrong to overstate – and no less wrong to ignore – what was distinctive about her responses.

As was customary at this time, she seems to have devoted only limited attention to the skin colour of the various people she encountered during her life. In *The Female Captive* she had described the various Moroccans she had encountered – Moors, Arabs, Jews, Berbers, Bedouins, sub-Saharan military slaves and more – sometimes as 'dark' in complexion, and sometimes as 'sallow'; it was her publisher, and not her, who made use of the blanket term 'tawny'.[59] But, for all her elasticity of language in regard to complexions, Marsh had usually – though not invariably – insisted on the cultural, and especially the religious, gulf between her Moroccan captors and herself. In her book, the non-European peoples she meets in Morocco are sometimes 'infidels', whereas she is the 'fair Christian'. When she escapes from Marrakech and

Sidi Muhammad's attentions, and takes refuge in the house of a European merchant, her first thoughts, at least as she publishes them, are 'to return thanks to Providence for the happiness I then enjoyed, in being under the roof of those who professed the same faith as myself'.[60]

By the same token, although Elizabeth Marsh sporadically refers to indigenous inhabitants of the Indian subcontinent as 'black', as incomers from Europe had increasingly done since the fifteenth century, it was not skin colour that she focused on in her travel diary as the crucial mark of difference; and at no point does she ever refer to herself explicitly as 'white'. Instead, she had recourse to George Smith's military observations. She recorded how the old fort she saw at Vizagapatam was 'not capable of making any great defence, especially against European powers'. At Bimlipatam, too, she stressed that the local fort 'could only hold out against ... Country powers'; while the fort in the Maratha stronghold of Cuttack was 'small, and of no defence', its few guards 'chiefly supported for show'.[61] These are clearly George Smith's professional assessments, and – like Elizabeth Marsh's earlier remarks on the East Indian squadron in the Bay of Bengal – they bear witness to the swiftly shifting balance of power in this part of Asia. For Marsh, though, parroting Smith's opinions on indigenous fortifications in this fashion seems mainly to have been a way of asserting difference and superiority. She invoked, not Christianity this time, but rather Western military technology and might, as a means of distinguishing herself from the peoples amongst whom she was travelling.

Reacting in this manner was not always her instinct, however, and it became markedly less so as her journey progressed. Even in its early stages, Elizabeth Marsh's written reactions to travelling overland in a party that was overwhelmingly made up of indigenous soldiers and servants seem relaxed and even accepting when compared to the recorded responses of some other female incomers to the subcontinent at this time. 'I could not be reconciled to the vast numbers of black people who flocked to the shore on my first arrival,' Jemima Kindersley declared in her published account of her arrival in India in the mid-1760s. Some women never became reconciled. 'God knows what would become of me left *quite* alone with the black people,' wrote Mary Morgan in the 1770s, after living in Calcutta with her army officer husband for some years. 'God forgive me,' she went on, '. . . I cannot bear the sight of them.'[62] No outbursts of remotely this sort occur in Elizabeth Marsh's Indian travel diary, and there is no evidence that she felt apprehensive at the prospect of being left alone 'with the black people'. Indeed, towards the end of her progress she increasingly allowed herself to slip into precisely that situation. This relative absence of anxiety was due in large part to her peculiar background. Virtually all women and most men migrating to India from Europe in the mid-eighteenth century had little or no prior experience of different continents, peoples and cultures: but this was manifestly not Marsh's situation. Whatever the birth identity of her mother, *she* had arrived in the subcontinent having already been exposed not simply to Morocco, but also to the markedly cosmopolitan populations of Portsmouth, Menorca, Gibraltar and Bishopsgate; and, ever since childhood, she must have encountered stray black and Asian seamen on Royal Navy ships. Elizabeth Marsh might proclaim her own difference on occasion. But she was also sufficiently used to living among difference for it sometimes to recede in importance in her mind.

The sort of woman that she was, and what she was not, shaped her experience of indigenous culture and society during her Asiatic progress in another respect. The almost complete absence of detail in her travel diary about even elite male Indians may well be a reflection of her racial, religious and national prejudices; but it was no less a product of her own insignificance and powerlessness, of the degree to which *she* was looked down upon. When Jemima Kindersley published her account of her Indian travels in 1777, she was able to preface it with an image of a *zenana*, the harem of 'a great Mussulman' in Allahabad who had extended hospitality to her and her officer husband. The hospitality from local elites that Elizabeth Plowden received when she visited Lucknow in the company of her husband Richard Chicheley Plowden in the 1780s was far more protracted and lavish. As her diary makes clear, Lucknow's Nawab, Asaf ud-Daula, invited her to a succession of breakfasts, feasts, elephant-fights and displays of dancing and fireworks. He showed her some of his collection of precious stones, and poetry that he had written. And in 1788, towards the end of her stay, he presented her with a *sanad* (a deed of grant) awarding her the title of *begum*, or noblewoman. Even Mary Morgan was obliged to stifle her prejudices and fears when, in 1778, she and her husband received a visit in Calcutta from a local Nawab, with his two hundred attendants, 'eight elephants, some fine palanquins, [and] a great many horses'.[63]

By contrast, Elizabeth Marsh experienced no elite attentions of this sort. At no time during her stay in Madras, for instance, does she seems to have been invited to the Nawab of Arcot's new palace at Chepauk. The Nawab, Muhammad Ali Khan Walajah, combined a deep interest in Sufism and in Persian scholarship and poetry with a taste for European, and specifically British, art and commodities; and he is known to have admitted European women to his presence, the painter Catherine Read amongst them. If Elizabeth had visited Chepauk, she would surely have included this coup in her diary. But she does not. Nor, on the basis of what she writes, do any other indigenous aristocrats appear to have invited her into their presence, even on those occasions when they allowed her a place in which to stay. When the ruler of Cuttack, in Orissa, granted her brief shelter in his town, she recorded how 'his palace, from description, is magnificent'. She herself was evidently never given the opportunity to find out.[64]

As in the house she sometimes lived in with James Crisp at Dhaka, Elizabeth Marsh was surrounded on her progress by traditional signifiers of high status in the subcontinent. She travelled in a palanquin, as Indian elite individuals and top East India Company officials customarily did, and amidst a very large retinue. On some occasions her party was even preceded by a *chobdar*, a ceremonial stick-bearer. Yet it would have been easily apparent to any interested indigenous witnesses that she was not noble in fact, but an outsider, religiously impure and meat-eating. They would likely have seen her too as a woman who was evidently of no great propriety, since she did not remain decently hidden behind the covers of her palanquin, but got out and walked at regular intervals, and talked, or laughed, or danced, or consumed alcohol in the open air with a variety of men. Along with her own prejudices, the suspicion and contempt that Elizabeth Marsh would have aroused among many Asians inevitably circumscribed what she could do, and what she could get to see and understand.

It was ignorance, though, which constituted her greatest obstacle. 'Books of travels of Thevenot, Bernier, Tavernier, P. de la Valle,' wrote James Rennell grandly in 1783, '. . . are in every body's hands.' He was referring to some of the best-known European authorities on the subcontinent: Jean de Thévenot (1633–67), François Bernier (1625–88), a physician who visited the Mughal court in Delhi, Jean-Baptiste Tavernier (1605–89), and Pietro della Valle (1586–1652), all of whom, and more, a highly educated and/or highly ambitious Western incomer to India was likely to have heard of, if not read.[65] One may safely assume, however, that these men's writings, and other expensive learned works, rarely if ever passed through Elizabeth Marsh's hands. She was, anyway, an intelligent and curious woman, not remotely a scholarly or a studious one. As the rest of her Asiatic progress demonstrates, she had been deeply intrigued by Quintin Craufurd's conversations about Indian mythologies and religions. But she remained profoundly uneducated about them. And she was linguistically hobbled, shut off not just from the writings of Indo-Persian and Hindu scholars, but also from easy verbal communication with such native inhabitants as she encountered. By now, men who aspired to the East India Company's senior ranks, such as her son Burrish Crisp, were investing more time in acquiring Asian languages, though few European males at this stage were familiar with the dominant spoken languages of those parts of the subcontinent Elizabeth Marsh progressed through: Tamil, Telagu, and Oriya in Orissa. She herself seems to have known enough 'Moors', or pidgin Hindustani, to tell her servants and slave women what to do, and to ask them questions. But she had limited opportunities, and crucially no career incentive, seriously to learn indigenous languages and customs.

❧

All of this, her prejudices, her social and economic insignificance, her substantial ignorance, but also her unusual experience of different kinds of people and places and her curiosity about them, influenced what Elizabeth Marsh could see and do when, from the spring of 1776, she finally began on her Asiatic progress to look outwards. The vigour and eagerness of her vision, and the various and inevitable blinkers on it, emerge from her account of her first self-conscious effort to investigate the cultures through which she was travelling. This was on 20 April, on the route to Aska, and near the place the British usually referred to as 'Chicacole', because they found it so hard to pronounce Srikakulam. It was already hot, and she was 'almost dying with fatigue'. But she

> rose early, and accompanied by some gentlemen, went to see a famous mosque – I ventured (where no woman ever had) to the top – the steps were placed on one side, and not more than 1 foot 8½ width, and about half yard broad – these joined to the mosque on one side, and a very deep precipice on the other, no railing to support the footsteps – The gentlemen who were with me could afford me no assistance, except that I took hold of the skirts of one of their coats – and kept my eyes fixed on the steps – when we reached the top, which is a great height, I was delighted

with the view, as it commanded one of the finest prospects that can be imagined – the returning was most to be dreaded – for our danger was exceedingly great – happy was I when I found myself safe at the bottom.[66]

It is impossible to be certain which of the important religious sites near Srikakulam this was, since the region contains so many. Almost certainly, however, it was not a 'mosque' that Elizabeth saw, but a Hindu temple. She may have gone to Arasavalli, a couple of miles from Srikakulam, the only temple in the subcontinent devoted to sun worship. It is rather more likely that she and her companions travelled to see the Srikurmam temple, and that what she climbed was part of its soaring *gopuram*, its remarkable five-storey gateway tower. Whichever temple it was, it would have been ornamented with sculptures and carvings of deities, semi-demigods and mythological figures and creatures, and possibly wall paintings, but she makes no mention of any of these. Elizabeth Marsh focused only on what she could understand, her own physical toughness, and the beauty of the scenery.

She did much the same when she explored another 'mosque' six days later, writing of how she had climbed a mountain for two hours in order to view it, and once again letting herself become absorbed in the scenery and the picturesque. It was 'a fine night', she recorded when they finally reached Aska:

> Went through several extensive villages, which had every appearance of opulence – the moon was high, and most of the towns surrounded by noble topes – rivers and fields of grain – in short, as we drew near to Aska, it was all enchantment – so delicious a country, stately trees, fine pasture, rising hills, fertile vales, winding rivers, that I never beheld any prospect so heavenly. To sleep was impossible, as the eye (though moonlight) was constantly engaged by a new object.

Yet, although she resorted to clichéd words from English novels ('enchantment', 'delicious', 'heavenly'), she also noted how the scorching heat and wind made the bleached shrubs and under-growth on the outskirts of the town brush against each other, and sometimes catch fire: 'a pleasing yet awful sight'.[67] And, as soon as George Smith's court martial proceedings at Aska were over, they started travelling again.

They set out on 15 May, stopping at about 2 o'clock the following morning 'to get a little sleep, and [we] did not wake till the daybreak; the other palanquins had passed us un-noticed, and missing us, hastened on to Ganjam, thinking we were before'. Alone, barring their immediate servants, the couple travelled on to an unidentified place 'which was only inhabited by Brahmins', a vast complex of (Elizabeth thought) over a hundred Hindu temples and sacred sites, some of which were underground. It is the first time that an element of guilt enters her diary. Because it was so hot, Smith escorted her into one of the underground temples. By now she knew that unbelievers were forbidden the interior of such places, and that one worshipped at a temple only after a ritual bath in a nearby tank or river. So this time she took note of 'the great distress of the poor Brahmins, who no doubt had much trouble to purify it after us. It would take many sacrifices etc. before they could possibly make use of it again.' And although she still referred to the place as a 'mosque', she observed some of the interior detail. Each of the subterranean temples, she wrote, had a 'Swammy, or God in it', a reference to *Swami*, a title of the Hindu deity Krishna. Exposure to scenes so utterly divorced from her knowledge did not tempt her to back off. When they reached Ganjam, she decided again not to wait in the settlement for a ship that would take her back to Calcutta. Instead, she would 'pursue my journey by land', on a route, she wrote carefully, which 'no European lady had ever undertaken . . . before'.[68]

Although Ganjam was only 370 miles from Calcutta, this was an extraordinarily rash decision. Ganjam itself had only been brought under an uncertain degree of British administration since 1767. There was now a garrison of two thousand Company troops, but the place remained under threat of attack from the north by Maratha armies, 'a lawless tribe, who are forever breaking treaties', as Elizabeth wrote with the utmost conventionality. In order to reach Calcutta, her party would have to travel northwards through Orissa, and 'we had not a clear plan of the journey we were going'. Outside of Midnapur, Orissa was substantially under Maratha, not Company, control. Moreover, since 1775, the Marathas and the Company had been in a state of open war. For the first time since leaving Dhaka, Elizabeth Marsh was committing herself to moving beyond the limits and the effective coercive reach of the Company state.[69] Over the course of the month that remained to her as a traveller, a period that fills almost a third of her diary, she progressively cast off a succession of other supports.

On 30 May, she, George Smith and their party reached Lake Chilka, at forty miles long, Asia's biggest salt-water lake, separated from the sea only by narrow strips of land and shale. For fear of getting stuck in the surrounding sands, they decided not to travel around it, but to cross part of it by ferryboat, and move decisively into Orissa that way: 'our palanquins were placed across the boat, the baggage and servants under them; the night passed very well'. When they disembarked at midnight on 31 May on the beach at Manickpatam, it was to learn that a famine was in progress inland, and that obtaining sufficient new supplies of rice for the whole of their retinue was out of the question. This forced another sloughing off. They decided to send most of their coolies back to Ganjam on the same boat. This necessarily also meant that they had to let go of many of their heavy European artifacts and comforts: 'our tents, table, chairs, and a large chest of linen belonging to me'. It is an indication of how strangely privileged her progress had been at one level that even after this, their travelling party still seems to have numbered about sixty, of whom all but she and Smith were Asian. As they entered the town that she called 'Jaggurnaut' on 2 June, she recorded yet another falling away: 'the *chowkey* people, or customs officers stopped us . . . enquiring for our pass, and doubting our right to proceed'. George Smith eventually smoothed things over, but this seems to have been the first time she was brought face to face with outright indigenous opposition, explicit non-deference.[70]

'Jaggurnaut' was the modern Puri, with its extraordinary two-hundred-foot-high twelfth-century temple to Vishnu in his form as Jagannath, or Lord of the World. It is in relation to this place that Elizabeth Marsh's limitations as a witness and reporter – and some of her strengths – emerge most strongly. The 'high street' here, she wrote, was 'about as broad as the Haymarket in London – and as the moon was at full, the people were all out, conversing in the street, and the crowd was prodigious'. Easing their way through the crowds, the pilgrims, the temple functionaries, the sellers of palm-leaf paintings, jewels and food, they passed what she called 'the grand pagoda, where the famous God, Jaggernaut is deposited'. But, she was told, 'as the natives are never suffered to see the image, no stranger is permitted even to approach its walls': that is, the fortress-like stone wall surrounding the temple complex with its elephant, lion, horse and tiger gates. Typically, she was unsatisfied, and sought to find out more: 'I had a description of the God from a Brahmin, who said it has only one eye, and that is a diamond, of immense value, in the middle of its forehead, other riches surround it.' In other words, this man spun her a line that was intended to impress and to provoke wonder in someone who was ignorant or, as in her case, an unbeliever. This, at least, she perceived. There were, she grumbled, five hundred Brahmins in Puri, and 'the truth is not to be obtained, every Brahmin telling you a different story'.[71]

There was much going on, though, that she was unable to perceive. A learned, often inaccurate literature existed in English, going back to at least the early seventeenth century, on Puri's massive significance as a pilgrimage site. Naturally, Elizabeth Marsh was ignorant of it.[72] She was able to discover that their arrival had coincided with 'the high festival, when pilgrims (from the most distant parts of India) go . . . with presents to the God Jaggurnaut', and she sensed that the Brahmins whom she tried to converse with were withholding vital information of some kind. But neither she, nor apparently Captain George Smith, understood that the *Ratha Yatra* was imminent, the car festival of Lord Jagannath. Nor did they understand (and their Hindu servants seemingly either did not know or, more likely, chose not to tell them) that, far from 'the natives' never being suffered to see Jagannath, they were about to do so, and that she and Smith were being hurried out of the town as it prepared for one of the most spectacular and important Hindu religious festivals in the subcontinent.[73]

Jagannath's eyes are large, staring, and round like lotus flowers. His complexion is blackish, and he smiles and his emblematic arms are cast wide because he is all-merciful as well as all-seeing. Customarily his image is about five feet tall, but that is not how he appears at the *Ratha Yatra*. The great central road through Puri that reminded Elizabeth Marsh of the Haymarket, the *Bada Danda*, is wide because it has to be. During the festival, it must accommodate the forty-five-foot-high car or chariot of Jagannath, with its sixteen wheels, each seven feet wide, and the only somewhat smaller chariots of Jagannath's brother, Balabhadra, and his sister Subhadra. These are all three storeys high. Constructed and painted anew every festival, they are covered with carvings, mirrors, pictures, brass bells and iron gongs; it is on these huge chariots or *rathas* that the images are hauled ceremoniously through Puri, covered in brilliant fabric canopies.[74] Because she was a stranger and hobbled by ignorance, Elizabeth Marsh missed seeing all of this. But she persisted in looking. Her diary over the next few days is full of references to the pilgrims whom she watched moving relentlessly towards Puri as her own party increasingly left it behind. There were 'prodigious numbers of people, all loaded with different presents'; 'thousands of pilgrims, going to pray to Jaggernaut'; 'many with old and decrepit men and women upon their backs, carrying them to die at Jaggernaut'. As she correctly observed, a disproportionate number of the pilgrims were women, many of them 'with a pot of Ganges water, neatly tied up'. Elizabeth Marsh seems to have found it easy, up to a point, to sympathize with her indigenous servants, organizing fires to warm 'the poor people who carried us', for instance, when they got drenched in the monsoon rains. But her comments on the Puri pilgrims are the closest she comes to expressing some sense of common humanity with, and curiosity about, ordinary Indians outside her employ, perhaps because these people too were involved in motion across vast distances. Some of them, she discovered, 'had already travelled upwards of 1000 miles'. 'They appeared perfectly harmless, and suffered us to pass without interruption,' she recorded: 'I did not expose myself to view, but cut a hole in my *bulker*, or cover of my palanquin, from whence I could see, and not be seen.'[75]

As they moved nearer to Cuttack, however, her party began to encounter physical harassment and open hostility. On 5 June, when a 'severe hot wind ... almost took the skin off', the only *choultry* they could find to shelter in was 'occupied by some Maratha horsemen, and they would not quit it. They behaved rather insolently to Captain Smith, but nothing would do but temporizing with them, and leaving them as fast as possible.' The few sepoys who remained with them wanted to make a fight of it, but Smith ordered a retreat. On seeing this, an East India Company army officer and Company sepoys backing away from an armed encounter, their own remaining coolies became in turn 'distressingly insolent, [and] refused to take the baggage, unless we gave them double pay, which we were obliged to comply with'. When they reached Cuttack, Orissa's capital and a Maratha power centre, 'large and irregular [and] crowded with inhabitants', the pressure on them increased. One morning they 'were refused liberty to pass through their town'. The next, some local officials slapped 'a heavy tax upon our baggage'. When they finally extricated themselves from the city, 'the palanquins could hardly be squeezed through the crowd of men and boys, each with a drawn scimitar or knife in his hand, loading us with every abuse'.[76]

The famine, and the seething hostility of the villages they were now passing through, obliged them to begin rationing food. The days of Madeira and oysters were long over, and for a period – as they all did – Elizabeth ate nothing but a few water-sodden biscuits. There were other changes to her body at this time, and other types of discarding. Since the heavy monsoon rains had now set in, she purchased some rolls of muslin from a Maratha 'peddler', and wound the open-weaved fabric loosely around herself and over her Western clothing. It is unlikely (though, since her husband dealt in textiles, it is not impossible) that Elizabeth Marsh understood that, in Indian society, the cloth that individuals selected and wore could be understood as part of their substance, as almost as integral to them as their very skin. But she did now begin experimenting with different modes of dress and cloth in a manner that was unusual among European women in the subcontinent, and in ways that she had not done in the Madras region, irrespective of the weather. When they stopped for the night at Balasore, for instance, the main port of Orissa, she accepted the loan of a dress belonging to a 'Portuguese', a term that usually signified someone of mixed race, and was sometimes a euphemism for the indigenous concubine of a white official.[77]

What seems, but may not have been, her most significant relinquishing of familiar things occurred shortly after this. According to her diary, Captain George Smith had been acting without orders in continuing to accompany her through Orissa. For the sake of his career as an officer of the Madras army, he could not afford to go any further and cross into Bengal and another Presidency without his superiors' permission. She had been anticipating their imminent parting for some weeks by now: 'the thought of being soon separated from my dear cousin embitters every moment', even though she tried hard to 'reconcile myself to that common event in life, parting with those we esteem and admire'. 'The dreadful hour of separation' occurred 'about 5 o'clock' on the morning of 13 June. 'I parted from my dear, dear cousin – he for Ganjam, and I for Calcutta,' she wrote: 'some hours my whole soul was absorbed in grief.'[78]

Yet it is not so much grief as irritation and a sense of mounting constraints that are most evident in her account of the last phase of her journey. When she reached Midnapur, the settlement that marked her formal return to safety and to the East India Company's dominion, she sat on the ground alone for a while 'under some trees, near the fort', before going to present herself to the local chief, Mr Pearce. He received her 'politely' enough, and they 'walked and chatted'. But it seemed 'stiff and formal', and she wished herself 'seated again under the large tree I had just left, enjoying freedom and ease'.[79] She was exasperated, too, by having to cope with a Mr Brishen, whom they had encountered in Orissa, lost and virtually penniless. George Smith had insisted on Brishen travelling with them so that Elizabeth would have a European male to protect her after his own departure. But she did not want him. He was 'extremely illiterate', 'an over-grown boy of about 20' without money who insisted on sharing her own scant supplies of food. 'He . . . found me very convenient,' she snapped, 'and I found him a very useless piece of baggage.' Earlier in her progress she had noted acidly in her diary how on one occasion the sight of a tiger caused their native servants abruptly to 'set down our palanquins' and run off: 'Capt. Smith threatened them . . . but it was in vain, for they would have done the same the next moment.' By now, though, she was less dismissive and more trusting, and she no longer felt the need for any European chaperone, 'having sepoys and peons sufficient to protect me'. Understandably, Brishen hid in his palanquin for much of the time. So in the end it was substantially left to her, and above all to her sepoys, coolies and palanquin-bearers, to find the safest way back into the heart of Bengal, 'wading through the wet ploughed ground' of paddy fields.[80]

The end of Elizabeth Marsh's journey also meant an end to her interlude of escape. Her experience and knowledge were now far wider, and so were certain fractures in her thinking and in her sense of herself. Her Indian diary is eloquent about her delight in company and her yearning for acceptance by what passed for 'European' genteel society. It also documents her desire at times to get away from both. It discloses her extensive ignorance and her capacity for racial disdain and ruthlessness. It also reveals at times a hunger to learn, and a capacity for curiosity about, and for occasional empathy with, indigenous sites and people. And it shows how she was bound up with the East India Company's power, and with the British Empire and nation, but not always assertively or unambiguously so. It is what is left out of the journal that illustrates this most clearly. If Elizabeth Marsh attended Christian worship at any stage of her progress, or made a private act of devotion, she never mentions it. Temples, or what she persists in calling 'mosques', progressively intrigue and interest her. But the Bible and prayer book are always missing. Nor, once she arrives at Madras, does she mention a single patriotic celebration on the part of the Company or its army. At the military cantonment at Ellore, and elsewhere, she would have been bound to see flags waved, guns fired, troops lined up in honour of royal birthdays and other canonical British anniversaries. Such occurrences are absent from her account, shrugged off in the course of her journey like so much else as she became increasingly deciduous.[81]

The silences and elisions in her text – what she leaves out or quickly passes over – are also suggestive about some of the contradictions in Elizabeth Marsh's relationship with James Crisp. She returned to Calcutta on 20 June 1776. Instead of immediately hiring a river boat to take her back to Dhaka, and the husband and son she had not seen for eighteen months, she remained in the city for six weeks, staying in the garden house of her friend Johanna Ross. The likely reasons for this cast light on her journey more broadly. Johanna Ross was not just a connection of Elizabeth

Marsh's powerful kinsman, General Richard Smith, but a wealthy woman in her own right, with commercial interests. It was at one of her houses in Calcutta back in December 1774 that Elizabeth had said farewell to her husband and son, 'who had been there upon business some time', before embarking on her Asiatic progress with George Smith. Around this time, the mid-1770s, Johanna Ross is known to have lent James Crisp a substantial sum for his textile business.[82] Elizabeth Marsh may have lingered in her house in late June and early July 1776 therefore not just (and perhaps not at all) so as to prolong her absence from her husband, but in order to assist him by facilitating this loan in some way. This possibility is reinforced by the likely identity of the man who went out to meet her on the outskirts of Calcutta at the end of her progress, and who escorted her into the city. He was a 'Mr. Ross of Calcutta', not as it happens a relation of Johanna Ross, but almost certainly Johannes Mathias Ross, the chief of the Dutch East India Company in Bengal, who is known to have done extensive business with many British Company and private traders.[83]

The closer one looks at Elizabeth Marsh's Indian diary, the more one notices – not merely her delight in socializing and attention, her evident pleasure in the company of a younger and military male 'cousin', her growing, though uninformed, curiosity about indigenous religions, peoples, townscapes and landscapes, and her relish for distance and movement – but also her persistent interest in economic life, in business. She was particularly and understandably attentive to places where 'a very considerable cloth trade . . . is carried on': Machilipatnam; Madapolam; Pulicat; Ichapur, a centre for indigo; Cuttack; Ganjam and the like. She took note as she went along too of other kinds of economic activity: the 'great trade carried on in brass and copper' in Aska, where she noticed how the local inhabitants 'feed well, and save money'; the salt pans outside Injuram, with 'large mountains heaped up with that valuable article, ready for exportation'; the manufacture and export of fine furniture carried out at Vizagapatam, where 'a great number of artificers ... nicely inlay in ivory and black wood', and that town's 'stocking manufactory' from which an 'abundance [is] sent to all parts of the country'.[84]

Elizabeth Marsh clearly did not view the parts of the subcontinent she travelled through only as a 'vast museum, its countryside filled with ruins, its people representing past ages'.[85] She took note of certain ruined bridges, forts and palaces along her route, to be sure, but like other incomers to India at this time, she also saw some of the towns and settlements she passed through as flourishing environments for commerce, manufacturing and making money. It is possible, indeed, that sections of her Asiatic progress, and not just the end of it in Calcutta, were carried out in order to assist her merchant husband. The evident care she took at different stages to cultivate influential East India Company men, for instance, may have been designed to benefit James Crisp's dealings in some fashion, and not just to cater to her own vanity and insecurities. And when, occasionally, she slips enigmatic lines into her diary like 'finished all our business', she may have been referring to more than just the personal business of packing up her chests and organizing her clothes.[86]

This is the final paradox of her Asiatic progress: that, despite all the time she spent away from James Crisp and in the company of George Smith, her marriage may still have been something that at a certain level she took seriously. Her husband's bankruptcy, her own authorship, and perhaps his slave dealings and the original circumstances of their marriage, had put her relationship with Crisp under strain even before she arrived in the subcontinent. In every sense, her extraordinary travels widened the distance between them further, not least because of how much she changed over the course of them. Neither she – nor indeed Crisp – was likely now to remain content for long with staying amidst the waterways of Dhaka. Yet the evidence suggests that she still saw herself as caught up with Crisp in a joint enterprise, and that she was prepared to invest some effort in this. She might not live with him. She would not even necessarily stay close to their children. But she would strive to help him to make money, and to aid their collective survival and worldly advance. It was late July 1776 when she eventually returned to 'my dear Crisp and precious boy', barely a fortnight after the signing of the American Declaration of Independence.

6

World War and Family Revolutions

THE EVENTUAL SCALE of what began as a rebellion and a civil war along the eastern coastline of North America shattered Elizabeth Marsh's life, and obliged her to reconfigure it. The American revolutionaries' success in securing first covert, then open support from some of the main European colonial and naval powers – France, Spain, and the Dutch – together with Britain's own imperial and naval reach, ensured that the war proliferated across multiple land boundaries, and reached into every one of the world's oceans. Almost immediately sweeping into Canada, and soon into various Native American lands, the conflict spread progressively into British, French, Spanish and Dutch territories and areas of rivalry in the Caribbean, the Mediterranean, and northern Europe, sections of the Indian subcontinent, and parts of northern and southern Africa and Central America; while its economic and diplomatic ramifications, and in some cases its demographic repercussions, extended still farther, into South America, Russia, West Africa, China, and ultimately New South Wales.[1]

Since the livelihoods of so many of them were bound up with the British state, the British Empire, the Royal Navy and the sea, the East India Company and long-distance commerce, the men of the Crisp and Marsh families were ineluctably caught up in the disruptions and violence of this war, and in some of the issues and ideas involved in it. This in turn affected Elizabeth Marsh, not least because of a persistent paradox of her life. Original, determined, selfish and irrepressibly mobile, she was also a dependent being. There was a sense indeed in which her deviations from customary female norms actually rendered her *less* self-sufficient, not more so. The publication of her personal testament as *The Female Captive*, like the free passages she repeatedly sought out aboard naval ships, like her ambitious travels overland with scores of guards and guides, all required her to have recourse to, and to seek aid from, men. Consequently, the onset of transcontinental warfare that increasingly sucked in and distracted very large numbers of men necessarily curtailed and changed the quality of her activities. There could now be no further explorations of the Indian subcontinent on her part, along routes of her own choosing, and with a uniformed escort, because the East India Company's troops soon had more urgent and dangerous things to do. The war's onset cost her auxiliaries in a more intimate fashion. It coincided with, and contributed to, the deaths of some of her closest relations and supporters. As a result she was forced to hunt out additional sources of income, to embark on new, grimly functional rather than revelatory voyages, and to adjust the conditions of her own and her children's lives.

These shocks and alterations may help to explain why her extant writings come to an end along with her Asiatic journey, and her return to Dhaka and her husband, in July 1776. Her intense, intermittent accounts of her evolution in the face of new encounters and sceneries cease abruptly at this point, and no further journals or copies of her manuscripts are known to exist, and there are no letters. So her ideas and emotions after mid-1776 have to be deduced substantially from her actions; and these in turn have to be reconstructed at one or more removes, by drawing on and patching together the records and accounts of others. In particular, Elizabeth Marsh's experiences during her final years have to be recovered from the testimonies of a series of men who powerfully influenced what happened to her and what she was able to achieve, but whom she was also able at times to turn to use.

The first of these witnesses who both determined and eased her progress is necessarily her husband, James Crisp. While Elizabeth was travelling and exploring in eastern and southern India, he had remained behind in Bengal making money, for himself and his family through his dealings in north Indian textiles, and for the East India Company by overseeing the local production and sale of salt.

❀

Gandhi's complaint that the taxes on salt levied by the British Raj were 'the most iniquitous of all from the poor man's standpoint' conveys exactly why so many rulers over the centuries and in different parts of the world have found it advantageous to impose them. Salt lent itself to taxation for the same reason that it served in some societies as a form of payment in kind, and as an instrument of barter: it was an article that no one, however impoverished, could entirely do without.[2] Salt is found in virtually every part of the human body, and is essential to life. In the past, it was also vital for the manufacture of gunpowder; and before refrigeration, it was indispensable for preserving food. The Nawabs of Bengal had acknowledged the mineral's indispensability by establishing a monopoly on it; and after the East India Company assumed authority over the province, it treated salt in a similar, but more rigorous, fashion. In 1772, salt production in Bengal, which was estimated conservatively at some ninety thousand tons annually, became a Company monopoly. Indian salt-farmers were introduced throughout the province to supervise production on the Company's behalf, shunting aside much of the authority traditionally exercised over the industry by local landholders.[3]

In his official employment as salt agent for Bhulua, a huge, partly waterlogged region that approximates now to the Noakhali district of Bangladesh, James Crisp was thus in a position that was at once politically sensitive, economically significant, and physically very arduous. He had to monitor the productivity of thousands of *malangis*, the peasant workers who produced the salt, and collect regular samples of it in order to check for quality. He had to oversee the condition of the salt stores, or *golas*, of which he calculated there were at least 286 in Bhulua. Many of them, he complained, searching for a simile from home, looked 'more like cow-houses than *golas*'. It was Crisp's job to ensure that these low-lying, tumbledown structures were not overwhelmed by water from Bengal's latticework of rivers, especially during the 'inundations in the time of the rains', between June and September. He also had to arrange for his region's salt to be weighed, and for its transportation by boat and bullock cart to set locations on certain dates, so that it could be auctioned; and notices of these salt sales had to be prepared and displayed throughout the region in Persian, Bengali and English. Finally, it was Crisp's responsibility to ensure that indigenous merchants purchasing salt at auctions received what they paid for promptly, and did 'not have any cause to complain'.[4]

In order to accomplish these tasks James Crisp was assisted by a deputy, and together they oversaw forty Bengali assistants, without whom this system had not the slightest chance of working. Crisp himself was expected to tour Bhulua on horseback, elephant and by boat, make monthly (sometimes fortnightly) reports to his immediate superiors in the Provincial Council of Dhaka, and submit detailed accounts. Once checked, these accounts were dispatched to the Governor General, Warren Hastings, and his Council in Calcutta, who had every reason to scrutinize them in turn, since profits on salt made up a substantial part of the Company's Bengal revenue. As Hastings warned James Crisp and his fellow salt agents in a circular in March 1775, any negligence 'or any connivance' on their part, any failure of 'vigilance and punctuality', would 'injure an important branch of the government's revenue, [and] will subject you to our severe displeasure and must consequently be attended with disgrace and loss of station'.[5]

Initially, Crisp's salt agency in Bhulua went well. Production levels seem to have risen under his stewardship; and, like most people who met him, the members of Dhaka's Provincial Council were immediately impressed by his energy. 'We have every reason to be satisfied with his industry and regularity,' they assured Hastings late in 1775.[6] In some respects, too, Elizabeth Marsh's husband was fortunate in his new position. Salt agents did not enjoy job security, and they were not covenanted servants of the East India Company, the self-regarding aristocracy of the British community in the subcontinent. But, at the equivalent of £450 per annum, Crisp's basic salary was generous; and while the terrain and the manufacturing networks he now had to deal with were in every sense alien, he possessed experience in the salt trade, and in dealing with different peoples and different languages. Elizabeth Marsh might strive to get by for much of the time in pidgin 'Moors', but in addition to Hindustani, her husband had little choice but to learn some Bengali, and to acquire a smattering of Persian, the embedded language of administration, law and revenue-collection.[7]

Despite all of James Crisp's efforts, however, success in his new post progressively eluded him, in large part because the most relentless challenges confronting him were beyond the scope of any individual's competence. As a leading north Indian intellectual, Ghulam Hussain Khan Tabatabai, subsequently argued, East India Company officials had only very recently shifted from working mainly as traders and soldiers on the coastal fringes of the subcontinent to assuming the roles of governors and administrators within Bengal. 'Oppressive, irregular, capricious, unsteady, and peculating' in some cases, with no developed ethos of public service, and manifestly no accumulated bureaucratic memory, the Company's men were almost invariably also out of their depth. They were 'quite strangers to the methods of raising tribute' in Bengal, Ghulam Hussain complained, and 'to the maxims of estimating the revenues, or of comprehending the ways of tax gathering'; and these strictures certainly applied to James Crisp and to his immediate superiors in Dhaka.[8]

Himself a recent migrant to the subcontinent, James Crisp had to implement a salt monopoly that had only been introduced by the East India Company in 1772, in a district, Bhulua, it had only started to govern since 1765, working directly to Dhaka's Provincial Council, that had itself only been put in place in 1774, and whose British members possessed only limited local knowledge. Not just Crisp himself, but also his Company superiors were substantially making it up as they went along. Partly as a result of this, there was often a striking absence of capacity to get things to work. In response to an early request by him on behalf of his Indian clerks and auditors for essential office supplies, for instance, Dhaka's Provincial Council informed Crisp that it was 'not in our power to furnish you with a supply of stationery'. By the same token, Crisp's Company superiors demanded that he construct new, water-resistant *golas* throughout Bhulua in which to store the region's salt. Since 'the land is so very low all over that country', this meant employing large numbers of men to raise the riverbanks on which the *golas* were situated; yet, as Crisp complained, he was expected to pay for this entirely out of his own funds.[9] The gulf between what he was expected to accomplish and the means afforded him was torture to an enterprising man who knew he must perform well and show a profit to have any chance of his contract as salt agent being extended.

Ill-informed and ill-equipped in its implementation, the East India Company's salt monopoly was further undermined by some of its own officials. After 1773, it was illegal for Europeans in Bengal to be 'concerned directly or indirectly with the salt trade', unless they were working on behalf of the Company. By contrast, Bengal's native inhabitants were to possess 'a natural right to an open trade'. Within the necessary and benevolent framework of the Company's overall monopoly, or so the theory went, trade in salt in Bengal was to be the business of Indians only, and it was to be free. In reality, individual Company officials continued to take a cut, often operating behind a front of indigenous agents. A

A salt digger. Anonymous painting, *c.*1825.

Above John Perceval, later 2nd Earl of Egmont, by Francis Hayman. As First Lord of the Admiralty, Egmont sponsored two voyages of circumnavigation. He also supplied James Crisp and Elizabeth Marsh with the prospect of 20, 000 acres of land in East Florida.

Left Sir William Musgrave, by Lemuel Francis Abbott. The bibliophile and Commissioner of the Customs who discussed *The Female Captive* with Elizabeth Marsh, and whose annotated copy still survives.

Left The future General Sir
Eyre Coote, attributed to
Henry Morland, *c.*1763. A
boyhood friend of James
Crisp who assisted his flight
to the Indian subcontinent
in 1769 and initial progress
there.

Below Admiral Sir Edward
Hughes, watercolour in
Madras style, *c.*1783.
An Indian artist's caricature
of the Commander-in-Chief
of the East Indian squadron,
whom Elizabeth Marsh
encountered during her
Asiatic progress in 1775, and
possibly had recourse to for
her voyage back to Britain
in 1777-78.

REACHING OUT AND OVER-REACHING

Top Engraving of Hamburg by Johann Georg, *c.*1750.
Bottom 'A view of a section of the Port of Barcelona including Moorish and European merchants and their ships'. Eighteenth-century engraving by Moulinier.
Two nodes of James Crisp's far-reaching commercial web: note the presence of Muslim traders in the view of Barcelona.

The land that was theirs:
Above The Lower Crisp in Florida as it now is.
Below The Upper Crisp, which encompasses today's Creighton Island and the northern part of Fleming Island.

Above 'Examination of a bankrupt before his creditors in the Court of King's Bench, Guildhall', by Augustus Charles Pugin and Thomas Rowlandson.
An early-nineteenth-century rendition of the ordeal through which James Crisp passed in 1767.

Left Money lenders in Calcutta. The degree to which incoming Europeans easily became dependent on indigenous sources of capital and credit in the sub-continent accounts for some of the bitter racism evident in this print.

Bk 4   6

MULTIPLE CROSSINGS

Above left 'In India on the March', by Samuel Davis.
A scene that would have been familiar to Elizabeth Marsh on her progress: a halted palanquin, and a critical supply of Indian guides, servants and armed retainers.

Left 'Procession at the Great Temple of Jagannath, Puri', British school, *c*.1818-20.
One of the major Hindu pilgrimage sites and festivals which Elizabeth Marsh tried to observe in 1776.

Above Lockleys: the Hertfordshire mansion acquired by Elizabeth Marsh's daughter and Sir George Shee.

Captain John Henry Crisp, Elizabeth Marsh's half-Indian grandson, represented as indistinguishable from three British colleagues during part of his scientific expedition to Sumatra.

Preparing for the expedition at the Madras observatory.

fellow salt agent described the kind of subversion from within the Company machine that James Crisp was obliged to contend with:

> At certain periods it [the salt] is brought up in large boats to Dacca, and there exposed to public sale . . . In the mode of exposing the lots to sale I could perceive no small intrigue was carrying on, for I saw that the natives had not that free access to the public sale to which they were entitled, and that the lots fell, as they were put up, to the dependents of the members in Council, who by this means gained to themselves a considerable advantage.[10]

Even if Crisp himself refrained from such illicit salt dealings (and there is no proof either way), he would still have needed to tread very deftly around the sharp practices of some of his Dhaka superiors.

The passive and active resistance he encountered from some of Bhulua's native inhabitants was a still more pervasive challenge. His problems in this regard began with the *malangis*. These were the desperately poor people whose job it was in late autumn to dig salt ponds near the sea and salt-water rivers. This was the start of the salt-making cycle. The men would then build

> sluices to let in saltwater during high tide. Salt was absorbed into the earth and then more saltwater taken in with the spring tides. The additional seawater combined with the salty soil to produce concentrated brine, which they put in oblong pots, about 200 of which were cemented together by mud in a dome-shaped kiln. The salt makers placed vents at the north and south ends of each kiln so that fire would be fanned by prevailing breezes. As the brine in the pots evaporated, workers . . . added more brine, one ladle at a time, until each pot was about three-quarters full of salt crystals.[11]

Malangis often tried to supplement their incomes by making additional salt, working at night in Dhaka's dense woodlands, or in their own huts with the help of their wives, and then selling their 'illicit' product to smugglers. The *pykars* (agents) whom the Company employed to purchase salt from the *malangis* also subverted the system by frequently selling quantities of it on their own behalf. They would cover up these private sales by adulterating their remaining salt supplies with sand, or fiddling their accounts. Or, as James Crisp complained, *pykars* might simply refuse to produce any accounts at all ('after being deceived by their repeated promises of compliance, I find it is in vain any longer to expect the least satisfaction from them of this kind'). In addition, Bhulua's *golas*, which were generally unguarded earth buildings, leaked salt into the surrounding communities. About fifty thousand *maunds* of salt had been illicitly removed from his *golas*, Crisp reported in June 1775, much of it by boat at night-time.[12] Such raids on *golas* were sometimes sponsored by local landholders, who were angry at being stripped of their former profits from salt works. 'The people of these districts are a set of desperate smugglers,' Crisp wrote from Lakshmipur in 1776, 'who keep an armed force, and . . . pay no regard to so small a one as I have.' There were repeated reports from Bhulua, and from the other salt districts in Bengal, of attacks on the East India Company's salt boats as they sailed slowly towards the auction sites. On occasions, salt smugglers would fire at the boats' flags, blazoned with the Company's colours and with the Union Jack.[13]

⁂

It is important to remember that James Crisp had himself once been a smuggler. That he was having to function now as a fiscal enforcer, and deal with multiple levels of resistance from Britons and Asians alike, was a novel, thoroughly unwelcome experience that he increasingly came to resent. Yet, as he tried unavailingly and ever more from a distance to carry out his salt duties in Bhulua, Crisp was not simply a lonely individual operating out of his depth and out of his element in a particular imperial environment. He was also a single figure in a global landscape marked out both by more intensive revenue-raising expedients, and by sharper resistance to them.

In parts of the Americas, Asia, Northern Africa, and within Europe itself, levels of taxation and other fiscal duties were rising at this time, and so were serious protests against them. Growing competition and conflict between states, and a 'pre-industrial arms race in which fiscal strength was as essential to military power as advances in strategy and technology', had made rulers ever more hungry for additional revenue. It is open to debate just how far this raging fiscal hunger provoked a 'global crisis', but it is beyond dispute that increasing exactions by many different rulers were fostering popular revolts across the continents, and that these became more serious and more widespread during the second half of the eighteenth century.[14] Pugachev's revolt among the Ural Cossacks in 1773–74 and the *Comunero* revolt in New Granada (Colombia) in 1781 were both fired in large part by resentment at increased wartime taxation. In the former case, the spark was Catherine the Great's need for more money in order to pay for Russia's war against the Ottoman Empire. In the case of the *Comunero* revolt, one of the triggers was Spain's want of extra funds in part so that it could join the American Revolutionaries in their war against Britain. Nor was this drive to raise more revenue so as to finance greater military effort and effectiveness the preserve only of Christian rulers. In Morocco, Sidi Muhammad's policies of seeking out new commercial treaties, and of levying increased duties on incoming and outgoing trade, were also driven by the desire to build up his armies and his authority.[15]

In the same way, the American Revolution was partly (and notoriously) caused by Britain's attempts to tax its colonists more rigorously, so as to cover its debts from the Seven Years War and underpin its vastly expanded imperial role. Similarly, it was the huge costs of building new fortifications in Calcutta and Madras, of rapidly inflating its armies, and of fighting wars with Mysore and the Marathas in the 1760s and '70s that drove the East India Company to try imposing new taxes on land in northern India at this time, and to increase its profits from the manufacture and sale of salt and opium.[16] Indeed, these revenue-raising initiatives on different sides of the world were not just comparable in type, but also interwoven in practice. It was in order to ease the East India Company's financial difficulties in the subcontinent that the British Parliament passed the Tea Act in April 1773. This allowed the Company to export its surplus Chinese tea for the first time, in its own ships, directly to four ports in Britain's American colonies. It was because they viewed this, rightly, as a threat to their own private smuggling, and 'as a badge' of imperial sovereignty over them, that angry citizens in one of these ports, Boston, threw ninety thousand pounds of East India Company tea into their harbour in November 1774.[17]

As far as his salt agency in Bhulua, and many of the difficulties he encountered there, were concerned, then, James Crisp was very much a man of his time. He was one of a multitude of agents, active in widely different parts of the world, who were seeking to extract extra revenue for their respective cash-hungry and authority-hungry political masters, and – in the process – were provoking haggling, obstruction and occasionally violent protest. Crisp was not tarred and feathered or beaten up as he went about his salt agent's duties in Bhulua. But, like those customs officers in Rhode Island and Massachusetts who did experience such treatment at the hands of irate American colonists, he suffered personally on account of his revenue-raising work, even as he tried to extricate himself from it.

Just as customs officers in the American colonies had been wont to do, Crisp frequently complained that opposition to the East India Company's salt monopoly in Bhulua cried out for more coercive power. As early as 1775, he warned the Provincial Council at Dhaka that he needed at least three more sepoys to aid him, 'which the duty I am upon absolutely requires'. A year later, he was requesting 'a reinforcement of about 12 sepoys'.[18] As on this last occasion, his demands for extra military support were usually rejected. Under economic pressure, and faced with the prospect of an already international war soon seeping into the subcontinent, Crisp's superiors in Dhaka and Calcutta preferred to believe that all would be well if only he intensified his own efforts and application. From early on, they urged him to spend more time on-site and on duty in Bhulua: 'It is only you that can be called upon to answer . . . and therefore if you have not hitherto, you must now take charge of the Company's salt and be careful that there be no delay in the delivery thereof.'[19] To the extent that James Crisp was being asked to administer a system that was structurally flawed, insufficiently supported, and deficient in legitimacy, this was unfair. But the Company was right in thinking that he was often absent from his post. His letters to his superiors during the course of Elizabeth Marsh's leisurely journeying with George Smith show that Crisp spent more and more of his time in Lakshmipur: 'Luckipore', as the British commonly referred to it. This town was about sixty-eight miles by river from Dhaka, close to the junction of the Meghna and the Ganges, and it was not a centre of salt production. Lakshmipur was supremely a place of cloth-making. Its weavers enjoyed an illustrious reputation for producing fine-quality textiles both for elite consumption within the subcontinent and for markets overseas.[20]

It was to this place and its commercial potential that James Crisp was increasingly drawn in preference to his Company salt duties in Bhulua. He was not a natural bureaucrat, or a man who enjoyed working to others. Nor, as he had already shown in Barcelona and London, was he someone who willingly accepted the confines of a single empire. Necessity had driven him, as a new migrant, to seek employment with the East India Company, just as bankruptcy had earlier tempted him to become involved in colonial projects in East Florida. But quintessentially James Crisp was a merchant: 'that is to say, a man whose operations are not confined within any region but spread over the whole globe and who constantly behaves as if he regards himself as a burgher of the whole world'.[21] True to such an outlook, his interests and aspirations extended far beyond damp Bhulua. Even before he arrived in Dhaka and became a salt agent, Crisp had begun trading with Persia. This was traditionally an important market for Bengal cloth both in its own right, and because of the access it afforded to Ottoman territories. By 1774, East India Company records show Crisp importing raw materials into Calcutta from England for cloth production and finishing, cases of starch, soap, oil and the like. And about this time he found himself a new business partner, joining up with Henry Lodge, a Company servant who was then secretary to the Provincial Council in Dhaka. Their joint business was sufficiently well known for the two men to be asked in 1775 to give evidence on the state of Dhaka's textile industry in a case brought by indigenous weavers in Calcutta's Supreme Court.[22]

Thus far, there was nothing in any of this that was unusual, or to which the East India Company could reasonably object. Its senior officials took it for granted that full-time employees in the subcontinent, men like Henry Lodge, would supplement their salaries by trading on their own account. And while James Crisp was not a covenanted servant of the Company, he was known to possess a licence from its directors allowing him to engage in private trade in Bengal and off its coast. That he was combining his work as a salt agent on the Company's payroll with trading in Bengal textiles to Persia and elsewhere in Asia was therefore understood and accepted. But in 1775–76, while Elizabeth Marsh was away travelling, James Crisp crossed an important line. He started spending conspicuous amounts of time in Lakshmipur, where the East India Company itself controlled a substantial textile manufactory. He also appears to have begun competing with the Company's agents to purchase high-quality fabric from Lakshmipur's weavers, exactly the sort of cloth that the Company relied on to meet its export targets for markets beyond Asia. In short, and just as he had in Barcelona and London, James Crisp began pressing against the rules, and testing the barriers on free trade.

A single building in Lakshmipur became the physical embodiment of these barriers, and the site for struggle between Crisp and the Company's powerful and disapproving local factory chief, one Henry Goodwin. The building was an unprepossessing bungalow, 'with a small veranda round it closed in with old mats', and with a surrounding open ditch its only gesture to sanitation. Its attraction lay in its location. It was just 250 yards from the entrance to the East India Company's cloth factory. Whoever occupied this Lakshmipur bungalow was in a position to watch the daily stream of indigenous weavers and cloth-traders entering and leaving the Company's factory – and to intercept any of them and try to cut his own commercial deals. As Henry Goodwin told the tale, the first time James Crisp had visited Lakshmipur, there was nowhere for him to sleep except his *budgerow*, the covered boat that served as his mobile home as he travelled Bengal's river system carrying out his salt duties. He, Goodwin, had generously offered him the loan of the bungalow, which was then standing empty, 'for the short time he should stay at Lakshmipur which he supposed would not exceed a month'. But no sooner had Crisp returned to Dhaka than he had fired off a letter to Goodwin setting out a claim to live in the bungalow permanently, 'as he found . . . [it] was at the disposal of the Dhaka Council, and he wished to make such alterations in it as would render it a comfortable dwelling'.[23]

Goodwin reacted with fury. This was no mere bungalow, he insisted. It was a *cutcherry*, an office. Dhaka's Provincial Council had no rights over it, because it belonged to the East India Company's commercial department, and was intended for Company servants employed in collecting revenue in Lakshmipur. As for James Crisp, who was he, and what claim could he conceivably have on the Company's accommodation? He was 'a person who is not in the service and no ways entitled to an habitation from the Company by being salt agent'. Spurred on by Crisp's new business partner, Henry Lodge, Dhaka's Provincial Council initially swept Goodwin's objections aside. The bungalow was situated within the Dhaka district. It was accordingly the Council's right to allocate it as they saw fit, and their wish was for James Crisp to occupy it whenever his salt duties took him to Lakshmipur. It followed that no one else could live there. The correspondence over this matter became increasingly bad-tempered, went on for over a year, and reached the desk of Warren Hastings several times over. To begin with, he came down on the side of James Crisp.[24]

Yet Henry Goodwin was right to insist that far more was at stake than a mere bungalow. At a personal level, this protracted tussle over an 'uncomfortable habitation . . . made entirely of mats' illustrates the resentment and suspicion that Elizabeth Marsh's husband seems often to have provoked by his brand of impatient, improvisory enterprise.[25] To some he came in contact with – and especially to those of a more conventional and pompous disposition, like George Marsh in London or Henry Goodwin in Bengal – James Crisp's business style, which was an outcrop of his intense ambition and his lack of secure capital, could seem mere ruthless opportunism, arrant rule-breaking, even dishonesty. He 'had not been genteely treated' by Crisp, Goodwin complained. Part of what he meant by this was that Elizabeth Marsh's husband was not a gentleman. Crisp, he wrote, had 'acted a very disingenuous part'. A Company revenue officer who had been hoping to move into the Lakshmipur bungalow himself was just as scathing: 'It appears to me Mr. Crisp does not like to put himself to any expense when it can be done at another's cost.' The revenue officer and Goodwin did not send these accusations directly to James Crisp, since to do so would have been to invite a duel. But, almost as dangerously, his accusers did send copies of their letters of complaint to the Board of Trade in Calcutta, the body that was responsible for overseeing the Company's commercial ventures and investments.[26]

Neither Henry Goodwin nor the disgruntled and homeless

revenue officer was in any doubt as to why James Crisp wanted the bungalow so badly – wanted indeed, so they claimed, to move to Lakshmipur permanently, even if he had to build himself a new house there in order to do so. As Goodwin wrote, nastily, to the Board of Trade in May 1776:

> I cannot help adding . . . with respect to Mr. Crisp's residing at Lakshmipur, that this appears to me incompatible with the duty of the salt agent's office, and contrary to the meaning of his appointment which I think requires his residing at, or near the places where the salt is made, that it may be under his immediate superintendancy, whereas I do not see for my part the use he can be of to the Company if the business which he should look after himself is delegated to others, and he might as well reside altogether at Dhaka, or even in Calcutta as at Lakshmipur. Indeed . . . [for] fourteen months, the salt agent has not to my knowledge once visited the places where the salt is manufactured.

As a *coup de grâce*, Goodwin included with this letter the revenue officer's own essentially accurate assessment of James Crisp's behaviour: 'it is more for the sake of carrying on his own private trade than any real service he can render to the Company, that induces him to reside here'.[27]

As it happened, the prospect of expanding his private trade in new directions may not have been all that was enticing James Crisp in the direction of Lakshmipur. If Henry Goodwin and the revenue officer were correct, and he did contemplate moving there permanently, and abandoning the elegant house in Dhaka, Crisp may have had other, more personal incentives. By this stage, the early summer of 1776, Elizabeth Marsh had been absent travelling with George Smith for almost eighteen months; this after having also been apart from her husband for most of 1769, 1770 and early 1771. James Crisp may have had enough. He may have looked for and found female companionship and sexual consolation in Lakshmipur, as well as a rich source of luxury fabrics, though this can be no more than speculation. What is certain is that he was pulled in this new direction not simply by a variety of pressures and temptations, but also by his instinct for potentially lucrative ventures that came freighted with risk.

By the early 1770s, East India Company officials in the subcontinent were finding it increasingly difficult to meet their export targets for textiles, particularly in regard to the finer varieties of cloth on which profits in Europe, North America, the Caribbean and elsewhere were highest.[28] Despite the Company's considerable capacity for harassment and coercion, there were frequent complaints from its agents throughout Bengal that native weavers were defying them, and choosing to sell their cloth to rival Asian merchants, or to European private traders. Some Bengal weavers simply refused to work for the Company any more. Others reportedly cut back on the quality of the cloth they were producing for the Company, and many weavers complained that the prices it was offering were no longer sufficient to cover their costs for yarn and food, which had risen since a terrible famine in Bengal in 1769–70. The fact that large numbers of weavers had starved to death in this famine may have increased for a while the bargaining power of those who remained healthy and at work. At the same time as the East India Company was confronted in Bengal with these challenges from native textile workers and rival merchants, there were signs that consumer demand for its exports in Britain and elsewhere was flattening off. Quantities of unwanted goods began to pile up ominously in the Company's warehouses.[29]

One of the places where anxiety over these developments was felt acutely was Lakshmipur, with its Company factory and its tradition of producing superlative, brilliantly coloured cloth for Western markets. In April 1776, a month before he composed his character assassination of James Crisp, Henry Goodwin had written to the Board of Trade in Calcutta warning that the Company's hold on Lakshmipur's weavers was slipping. He could no longer guarantee to procure the requisite quota of fine textiles, since the

Hindu weavers. Anonymous watercolour, *c.*1798–1804.

prices the Company was offering had fallen below the 'real cost of cloth to the weavers'.[30] Some of Lakshmipur's traditionally independent weavers, Goodwin reported, were making up for their losses in regard to the Company by selling their cloth to private traders – to men like James Crisp. In this year of revolutions, Crisp was seemingly no longer content to confine himself to trading within Asia. He also wanted – and perhaps needed – to win access to the overseas export trade in top-quality Bengal cloth. Dissatisfied with his situation in Dhaka, with his difficult and disputatious work as a salt agent, and with his long-absent wife, he wanted the bungalow in Lakshmipur, or at least a house of his own there, among other things so as to be within easy reach of the best textiles that its rebellious weavers could produce.

Later in 1776, in *The Wealth of Nations*, Adam Smith would famously urge the desirability of such challenges to the East India

Company's commercial grip on sectors of the Indian subcontinent, for the sake of their inhabitants, and for the sake of freer trade. The Company and its servants were 'plunderers', Smith wrote. Their 'perpetual monopoly' on so much British trade around Calcutta, Madras and Bombay was unnecessary and commercially iniquitous. 'That a joint stock company should be able to carry on successfully any branch of foreign trade,' he insisted, 'when private adventurers can come into any sort of open and fair competition with them seems contrary to all experience.'[31] Adam Smith had little to say, however, about the sort of risks such 'private adventurers' might incur if they tried competing against the East India Company on territory that it regarded as its own. Given James Crisp's temperament and business style, his earlier involvement in smuggling on the Isle of Man, and the varied pressures he was under in Dhaka as a bankrupted newcomer with no permanent position and with a family to support, it was less than surprising that he should have chosen to venture himself this way.[32] Working as a salt agent, and observing how often the Company's authority was flouted in Bhulua by native inhabitants and by some of its own officials, may also have encouraged Crisp to attempt defying the rules himself, and to believe that he could get away with it. He had already witnessed at close quarters some of the Company's weaknesses and inefficiencies. In late autumn 1776, he experienced the power of the Company's displeasure.

Although Warren Hastings concluded, after surveying some of the complaints against him, that James Crisp's conduct as a salt agent did 'not appear culpable', the Board of Trade in Calcutta insisted on his dismissal.[33] Not, in reality, on the grounds of incompetence, or even his intermittent absenteeism, but rather because Crisp had been caught out in commercial poaching. It was not his failure fully to implement the Company's salt monopoly (something he shared with every other salt agent) that earned him the sack, but his attempts to succeed as an interloper in Lakshmipur. For some months Crisp managed to keep the man appointed as his replacement at Bhulua, William Justice, at bay by refusing to yield up his accounts or any of the salt he had already collected from the region's *golas*, but this could be no more than a delaying tactic. 'Your agency with the allowances annexed thereto will expire the last day of March,' Crisp was reminded sternly in February 1777, so 'you will see the necessity of using dispatch'. When he persisted in holding out into March, he was dispatched a more explicit warning: 'no delay in this business will occasion a continuance of your salary after the 31st of this month'.[34] After that, from 1 April 1777, James Crisp's only source of income became whatever he could make from trading in textiles on his own account, in parts of the world he was in no position fully to understand, and at a time of contagious warfare.

Trying to live in the Indian subcontinent as a European immigrant but 'without an appointment', wrote a senior East India Company official later in 1777, was 'a woeful extremity. It gives me a shivering to think that . . . a man should be reduced to it.'[35] The loss of his semi-detached association with the Company, with its comfortable regular salary, did not however affect James Crisp alone. The insecurity of his position now also involved his only recently returned, but still considerably dependent wife.

In the immediate aftermath of his dismissal, Crisp's Asian commerce seems to have continued to expand. Even in 1778, a Company official included him in a list of European private merchants resident in Dhaka whom 'we understand to have considerable dealing in trade'.[36] Yet, well before this, some of those close to the Crisps seem to have regarded the couple's situation as being under stress from more than just their respective wanderings. It is suggestive that in late 1776 Johanna Ross, the rich Calcutta widow, left Elizabeth Marsh five thousand rupees (about £500) in her will, the same sum she bequeathed Warren Hastings, who had acted as one of her executors. Initially Johanna had allowed Elizabeth only four thousand rupees, but she later evidently decided that her friend either deserved or needed an additional sum.[37] These five thousand rupees were probably the largest single cache of money that Elizabeth Marsh received in her life, though since she was a married woman, ultimate control over it and any other money she might be bequeathed belonged by law to her husband. Characteristically, James Crisp seems to have allowed his wife to use the bequest as she wished. But, together with her husband's loss of a reliable Company salary, Johanna Ross's generosity prompted Elizabeth Marsh to begin thinking more concentratedly about money and about the future.

The determination she exhibited from now on in this regard had several roots. She was driven in part by memories of Crisp's bankruptcy in 1767 and what this had meant: an eventual loss of home, precious objects and social status, and her and the children's enforced reliance on her parents in Chatham in the aftermath of her husband's flight. Her instinct to take action in the wake of Crisp's new economic difficulties owed more, however, to her own temperament and to the nature of her family background.

The seafarers' womenfolk in Portsmouth amongst whom Elizabeth Marsh had grown up – like their counterparts in other ports – were obliged to hold rather different attitudes to money, marriage and woman's sphere of action than the generality of females whose menfolk worked on land. By the conventions of English common law, which also applied to incomers to Bengal, a husband and his wife were accounted one legal person, and that person was emphatically the man. Legally, a wife was enmeshed in and defined by her dependence on her spouse.[38] But these legal fictions made absolutely no sense in maritime communities, where women might have to cope on their own for months or even years on end, while husbands, fathers or brothers were away on voyages from which they might never return. Consequently, seafarers' womenfolk had often strenuously to make do. This might involve them taking some kind of paid employment, or petitioning the navy or civilian ship-owners for access to a male relation's back pay, or getting their menfolk in advance of setting sail to confer on them power of attorney. Men who went to sea frequently came under community and family pressure to cooperate with these female expedients. Sailors' sexual loyalties might waver in distant ports, but in regard to making some provision for their women back home, they were expected not to be unduly feckless. For how else could women who were linked to such a dangerous trade through their men possibly survive? Elizabeth Marsh had come a long way from Portsmouth, geographically, socially and culturally. But in her responses to the potential economic dangers facing James Crisp and herself in Bengal after 1777, she was influenced by this maritime tradition of women taking the initiative, and shifting for themselves.[39]

Her mother, Elizabeth Marsh senior, had died in Chatham in January 1776 (the family's surviving letters on this event reveal sorrow, but nothing more about this lost woman).[40] Elizabeth only received the news after her return to Dhaka in July of that year, and she made no effort at this stage to return to Britain to comfort her father or pay her respects. For the rest of this year, and for much of 1777, she seems to have remained in Dhaka. James Crisp was sometimes present, and sometimes away on business; and she was in a position to reflect on their situation, and on the regular, six-month-old letters she received from members of her family in Britain and Spain. Over the months these would have informed her of her father's courtship of another, younger woman, and eventually of his remarriage. Once again, Milbourne Marsh had sought out a bride with money, marrying a respectable, propertied widow called Katherine Soan in December 1776. He may have sought out this new wife as a nurse, since Elizabeth's correspondents informed her that Milbourne too was now beginning to fail: he was 'in a very declining state of health'.[41] By contrast with her mother's demise, these two subsequent family developments – her father's remarriage and his physical deterioration – determined Elizabeth to attempt the voyage back from Bengal to Britain. She had been back with James Crisp in Dhaka for barely a year. Now she determined once again to set out without him.

Elizabeth Marsh's decision to attempt another protracted sea passage, which she may have paid for out of Johanna Ross's bequest, was influenced by her family's characteristically maritime attitude to women and money. Inured to work, risk, and conspicuous mobility at sea, the Marsh clan exhibited over the generations a marked commitment to providing its women with some independent source of income. In their wills, men of the family often named their wives as their sole executrix and legatee. George Marsh senior, for instance, the ship's carpenter who was Milbourne Marsh's father, left all of his very modest fortune to his wife when he died in 1753, named her as sole executor, and got two other women to witness this.[42] The strength of the family's adherence to the maritime code of safeguarding female survival is suggested by the fact that even those of its members who did not work at sea still demonstrated a testamentary concern for women's independence. Thus when Elizabeth's brother, Francis Milbourne Marsh, an army officer, left money in his will to an illegitimate daughter in 1782, he was careful to specify that this was 'for her own sole and separate use and not subject or liable to the debts, engagements or control of any husband she may marry'.[43] By the same token, when men of the family divided their property among legitimate children at death, they rarely did so according to the conventions of male primogeniture. Instead, a recurring phrase in the family's wills is 'share and share alike'. Not always, but very often, Marsh fathers left each daughter the identical sum they bequeathed to each of their sons.

Fully aware of these family strategies, and pondering the likely consequences of her father's remarriage and physical decline, Elizabeth Marsh was bound to feel anxious about the likely provisions of his future will. What if Milbourne Marsh were to die and leave his estate entirely or substantially to his new, younger wife, Katherine? Given his profound attachment to his family and its traditions, this was scarcely likely. But it *was* probable that Milbourne would act according to Marsh family custom and, having made a decent provision for his second wife, leave his remaining estate to be divided equally between his three children, Francis Milbourne Marsh, John Marsh, and his beloved only daughter, Elizabeth herself. In that event, she might well be a substantial beneficiary on paper. Any such bequest to her, however, would naturally fall under the authority of her husband. And this time, given the pressures he was under in Bengal, and the commercial repercussions of expanding warfare, James Crisp might not be willing to let such a windfall go.

Elizabeth Marsh's worries about her possible inheritance were not simply on her own account. It scarcely mattered how Milbourne Marsh bestowed his money as far as her son Burrish Crisp was concerned: his formidable language skills were expected soon to secure him a Writer's position with the East India Company, the first step on the career ladder of its civilian hierarchy. But while Burrish could be left to look after himself, the same could not be said of her daughter, Elizabeth Maria Crisp, who was thirteen in 1777. Since returning from India five years earlier, she had lived on Milbourne's charity in Chatham, receiving an expensive female education. Who would support Elizabeth Maria when Milbourne died, and where would she go? How were a suitable dowry and husband to be found for her, if James Crisp's commercial ventures failed again? There were other issues to do with mortality crowding in on Elizabeth Marsh's mind. Most incomers to the Indian subcontinent from Europe died prematurely, and often very suddenly. If James Crisp were to perish, what of her? And, since she herself was now over forty, and had already suffered serious illness, what if she were to die in the near future? Who would take care of Elizabeth Maria then?

Seeking out solutions to these questions against a background of transcontinental warfare would preoccupy Elizabeth Marsh for most of her remaining life. She set sail from Calcutta some time in late 1777 or early 1778, arriving in Portsmouth promptly enough to see her father and to settle arrangements with him.[44] The new will that Milbourne Marsh signed several months before his death on 17 May 1779, at the age of sixty-nine, followed family tradition in displaying a markedly creative concern for his womenfolk. He asked to be buried 'in the same manner as my late dear wife . . . and in the same grave', but he also gave thought to his widow. Since the new Mrs Katherine Marsh would be unable to remain in the fine Agent Victualler's house in Chatham, which belonged to the navy, Milbourne had purchased some houses and land in nearby Rochester to guarantee her a regular income. In addition, his will allowed Katherine the choice of all of his linen, china, plate and household goods, his 'best furniture', and the interest on £700 of consols, government stock. Francis Milbourne Marsh, his eldest son, was to receive the interest on £900 worth of consols, while John Marsh was to be forgiven the bulk of an extensive debt he owed his father.[45]

By contrast, Elizabeth Marsh herself received nothing: but this was exactly what she and her father had planned and agreed on together, since any money left directly to her might pass to James Crisp, or to his creditors. Consequently, in her case, Milbourne's will skipped a generation. Leaving Elizabeth out, it provided instead for £300 to be inherited by her daughter, Elizabeth Maria, when she was twenty-one. If Elizabeth Maria married sooner than this, Milbourne's executors were instructed immediately to pay her 'the said three hundred pounds trust and all arrears of interest'. Nor was this the only provision that Milbourne Marsh made in his will for Elizabeth's daughter. When his second wife died, all of the stock and property he had bequeathed her was to be divided equally between his two sons and his granddaughter Elizabeth Maria, according to the family convention of 'share and share alike' between menfolk and womenfolk. In other words, one of Elizabeth

Marsh's concerns – though not her own future security – had begun to be addressed. She had managed to ensure a modest dowry for her daughter, with the possibility of more to come.

Wills are compact autobiographies, condensed accounts not just of individuals' levels of wealth or poverty, but also of their primary concerns in life, of their networks of intimates, and of intimacy's limits. The silences in Milbourne Marsh's will – its omission of anyone by the name of Crisp except for his granddaughter Elizabeth Maria – are eloquent testimony to his lack of confidence and trust in his striving, erratic son-in-law, who was now geographically as well as temperamentally far away. By contrast, the length of his will (four pages) as well as its content make clear Milbourne's own substantial success in life. The victualling post he had occupied at Chatham since 1765 had been unchallenging, too much of a retirement job for a still creative and energetic man. He had none-theless designed and built a new wharf in Chatham's victualling yard, set up a new seventy-two-foot-long storehouse, extended and improved many of the yard's other offices and, at the onset of the war, promptly organized a system of offshore defences.[46] And not being so stretched at work had meant that he was able to devote more time to consolidating a respectable fortune. In the 1720s, his mother had received just five shillings from her father's will. Half a century later, Milbourne Marsh left behind investments and property worth more than £5000 (close to £500,000 in today's purchasing power). There was also a sense in which he was fortunate to die when he did, in advance of the end of the war. By the Peace of Paris in 1783, negotiated between Great Britain and the new United States and its Continental European allies, Menorca was returned to Spanish rule. Saffron Island was also handed over to the Spanish, along with its spare, immaculate, expensive new naval facility, Milbourne Marsh's brainchild and masterwork.

The contribution that Milbourne made to his only daughter's welfare over the years had been extensive: it had indeed been a constant in Elizabeth Marsh's life. He had sacrificed his work on

Saffron Island in order to return to England so as to be nearer to her in 1765. The legal papers regarding her and James Crisp's East Florida enterprises reveal how frequently Milbourne subsequently made himself available as a witness, and doubtless too as a lender of money.[47] It was Milbourne who had given securities for Elizabeth Marsh's first passage to India in 1770; and it was Milbourne who paid for her son's lonely voyage to the subcontinent in 1771, and who supported Elizabeth Maria Crisp in Chatham when she returned from there the following year. Elizabeth Marsh had also regularly had recourse to Milbourne's naval contacts, drawing on them for introductions in different ports and continents, and in order to gain free or cheap access to ships.

But now her father was dead. Her husband was on the other side of the world, in Bengal; and war separated her from her two closest remaining male relations. Her elder brother, Francis Milbourne Marsh, was by now a major in Britain's 90th Regiment of Foot. Viewed within the family as a 'sensible man and a good scholar', Major Marsh had been shipped out with his regiment to the Leeward Islands (which included Antigua, St Kitts, Montserrat and Nevis), an expedition that brought about his death in 1782.[48] Her younger, closer, brother John Marsh was also tightly enmeshed in war, though in a civilian capacity and in a different part of the world. Since 1768 he had been British Consul at Málaga, on the southern Spanish coast. As most consuls did at this time, he had raised his own salary there by carrying out commercial duties and by engaging in trade himself. In addition to the services they rendered to incoming ships and individuals from the states they represented, Consuls were also professional magpies, men whose brief it was to snatch pieces of intelligence from as many sources as possible. Even before the formal outbreak of the war, John Marsh was mutating into a spy and spymaster. Six months before the Declaration of Independence he was transmitting reports to London of how American merchant ships off the Spanish and French coasts were already endeavouring 'to carry on their own commerce independently' of the navigation laws passed by Parliament. He also corresponded regularly with the British Embassy in Madrid, and with the authorities in Gibraltar about any information he could glean about developments in Spanish and Portuguese America; and he set up strings of agents and informers in some of the leading Iberian and French ports, Seville, Cartagena, and Toulon, who smuggled him political pamphlets and occasional philosophical texts as well as secrets. So Elizabeth Marsh's younger brother was able to keep his political masters informed of some of the processes whereby the Continental powers prepared to enter the war, and thus dramatically extend its scope. How, in April 1778, 'a large supply of warlike stores and four thousand infantry supposed bound to North America' had been shipped out from Toulon; how the bakers in 'Seville and other places' were working 'day and night, making ships biscuit' in readiness for a Spanish naval offensive; how 'warlike stores, such as battering guns, sand bags and implements commonly used for throwing up entrenchments, were preparing on the coast of Catalonia'; and how the Dutch Consul in Málaga had let slip to him 'in a confidential manner' that the States General in The Hague was also giving 'orders for equipping thirty sail of men of war'.[49]

It was not until July 1779, when Spain formally declared war on Britain, that John Marsh was forced to leave Málaga. Even then, he remained in Portugal gathering intelligence for some months; and so he too was unavailable to aid his sister in the immediate aftermath of Milbourne Marsh's death. Instead, Elizabeth Marsh turned to yet another male relation undergoing the transformations of war. She turned to her uncle George Marsh.

Before 1776, George Marsh had never travelled overland outside southern England, or made more than very brief maritime journeys off its coast. It was this relative stillness that allowed him to act as custodian and chronicler of his family's history. Traditionally, it has often been women who have taken on this archival and memorializing role within families, because their more restricted lives have given them the time to bear witness, and perhaps a desire, in this indirect way, to impose a stamp and form on past events.[50] Although George Marsh's form of sheltered sphere was essentially masculine – dealing with the global reach of a paramount navy, but only with pen and ink and paper – it still cordoned him off from the disruptions and extensive journeys experienced by so many of his relations. Safe and busy on shore, he enjoyed quoting (inexactly) some lines from *De Rerum Natura* by the Epicurean poet Lucretius: 'It is pleasant to see a shipwreck, which we are not in fear of.' A more accurate translation was beyond his reach, since George Marsh possessed no Latin, but it would have encompassed his philosophy more comprehensively: 'Sweet it is, when on the great sea the winds are buffeting the waters, to gaze from the land on another's great struggles.' A landlubber in a thoroughly maritime dynasty, 'content in an easy chair, fortune in our pockets', as he liked to remark, George had only once before 1776 contemplated voyaging overseas. As a still-struggling naval clerk in his twenties, he had briefly considered advancing his career by going to work in Antigua.[51] This venture did not materialize, and he had remained contentedly and profitably at home. But now, the onset of extensive warfare forced him outside his customary regime and posture.

Since he had ceased to be Lord Egmont's secretary at the Admiralty, George Marsh's administrative career had continued ever upwards. In 1772 he had become a Commissioner of the Navy Board, the agency with overall responsibility for building, supplying and repairing the Royal Navy's ships and stores and for administering its naval dockyards at home and overseas. A year later, George was made Clerk of the Acts, the second most important officer on the Navy Board, with a basic annual salary of over £830. His new post required him to be present whenever the Board met, which after 1775 was six days a week, from at least 10 a.m. until the early evening:

> The special duty of the Clerk of the Acts is to receive, arrange, register, and keep safe all orders and letters from the Admiralty, Treasury, and from the various correspondents of the Navy Board, to prepare answers thereto . . . to keep a register of all the proceedings of the Board . . . to forward directions pursuant to orders from the Admiralty or Navy Board . . . for the equipment, victualling and storing of the ships and fleets . . . to frame, from the Board's minutes of agreement, all contracts for ships stores, and charter parties; to enter them, and forward copies thereof . . . to keep a register of all bills drawn upon the Board . . . to examine the vouchers for, and make out bounty bills to, widows and orphans of those men slain in fight . . . to keep an entry of the certificates of such gentlemen as pass for lieutenants of the Navy; to grant certificates to the captains of ships of war, lieutenants and masters, to enable them to receive their wages; to receive, arrange, and deposit the journals and log books delivered in by the several officers; to examine and check the accounts of purveyors employed to survey timber.[52]

Since, at the height of the war, the Royal Navy possessed 310 ships, including over a hundred ships of the line, and employed 106,000 seamen, on top of the more than eight thousand men at work in its naval dockyards, with yet more employees in its bases overseas, the volume of George Marsh's business, even with several clerks to help him, was immense.[53] He was working harder than ever before in his life.

Overseeing the provisioning, the matériel, the accounting, the compensation for human damage, and the archiving involved in a transoceanic conflict was only part of his changing experience. In February 1776 he was suddenly ordered to Hamburg, 'the most disagreeable and dangerous a journey as I could possibly have had'. He and a fellow member of the Navy Board, Jonas Hanway, remained there until late May, 'surmounting many difficulties and an infinite deal of trouble'. Marsh's subsequent entering (and misspelling) in his Family Book of the forty German, Belgian and French towns he passed through on his return journey, which read like the tolling of some ponderous bell, bear witness to how reluctant, indeed resentful, he was at being forced for once into travel: 'Zarendorff, Osnaberg, Rosamond, Burcan, Wickendorf . . . Halle, Zell, Munster', and so on, through Hanover, Louvain, Brussels, Lille and St Omer, and finally to Calais and the ship home.[54] As far as the British government was concerned, this mission was a success. By this stage it was busy concluding treaties with Brunswick-Wolfenbüttel, Hesse-Cassel, Ansbach-Bayreuth and other principalities to provide for the hire of additional, German, troops for the war. The business of sending men, weapons and supplies to so many diverse overseas destinations was already occupying 138,000 tons of British shipping. In Hamburg, George Marsh and his associates succeeded in negotiating the hire of an additional thirty-four thousand tons of shipping so as to transport seventeen thousand German soldiers to North America, 'who all arrived there in perfect health'.[55] Other than as a tribute to his professionalism, George, however, found little comfort in this logistical coup, for his sympathies lay with the Americans.

On this point, his private papers are unambiguous. The war with the former colonies, he wrote, was 'a very unhappy business'. As a career civil servant, he was not permitted to pronounce on policy. Nor, lacking inherited wealth, was he prepared to risk his livelihood by doing so: 'I had nothing to do with that.' In his official capacity, he continued prosecuting the war on paper at a high, relentless level. But 'as an individual', he recorded, 'I was sorry for it, or that the government judged it necessary'.[56] It was not simply the incestuous nature of the conflict that appalled him, or its growing human and monetary costs, which his position obliged him to document every working day. His temperament and prejudices also inclined him towards sympathy with the American enemy. Devotedly Anglican in terms of religion, George Marsh was decidedly puritanical in personal style. Self-made, he was still easily stung by allusions to 'how low bred and of what poor parents' he was, and his concealed support for the Americans may have been assisted by their rejection of the hereditary principle. Although he presented himself at court on his appointment as Clerk of the Acts, and acted as an escort to George III and Queen Charlotte when they visited Portsmouth for a naval review in 1773, and again in 1778, George never committed to paper at this stage an effusive comment about the institution of monarchy. Nor did he accept subsequent invitations to the royal court: 'I was not of the type of mind to make the most of it.' Indeed, he felt inclined to blame the King for insisting that he accept the post of Clerk of the Acts, 'a little empty honour' that brought him even more drudge-like labour, with no higher salary than his previous position.[57]

A wartime portrait (one of three he commissioned during his lifetime) captures George Marsh's mixed perception of himself as a public servant who was also at this time privately detached. The artist he selected was a Benjamin Wilson, who had painted Benjamin Franklin during the visit he made to London in the 1760s to argue the American colonists' cause. Like Franklin, Wilson was an avid amateur scientist, who performed his own experiments with electricity: and this interest in experimental and scientific matters may have been part of his appeal to George Marsh. Wilson was also, like Marsh, both a British placeman (he was painter to the Board of Ordnance) and, seemingly, possessed of opposition sympathies. Certainly, Wilson painted leading figures associated with British opposition to the war and support for the Americans, such as the Marquess of Rockingham.[58] In his portrait of George Marsh, the Clerk of the Acts is shown standing, wearing sombre, well-cut clothes, and still reasonably slender in his fifties, though a pronounced double chin suggests why Elizabeth Marsh's uncle was always careful to monitor his weight and diet. He looks, as he was, intelligent, shrewd, powerful, and intensely watchful. One leather glove is already removed, and he is just taking off the other. To his right are papers, ledgers and quill pens. George Marsh is preparing once again to set about the pressing naval business of His Majesty George III, but there are no emblems of that monarch in evidence on the canvas.

Her uncle's willingness to continue administering at a senior, well-paid level a war of which he thoroughly disapproved was vital for Elizabeth Marsh's interests and prospects. It ensured that for the rest of her life she and her daughter received occasional, essential gifts of money; and it meant that she retained, even after her father's death, a relation who was able to organize cheap berths for her aboard Royal Navy ships. This was just what George Marsh did in November 1779, securing places for her and Elizabeth Maria on the *York* storeship, a 664-ton, Caribbean-built vessel that was bound for Madras. They were not the only women aboard. Two of Elizabeth Marsh's Indian slaves, 'Phillis' and 'Mary', had accompanied her to England, and they now sailed back with her. They watched as she disembarked briefly in Madeira to deliver by hand some of her uncle's official correspondence to a navy official, part of the price for her free passage. They helped to unpack the wrought metal she was carrying to the subcontinent on behalf of a Crisp in-law in the jewellery trade. They stared at the *York*'s fourteen guns and twelve swivels, which were essential armament now that the French and Spanish war fleets were engaged on the Americans' side (Captain Bechinoe, the *York*'s commander, caught sight of a Spanish frigate in late December).[59]

Picking a course so as to avoid such perils, and waiting at intervals for convoys, meant that the *York*'s voyage lasted over seven months, but there was little reason for Phillis, Mary, Elizabeth Maria or Elizabeth Marsh to feel in much hurry. Because of the Somerset decision in London in 1772, it was now illegal for any slave to be forcibly removed from England, and it was becoming widely believed that slavery could not and should not exist on its soil. As a result, the East India Company tended to refer to any slaves who arrived from the subcontinent along with their employers after this date as 'servants' for the duration of their stay in Britain.[60] Briefly liberated (at least in name) by their residence on another shore, returning to the Indian subcontinent, as far as Phillis and Mary were concerned, meant a reversion in title to slaves. They were sailing back to bondage. The voyage out also involved Elizabeth Marsh's own, far more privileged, status in flux. The East India Company directors' written licence allowing her to embark once again for the subcontinent 'permitted [her] to proceed to her friends in Bengal and to take her daughter . . . and two black servants . . . with her'. The significant phrase, as far as Elizabeth was concerned, was *'to her friends'*. As on her Asiatic progress, she showed herself willing on this journey to carry out some Crisp commercial business, but the *York* was bound for Madras, close to where Captain George Smith was stationed. The ship was not proceeding directly to Bengal; and, while she chose to put herself (and others) at risk by embarking on a further transoceanic voyage at a time of war and growing maritime danger, this was not out of conjugal duty. As the wording of the Company's licence makes clear, Elizabeth Marsh was not proceeding to James Crisp.[61]

❦

For what was there for her to go back to? By now, the widening range and repercussions of warfare had devastated the commercial dealings that were her husband's sole means of support. As a private merchant exporting textiles from Dhaka to the Persian Gulf region, James Crisp must have been damaged by the Persian siege and invasion of Basra in 1775–76. A Livorno of the Indian Ocean, a transit area for East–West trade, with Arab, Armenian, Jewish, Indian, Portuguese, Dutch, Greek, Venetian, French and British merchants all buying and selling within its mud walls, and in the shelter of its 131 watchtowers, Basra had traditionally been an important entrepôt for the export of northern Indian textiles into Ottoman territory. Twice a year, one of the best-organized caravans in Asia would transport textiles and other goods from Basra to Aleppo, the largest city in the Fertile Crescent, and the third largest in the Ottoman Empire after Istanbul and Cairo. Some 3000–3500 bales of north Indian cotton goods are estimated to have entered Basra annually in the early 1770s, mainly coming from Bengal, and mainly carried in British vessels. This trade was almost entirely halted by Persia's invasion and subsequent occupation of Basra that lasted until 1779.[62]

Like many other European and Asian merchants in Bengal, James Crisp was affected even more severely by the increasingly transcontinental nature of the American war. This struck at the finances of the East India Company itself, which were already under pressure before 1776, and consequently at the availability of cash and credit in northern India. Much of the tea, textiles, spices, ceramics and luxury furniture carried to Britain on Company ships was habitually re-exported to other parts of the world, especially to Continental Europe and to the Caribbean and the Thirteen Colonies. After 1775, and for the duration of the war, the inhabitants of the one-time mainland American colonies were rarely in a position to buy these luxury re-exports. Moreover, in the Southern colonies, the war severely cut back on plantation owners' purchase of Africans from British slave ships. This further damaged the East India Company, since British slave-traders were accustomed to taking large quantities of Asian textiles to serve as barter for captive human beings in West Africa. As the war expanded, and as American privateers grew more daring and lethal, the Caribbean market for the Company's goods also suffered. The entry of France, then Spain, and ultimately the Dutch into the war was even more serious. The antagonism of these powers severely restricted the Company's access to Western European markets; and the ensuing fighting between European and European-backed forces in southern India and in the Indian Ocean necessarily deflected the

Company's resources from commerce into war.[63] Even in 1776, there had been complaints among British traders in Bengal of a 'scarcity of specie', and of silver bullion draining away to China. By the following year, credit was becoming far more difficult to obtain, and Calcutta's trade was worth little more in value than it had been forty years earlier. By 1779, both the volume and the value of textile exports from Bengal were plummeting.[64]

James Crisp's initial response to these successive blows was typically aggressive. He 'extended his trade so much as to ruin himself and others who were concerned with him', recorded George Marsh, with all the censorious satisfaction of a man whose warnings have proved fully justified by events.[65] His bias apart, it is clear that Crisp worked furiously hard in this emergency to put together a syndicate of creditors and associates and a package of loans that might enable him to stay afloat. His partner Henry Lodge was now in a position of some influence, as a member of Dhaka's Provincial Council. Some of Crisp's other known business allies were also selected because they were potentially well placed to assist him. William Cator, for instance, was fluent in Persian, as Crisp was not, worked as assistant to the Collector of Customs at Dhaka, and had family links with one of Calcutta's Agency Houses that lent out money to traders. Crisp is also known to have sought out loans from private individuals. He borrowed over eighteen thousand rupees on bond from Johanna Ross, and refused to return this money after her death. It would have been astonishing had he not also borrowed substantial sums from indigenous merchants and bankers.[66]

But by the end of 1778, Crisp's affairs were becoming desperate. So much so that he began pestering the East India Company for expenses that he claimed were still owing from his time as a salt agent. 'It appears to us very extraordinary,' Warren Hastings wrote icily in response to one such request, 'that Mr. Crisp should have so long neglected to make his demand for the article, if he had a right to it.'[67] This act of self-humiliation, appealing to the

Company that had dismissed him in a fashion that could have little chance of success, bore witness to the level of pressure Crisp was under as his debts mounted, and as one commercial initiative after another foundered. By mid-1779, bitterness, terror and the multiple cases of port wine and Madeira that he kept in the half-empty Dhaka house had 'destroyed his health and spirits'.[68] His wife was not only absent, but actively plotting to ensure that her husband did not receive any money from Milbourne Marsh's will. Even after her father's death, Elizabeth Marsh exhibited no eagerness to return to Dhaka, but lingered for months in the smart house that George Marsh now leased at Blackheath, south of the Thames. So, as her husband sickened and failed, it was their son who was summoned to see to his affairs.

Early in 1778, when not yet sixteen, Burrish Crisp had obtained a Writership in the East India Company, ranking third out of a new intake of twenty-one candidates.[69] His precocity and hard work soon drew him to the attention of Warren Hastings, who was already aware of his linguistic skills, and in June 1779 Burrish was summoned to Fort William in Calcutta. A stable of bright young men were at work there, translating Hindu and Persian legal and administrative texts into English for the sake of the East India Company's future rule, and it seems probable that Hastings intended to recruit Burrish Crisp for this enterprise. As it was, he had to sacrifice this career opportunity, and in August seek permission to leave Calcutta for a post in Dhaka so as to be nearer to his father.[70] It was Burrish who paid the native servants who were the only people available to look after James Crisp 'during his sickness'. And it was Burrish who helped Henry Lodge dispose of what was left after Crisp's death. This probably occurred late in October, or perhaps in the following month, since Lodge was granted the letter of administration for Crisp's estate on 23 December 1779.[71]

The exact date is unknown because all that remained of James Crisp was systematically dispersed and obliterated, including his memory. Since he died intestate, his entire belongings were put up for auction early in March 1780.[72] The house at Dhaka and its furniture were sold. So were its culturally eclectic consumer goods, jelly glasses and bread-and-butter plates on the one hand, and the Crisps' four peacock fans on the other, the latter purchased by an Asian bidder, as were nineteen other lots. James Crisp's silk suits, ruffled shirts and cotton underwear were also knocked down. So were his gold watch and chain, and even his shaving box, complete with razors, hone, soap box and 'some pigtail', which together fetched just seven rupees. As with some of the other articles put up for auction – Burrish's baby clothes, for example, or Elizabeth Marsh's old riding dress and petticoat – the overwhelming impression is of a family eager to make whatever money it could, and also anxious to cast off reminders of the past. The need for money was acute. Paying off the arrears owed to James Crisp's servants in Dhaka, and returning over eighteen thousand rupees in two instalments to Johanna Ross's estate, soaked up all of the proceeds of the auction and more. A final search of the Dhaka house turned up another 720 rupees, which seems to have been all the liquid capital that Crisp possessed at his death. With this, and by dint of leaving his male creditors unpaid, the family was able on paper to balance his final account.[73]

This marked the end of Elizabeth Marsh's marriage in more than a physical sense. Even when she arranged to set out on the *York*, probably still unaware that James Crisp was mortally ill, it does not seem to have been with the intention of returning to live with him in Dhaka. By the time she landed in Madras in June 1780, her former husband had been dead for more than six months, and virtually all the worldly goods of their life together in the subcontinent had been dispersed. To her mind, James Crisp had conspicuously failed in his duties, in a manner that seemed particularly reprehensible given her maritime background. The men of her clan looked after womenfolk in their wills, and were expected to make some reliable provision for them in life. Yet Crisp had died intestate, leaving her penniless for a second time. Once again, their home and their belongings had been lost, right down to her 'cruet stand compleat with silver tops'. Whatever scruples Elizabeth Marsh may have felt about her own diverse lapses from marital duty, this probably wiped them out. If James Crisp's unlucky creditors left any of his papers behind in Dhaka, neither she nor her children seem to have troubled to preserve them. His name would not even appear on Elizabeth Marsh's gravestone. Burrish Crisp could afford – or perhaps chose to afford – only one item at the auction of the family's effects, a silver cup that may have been a christening present. He paid out 172 rupees for his father's funeral, about £17. If James Crisp was buried at Dhaka, and if a monument was ever erected to him there, it no longer exists.[74]

❁

When Elizabeth Marsh and Elizabeth Maria eventually returned to Bengal from Madras, they took refuge in Hooghly, in a small house prepared for them by Burrish. Hooghly was a place of forgetting, a centre of opium production, fortified, waterlogged, and twenty-five miles north-west of Calcutta and relatively inexpensive. The two women 'lived very happily together' there, George Marsh was informed, with Burrish looking after the bills, and paying extended visits whenever he could get away from his Company duties in Dhaka.[75] Yet if the three of them now felt moderately secure, successfully exorcising memories of the missing member of their family quartet, they were still only imperfectly settled. Burrish Crisp's Company earnings, together with what he made by trading on his own behalf, were sufficient for him to support his mother and his sister. As an only recently appointed Writer, and a neophyte trader contending with the commercial repercussions of rampant war, he was in no position to augment Elizabeth Maria's modest inheritance from Milbourne Marsh into the more substantial dowry that ideally she required.

Given the paucity of young single white women in Calcutta, Elizabeth Maria, who was sixteen in 1780, was unlikely to lack for masculine attention. Especially since she had inherited the good looks of both of her parents, as well as her mother's musicality. George Marsh, whose only daughter died of consumption in her teens, and who relieved some of his grief by doting on Elizabeth Maria, memorialized his niece in his Family Book as 'well educated and accomplished [and] very handsome'.[76] She was 'a young lady of the most amiable and accomplished manners', wrote Edmund Burke, the Member of Parliament and political philosopher, when recommending her later to the attention of some aristocratic friends. Elizabeth Maria was already into middle age when the Indo-Persian traveller Abu Talib Khan encountered her in Ireland in 1800. He subsequently paid tribute in print to her 'remarkable . . . mildness of disposition, elegance of manners, skill in music and sweetness of voice'. Behind this graceful, accommodating façade, a mode of self-presentation and self-concealment that was initially dictated by disadvantage and need, there was an 'uncommonly sensible', even forceful temperament.[77] But none of these qualities was sufficient to resolve the dilemma she confronted – and that Elizabeth Marsh confronted on her daughter's behalf – in the immediate aftermath of James Crisp's destruction.

The nature of Elizabeth Maria's dilemma was made clear in issues of *Hicky's Bengal Gazette*, a scabrous weekly newspaper published in Calcutta by a one-time surgeon, James Augustus Hicky. Until Warren Hastings closed it down in 1782, Hicky employed his paper to scarify and expose prominent members of the 'European' community in Bengal. Drawn to devote space to Elizabeth Maria Crisp on account of her looks and her social impact, he relished probing and divulging the nature of her predicament. He published some of the bad, even indelicate verses that were submitted to the paper by her many admirers:

> Come push about the bottle, my bucks let's be brisk,
> Let's toast the fine girls that grace India's soil.
> Here's a health to the matchless, and pretty Miss C---p
> All beauties to her, are no more than a foil.

After all, this was a relatively poor, unprotected young woman, someone who was scarcely in a position to retaliate:

> Dear me, how I long to be married,
> And in my own coach to be carried!

This, Hicky suggested in print, was what Miss Crisp was invariably and privately thinking as she dutifully did the rounds of Calcutta's balls and suppers, chaperoned sometimes by her mother, and sometimes by her brother, but always arriving and leaving in someone else's transport. She evidently needed a husband, and she required money and a secure status even more. But even Hicky took note of Elizabeth Maria's caution as well as her suppressed desperation, of the social distance and conventions she worked hard to preserve: 'Miss C---p,' he reported punningly of her performance at a masquerade in 1782, 'was in a Geor gain [i.e. George-gain] dress called *hoity toity*.'[78]

Elizabeth Maria Crisp's task was to identify and secure an eligible male who would be affluent enough to rescue her from Hooghly, and from the insecurity her mother had experienced, and willing to marry her, a woman from a compromised family with scant financial resources. Moreover, she had to accomplish this under close scrutiny, without compounding her family's already mixed reputation by seeming to behave rashly, and in a place – Calcutta – that for all its size, populousness, occasional architectural grandeur and extensive, unequally distributed wealth, was still very much a frontier town. Female virtue and female safety here, both among those regarding themselves as whites and among non-whites, could be vulnerable to more than usually ruthless pressures.

Obtaining a suitable spouse for her daughter in these circumstances constituted Elizabeth Marsh's penultimate ordeal. This was what progressively obsessed her as deteriorating health, limited funds, widowhood and war constricted her mobility and her options. It seems a trite, irremediably domestic conclusion to a thoroughly original and venturesome odyssey. Yet Marsh's actions and schemes had usually been driven both by the basic imperative to survive, and by a desire to change and enhance her own condition. Getting her remaining unprovided child well settled, which in the case of a daughter could only mean a good marriage, would have seemed a continuation of these ambitions, not a departure from them. The project turned out anyway not to be a purely domestic one at all. Securing a husband for Elizabeth Maria was rather the last discrete episode in Elizabeth Marsh's life in which her personal circumstances and familial ambitions became interlaced with public events, and with an array of conspicuously polyglot actors.

George Shee, the man who ultimately married Elizabeth Maria, was born in Castlebar, County Mayo, in western Ireland in 1754. He was the eldest son of a minor Catholic landowner, and his mother was related to Edmund Burke. It was Burke's influence that obtained Shee a Writership in the East India Company in 1770, initially in Bombay. Burke liked the young man and took the trouble to send him out regular parcels of books from London, and to encourage his political journalism.[79] So when Shee moved to Bengal in September 1776, during the last full year of James Crisp's salt agency, he was already at a different level from the family of his future bride. Of landed background, and a covenanted servant of the East India Company, he was expected to climb rapidly in the service, was 'much liked, and well received in the first houses' in Calcutta, and seems to have had money to spare. 'His present occupations', wrote a friend shortly after Shee's arrival in Bengal, 'are divided between military storekeeping, music, and riding the finest horse in India.' Shee also involved himself in political debate and partisanship. Unapologetically committed to 'the interests of Britain in the East', he liked to believe that he was also concerned about 'the security and happiness of [Britain's] sixteen millions . . . subjects' in Bengal. Any disdain for the Mughal Empire's achievements here and elsewhere in the subcontinent, he would come to argue, was profoundly misplaced:

> This censure . . . I could with ease repel. We [the East India Company] have never succeeded to a Mahometan government in the possession of any territory that we did not find the country populous and rich. We have never acquired territory [in the subcontinent], that the length of our possession has not been marked by the progress of its decline.[80]

The individual in Calcutta to whom George Shee chiefly owed such arguments and perspectives was Philip Francis (1740–1818). The two men were initially attracted to each other by their common Irishness, and soon by a mutual attachment to Edmund Burke. And they shared a taste for politics, albeit with very different levels of expertise, and from very different levels of power. Fourteen years older than Shee, Philip Francis was a Dubliner with experience in diplomacy, government bureaucracy and vituperative journalism. In 1773 he had been appointed to the new five-man Supreme Council in Calcutta, and on his arrival there swiftly became Warren Hastings' fiercest and most dangerous critic within the Company. Francis was intellectually sophisticated, a natural, vivid polemicist, and a politician characterized by an unusual, ultimately self-defeating mix of high ambition and determined radicalism. Over the course of his career he came to support the American Revolution, the abolition of the slave trade, and the French Revolution – and as this suggests, he thought in geographically expansive terms.[81] It was clear to Francis, for instance, that there were significant parallels between some of Britain's troubles in its American colonies, where he himself owned land, and the failures and iniquities of the East India Company's rule on the other side of the world. 'The loss of America', he wrote some weeks after the

Declaration of Independence – and it is suggestive that he anticipated even then that it *was* lost – 'is only the forerunner of the
loss of Bengal.'[82]

A sinuous political shark to George Shee's eager, unaware min-
now, Philip Francis soon came to characterize the younger man as
'part of my family' in Calcutta, enjoyed and fostered his rashness
('you are a violent gentleman'), tossed him useful pieces of Company patronage, and exploited his admiration.[83] It was important,
Francis had written in a private memorandum before embarking
for Bengal:

> to encourage the resort of young people to me, from whom
> I may learn the current opinions with respect to persons
> and things. Their openness will more than make good their
> want of judgement.

In Calcutta, he and Shee collaborated on political schemes and
journalistic enterprises. The two men also seem to have pursued
women and pleasure together: 'You and I', wrote Francis on one
occasion, '. . . are agreed that we are sure of nothing but our sen-
sations.'[84] It was partly because of this intoxicating, unequal friendship with one of the most powerful political actors in Bengal, that
George Shee, prosperous, ambitious, well-connected and highly
eligible, became instead someone whom Elizabeth Marsh could
secure as a son-in-law.

※

About 10.30 p.m. on Tuesday, 8 December 1778, a man called
Meerun saw 'a strange thing', a peculiar ladder propped against
the compound wall of a red house in a fashionable district of
Calcutta. He reported it to the *jemadar*, the establishment's chief
servant. As the two men were studying the bamboo contraption,
which had 'movable steps to it inside', they noticed a tall figure
dressed in black slipping out of the house. The *jemadar* recognized

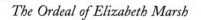

Philip Francis. Etching by James Sayers, 1788.

278

him 'by his figure, his face, and his colour' as 'Mr Francis the Counsellor', a friend of his own employer George Grand, who was a Franco-Swiss servant of the East India Company. The *jemadar* also knew that Grand was away from the red house at his club, and that his sixteen-year-old wife, Catherine, had been left alone in her apartments. 'Give me that thing,' Meerun remembered Francis saying in Hindustani as the two Indians seized hold of the ladder; 'I will give you money. I'll make you great men.'[85]

Instead, they hustled him into the house, 'in the part that leads to the upper part; there is a lanthern there and a staircase'. Francis continued to press coins on the two men, and even in the semi-darkness they knew from the 'light sound' that these were gold *mohurs*, not rupees. They forced him into a chair, and the *jemadar* put his 'hands on the arms of the chair to keep him there'. When Catherine Grand came downstairs and ordered the servants to set Francis free, the *jemadar* refused: 'I will not hear you,' he told her. 'You may go to your room.' Meerun was dispatched to fetch George Grand. While he was away, two Europeans broke down one of the doors to the house. One of them was George Shee. He threw the *jemadar* to the ground, but was promptly wrestled to the floor himself by another Indian servant. In the confusion, Philip Francis escaped, but Shee was seized and tied to a chair. They would not let him go until George Grand returned and saw it all.

These events in Calcutta became for several months, as Philip Francis subsequently complained, 'the clamours of this cursed place'.[86] As far as Elizabeth Marsh and her daughter are concerned, what happened on the night of 8 December 1778 helps to explain why the business of finding a husband in this city could seem to them a more than usually delicate and perilous business; why Elizabeth Maria Crisp, as an unmarried, troubled young woman venturing into what passed for Calcutta's European high society, felt obliged to be watchful and to practise the arts of 'hoity toity'. In the legal action that George Grand subsequently brought in

Calcutta's Supreme Court, both indigenous and European witnesses were agreed that Philip Francis had long been attracted by,
and had paid conspicuous attention to, Catherine Grand. But no
conclusive evidence was produced that she herself had known of,
'or previously consented to', Francis's illicit evening visit, 'for any
purpose, much less for the purpose of adultery'. Her lack of proven
complicity made no difference. George Grand immediately repudi-
ated his wife.[87]

There were significant respects in which Catherine Grand's
position in 1778 resembled that of Elizabeth Maria Crisp at the
time of her entry into Calcutta society two years later. Both
women were very young and very attractive. Both had suffered multiple physical and cultural uprootings, since Catherine Grand was
born of French parents in a Danish settlement in southern India
(Tranquebar), and had been transplanted to British-dominated
Calcutta on her marriage to the Franco-Swiss George Grand. And
both women were potentially vulnerable: Elizabeth Maria because
she was without a father, had little money, and came from a
substantially ruined and disordered family; and Catherine Grand
because – at a time when Britain and France were at war across
continents – she was a French Catholic living in British-dominated
space, and married to an older, seemingly unstable and violent
man.[88] The predatory behaviour of Philip Francis, and the in-
temperateness of George Grand's subsequent response, which left
his wife with her 'character entirely destroyed', and with little
choice but to agree subsequently to become Francis's mistress,
indicate how perilous Calcutta might be for the weak and the
inadequately guarded – even if they were viewed and viewed themselves as European, and even in higher-ranking households. They
also suggest how much, at this time, Calcutta was still a frontier
town.[89]

This point is underlined by the contrast between the manner in
which Philip Francis felt he could behave in Calcutta, and how
he normally presented himself in London. Like most political

revolutionaries in the former American colonies, and like most future French revolutionaries, Francis, in both his British and his Indian politics, combined an abstract commitment to extensive liberty and radical change, with a belief that women were necessarily a special case. A student of Montesquieu and Rousseau, he took it for granted that free, well-governed societies 'required of women a particular gravity'. 'If the time should ever come when there shall be no prostitutes in London streets,' Francis subsequently wrote in a set of observations intended for his son, 'depend upon it, it will be a sign of a general corruption of woman, and a prelude to the decay of the empire.' Prostitutes, in his view, were the necessary sewers that enabled decent women to remain clean and virtuous: 'we sacrifice a part to save the rest'. And safeguarding virtue among decent females was an essential public and political good – at least in certain favoured locations – since 'where there is no female virtue, there will soon be no male virtue left'.[90]

Accordingly, Francis had been careful before leaving London in 1774 to instruct his wife on her own conduct and on the proper upbringing of their daughters, stipulating what books they should read, what plays they might appropriately see, and how few people ideally they should mix with: 'Let the girls be taught a grave, modest, reserved carriage,' he insisted. 'I dislike hoydens.' Once en route for Bengal, however, he allowed himself to write to a male friend of his craving for 'the command of half the beauty' in the ship, champing against the 'state of privation in one of the most essential articles of life'.[91] This hungry, sexual aggressiveness, which was more than hypocrisy, and was linked both to his polemical style and to his political beliefs, was given much freer vent when he arrived in Calcutta, not just at the expense of some native women, but – as on his voyage out – in regard to some Europeans. Catherine Grand was the formerly respectable, too-young wife of a fellow East India Company official. It did not stop him.

Those who were chiefly responsible for stopping Philip Francis's initial pursuit of Catherine Grand, and for catching out George

Shee in the process, so that he was driven temporarily out of polite Calcutta society, and thus became available for Elizabeth Marsh's daughter, were labouring Indians. It was some of George Grand's house servants, men whom he referred to approvingly as Rajputs (a traditionally warrior grouping), who made sure that Shee was 'seized and thrown down' when he tried to free his friend and patron. Immediately after, Shee left Calcutta abruptly on Francis's instructions in an attempt to avoid having to give evidence in the Supreme Court; and it was 'one of the peons in the service of the Sheriff of Calcutta' who helped to track him down and bring him back. 'Shaike Doornah', as he appears in the East India Company's records, along with other officials, eventually discovered the Irishman hiding in a house at Chandernagore.[92] Shee had adopted this desperate strategy because what had begun as an undignified sexual escapade was evolving into a serious political scandal. Warren Hastings made sure that Philip Francis's embarrassing conduct was regularly discussed in Calcutta's Supreme Council, and that the Company's directors in London were kept well informed of the progress of the affair. When the trial opened in Calcutta's Supreme Court on 8 February 1779, a succession of Grand's native servants gave their names, and told their stories of the night of 8 December, among them Meerun, who was a *kitmutgar* or table servant, the *jemadar*, who was literate and, unlike the rest, could sign his testimony, and Catherine Grand's mixed-race maid, Anne Lagoorda.[93]

The reverberations of these Indian acts and testimonies in Calcutta in late 1778 and early 1779 affected many more people than just Elizabeth Marsh, a fading widow in Hooghly burdened with an unmarried daughter. On 5 March 1779, the Supreme Court found Philip Francis guilty of 'criminal conversation' with another man's wife, and fined him fifty thousand rupees (about £5000). The episode undermined his political standing in Calcutta, and further embittered his relations with Warren Hastings, and in December 1780 he returned to Britain. A disgraced Catherine

Grand had already left Bengal for France, where she eventually became the wife of Charles Maurice de Talleyrand, Napoleon's Minister of Foreign Affairs, while George Grand ended his career working for the Dutch at the Cape of Good Hope.[94] But as far as Elizabeth Marsh and her daughter were concerned, it was the scandal's impact on George Shee that mattered most, and that changed everything. Forcibly brought back to Calcutta, and with his conduct already outlined and denounced by a succession of Indian witnesses, Shee was obliged to testify to the city's Supreme Court. He confessed that Philip Francis had told him in advance of his plan of 'going to Mr. Grand's house'. He admitted to receiving and looking after the black clothes that Francis had worn for camouflage on the night of 8 December 1778. He even described to the court how his powerful friend had told him 'he would take it as a particular favour if I would get a ladder made for him'. A 'black carpenter' had duly built the contraption – Meerun's 'strange thing' – in the compound of George Shee's house. As a Company servant who knew him subsequently recorded: 'Mr. Shee . . . cut an awkward figure, the Chief Justice observing that his behaviour had been reprehensible as it was derogatory to the character of a gentleman.'[95]

As a result, George Shee too was forced into retreat and into motion. As some recompense for favours owed, Philip Francis secured him the post of Resident and Collector of Revenues at Ferruckabad (Farrukhabad), 'a city on the western bank of the Ganges, not very far south of Delhi'. The position enabled Shee to make a considerable sum of money from his salary and from trade, but it took him for a while out of Calcutta's more fashionable circles and its partisan Company politics. 'This,' as Francis advised him, 'is the time for you to be humble.'[96] Shee does not seem to have returned to Calcutta until early in 1782, and almost immediately *Hicky's Bengal Gazette* began reporting his pursuit of Elizabeth Marsh's daughter:

In [Elizabeth] Maria's praise what a song could I write,
Would the muses but lend me their aid;
For in Maria's form all the graces unite,
And every perfection displayed.
In her bosom fair virtue, and sweetness of soul,
Wit, judgement, and modesty shine;
No vanity vexes, no passions control.
But all is serene and divine.[97]

Elizabeth Marsh seems to have owed the beginnings of her and her daughter's acquaintance with Shee in part, like so much else, to one of her relations. By now her younger brother John Marsh had moved to a new government post in Cork, a major port in the south-west of Ireland, where he oversaw the transport of victuals and supplies to British and allied troops in North America and the Caribbean. For all that he was a cog in the war against America, John Marsh's utter efficiency and conspicuous lack of corruption in this post brought him to the notice, and swiftly into the favour, of Edmund Burke, who had political interests and close family associations in Cork – and who was a kinsman and still devoted patron of George Shee.[98] So it was natural that, when a badly compromised and subdued Shee finally drifted back to Calcutta, he should have gravitated towards the company of Elizabeth Marsh and her daughter, people who were also damaged in their own way, and who were glad and willing to receive him. But it still took the two women over a year to secure him. 'Were I to deny that the superior and most uncommon merit of Miss Crisp has made a strong and lasting impression upon me,' Shee admitted in March 1783, 'the whole tenor of my conduct towards her would flatly contradict my words.' But he had been held back by concern about 'the contracted scale of my fortune, and uncertain state of my prospects'.[99] He might have added, but did not, that Elizabeth Maria's own very limited fortune and prospects were also a drawback.

'You will then ask,' he wrote to Elizabeth Marsh in a long,

indiscreet letter outlining the evolution of his sentiments, 'why this consideration did not at an earlier period influence my conduct.' With a wholly characteristic blend of naïveté and ruthlessness, and a genuflection to 'the unreserved candour you permit me to use', Shee admitted that initially, and 'for some time', his attentions to Elizabeth Maria had been 'without meaning'. But now, 'Should fortune befriend me, there is no farther gift I should so anxiously desire of her as a certainty or essential proof that I possessed the good opinion of your daughter.' Should she, Elizabeth Marsh, 'think my presence at Hooghly likely to cause a continuance of that anxiety you have felt', however, he would desist and retire. So she was obliged to be patient and play him, while Elizabeth Maria Crisp had to ensure that 'the difficulty' that George Shee 'found in restraining my inclination' did not entrap her, that she did not suffer the sort of ruin (temporarily) experienced in Calcutta by Catherine Grand. On 2 August 1783, the two women achieved their aim. In a private ceremony in the house at Hooghly, George Shee married Elizabeth Maria and became Elizabeth Marsh's son-in-law.[100]

It was a substantially compromised achievement, and an act of some desperation. Just as Burrish Crisp had been dispatched to Persia as a ten-year-old boy, so now Elizabeth Marsh married off her still under-age daughter to a man of questionable reputation, out of economic need and ambition. Yet, to those who were his friends, George Shee could still seem 'possessed of . . . great activity of mind and highly prepossessing manners', full of 'uprightness and integrity' even; and at this stage he was a driven man capable of political idealism.[101] After marrying Elizabeth Maria and taking up a Company judicial post in Dhaka, he busied himself collecting information about Warren Hastings' administration in Bengal, determined to visit upon him some of the scandal and ruin he himself had experienced. Shee would dispatch this intelligence sometimes directly to Philip Francis in London, sometimes to Edmund Burke, and sometimes to his own uncle, John Bourke, a City merchant who acted as link-man between these two politicians. Shee thus became a minor player in the subsequent campaign against, and Parliamentary impeachment of, Warren Hastings, the most sustained public inquisition up to this point into the East India Company's conduct in the subcontinent, and – in Edmund Burke's mind – a much broader assault on some of the practices and assumptions of empire, and on what he styled 'geographical morality'. General Richard Smith, another of Elizabeth Marsh's kinsmen, also took part in the prosecution of Hastings, and so, in a secretarial and advisory capacity, did the newly married Elizabeth Maria Shee. 'You draw pictures to admiration,' wrote Philip Francis to George Shee at the close of 1786, having received from him yet another packet of Bengal information:

> As long as the scenes shift, pray let your pencil be employed
> . . . Observe you are never to show this letter to anybody
> but Mrs. Shee, on whose friendship and discretion I place
> a particular dependence. The prosecution of your friend Mr.
> Hastings will be revived with a renewal of vigour as soon as
> Parliament meets.[102]

How much Elizabeth Marsh was aware of her new son-in-law's political ventures, or cared about them, is unknown. She would have known and cared that, by his own estimate, before marrying, George Shee was making 'a *certain* income of between two and three thousand pounds a year', mainly by means of trade in saltpetre and opium in the subcontinent and with China.[103] The former Elizabeth Maria Crisp was thus more than amply provided for; and since Shee was a covenanted Company servant, not a private merchant acutely at the mercy of external events, his new wife was assured of a measure of both status and security. So, if this matrimonial outcome was flawed, it was also far more than Elizabeth Marsh could have dared to hope for. War in sectors of the

Americas, Asia, Africa and Europe, and some of the issues bound up in it, had combined to alter and divide members of her own birth family, and to destroy her husband, James Crisp. She had been first imperilled, and then widowed and reduced to want; and she had been obliged to have recourse again to her own inventiveness and ruthlessness, to her extended family, and to transoceanic journeying. But now, as a result of a scandal involving both miscellaneous Asians and miscellaneous Europeans, her remaining dependent child was safely married to a rich man, in a ceremony attended by John Shore, Elizabeth Marsh's former fellow passenger on the *Goodwill*, and a future Governor General of India. Surely a happy ending was finally in prospect.

Ending – and Continuing

ACCORDING TO GEORGE MARSH, it was only a short period after her daughter's marriage in August 1783 when Elizabeth Marsh first noticed 'a violent cancer' developing in one of her breasts. He set down this piece of information in old age, when the passage of time had probably become telescoped in his memory, but it does seem that Elizabeth became ill in 1784, and that she concealed her ailment and tolerated the pain for several months. Burrish Crisp would later try to sanitize this phase of his mother's life, and soften his own memories of it, by characterizing her as 'the patient martyr of a cruel and unrelenting malady'. In reality, she was probably not patient in the face of her cancer at all: merely in terror of the only available alternative to passive endurance and pretence. By early 1785, though, she had summoned up 'resolution enough' to take action. She waited until a day when both her son and her daughter were away out of town, and then she called in the surgeon.[1]

It was still common for incomers to the Indian subcontinent from Europe, women as well as men, to resort to indigenous physicians, particularly in the smaller settlements.[2] But Elizabeth Marsh seems to have had her mastectomy in Calcutta, where Burrish had a house; and thanks to him and her son-in-law, George Shee, she was now affluent enough to afford a European doctor. The ritual of a Western-style mastectomy without anaesthetic was designed to preserve some decorum amidst surgery that was at once drastic and almost unavoidably possessed of sexual overtones. The patient would usually remain fully clothed, except for her exposed breast. She might be tied or belted to a chair. Her arm would be held up throughout in order for the pectoralis major muscle to lift the offending breast. Servants, or the physician's assistants, would also endeavour to keep her neck and shoulders pressed as firmly as possible to the back of the chair or the mattress of a bed. The surgeon meanwhile would straddle the patient's knees, and set to work:

> I began a scream that lasted intermittently during the whole time of the incision ... When the wound was made, and the instrument was withdrawn, the pain seemed undiminished, for the air that suddenly rushed into those delicate parts felt like a mass of minute but sharp and forked poniards, that were tearing the edges of the wound – but when again I felt the instrument – describing a curve – cutting against the grain, if I may so say, while the flesh resisted in a manner so forcible as to oppose and tire the hand of the operator, who was forced to change from the right to the left – then, indeed, I thought I must have expired. I attempted no more to open my Eyes, – they felt as if hermetically shut, and so firmly closed, that the Eyelids seemed indented into the Cheeks. The instrument this second time withdrawn, I concluded the operation was over, – Oh, no! presently the terrible cutting was renewed – and worse than ever, to separate the bottom, the foundation of this dreadful gland from the parts to which it adhered ... yet again all was not over ... I then felt the Knife rackling against the breast bone – scraping it!³

Fanny Burney's famous account of *her* mastectomy in 1811, which lasted twenty minutes from the first incision to the dressing of the wound, is an exceptional testimony, and not just because of its gruesome detail and literary power. Women who underwent this operation during the eighteenth and early nineteenth centuries rarely survived long enough, or were left in any condition, to write about their experience. Some succumbed immediately to the pain and shock. Far more died of infection, even though surgeons might cauterize the wound with a red-hot iron. But, as may have been true in Elizabeth Marsh's case, what most caused these operations for breast cancer to fail was that, for obvious reasons, women tended to put them off for too long. As a result, the cancer often spread to the lymph nodes, far beyond the reach of even the most heroic surgery at this time.

Elizabeth Marsh survived the ordeal of her operation. 'In it, she suffered excruciating pain', confirmed George Marsh unnecessarily, which she endured – her children were later informed – 'with heroic constancy'. After it was finished, the surgeon, whoever he was, took out his medical scales and established that the excised tumour with its attaching breast tissue 'weighed upwards of five pounds'. It is a measure of her physical toughness that, despite the encroaching heat of a Calcutta spring, Elizabeth lived for 'a few months' after this.[4] It was probably also a measure of her powerful will to keep going. She was only forty-nine, and she had recently acquired an additional stake in the future. In July 1784, her daughter had given birth to a son, who was named George Shee after his father. So, as grandmother to 'one of the finest urchins you ever saw', Elizabeth Marsh had good reason to live, and she managed to do so until 30 April 1785.[5]

No account exists of her death, or of who was with her at the end. The day after, they buried her in what later became known as South Park Street cemetery, a forested area about a mile south from the old town of Calcutta. It seems to have been her son Burrish Crisp who composed her epitaph. He described her as 'the best of mothers', and recorded her steadfastness in the face of 'one of the severest chirurgical operations'. But he made no mention of Elizabeth Marsh's travels or writings. Nor did he refer in her regard to any single place, or nation, or religion, or to James Crisp. This only partially appropriate memorial scarcely signified. Like most modest tombs erected in South Park Street cemetery – as distinct from the elaborate monuments of the rich and the powerful – the gravestone of Elizabeth Marsh has long since disappeared.[6]

✿

Resurrecting this obliterated life has been absorbing. It has also been challenging. More even than is true of the generality of biographical subjects, there is no possible owning of all the facts of Elizabeth Marsh's existence. Some of her life-parts, like her bones, like her image, are gone forever. How then should she be seen? And what came after?

It was more than ten years after her death that George Marsh began compiling his Family Book, a random assemblage of anecdotes, observations and stories about himself and his relations. He was in no doubt that he and they had lived through a world of change and a world still in change, and he experimented with various devices in order to represent the scale of these changes on paper. Understandably, given its significance for connecting different portions of the globe, and his own involvement with it, the first index of transformation he seized on was the rapid growth of the Royal Navy. The vellum-covered Family Book opens with a page of statistics. In 1741, George noted, there had been 740 admirals, captains, masters and commanders, and lieutenants serving in the navy. By July 1756, the month in which Elizabeth Marsh set out from Gibraltar on the *Ann*, the number of naval officers had already risen to 929. By 1790, he calculated, there were close to three thousand.

He also summoned up the more violently interconnected world that he and – far more directly – his niece had inhabited, by describing in the Family Book a succession of objects and artifacts. Some of these were items that he kept near him, on shelves in his house and office. There was the '£70 worth of Dresden china' he had bribed the customs officers to ignore on his return to England from Hamburg in 1776. There was the 'silver hammered punch bowl made by an Indian' he kept in his study, that had originally been given to Milbourne Warren by the crew of the *Norfolk* after his goods were swept overboard on the voyage back to Madras from Manila in 1764. Then there was Nicholas Owen's manuscript account of slave trading in West Africa, which George Marsh had acquired during his time at the Navy Board. And in addition to these items, that he could see and touch, there were others he had only heard of from others, or that were lost. He recorded Elizabeth Marsh's description of the bracelets 'which were of silver and more like horse shoes than anything else' that Sidi Muhammad's women offered her in Marrakech. He recalled the 'vast and continued expense' of an Arab stallion, which had been dispatched as a present from Cairo to a Marsh relation in Menorca, but had somehow ended up with him in London. He remembered the plans and provisions that he himself had prepared in readiness for John Byron's voyage to the Pacific in 1764 and, less happily, the plats of East Florida land that had tempted him into investing (and losing) £1000 in the colony.[7]

Continental Europe, the Indian subcontinent and South-East Asia, Western and Northern Africa, the Mediterranean, the Pacific, North America: locations in all of these were caught up in the texture of George Marsh's memories. In the early eighteenth century, his parents too had carefully preserved significant emblems of family history: their print of the Marquess of Montrose, for instance, and the Bible that Francis Marsh had clung to when he was shipwrecked off the coast of the Isle of Wight. But their horizons, like the objects they cherished, had remained bounded by the island of Great Britain and its adjacent seas. For all that he had hardly ever travelled, George Marsh's horizons by contrast incorporated by the 1790s every continent of the globe.

Elizabeth Marsh, who was in motion for most of her life, was shaped and ravaged far more intimately by contact with different continents and oceans. Although she was unlike her uncle in temperament, as in her travels, she cannot be understood in isolation from him, which is why their stories have intertwined so frequently in this book. Both of them lacked formal education. Yet both compiled narratives as a way of trying to understand the shocks and transitions through which they were living, and to help them work out who they were becoming in the face of them. Niece and uncle possessed something else in common. George Marsh was able to encompass large stretches of the world in his imagination and possessions, thanks to his close association with an aggressively expansionist British state. The same was true of Elizabeth Marsh, though it was not the whole truth.

Without Britain's empire, maritime reach, and slave trade, she would never have been conceived. And without the resources of the British imperial state to which her uncle and other male relations afforded her repeated access – its warships and naval bases, its consuls and ports, its expanding colonial territories, and the East India Company – her career would never have unfolded as it did. Empire continued to preoccupy many members of her family after her death. Some of them, her surviving brother John Marsh for instance, participated in its business only on paper. In recognition of his work in Spain and Ireland during the American War, he was appointed to the five-man commission set up in London in 1783 to investigate the claims of loyalist refugees from the former colonies. Over the next seven years, John Marsh interviewed almost three thousand white and black American loyalists, familiarizing himself in extraordinary detail with the lives of some of empire's losers. 'It was a rule with him, on enquiries of this kind,' he later remarked, 'to make himself master of every thing relative to the main subject.' So conscientious was he that, at the end of this commission, John Marsh was promptly switched to another. He was ordered to inquire into the losses of those Britons who had been evacuated in 1787 from the Mosquito Shore, a four-hundred-mile stretch of land from Cape Gracias a Dios in the north to the San Juan River in what is now Costa Rica, that had been 'transferred' to Spain.[8]

Other Marsh family members became directly involved in Britain's imperial diaspora. This was true of several of George Marsh's grandsons. One of them, another George Marsh (1790–1868), emigrated to the Cape of Good Hope, where he lent his surname to a street in Mossel Bay, married a Dutch woman, and seems to have given refuge to a black American sailor called John Washington, who had been discharged from his ship and wanted to settle in his ancestral continent.[9] It was an illegitimate grandson, 'a very bad youth', though, who travelled farthest. The Marsh family got rid of him by securing him a place as a seaman on the First Fleet that set out from Portsmouth for New South Wales in May 1787, with 750 convicts. So it was that a member of their clan, albeit an unwanted one, reached Australia. Making landfall there was only the beginning of this young man's journeying. In August 1788 his ship, the *Scarborough*, set out from Port Jackson (the site of what is now Sydney) for China, and he sailed with it. He made 'several other voyages without the least amendment', recorded George Marsh dolefully in the Family Book, and at 'last entered for a soldier in the East India Company's service'. Before disappearing in the Indian subcontinent, this unwelcome, unauthorized grandson changed his name from Marsh to George Smith.[10] It illustrates the point that 'George Smith' – the name, apparently, of Elizabeth Marsh's escort during her Asiatic progress – was not simply common. It was also commonly employed as a pseudonym.

Elizabeth's daughter, Elizabeth Maria, and her husband George Shee secured the most conspicuous advantages from servicing state and empire. Along with their young son, they left Bengal for Britain in 1788, which was when Elizabeth Maria passed on to John Marsh some of her mother's manuscripts, a draft in another's hand of her Moroccan experiences, and her Indian journal.[11] Shee was now rich, and he acted the part of returning nabob with conviction. He secured a baronetcy in 1794, spent over £1300 on a rotten Irish borough in 1797, and supported the Act of Union between Ireland and Great Britain in 1800, which he viewed as

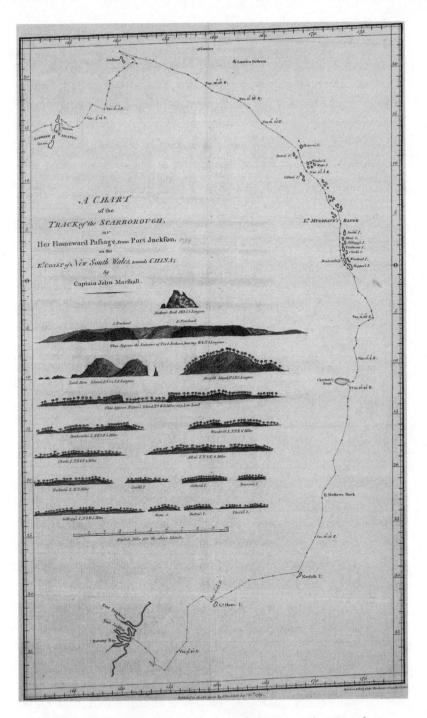

'A chart of the track of the *Scarborough*, on her homeward passage, from Port Jackson, on the E. Coast of New South Wales, towards China', by Captain John Marshall. Engraving, 1789.

'advantageous ... to the empire at large'. Shee seems to have believed ('I never was more certain of any truth in my life') that union would benefit Ireland and his fellow Catholics: but his enthusiastic advocacy of the measure also benefited him. He received £8000 of secret-service money for his pains, plus a succession of minor government posts, including the Under Secretaryship for War and the Colonies in 1806.[12]

As a result, Elizabeth Marsh's daughter acquired a lifestyle that her mother, for all the ambitions she entertained for her, can never have envisaged. There was a house in Galway, Ireland, and a much bigger house, Lockleys, in Hertfordshire in England. It boasted a 'handsome principal stair-case ... a library 20 feet by 16, and a dining parlour 24 feet by 16 wainscotted'. There were eight bed-rooms (and four more dormitories for the servants), a schoolroom and nursery for the children, a double coach-house, a gravelled terrace and a pleasure garden.[13] When the Shees tore themselves away from this residence, they could take refuge in yet another house in London, which held many of their prints and paintings, as well as Elizabeth Maria's range of musical instruments. Their eldest son, George Shee junior, went to St John's College, Cambridge. One of the closest friends he made there was Henry John Temple, Viscount Palmerston, the future British Prime Minister. This second George Shee, great-grandson of Milbourne Marsh, a shipwright, would become – in part through Palmerston's patronage – a Member of Parliament, a career diplomat, an art collector and a hopeless rake.[14]

※

Elizabeth Marsh's own story however is more than an imperial one. Britain's empire provided for her birth and for much of her mobility, to be sure, but it made up only a sub-set of the geographical range of her experience and influences. Nor were the multifarious changes and cultural shifts that this woman lived through an outcrop only of an 'omnipotent West as the main locus of historical initiative'.[15] From the outset, people who were not European determined key stages of her life. It was fear of African slaves on the run from sugar plantations that worked to persuade her parents to leave Jamaica, thus ensuring that she was born in Portsmouth, England. Had the family remained in the Caribbean, it is unlikely that Elizabeth Marsh would have grown up with the physical hardiness she was able to draw on so often. She might not have grown up at all.

Nor was the impact on her of peoples and societies beyond Europe only serendipitous. By ordering his corsair ships to seize British vessels in 1756, Sidi Muhammad set in motion a sequence of events that ended Elizabeth Marsh's first engagement, and drove her into a different marriage and a different future. The significance of this remarkable ruler for the story of this book, however, is far more extensive than this. Sidi Muhammad's reign in Morocco illustrates how in this period – the middle decades of the eighteenth century – the work of forging economic and cultural connections across very long distances was not only carried out by Western powers. Nor was it carried out just in the West's image. The Sultan's world-view was pan-Islamic and broadly African, though it also made room for exchanges of goods, services and knowledge between Morocco and sites in Western and Eastern Europe, and ultimately in the United States. Settling in Bengal in 1774 allowed Elizabeth Marsh and James Crisp contact with a still more signifi-cant extra-European centre of enterprise. For a time, and in dif-ferent ways – he through trade, and she by drawing on his earnings to travel – husband and wife both profited from Dhaka's textile manufacturing, and from the global extent of its markets.

In retrospect, it is possible to view Elizabeth Marsh's life as poised on a cusp between phases in world history. On the one hand, she was involved in some of the key developments that are traditionally viewed as bringing into being, for a while, a more Western-dominated world: the rise of British naval power, the territorial transformations of the Seven Years War, the American

Revolution and the making of the United States, and the more concerted European invasion of the Pacific after 1750. On the other hand, her story also makes clear some of the limitations on Western power during her lifetime, and the continuing creativity of non-Western centres of initiative, innovation and communication.

By 1800, many of these non-Western dynamic centres were fading. Even before Sidi Muhammad's death in 1790, European trading houses and diplomats had begun to subvert his campaign to exert decisive control over Morocco's overseas trade. Dhaka's weavers and Bengal's cotton trade, too, were in the doldrums by the end of the century (though how much is still in dispute).[16] Bengal's textiles were under pressure both from Britain's own mechanizing cotton industry, and from the scale of exterminatory warfare between imperial Britain and Napoleon's French empire, which badly disrupted overseas markets. There were many other casualties. In the 1750s and '60s, James Crisp had been able to work profitably with Sephardic Jewish merchants and bankers, taking advantage of their business and family networks that spanned parts of Asia, North Africa, the Caribbean and European free ports such as Livorno and Hamburg. But the Sephardim, who had flourished during the seventeenth and early eighteenth centuries because of their capacity and willingness to bridge different societies and cultures, were also in evident commercial decline by 1800. With a few conspicuous exceptions, their role as intermediaries was no longer so valued – or so possible – in a world characterized by more bureaucratic, and more aggressive, imperial and nation states.[17]

One of the underlying themes in this book, indeed (and this would scarcely have surprised Adam Smith), has been the uncomfortable relationship that could exist between imperial ambitions on the one hand, and transcontinental commercial enterprise on the other. Empire is about exercising and extending power across oceanic and territorial space. So it is hardly surprising that the British Empire has been credited (not without some justice) with fostering worldwide economic connections and proto-globalization.[18] Yet, in practice, and as the dual stages of James Crisp's commercial ruin illustrate, the disruptions and wars that accompanied empire could also sabotage international trade, even for the British themselves. Empire, both the British and the Spanish varieties, gave to James Crisp. It afforded him access to Caribbean products and ultimately African slaves. It gave him markets for his salted fish, a brief prospect of an estate in East Florida, and for a while profitable access to Bengal's textiles. But empire, and the changes it imposed on the world, also took away. Crisp's bankruptcy in 1767 was due in part to the economic dislocations caused by the Seven Years War, and to a more aggressively imperial British state's determination to clamp down on the Isle of Man's flexible and extensive trade. The disruptions caused by another imperial war after 1775, along with the East India Company's determination to safeguard its monopolies, helped to kill him.

This, too, has been a recurrent theme of this book: the enhanced opportunities that increasing connections and exchanges between continents and distant societies made available to some individuals, but also the terrible risks. In 1824, William Marsh, George Marsh's eldest son, was ruined along with his banking house, Marsh, Stacey, Fauntleroy & Graham of Berners Street, London. The collapse was partly the result of acts of forgery by one of William Marsh's partners. It was made worse, however, by the strains caused to the British banking system at this time by a rash of loans to the newly independent Latin American states that were emerging from the ruins of the Spanish Empire. As William wrote, his father had made a fortune: he had lost it. George Marsh had risen from mariner to riches through servicing for over sixty years the world's most powerful navy. William Marsh came to grief through dealing in the world's biggest and most outward-looking capital market.[19]

As the novelist John Galsworthy recognized, tracing the fortunes of a family's multiple members over time can be a good way of compressing and rendering history.[20] This micro strategy – using the perspectives on the past afforded by a family – becomes paradoxically more, and not less, valuable when dealing with historical developments that extend over vast territorial and oceanic spaces. Some of the changes in which Elizabeth Marsh was involved were so large, so momentous and far-reaching, that they can seem hard to grasp except in anonymous and abstract terms. Yet adopting a purely abstract approach to changes and influences that transcend continents means that we understand them only imperfectly. There can and should be no Olympian version of world history, and there is always a human and individual dimension. In this book I have been concerned to examine how a momentous and disruptive period of global history was experienced by one extended family. I have sought to reveal the many and diverse connections that existed between 'impersonal and remote transformations' on the one hand and, on the other, 'the most intimate features of the human self'.[21]

This has also been the story of a woman who was more, of course, than the puppet of impersonal forces. For all of her ordeals, Elizabeth Marsh cannot plausibly be viewed as a victim. She was often endangered and challenged by external events, but she also made a succession of choices that took her across boundaries, and into danger. And although her existence was sometimes harsh, and she knew terror and persistent insecurity, she also knew discovery and exhilaration: 'the life was new and by no means unpleasant'. It was an infinitely more diverse life than would have been her lot had she stayed in England; and hers was a more privileged existence than that enjoyed by those slaves whom she and James Crisp owned at intervals, or by the slaves she might have joined inside Sidi Muhammad's palace.

I have sought to extract Elizabeth Marsh's mixed qualities, which reflect her fractured origins and life, from her extraordinary actions and from her writings. She was highly courageous and enterprising, and often ignorant; intensely curious, shrewd and enquiring, and simultaneously prejudiced; socially insecure and avid for approval, but willing to disregard the bonds of polite womanhood when it suited her; devoted to the interests of her birth family and off-spring, and sporadically eager to get away from them; at once selfish and ruthless, and possessed always of a capacity to pick herself up in the wake of crisis and disaster, and to try something new. There remain two significant gaps in our knowledge about her private world. One is the birth identity of her mother, and the other is the quality of her own marriage. Her growing alienation from James Crisp can be charted and speculated about, but it cannot be fully explained. Nor is it knowable whether she absented herself from him so often in part as a rudimentary but very effective means of birth control. Their two children represented a very small family by eighteenth-century standards.

The powerful influence that this 'very engaging woman with great abilities' exercised over others, however, *is* clear. Her encounters with Sidi Muhammad (for all her literary embellishments) suggest this, and so do her dealings with various Royal Navy admirals and captains. The force of her personality and her capacity to inspire attachment are also evident in the behaviour of her male relations. Elizabeth Marsh was always economically dependent: but far from confining her, her male kin frequently went out of their way to assist her enterprises. George Marsh disapproved of her, but gave her money and access to ships. John Marsh ensured the survival of some of her writings, while possibly also censoring them. General Richard Smith used his influence to ease her Asiatic progress. So, even to the extent of defying military orders, did Captain George Smith. Milbourne Marsh aided his daughter repeatedly, and even compromised his career for her, just as James Crisp compromised his mercantile prospects by renewing his proposal to Elizabeth in December 1756.

There was another man who was devoted to Elizabeth Marsh

and who was profoundly damaged on her account, and that was her son Burrish Crisp, who purchased the burial site adjacent to hers. In 1779, he had been obliged to give up the chance of working in Warren Hastings' powerful orbit, so as to return to Dhaka and look after his dying father in the absence of his mother. A comparable chance for his marked linguistic skills to win recognition from the Company's hierarchy never came again. Burrish Crisp became a founding member of the Asiatic Society, the leading European intellectual club in Calcutta, and he produced learned translations of some important texts; but he remained for the rest of his life a merchant, and a minor judicial official in Dhaka.[22] He also fathered two children, a boy and a girl, on an Indian companion of whom we know nothing.

To end Elizabeth Marsh's story with this lost woman seems appropriate, because her own life had begun with another ghost in the family tree. Her mother Elizabeth Bouchier (or Boucher, or Bourchier) may have been African in ancestry, or as conventionally English as her daughter chose on occasions to proclaim herself to be. Burrish Crisp's Indian companion is an even more elusive character, because in her case we do not even know her name. As was often the case in relationships of this sort, Burrish made no mention of the mother of his son when he had him baptized in Calcutta in 1794, and named John Henry Crisp.[23] This other, half-Indian, grandson of Elizabeth Marsh grew up very differently from the younger George Shee. Although Eurasians were officially excluded after 1791 from positions in the East India Company's service, John Henry Crisp went on to become a Captain in the Madras army. Like his father (and perhaps his Indian mother), he was naturally studious and highly intelligent, 'particularly assiduous in the study of the Hindoostanee language' and 'distinguished . . . by his scientific acquirements'. It was this scientific ability that led him to be put in charge of a special mission to Sumatra in 1822. Combining Western and Indian astronomical techniques that he had acquired at the Madras Observatory, John Henry Crisp carried out eight hundred experiments on Sumatra, and subsequently published a dense treatise on determining 'terrestrial longitudes by the moon's right ascension'.[24]

It may have been before or after this scientific mission that he, in his turn, had an affair with an Indian woman whose name has also been lost. They had a child, a girl. In due course, she was given over to the care of the Madras orphanage for 'illegitimate children of European officers and soldiers of the King's and Company's service'. Before abandoning her there, John Henry Crisp bestowed on this daughter the married name of Burrish Crisp's mother, the remarkable grandmother whom he had never met. The girl, however, proved restless. At some point between 1829 and 1838, the archives reveal, she absconded.[25] Thus it was that a new and now almost entirely Indian Elizabeth Crisp one day opened the door of the Madras orphanage that was confining her, and set out on her own journey in the streets of Chennai.

FAMILY TREES

These are streamlined genealogical tables. For more details about members of these families, see the website: http://www.jjhc.info/ Individuals discussed in detail in this book are given in bold print and with such dates as are available. The fact that the dates of several of these characters are unknown reflects in some cases their race, gender, or poverty. In other cases, their omission from known official records is due to their own or their parents' transnational and transcontinental journeyings.

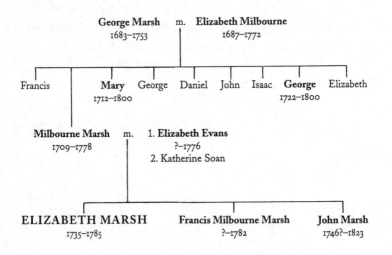

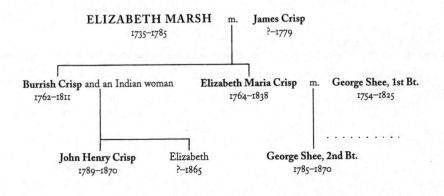

ELIZABETH MARSH   m.   James Crisp
1735–1785   ?–1779

Burrish Crisp and an Indian woman   **Elizabeth Maria Crisp**   m.   **George Shee, 1st Bt.**
1762–1811   1764–1838   1754–1825

John Henry Crisp   Elizabeth   **George Shee, 2nd Bt.**
1789–1870   ?–1865   1785–1870

NOTES

ABBREVIATIONS

The following abbreviations are employed in the notes:

a) INDIVIDUALS

EM – Elizabeth Marsh
GM – George Marsh
GS – George Shee
JC – James Crisp
JM – John Marsh
MM – Milbourne Marsh

b) FAMILY WRITINGS

CB – Commonplace Book
A two-volume commonplace book and scrapbook compiled by Elizabeth Marsh's uncle, George Marsh. It contains notes on a wide variety of topics and various literary and newspaper extracts, and is held by the Wellcome Library, London (MSS.7628–9).

FB – Family Book
This is an unevenly-paginated compilation of Marsh family histories, contemporary observations and autobiographical notes compiled, again by George Marsh, in the 1790s. The original manuscript, which is a volume half bound in white leather with marbled covers, and containing almost two hundred pages, remains in private ownership. An online version is available at www.jjhc.info/marshgeorge1800diary.htm.

FC – *The Female Captive*
Page references to this work, published anonymously by EM in

1769, are taken from the edited version produced by Khalid Bekkaoui (Moroccan Cultural Studies, Casablanca, 2003). Professors Bekkaoui and Felicity Nussbaum are currently at work on a new edition of this book together with EM's Indian Journal.

FCMS – Manuscript draft of *The Female Captive*

The provenance of this manuscript is unknown. Although its manuscript title is 'Narrative of her Captivity in Barbary', it is not in EM's handwriting. It appears to be a copy of an early version of *The Female Captive* which EM wrote in Chatham, England, in 1769, not in Morocco in 1756, and it contains factual errors but also some material not repeated in the published work. It is held by the Special Collections department of the Charles E. Young Research Library, University of California, Los Angeles (Bound Manuscript 170/604).

IJ – Indian Journal

This was compiled by EM during her progress in eastern and southern regions of the Indian subcontinent between December 1774 and July 1776. For a description of this manuscript, see *infra*, pp.187–8, 203. It is bound together with *FCMS*, and held at the Charles E. Young Library as above.

c) ARCHIVES AND LIBRARIES

AHPB	–	Arxiu Històric de Protocols, Barcelona, Spain
BL	–	British Library, London, England
GL	–	Guildhall Library, London, England
IOL	–	India Office Library in the British Library, London, England
IRO	–	Island Record Office, Twickenham, Jamaica
JA	–	Jamaica Archives, Spanish Town, Jamaica
LC	–	Library of Congress, Washington, DC, USA
MNHL	–	Manx National Heritage Library, Douglas, Isle of Man
NA	–	National Archives, Kew, England
NAS	–	National Archives of Scotland, Edinburgh, Scotland
NMM	–	National Maritime Museum, Greenwich, England
RO	–	Record Office

d) PRINTED WORKS

HMC	– Reports of the Royal Commission on Historical Manuscripts
ODNB	– Oxford Dictionary of National Biography (online version)
Parl. Hist.	– William Cobbett, *The Parliamentary History of England from the Earliest Period to 1803* (36 vols, 1816)

INTRODUCTION

1 *The Theory of Moral Sentiments* (4th edn, 1774), p.272.

2 See V. Carretta, *Equiano the African: Biography of a Self-Made Man* (2006).

3 Quoted in P. Horden and N. Purcell, *The Corrupting Sea: A Study of Mediterranean History* (Oxford, 2000), p.27.

4 J.L. Abu-Lughod, *Before European Hegemony: The World System A.D. 1250–1350* (New York, 1989); D.O. Flynn and A. Giráldez, 'Born With a "Silver Spoon": The Origin of World Trade in 1571', *Journal of World History* 6 (1995), pp.201–21.

5 For an elegant argument about the importance of this mid-eighteenth-century period for belief in global connections, see R. Koselleck, *Futures Past: On the Semantics of Historical Time*, trans. K. Tribe (Cambridge, Mass., 1985); *Philosophical and Political History of the Settlements and Trade of the Europeans in the East and West Indies*, trans. J.O. Justamond (6 vols, 1798 edn), I, p.2; T.W. Copeland *et al.* (eds), *The Correspondence of Edmund Burke* (Cambridge, 10 vols, 1958–78), III, pp.350–1.

6 The Pacific Ocean basin 'was the site of frequent interaction well before modern times', but in the main only among non-European sailors: see E. Manke, 'Early Modern Globalization and the Politicization of Oceanic Space', *Geographical Review* 89 (1999), pp.225–36; *The Universal Pocket Companion* (1760), p.3.

7 C. Tang, 'Writing World History: The Emergence of a Modern Global Consciousness in the Late Eighteenth Century', Columbia University Ph.D. diss., 2000, p.102.

8 Thomas Salmon, *A New Geographical and Historical Grammar: Wherein the Geographical Part is Truly Modern* (12th edn, Dublin, 1766), preface.

9 My appreciation of this point was much enhanced by Emma Rothschild's Tanner Lectures on 'The Inner Life of Empires' at Princeton University in April 2006.

10 For two recent surveys of the enormous amount of work now in progress, see R. Grew, 'Expanding Worlds of World History', and M. Lang, 'Globalization and its History', *Journal of Modern History* 78 (2006), pp.878–98 and 899–931. The argument that global history tends only to universalize Western experience – something that EM's own experience challenges – is made powerfully in F. Cooper, 'What is the Concept of Globalization Good For? An African Historian's Perspective', *African Affairs* 100 (2001), pp.189–213.

11 C. Geertz, *Local Knowledge: Further Essays in Interpretive Anthropology* (New York, 1983), pp.68–9.

12 C. Wright Mills, *The Sociological Imagination* (New York, 1959), pp.4–5, 7.

CHAPTER 1 : *Out of the Caribbean*

1 See the Lieutenant's log: *NMM*, ADM/L/K 40A.

2 'State of Jamaica', c.1735: *NA*, PC 1/58/3. For the shifts in land ownership and sugar production on the island, see B.W. Higman, *Jamaica Surveyed: Plantation Maps and Plans of the Eighteenth and Nineteenth Centuries* (Kingston, 1988); and R.S. Dunn, *Sugar and Slaves: The Rise of the Planter Class in the English West Indies, 1624–1713* (Chapel Hill, NC, 1972).

3 For the Caribbean region as 'precociously modern' see, for instance, P.D. Morgan, 'The Caribbean Islands in Atlantic Context, circa 1500–1800', F. Nussbaum (ed.), *The Global Eighteenth Century* (Baltimore, MD, 2003), pp.52–64, and R. Drayton, 'The Collaboration of Labour: Slaves, Empires and Globalization in the Atlantic World, c.1600–1850', in A.G. Hopkins (ed.), *Globalization in World History* (2002), pp.98–114.

4 D. Eltis, *The Rise of African Slavery in the Americas* (Cambridge, 2000), p.136; T. Burnard and K. Morgan, 'The Dynamics of the Slave Market and Slave Purchasing Patterns in Jamaica, 1655–1788', *William and Mary Quarterly* 58 (2001), pp.205–28.

5 M. Pawson and D. Buisseret, *Port Royal, Jamaica* (Oxford, 1975), pp.98–9 and *passim*; and see N. Zahedieh, 'Trade, Plunder, and Economic Development in Early English Jamaica, 1655–89', *Economic History Review* 39 (1986), pp.205–22; and her 'The Merchants of Port Royal, Jamaica, and the Spanish Contraband Trade, 1655–1692', *William and Mary Quarterly* 43 (1986), pp.570–93. There is a need for a new survey history that will locate Port Royal firmly in its broader American, African, European *and* Asian contexts.

6 *A Philosophical and Political History of the Settlements and Trade of the Europeans*, trans. J.O. Justamond (6 vols, 1788 edn), VI, pp.340–1.

7 C. Leslie, *A New History of Jamaica* (1740), p.25.

8 A.D. Meyers, 'Ethnic Distinctions and Wealth Among Colonial Jamaican Merchants, 1685–1716', *Social Science History* 22 (1998), pp.47–81.

9 Quoted in Morgan, 'Caribbean Islands', p.63; H.C. De Wolf, 'Chinese Porcelain and Seventeenth-Century Port Royal, Jamaica', Texas A & M University Ph.D. diss., 1998.

10 T. Burnard, 'European Migration to Jamaica, 1655–1780', *William and Mary Quarterly* 53 (1996), pp.769–96.

11 For the pervasiveness of death in early modern Jamaica, see V.A. Brown, 'Slavery and the Spirits of the Dead: Mortuary Politics in Jamaica, 1740–1834', Duke University Ph.D diss., 2002.

12 *NMM*, ADM /L/K 40A: entry for 22 July 1732; Edward Long subsequently claimed that a total of 4570 slaves were unloaded at Port Royal during 1734: *BL* Add.MS 12435, fol. 17.

13 Quoted in K. Brathwaite, *The Development of Creole Society in Jamaica, 1770–1820* (Kingston, 2005 edn), p.223.

14 The human damage can be tracked in the *Kingston* muster book for 1732–33: *NA*, ADM 36/1662; *BL* Add.MS 12427, fol. 102.

15 N.A.M. Rodger, *The Wooden World: An Anatomy of the Georgian Navy* (1986), pp.98–9.

16 *Regulations and Instructions Relating to His Majesty's Service at Sea* (1746 edn), p.113; and see Rodger, *The Wooden World*, pp.20–1, 39, 66.

17 *NA*, ADM 36/727 and ADM 36/3166: muster books of *Deal Castle* and *Rupert*.

18 *IRO*, Kingston copy register 1721–1825: Marriages, I, fol. 9. On her church monument, MM claimed that his first wife was sixty-eight when she died in 1776. This is not corroborated by any other known source.

19 *IRO*, Court wills, Liber 19, Part 2, fol. 188. The will was entered into the record on 4 December 1734, so Evans would have died at least several weeks before then; T. Burnard, 'Inheritance and Independence: Women's Status in Early Colonial Jamaica', *William and Mary Quarterly* 48 (1991), pp.95–6.

20 *JA*, 2/19/1–4 (unfol.): permission recorded 13 August 1734.

21 See T. Burnard, 'Slave Naming Patterns: Onomastics and the Taxonomy of Race in Eighteenth-Century Jamaica', *Journal of Interdisciplinary History* 31 (2001), pp.325–46; Evans' inventory is at *JA*, 1B/11/3/17, fols 132–3.

22 'A list taken . . . of all and every negro slave', *JA*, 2/19/1–4 (unfol.).

23 *JA*, Letters Testamentary, 1B/11/18/4, fol. 91; *IRO*, Kingston Copy Register 1721–1825: Marriages, I, fol. 91.

24 She is not listed for instance in J. and M. Kaminkow, *A List of Emigrants from England to America, 1718–1759* (Baltimore, MD, 1964); or in David

Galenson's addendum: 'Agreements to Serve in America and the West Indies, 1727–31', *Genealogists' Magazine* 19 (1977), pp.40–4.

25 *FB* (unfol.).

26 This may or may not be significant. As John Gillis writes, in early modern England 'the epitaph was not meant to remember the person but to remind everyone of a certain type of person': *A World of Their Own Making* (New York, 1996), p.35.

27 *JA* 2/19/1–4: 'A list of the white inhabitants of this parish'; widow Boucher is also listed in Port Royal's poll tax lists for 1739, 1740 and 1741.

28 In 1678, a Jane Bourchier is listed as owning 1020 acres on the island: *JA*, 1B/11/1, index to patents; for Charles Bourchier, whose land was in St Catharine's parish, see *IRO*, Court wills, Liber 17, Part I, fol. 60.

29 Brathwaite, *Development of Creole Society*, p.301.

30 Sir John Fielding quoted in P. Earle, *Sailors: English Merchant Seamen 1650–1775* (1998), preface.

31 P. Wright, *Monumental Inscriptions of Jamaica* (1966), p.vi. For a classic account of sailors' lives, stressing their distinctiveness, see M. Rediker, *Between the Devil and the Deep Blue Sea: Merchant Seamen, Pirates, and the Anglo-American Maritime World, 1700–1750* (Cambridge, 1987).

32 Raynal, *Philosophical and Political History* (4 vols, 1776, Dublin edn), IV, p.464.

33 For one of the best-known beneficiaries of the Royal Navy's relative openness, see V. Carretta, *Equiano the African* (2006); and W.J. Bolster, *Black Jacks: African American Seamen in the Age of Sail* (Cambridge, Mass., 1997).

34 *NA*, ADM 33/342: pay book of *Rupert*.

35 H. Lee, *Body Parts: Essays in Life-Writing* (2005), p.6; the original image is Julian Barnes's.

36 K. Wilson, *The Island Race: Englishness, Empire and Gender in the Eighteenth Century* (2003), p.148.

37 B. Anderson, *Imagined Communities* (rev. edn, 1991), p.166.

38 See T. Burnard, 'A Failed Settler Society: Marriage and Demographic Failure in Early Jamaica', *Journal of Social History* 28 (1994), pp.63–82; *IRO*, Port Royal copy register, 1725–1835, I: entry for 2 July 1730.

39 *JA*, House of Assembly journals, 1B/5/1//10, fols 197 and 204; Michael Craton, *Testing the Chains: Resistance to Slavery in the British West Indies* (New York, 1982).

40 For Cudjoe's departure, see the muster book of the *Rupert*: *NA*, ADM 36/3167. By 1738, a 'John Cudjoe', still a slave, was working as a caulker for the navy at Port Royal: *NA*, ADM 106/901, fol. 22.

41 See *Calendar of State Papers Colonial Series; America and West Indies . . . 1734–1735* (1953), pp.32, 49–51, 91, 102–3, 188–90, 257–8, 321–2, and 407–9 for growing expressions of anxiety on the part of Jamaica's settler elite.

42 It is possible that MM retained some property in Port Royal for a while. A friend was still paying local taxes on his behalf there in 1737: 'A list of the deficiency tax for the parish and precincts of Port Royal', *JA*, 2/19/1–4 (unfol.).

43 Log of the *Kingston*, *NMM*, ADM L/K 40A; for women voyaging in Royal Navy warships, see Rodger, *The Wooden World*, pp.67–76.

44 Here and throughout – unless otherwise stated – I am relying on the Familysearch.org website for details of births, christenings, marriages, deaths and burials.

45 *NA*, ADM 6/14, fol. 221; MM's presence on the *Deal Castle* and *Cambridge* can be tracked in *NA*, ADM 36/730, 736, and 437.

46 C.R. Markham (ed.), *Life of Captain Stephen Martin 1666–1740*, Navy Records Society (1895), p.210.

47 D.A. Baugh, *British Naval Administration in the Age of Walpole* (Princeton, NJ, 1965), pp.262–340 ; J. Coad, *The Royal Dockyards 1690–1850: Architecture and Engineering Works of the Royal Navy* (Aldershot, 1989), pp.1–13.

48 Quoted in J.H. Thomas, *Portsmouth and the East India Company 1700–1815* (1999), p.34.

49 Coad, *Royal Dockyards*, p.3.

50 See Thomas, *Portsmouth and the East India Company*, *passim*; the pagodas, booty from Anson's circumnavigation of the world, are noted in J.J. Cartwright (ed.), *The Travels Through England of Dr. Richard Pococke*, Camden Society (2 vols, 1888–89), II, p.115.

51 *FC*, p.43.

52 This and successive paragraphs draw on 'Memorandums that I have heard of father's and mother's families' in *FB*; for George Marsh senior, see *NA*, ADM 7/810, fol. 15.

53 There may have been some truth to this. In John Milbourne's will, in which he refers to himself as a 'gentleman', MM's mother was left only five shillings: *Hampshire RO*, 1722, A 56.

54 In 1749 he was listed as one of the Portsmouth shipwrights who 'appear to be worn out': *NA*, ADM 7/658, fol. 49.

55 For Jean Duval, see *NA*, PROB 11/844; EM comments on her French in *FC*, p.90.

56 J. DeVries, 'The Industrial Revolution and the Industrious Revolution', *Journal of Economic History* 54 (1994), pp.249–70.

57 MM to Navy Board, 30 May 1765 (copy), *NMM* ADM/B/177.

58 *Regulations and Instructions*, pp.113–14.

59 R. Campbell, *The London Tradesman* (1747), p.299.

60 *IJ*, p.3.

61 *NA*, ADM 106/938, fols 222, 234–8.

62 MM's answer to the allegation, *ibid.*, fol. 236.

63 *Ibid.*

64 For MM's work in advance of Toulon, see his reports in *NA*, ADM 1/381; and ADM 36/2098: muster book of *Namur*.

65 Minutes of court martial of Admiral Thomas Mathews, 1746, evidence of Milbourne Marsh: *NA*, ADM 1/5279; for the background to and debate over Toulon, see N.A.M. Rodger, *The Command of the Ocean: A Naval History of Britain, 1649–1815* (2004), pp.242–5.

66 *NA*, ADM 1/5279: evidence of Milbourne Marsh; *A Narrative of the Proceedings of His Majesty's Fleet* (1744), p.63.

67 M. Hunt, 'Women and the Fiscal-Imperial State in the Late Seventeenth and Eighteenth Centuries', in K. Wilson (ed.), *A New Imperial History: Culture, Identity and Modernity in Britain and the Empire, 1660–1840* (Cambridge, 2004), pp.29–47.

68 *NA*, ADM 106/938, fol. 236; I am inferring that EM's two brothers were born at sea, since they seem not to be registered in any land parish.

69 Quoted in C. Flint, *Family Fictions: Narrative and Domestic Relations in Britain, 1688–1798* (Stanford, CA, 1998), p.143; for MM's wages at Chatham dockyard during this period, see *NA*, ADM 42/42 and 43.

70 *FB*, entries for February 1737 and May 1744; GM's account of his own early career differs in some details from that given in J.M. Collinge, *Navy Board Officials, 1660–1832* (1978), p.121.

71 *FB*, entry for 10 October 1745.

72 D.M. Peers, 'Between Mars and Mammon: The East India Company and Efforts to Reform its Army, 1796–1832', *Historical Journal* 33 (1990), p.389.

73 George Marsh MSS. (unsorted).

74 J.B. Hattendorf *et al.* (eds), *British Naval Documents, 1204–1940*, Navy Records Society (1993), p.461

75 GM, 'Rough memorandum book', c.1799, included in *FB*, at pages at the back of the volume.

76 *CB*, fols 47, 79, and prayer at the back of the volume; *FB*, fol. 78. For a characteristic example of GM's unctuousness, see his letter to Lord Sandwich, 13 May 1785: 'It will ever give me the utmost pleasure to shew by my actions, my sense of your truly great and noble turn of mind in all situations, who always am, with the greatest veneration, My Lord, Your Lordship's most obedient and most devoted, humble servant', *NMM*, SAN/F/40/27. By this stage, Sandwich owed GM money.

77 *FB*, entry for 1755; *NA*, ADM 6/18, fol. 120.

78 *NA*, ADM 7/813, fol. 25.

CHAPTER 2 : *Taken to Africa, Encountering Islam*

1 For the British presence on the island, see D. Gregory, *Minorca, the Illusory Prize* (1990).
2 *FC*, p.43, and see pp.78 and 109 for EM's riding clothes and capacity to read music by 1756; Hospital Island (*aka* Bloody Island), where the Marsh family lived in Menorca, is described in *The Importance of the Island of Minorca and Harbour of Port-Mahon* (1756), pp.25–6 and 60.
3 *Importance of the Island*, p.26; J.G. Coad, *The Royal Dockyards 1690–1850: Architecture and Engineering Works of the Sailing Navy* (Aldershot, 1989), pp.329–40.
4 *Importance of the Island*, p.40.
5 Quoted in Gregory, *Minorca*, p.108.
6 The Royal Navy began seizing French ships in the Mediterranean in early September 1755, having learnt of General Braddock's defeat at Monongahela in North America: D. Syrett, 'A Study of Peacetime Operations: The Royal Navy in the Mediterranean, 1752–5', *Mariner's Mirror* 90 (2004), pp.42–50; P. Gould, 'Lisbon 1755: Enlightenment, Catastrophe, and Communication', in D. Livingstone and C.W.J. Withers (eds), *Geography and Enlightenment* (Chicago, 1999).
7 H.W. Richmond, *Papers Relating to the Loss of Minorca in 1756*, Navy Records Society (1913), pp.208–9; Desmond, *Minorca*, pp.172–8.
8 Richmond, *Papers Relating to the Loss of Minorca*, pp.xxxi and xxxiv.
9 *NA*, ADM 1/383, fol. 335; Desmond, *Minorca*, pp.168–78.
10 'Boscawen's Letters to his Wife, 1755–1756', in *The Naval Miscellany*, 4, ed. C. Lloyd (1952), p.214. GM claimed in his Family Book that EM escaped first to Barcelona when the French landed in Menorca. Here I follow her own version of events.
11 *NMM*, ADM B/153, letter of 11 June 1756.
12 *NMM*, MRF/14: Journal of the siege of Menorca (microfilm) and ADM/L/P/327: Log of *Princess Louisa*.
13 *NA*, ADM 1/383, fol. 388; MM's report is quoted in *The Trial of the Honourable Admiral John Byng* (1757), p.9.
14 James Lind, *Three Letters Relating to the Navy, Gibraltar, and Port Mahon* (1757), p.115.
15 See, for instance, *BL*, Add.MS 35895, fol. 252.
16 *NA*, ADM 1/383, fol. 388.
17 *Ibid.*, fol. 473; for the Marsh family salaries, see *NA*, ADM 7/813, fol. 25 and 7/814, fol. 29.
18 The passengers and Master of the *Ann* are listed in *NA*, ADM 1/2108.
19 Logbooks for *Gosport* from Plymouth and on from Gibraltar: *NA*, ADM 51/406, and *NMM*, ADM/L/G/77.

20 *FC*, p.44.
21 *FC*, pp.45–7.
22 *NA*, SP 71/20, fol. 183.
23 *FC*, pp.47–53.
24 For copies of some of these early letters from Morocco by JC and Joseph Popham, see *NA*, SP 71/20, Part I, fols 65, 67 and 69; *FB*, fol. 21.
25 In mid-eighteenth-century English usage, 'dark' as a description of complexion, like 'black', possessed no *necessary* racial connotations; *FC*, p.54.
26 Intermediaries of this sort, who were selected and trained so that they could move easily between the Maghreb and various Christian powers and lobbies, together with Sidi Muhammad's recruitment and employment of them, merit more attention.
27 *FC*, pp.59–60.
28 *NA*, SP 71/20, Part I, fols 183, 187.
29 On the impact of this on English, and subsequently British, shipping and religious and political attitudes, see my *Captives: Britain, Empire, and the World, 1600–1850* (2002), pp.23–134.
30 See the sources listed in *ibid.*, p.391, and R.C. Davis, 'Counting European Slaves on the Barbary Coast', *Past and Present* 172 (2001), pp.87–124.
31 'Boscawen's Letters to his Wife', p.236.
32 Colley, *Captives*, pp.65–72.
33 General Thomas Fowke, Governor of Gibraltar, to London, 2 January 1756: *NA*, CO 91/12 (unfol.).
34 *NA*, ADM 1/383, fol. 279; for Arvona, see Fowke to Henry Fox, 12 March 1756: *NA*, CO 91/2 (unfol.).
35 *NA*, ADM 1/383, fol. 279.
36 Höst is quoted by Khalid Bekkaoui in *FC*, p.8; P.G. Rogers, *A History of Anglo-Moroccan Relations to 1900* (1970), pp.95–104.
37 *FC*, pp.65–73.
38 *FC*, pp.68–9, 72.
39 *FC*, p.73.
40 *FC*, pp.73–4.
41 The classic account is E.P. Thompson, 'Rough Music', in *Cultures in Common: Studies in Traditional Popular Culture* (1991), pp.467–538; *FC*, pp.74–5.
42 On Moroccan imperial ritual at this time, see A. El Moudden, '*Sharifs* and *Padishahs*: Moroccan–Ottoman Relations from the Sixteenth Through the Eighteenth Centuries', Princeton University Ph.D diss., 1992; *FC*, pp.75–7.
43 John Stimson, 'Misfortunes that Befell HMS Lichfield on the Coast of

Barbary', a naïve but extraordinary slave account: *NMM*, JOD/7 (unfol.); for another European comment on Sidi Muhammad's striking appearance, see *FC*, p.87n.

44 Stimson's account of the Sultan's daily routine: *NMM*, JOD/7; F. Harrak, 'State and Religion in Eighteenth-Century Morocco: The Religious Policy of Sidi Muhammad B'Abd Allâh 1757–1790', London University Ph.D diss., 1989, pp.231–4.

45 A.K. Bennison, 'Muslim Universalism and Western Globalization', in A.G. Hopkins (ed.), *Globalization in World History* (2002), p.84; and see El Moudden, '*Sharifs* and *Padishahs*', pp.224–300.

46 See the report in *NA*, SP 71/19, fol. 251; Bennison, 'Muslim Universalism', pp.74–97.

47 *FC*, p.77; R.L. Diaz, 'El sultán 'Alawi Sîdi Muhammad . . . y sus sueños de hegemonía sobre el Islam Occidental', in J.M. Barral (ed.), *Orientalia Hispanica* (Leiden, 1974).

48 See J. Caillé, *Les Accords internationaux du sultan Sidi Mohammed ben Abdallah* (Paris, 1960).

49 P.H. Roberts and J.N. Tull, 'Moroccan Sultan Sidi Muhammad Ibn Abdallah's Diplomatic Initiatives Towards the United States, 1777–1786', *Proceedings of the American Philosophical Society* 143 (1999), pp.233–65; *NA*, FO 52/1, fol. 47.

50 I am indebted here to a lecture delivered at Princeton University in 2005 by Professor Frank Stewart on 'The Tribal Background to the Contemporary Arab World'; *FC*, p.66.

51 Harrak, 'State and Religion', p.287.

52 *NMM*, JOD/157/1–3, fol. 2; Bennison, 'Muslim Universalism', p.93.

53 E.R. Gottreich, 'Jewish Space in the Moroccan City: A History of the *Mellah* of Marrakech, 1550–1930', Harvard University Ph.D diss., 1999; *FC*, pp.77, 113.

54 *FC*, p.78.

55 See *infra*, pp.134–60.

56 *FC*, pp.78–80; EM's reaction to the bracelets is recorded in *FB*, fol. 26.

57 *FC*, pp.81–3.

58 *FC*, pp.83–4.

59 *FC*, p.84.

60 John Stimson's slave's-eye view of the palace interior: *NMM*, JOD/7; for other comments on Sidi Muhammad's taste for Western exports and re-exports, see Bennison, 'Muslim Universalism', p.85.

61 *FC*, pp.87 and note, and 88.

62 *FC*, p.89.

63 *NMM*, JOD/7 (unfol.); *FC*, p.89.

64 *FC*, pp.90–3.

65 See my 'The Narrative of Elizabeth Marsh: Barbary, Sex and Power', in F. Nussbaum (ed.), *The Global Eighteenth Century* (Baltimore, 2003), pp.140–1.

66 W. Lempriere, *A Tour from Gibraltar to Tangier, Sallee, Mogodore, Santa Cruz, and Tarudant* (3rd edn, Richmond, 1800), p.259; the factual accuracy of this (undoubtedly biased) account has been questioned: A. Farouk, 'Critique du livre de Lempriere par un temoin de l'epoque', *Hésperis-Tamuda* (1988–89), pp.105–37.

67 *FC*, p.92; for British captives' treatment in Morocco, and the varied length of their stays there, see my *Captives*, pp.48–72, 88–98.

68 Professor Madeline Zilfi's forthcoming book on female slavery in the Ottoman Middle East will open up this subject, and I have learned much from conversations with her. In the interim, see the essays in C.C. Robertson and M.A. Klein (eds), *Women and Slavery in Africa* (Madison, Wisc., 1983), and J.O. Hunwick, 'Black Slaves in the Mediterranean World', in E. Savage (ed.), *The Human Commodity: Perspectives on the Trans-Saharan Slave Trade* (1992).

69 *FC*, p.91.

70 I am grateful to Madeline Zilfi for clarifying this point. For examples of Arvona's restraint, see *NA*, ADM 1/383, fols 510 and 512.

71 EM seems to be recording her gratitude to Arvona, in *FC*, p.94.

72 *FC*, pp.95–6.

73 The order, dated 7 October 1756, is at *NMM*, HWK/4 (unfol.).

74 Logs of the *Portland*, at *NA*, ADM 51/3941, and *NMM*, ADM/L/P/205.

75 *NA*, ADM 1/383, fols 508, 512.

76 See its log: *NA*, ADM 51/3941; and for Sidi Muhammad's communication, *NA*, ADM 1/383, fol. 514.

77 *FC*, pp.112, 116, 118.

78 *FC*, p.117.

79 *FC*, p.103.

80 *FC*, pp.83, 104.

81 *FC*, p.105.

CHAPTER 3 : *Trading from London, Looking to America*

1 *FC*, pp. 119–20.

2 *FB*, fol. 20; *FC*, pp.43 and 120.

3 L. Namier and J. Brooke (eds), *The House of Commons 1754–1790* (3 vols, 1964), II, pp.220–1; *NA*, PROB 11/829.

4 *FC*, p. 120.

5 *FB*, fol. 20.

6 *FC*, pp. 43–4, 120.

7 R. Porter, 'The Crispe Family and the African Trade in the Seventeenth Century', *Journal of African History* 9 (1968), pp.57–77; P.E.H. Hair and R. Law, 'The English in Western Africa to 1700': N.Canny (ed.), *The Oxford History of the British Empire. Vol I: The Origins of Empire* (Oxford, 1998), pp. 241–63.

8 For some of the complexities and the diaspora of this clan, see F.A. Crisp, *Collections relating to the family of Crispe . . . 1510–1760* (1882), pp. 1–76.

9 A. Farrington *et al.* (eds), *The English Factory in Taiwan 1670–1685* (Taipei, 1995), pp.3–16, 50–118.

10 For the Burrish connection (which JC and EM honoured in the naming of their son) see *NA*, PROB 11/958; there were Crisp relations in Menorca: John Crisp's letter from Mahón to John Russell, 12 January 1734: *NMM*, MS 83/135 (unfol.).

11 M. Ogborn, *Spaces of Modernity: London's Geographies, 1680–1780* (New York, 1998), p.20.

12 P. Gauci, *The Politics of Trade: The Overseas Merchant in State and Society, 1660–1720* (Oxford, 2001), p.74. Other valuable discussions of mercantile life and working assumptions at this time include J.M. Price, 'What Did Merchants Do? Reflections on British Overseas Trade, 1660–1790', *Journal of Economic History* 49 (1989), pp. 267–84, and D. Hancock, *Citizens of the World: London Merchants and the Integration of the British Atlantic Community, 1735–1785* (Cambridge, 1995).

13 *FB*, fol. 97; *NA*, PROB 11/1053.

14 *FC*, p.120; the *Elizabeth* entered Bristol from Gibraltar on 26 February 1757. I owe this information to Professor Kenneth Morgan.

15 *NA*, ADM 1/3833, fols 97 and 252.

16 *FB*, fol. 20; K. Ellis, *The Post Office in the Eighteenth Century* (1958), pp.34–6; *Postal Museum and Archive*, POST 103/5 and 1/8.

17 C.J. French, 'London's Overseas Trade with Europe 1700–1775', *Journal of European Economic History* 23 (1994), pp. 475–501.

18 J.K.J. Thomson, *A Distinctive Industrialization: Cotton in Barcelona, 1728–1832* (Cambridge, 1992); for Lavalée, see *AHPB*, Sebastià Prats, 272v.

19 For British traders in Livorno and elsewhere in Italy at this time, see the diplomatic reports contained in G. Pagano de Divitiis and V. Giura (eds), *L'Italia del secondo settecento nelle relazioni segrete di William Hamilton, Horace Mann e John Murray* (Naples, 1997).

20 K. Newman, 'Hamburg in the European Economy, 1660–1750', *Journal of European Economic History* 14 (1985), pp.57–93. Little is known about JC's trade in Hamburg, but in a memorandum in 1766 he described it as one of his main markets: *NA*, T1/453, fol. 304.

21 D.J. Withrington, *Shetland and the Outside World 1469–1969* (Oxford, 1983).

22 *Speech of Edmund Burke, Esq. on American Taxation* (2nd edn, 1775), p.34; R.H. Kinvig, *The Isle of Man: A Social, Cultural, and Political History* (Liverpool, 1975).

23 *NA*, T1/434, Pt 2, fol. 60.

24 *AHPB*, Sebastià Prats, 32 r–v, 35 r–v, 67r–68r, 440r–441r.

25 See, for instance, the references to Rowland Crisp's voyages in *NA*, CO 142/18; and *Boston Evening Post*, 31 December 1759.

26 *Lloyd's Register 1764* (1963 repr.), unpag. Where a ship was formally declared to be bound was not necessarily the sum total of the ports it visited.

27 *AHPB*, Sebastià Prats, 135, 8 April 1763; and see the other wartime letters in these papers of the Crisps' Barcelona notary.

28 *AHPB*, Sebastià Prats, 21, 343v–345v.

29 Divitiis and Giura, *L'Italia del secondo settecento*, pp. 285 and 288; F. Trivellato, 'Trading Diasporas and Trading Networks in the Early Modern Period: A Sephardic Partnership of Livorno in the Mediterranean, Europe and Portuguese India c.1700–1750', Brown University Ph.D. diss., 2004.

30 It is suggestive that these three men went bankrupt shortly after JC: see *London Gazette*, 7–11 July 1767.

31 See George Moore's letters to James and Samuel Crisp, e.g. 4 October 1752: *MNHL*, MSS 501C; and F. Wilkins, *George Moore and Friends: The Letters from a Manx Merchant (1750–1760)* (Kidderminster, 1994).

32 *MNHL*, Acc no.MS 09591: letters from JC and Jacob Emery to John Taubman, 1760–1765; and John Taubman's accounts for 1764 and 1765.

33 F. Wilkins, *The Smuggling Trade Revisited* (Kidderminster, 2004), p.14.

34 F. Wilkins, *Manx Slave Traders* (Kidderminster, 1999).

35 The Duke of Atholl later claimed that it was the geographical and economic scale of Taubman's 'extensive smuggling' that had chiefly persuaded London to impose its control on the island: Wilkins, *Smuggling Trade*, p.22.

36 *FB*, fol. 28.

37 I am grateful to Professors Michela D'Angelo and Gigliola Pagano de Divitiis for this information.

38 Egmont to J. Grant, 1 Sept. 1768, *LC*, microfilm 22671, box 16.

39 I am grateful to Professor Derek Keene for supplying me with an expert analysis of this part of London; for its extreme diversity, see the poor relief books for St Botolph Without Bishopsgate: *GL*, MS. 5419, vols 262–5.

40 She is listed among the subscribers to EM's *The Female Captive* in 1769: *BL*, 1417.a.5; for the Jewsons and Crisps as neighbours: *GL* MS 5419, vols 262–4.

41 *GL*, MS. 05038, vol.4.

42 I am assuming that this is the Dr Orme listed as a subscriber to *The Female Captive*: *BL*, 1417.a.5.

43 *London Evening Post*, 28 February–3 March 1767.

44 *FB*, fol. 28, and concluding jottings.

45 *FB*, fol. 153.

46 *Ibid.*, fol. 189.

47 In 1763, JC was offering £100 per annum to a clerk who could 'write French & Italian letters': *Liverpool R.O.*, D/Earle/3/3/5; for the linguistic range that British merchants were ideally expected to command, and the expectation that French, Spanish, German and Italian would ease their business far beyond Europe, see W. Beawes, *Lex mercatoria rediviva: Or, the Merchant's Directory* (2nd edn, 1761), pp.30–1.

48 *FCMS* (unfol.).

49 A.S. Skinner and R.H. Campbell (eds), *An Inquiry into the Nature and Causes of the Wealth of Nations* (2 vols, Oxford, 1976), I, p.426.

50 For some of these debates, see P.N. Miller, *Defining the Common Good: Empire, Religion and Philosophy in Eighteenth-Century Britain* (Cambridge, 1994), pp.88–213.

51 Raynal, *A Philosophical and Political History* (1788 edn, 8 vols.), VIII, pp.195–6.

52 For the effects of this on another London merchant at this time, see A.H. John, 'Miles Nightingale – Drysalter', *Economic History Review* 18 (1965), pp.152–63.

53 *Speech of Edmund Burke*, p.34; *NA*, T1/434, fols 65 and 67.

54 Wilkins, *Smuggling Trade Revisited*, p.149.

55 *NA*, T1/453, fol. 302 *et seq.*; Wilkins, *Smuggling Trade*, p.149.

56 *NA*, T1/453, fols 302–4, 310.

57 *NA*, T1/442, fol. 25.

58 *NA*, T1/453, fols 302–4.

59 This episode in JC's career can be followed in detail in *NA*, SP 79/23 (unfol.), especially in his memorial dated 13 June 1764.

60 *Ibid.*, translation of statement by Genoa's magistrates, 7 July 1764; *NA*, SP 44/138, fol.267.

61 *NA*, SP 79/23 (unfol.): Lord Halifax to the British Consul in Genoa, 25 September 1764, enclosing JC's reply.

62 JC to William Burke, 10 January 1766: *NA*, SP 46/151, fol. 5.

63 For a good account of bills of exchange in international trade, see L. Neal and S. Quinn, 'Networks of Information, Markets, and Institutions in the

Rise of London as a Financial Centre, 1660–1720', *Financial History Review* 8 (2001), pp. 7–26.

64 Wilkins, *Smuggling Trade*, p.149; printed delivery notice dated 26 September 1765, *MNHL*, Acc 09591, James Crisp and Jacob Emery letters.

65 *AHPB*, Sebastià Prats, e.g. 26r–v, 10r–v and 406v–407v.

66 *Ibid.*, 24, 67r–68r, 74v–77r, 115v–116r; James Clegg to JC, 18 May 1764, *NA*, SP79/23 (unfol.).

67 *London Gazette*, 14–17 March 1767; and see the notices on 18–21 April and 28 April–2 May 1767.

68 *NAS*, CS/226/5171/7.

69 See J. Hoppit, *Risk and Failure in English Business 1700–1800* (Cambridge, 1987); and M.C. Finn, 'Women, Consumption and Coverture in England, c.1760–1860', *Historical Journal* 39 (1996), pp. 703–22.

70 See R. Boote, *The Solicitor's Guide, and Tradesman's Instructor, Concerning Bankrupts* (3rd edn, 1768). JC's assignees in 1767 included John Motteux, a future Director of the East India Company, which suggests that JC was already becoming more involved in Asian trade by this stage: *NAS*, CS226/5171/3.

71 *London Evening Post*, 26–28 May 1767; *FB*, fol.28.

72 *FB*, fols 97–109; for the Victualling Board, see D.A. Baugh, *British Naval Administration in the Age of Walpole* (Princeton, NJ, 1965), pp.373–451.

73 *FB*, fol. 136; C. Wilkinson, *The British Navy and the State in the Eighteenth Century* (Rochester, NY, 2004), p.118.

74 C.L. Mowat, 'The First Campaign of Publicity for Florida', *Mississippi Valley Historical Review* 30 (1943), pp.361–2.

75 *FB*, fol. 116; D.L. Schafer, 'Plantation Development in British East Florida: A Case Study of the Earl of Egmont', *Florida Historical Quarterly* 63 (1984), p.172.

76 Letter of JC dated August 1765: *MNHL*, Acc no. 09591.

77 For the circumstances of JC's grant, see the Earl of Egmont's file in *NA*, T77/5 (East Florida Claims Commission); C.L. Mowat, *East Florida as a British Province 1763–1784* (Berkeley, CA, 1943).

78 Schafer, 'Plantation Development', pp.172–83.

79 Egmont to J. Grant, 5 January 1767, *LC*, microfilm 22671, box 13; Schafer, 'Plantation Development'.

80 Egmont to J. Grant, 1 September 1768, *LC*, microfilm 22671, box 16.

81 *To the King's Most Excellent Majesty, the Memorial of John Earl of Egmont* (1764), p.21; Schafer, 'Plantation Development'.

82 Egmont to J. Grant, 1 September 1768, *LC*, microfilm 22671, box 16; for these estate plans, see http://www.floridahistoryonline.com/Plantations. I

am grateful to Professor Daniel Schafer for directing me to this site, and for other assistance.

83 W. Stork, *A Description of East Florida* (3rd edn, 1769), pp.v–vii, 2, 21.

84 e.g. *NA*, T77/5/5, fol.104.

85 *Gentleman's Magazine* 37 (1767), p.21; Francis Warren died in St Augustine in East Florida in late 1769: see *NA*, ADM B/183.

86 D. Schafer, '"A Swamp of an Investment"? Richard Oswald's British East Florida Experiment', in J.G. Landers (ed.), *Colonial Plantations and Economy in Florida* (Gainesville, FL, 2000); cf. B. Bailyn, *Voyagers to the West: A Passage in the Peopling of America on the Eve of the Revolution* (New York, 1988), pp.430–74.

87 *NA*, T77/9, file 7, fol.57; Egmont to J. Grant, 1 September 768, LC, microfilm 22671, box 16.

88 *NA*, T77/5/5, fol.88.

89 *FC*, p.41.

90 *Ibid.*; P. Mathias, 'Risk, Credit and Kinship in Early Modern Enterprise', in J.J. McCusker and K. Morgan (eds), *The Early Modern Atlantic Economy* (Cambridge, 2000), p.29.

CHAPTER 4 : *Writing and Migrating*

1 John Locke's evocation of travel writing's appeal as quoted in J. Lamb, *Preserving the Self in the South Seas, 1680–1840* (Chicago, 2001), p.55; for the enhanced vogue for travel writing by the 1750s, see P.J. Marshall and G. Williams, *The Great Map of Mankind: British Perceptions of the World in the Age of Enlightenment* (1982).

2 For Williamson, see L. Colley, *Captives: Britain, Empire and the World, 1600–1850* (2002), pp.188–92.

3 J. Raven, *British Fiction 1750–1770* (1987), p.19.

4 *Letters of the Right Honourable Lady M—y W—y M—e written during her travels in Europe, Asia and Africa* (3 vols, 1767), I, p.viii; and see I. Grundy, *Lady Mary Wortley Montagu* (Oxford, 1999), pp.117–78, 625–6.

5 For Brooke, Kindersley, Parker and Falconbridge, see the articles in *ODNB*; for Schaw: E.W. Andrews and C. McLean Andrews (eds), *Journal of a Lady of Quality* (New Haven, CT, 1934).

6 Sir William Musgrave's copy of *The Female Captive*, complete with his manuscript notes, is at *BL*, 1417.a.5; for the work's longevity in libraries, see for instance *A Catalogue of the Minerva General Library, Leadenhall-Street, London* (1795), p.76.

7 *Critical Review* 28 (1769), pp.212–17; see too *Monthly Review* 41 (1769),

p.156. A. Forster, *Index to Book Reviews in England 1749–1774* (Carbondale, Ill., 1990), p.203.

8 P. Hulme and T. Youngs (eds), *The Cambridge Companion to Travel Writing* (Cambridge, 2000), p.6.

9 This phrase was often used by London publishers to signal the fact that an author was, for some reason, outside the number of those who normally wrote and published.

10 Navy Board to Philip Stephens, 1 October 1764: *NMM*, ADM/B/175; for MM's earlier plans for Gibraltar, see *NA*, ADM 140/1263 and 140/1264.

11 Commodore Spry to Navy Board, 5 March 1767, *NA*, ADM 106/1160/30; J.G. Coad, *The Royal Dockyards, 1690–1850: Architecture and Engineering Works of the Sailing Navy* (Aldershot, 1989), pp.331–3.

12 Coad, *Royal Dockyards*, p.4.

13 *Ibid.*, pp.13–17.

14 *NA*, ADM 7/660, fol. 55; 'Plan of the Agent's dwelling-house and offices', *BL* Add.MS 11643.

15 *NA*, CO 91/12 (unfol.).

16 The Master of the *Dolphin* in 1766, as quoted in R. Cock, 'Precursors of Cook: The Voyages of the *Dolphin*, 1764–8', *Mariner's Mirror* 85 (1999), p.42.

17 This description of storage and slaughtering procedures at Chatham's victualling yard is based on GM's notes in *CB*, I, fols 61–70, and evidence he gave to Parliament in 1779, as reported in T. Baillie, *A Solemn Appeal to the Public, from an Injured Officer* (1779), pp.30–3.

18 See Khalid Bekkaoui's introduction to *FC*, p.20.

19 For colonial American captivity narratives by women, see my *Captives: Britain, Empire and the World, 1600–1850* (2002), pp.137–67; *FC*, p.41.

20 Epilogue by Aaron Hill to Eliza Haywood's *The Fair Captive* (1721), p.xv; for the theme of sexual violation in 'Barbary' captivity accounts, see my 'The Narrative of Elizabeth Marsh: Barbary, Sex and Power', in F. Nussbaum (ed.), *The Global Eighteenth Century* (Baltimore, MD, 2003), pp.138–50.

21 *Critical Review* 28 (1769), p.213.

22 P.M. Spacks, *Imagining a Self: Autobiography and Novel in Eighteenth-Century England* (Cambridge, Mass., 1976), p.72; extract on 'Woman', in *CB*, I, fol. 79

23 H.R. Plomer *et al.* (eds), *A Dictionary of the Printers and Booksellers who were at Work in England, Scotland and Ireland from 1726 to 1775* (Oxford, 1932), p.20; and see J. Raven, 'The Book Trades', in I. Rivers (ed.), *Books and Their Readers in Eighteenth-Century England: New Essays* (Leicester, 2001).

24 *The Female Captive* was one of thirty-six books known to have been

published by subscription in England in 1769: R.C. Alston *et al.*, *Eighteenth-Century Subscription Lists* (Newcastle upon Tyne, 1983); for the system, see J. Brewer, *The Pleasures of the Imagination: English Culture in the Eighteenth Century* (1997), p.164.

25 *BL*, 1417.a.5.

26 It is held in the Mitchell Library of the State Library of New South Wales, Sydney, and bears the Marsh bookplate.

27 See J. Mullan, *Sentiment and Sociability: The Language of Feeling in the Eighteenth Century* (Oxford, 1988)

28 *FC*, pp.41–2, 60, 64, 67, 71, 92, 104, 106, 111.

29 *FB*, fol. 25.

30 *FC*, p.66.

31 *FC*, pp.47, 49 and 93.

32 *FC*, pp.49, 83, 121; *FCMS* (unfol.).

33 *FC*, pp.54, 69.

34 *FC*, pp.43, 95, 103.

35 *FC*, 109; Spacks, *Imagining a Self*, p.58.

36 *FC*, pp.108–9, 118.

37 *FC*, pp.118–19; Charles Bathurst, EM's publisher, had been one of the printers involved in issuing a nine-volume edition of Pope's works in 1757–60.

38 *FC*, p.108.

39 List of subscribers included at the beginning of *The Female Captive* at *BL*, 1417.a.5; for Court, see *NA*, PROB 11/1183.

40 *FC*, p.103 (my italics).

41 *FCMS* (unfol.); *FC*, p.88.

42 T. Shadwell to J. Marsh, 5 April 1774, *William L. Clements Library*, Thomas Shadwell letterbook. I am grateful to Maya Jasanoff for transcribing this letter for me. F. Nussbaum, *Torrid Zones: Maternity, Sexuality, and Empire in Eighteenth-Century English Narratives* (Baltimore, MD, 1995), pp.11–12.

43 *FC*, p.103; S. Tomaselli, 'The Enlightenment Debate on Women', *History Workshop Journal* 20 (1985), pp.101–24.

44 On *Pamela*, credit and debt, see M.C. Finn, *The Character of Credit: Personal Debt in English Culture, 1740–1914* (Cambridge, 2003), pp.26–34; and C. Flint, *Family Fictions: Narrative and Domestic Relations in Britain, 1688–1798* (Stanford, CA, 1998), pp.171–80.

45 *FB*, fols 24–5.

46 I have benefited in my thoughts on this point from discussions with Jonathan Spence.

47 *Kent's Directory for 1766*, pp.7, 34 and 54.

48 I am grateful to Gareth Hughes of English Heritage for this information.

49 D. Hancock, *Citizens of the World: London Merchants and the Integration of the British Atlantic Community, 1735–1785* (Cambridge, 1995), pp.144, 213; for these Caribbean players, see the entries in ODNB.

50 John Crisp was based near Camomile Street, the last London address of JC and EM; as late as 1770 there are references to a 'Crisp's plantation-office, London': *The Massachusetts Spy*, 27–30 October 1770.

51 See *http://floridahistoryonline.com/Plantations*, under 'English Plantations on the St. John's River'.

52 Hancock, *Citizens of the World*, pp.68n, 112–13.

53 *NA*, T77/5/5, fol. 104; Hancock, *Citizens of the World*, pp.203–4.

54 S.J. Braidwood, *Black Poor and White Philanthropists* (Liverpool, 1994), pp.103–4; GM owned, for instance, the manuscript of Nicholas Owen's slave-trading journal: see E. Martin (ed.), *Nicholas Owen: Journal of a Slave-Dealer* (Boston, Mass., 1930).

55 *FC*, p.60.

56 C. Hesse, *The Other Enlightenment: How French Women Became Modern* (Princeton, NJ, 2001), p.76.

57 L. Sterne, *A Sentimental Journey . . . to which are added the Journal to Eliza*, ed. I. Jack (Oxford, 1968), p.167.

58 His notes on his copy of *The Female Captive*: BL, 1417.a.5.

59 *IOL*, B/86, fol. 53.

60 William Hickey's account of Digby Dent and the *Dolphin*: *IOL*, Photo Eur 175/1, fol. 369; R.F. Mackay (ed.), *The Hawke Papers . . . 1743–1771*, Navy Records Society (1990), pp.441 and 447n.

61 *NA*, ADM 36/7581.

62 Quoted in N. Papastergiadis, *The Turbulence of Migration* (2000), p.21.

63 E. Rothschild, 'A Horrible Tragedy in the French Atlantic', unpublished paper; for two rather different approaches to the 'world in motion' after 1763, see B. Bailyn, *Voyagers to the West: A Passage in the Peopling of America on the Eve of the Revolution* (New York, 1988); and R. Blackburn, *The Making of New World Slavery: From the Baroque to the Modern, 1492–1800* (1997).

64 *IOL*, O/5/29, Pt II, fols 119 *et seq.* Attitudes to race and skin colour are always subjective, and – as contemporaries perceived – they were markedly so in the subcontinent at this time: see D. Ghosh, 'Who Counts as "Native"?: Gender, Race, and Subjectivity in Colonial India', *Journal of Colonialism and Colonial History* 6 (2005).

65 Bailyn, *Voyages to the West*, pp.126–203; N. Canny, *Europeans on the Move: Studies on European Migration, 1500–1800* (Oxford, 1994), p.274.

66 Cock, 'Precursors of Cook', pp.30–52; A. Frost, *The Global Reach of Empire: Britain's Maritime Expansion in the Indian and Pacific Oceans, 1764–1815* (Carlton, VA, 2003), pp.51–9.

67 *FB*, entry for March 1770.

68 P.J. Marshall, *The Making and Unmaking of Empires: Britain, India and America c.1750–1783* (Oxford, 2005), pp.119–228; and see R. Travers' forthcoming *Ideology and Empire in Eighteenth-Century India: The British in Bengal, 1757–93.*

69 *HMC: Report on the Palk Manuscripts* (1922), p.158; James Rennell writing 31 March 1771: *IOL*, MSS Eur D.1073 (unfol).

70 D. Dent to P. Stephens, 17 December 1771, *NA*, SP 89/71, fols 92 and 94.

71 *NA*, ADM 51/259: Captain's log of the *Dolphin*; *IJ*, p.5.

72 For Crisp family members' dealings with the Company in London in the early eighteenth century, see for instance *IOL*, L/AG/1/1/8, fols 76, 85, 379 and 427; and L/AG/1/1/10, fol. 352. I am grateful to Anthony Farrington for these references; for Phesaunt Crisp: *NA*, PROB 11/739.

73 *ODNB* (Eyre Coote); *FB*, fol. 28.

74 *IOL*, G/15/20, fol. 74, and B/84, fols 262–3, 318 and 326.

75 JC to John Taubman, 15 November 1768, *MNHL*, Acc. no. MS.09591; R.P. Patwardhan (ed.), *Fort William–India House Correspondence . . . 1773–1776* (New Delhi, 1971), p.38.

76 *IOL*, Photo Eur 175/1, fol. 277; *IOL*, E/4/304, fol. 31.

77 *FB*, fols 29–30.

78 See L. Lockhart, 'European Contacts with Persia, 1350–1736', in his and P. Jackson (eds), *The Cambridge History of Iran: The Timurid and Safavid periods* (Cambridge, 1986).

79 W. Jones, *A Grammar of the Persian Language* (2nd edn, 1775), p.x.

80 Patwardhan, *Fort William–India House Correspondence*, pp.274–5.

81 Hon. Robert Lindsay as quoted in *Lives of the Lindsays; or, A Memoir of the Houses of Crawford and Balcarres by Lord Lindsay* (2nd edn, 3 vols, 1858), III, p.159. These provincial councils, at Calcutta, Burdwan, Murshidabad, Dhaka, Dinajpur and Patna, were intended as a temporary measure.

82 Recent useful surveys include S.U. Ahmed, *Dacca: A Study in Urban History and Development* (1986), and N.K. Singh (ed.), *Dhaka: The Capital of Bangladesh* (Delhi, 2003); the most detailed British account of Dhaka as the Crisps would have known it is by John Taylor, the commercial resident there in 1800: *IOL*, H/456f.

83 James Rennell describing Dhaka, 3 August 1765: *IOL*, MSS Eur D 1073 (unfol.); B.Barui, *The Salt Industry of Bengal, 1757–1800* (Calcutta, 1985).

84 A. Prasad (ed.), *Fort William–India House Correspondence . . . 1752–81* (Delhi, 1985), p.104; *Lives of the Lindsays* (2nd edn, 3 vols, 1858), III, p.160.

85 *IOL*, H/456f, fol. 121.

86 For the global significance of cotton at this time, see the invaluable

'Cotton Textiles as a Global Industry' section of the London School of Economics online Global Economic History Network (GEHN). I am grateful to Dr Giorgio Riello for referring me to this site.

87 *IOL*, E/1/60, fols 420–34; see also R. Datta, *Society, Economy and the Market: Commercialization in Rural Bengal, c.1760–1800* (Delhi, 2000).

88 Prasannan Parthasarathi, 'Cotton Textile Exports from the Indian Subcontinent, 1680–1780', on the GEHN 'Cotton Textiles as a Global Industry' website; A. Karim, *Dacca: The Mughal Capital* (Dhaka, 1964), pp.1–108. An appendix in this book, an inventory of the house of one of Dhaka's local zamindars in 1774, suggests the wealth and eclectic consumerism of its indigenous elite (*ibid.*, pp.487–94).

89 O. Prakash and D. Lombard (eds), *Commerce and Culture in the Bay of Bengal, 1500–1800* (New Delhi, 1999); P. Parthasarathi, 'Global Trade and Textile Workers, 1650–2000', on the GEHN 'Cotton Textiles as a Global Industry' website.

90 Philip Francis in 1776: *IOL*, L/MAR/C/891, fols 37–8.

91 *FB*, fol. 29.

92 These and the following details about the Crisps' Dhaka house and wardrobes are taken from the inventory at sale 6–8 March 1780: *IOL*, L/AG/34/27/2, fol. 51 *et seq.*; for Calcutta rents, see P.J. Marshall, *East Indian Fortunes: The British in Bengal in the Eighteenth Century* (Oxford, 1976), p.159.

93 *IOL*, L/AG/34/27/2, fol. 51 *et seq.*; and see A. Jaffer, *Furniture from British India and Ceylon* (2001), pp.28, 34, 54 and *passim*.

94 Jaffer, *Furniture from British India*, p.40; cf. W. Dalrymple, *White Mughals: Love and Betrayal in Eighteenth-Century India* (2002).

95 *IOL*, L/AG/34/27/2, fol. 51 *et seq.*

96 *IOL*, G/15/20, fols 67–9.

97 J.B. Esteve to G. Ducarel, 23 February 1785, *Gloucestershire RO*, D2091/F14.

98 *Ibid.*

CHAPTER 5 : *An Asiatic Progress*

1 Indian Journal (subsequently *IJ*), pp.1, 4, 8; *IOL*, P/2/9, fol. 32.

2 See, for instance, A.K. Srivastava, *India as Described by the Arab Travellers* (Gorakhpur, 1967); and J.P. Rubies, *Travel and Ethnology in the Renaissance: South India Through European Eyes, 1250–1625* (Cambridge, 2000).

3 J. Rennell, *Memoir of a Map of Hindoostan* (1788 edn), pp.5 and 207.

4 J. Kindersley, *Letters from the Island of Teneriffe, Brazil, the Cape of Good*

Hope and the East Indies (1777); E. Fay, *Original Letters from India* (Calcutta, 1821); for Plowden's travel diary, see *IOL*, MSS Eur F 127/94.

5 Kindersley, *Letters from the Island of Teneriffe*, p.1.

6 On this, see G. Becker, *Disrupted Lives: How People Create Meaning in a Chaotic World* (Berkeley,CA, 1997); *IJ*, p.38. A *coss* was normally accounted the equivalent of two miles in Bengal, but (as was true of the mile itself within Europe at this time) interpretations of its length varied in different regions.

7 D.A. Washbrook, 'Eighteenth-Century Issues in South Asia', *Journal of the Economic and Social History of the Orient*, 44 (2001), pp.372–3.

8 *IOL*, P/2/11, fol. 161; *IJ*, pp.1–3.

9 *IJ*, pp.2, 4.

10 *IJ*, pp.3–5, 13. For the *Dolphin's* mission, see *IOL*, H/122, fol. 5; for the *Salisbury*: *NA*, ADM 1/164.

11 *IJ*, pp.1, 5.

12 *IJ*, p.3.

13 'Nawab' was originally a Mughal title for a provincial official. It was anglicized as 'Nabob' and applied to those British- and Irish-born males who were accused of acquiring 'oriental' manners and undue Asian wealth. S. Foote, *The Nabob* (Dublin, 1778 edn), pp.4 and 31; L. Namier and J. Brooke (eds), *The History of Parliament: The House of Commons 1754–1790* (3 vols, 1964), III, pp.449–51.

14 *Parl. Hist.* 21 (1780–81), pp.1201–2.

15 *NA*, PROB 11/1396. Richard Smith claimed to be the real father of Amelia Cuthbert, who was born in Madras in 1766, and who married George Marsh junior in 1785. Given that 'Smith' is such a common surname, it is impossible to be certain exactly how Richard Smith was related to the Marsh clan. A member of the latter, yet another 'George Marsh', is known to have married an Elizabeth Smith in Rochester in 1705, and this may have been the origin of the connection. The crucial point is obviously that both Richard Smith and Elizabeth Marsh took some kind of kinship tie for granted.

16 Orme writes of dining with General Smith and 'a young lady whom he [Digby Dent] takes as a passenger' on 30 May 1770. 'Guard your heart,' he adds. Other than EM and her six-year-old daughter, no other women are known to have sailed on the *Dolphin*: *IOL*, MSS EUR/Orme OV., 202, fol. 37; for Johanna Ross and EM, see *IOL*, P/154/57, fol. 77.

17 *IJ*, pp.6–7.

18 S.M. Neild, 'Colonial Urbanism: The Development of Madras City in the Eighteenth and Nineteenth Centuries', *Modern Asian Studies* 13 (1979), pp.217–46.

19 *IJ*, pp.7–8.

20 G. Quilley (ed.), *William Hodges 1744–1797: The Art of Exploration* (2004), p.36.

21 *IJ*, pp.6, 20.

22 *Guide to the Records of the Ganjam District from 1774 to 1835* (Madras, 1934), pp.105–6.

23 Boswell is quoted in P.M. Spacks, *Imagining a Self: Autobiography and Novel in Eighteenth-Century England* (Cambridge, Mass., 1976), p.16.

24 *IJ*, p.10; F. Nussbaum, *Torrid Zones: Maternity, Sexuality, and Empire in Eighteenth-Century English Narratives* (Baltimore, MD, 1995), p.175.

25 *IJ*, pp.1, 7, 10, 26, 36, 39–40; for the significance of the minuet, see J. Eglin, *The Imaginary Autocrat: Beau Nash and the Invention of Bath* (2005), pp.43, 72–3.

26 H.F. Thompson, *The Intrigues of a Nabob* (1780), p.32. The description 'European' was often, though not invariably, applied by nominal Britons in the subcontinent to each other.

27 See D. Ghosh, 'Who Counts as "Native"? Gender, Race, and Subjectivity in Colonial India', *Journal of Colonialism and Colonial History* 6 (2005).

28 Thus a novelist had a character remark in 1789 how in Calcutta's theatre 'several country-born ladies figured away in the boxes . . . and their persons are genteel, and their dress magnificent': M. Clough (ed.), *Hartly House Calcutta* (1989 edn), p.204; L.E. Klein, 'Politeness and the Interpretation of the British Eighteenth Century', *Historical Journal* 45 (2002), p.879.

29 *IJ*, p.25.

30 *IOL*, MSS Eur E 25, fol. 19; *IJ*, pp.30, 33–4.

31 *IJ*, pp.16, 30, 33.

32 *IJ*, pp.8–9.

33 A Captain George Smith of Ellore appears regularly in the Madras army lists from 1765: see *IOL*, L/MIL/11/1, fols 28, 43, 74, 126, 177; for his likely birth, see *IOL*, N/2/1, fol. 455.

34 *IJ*, p.55; for the flexibility of early modern usages of the term 'cousin', see N. Tadmor, *Family and Friends in Eighteenth-Century England* (Cambridge, 2001), especially pp.149–52.

35 I am grateful to Felicity Nussbaum for some of these details about Elizabeth Marsh's Indian Journal.

36 *IJ*, pp.4 and 38.

37 'A Letter from a Lady in Calcutta to her Friend in England', published on 12 August 1784: W.S. Seton-Karr *et al.* (eds), *Selections from Calcutta Gazettes* (6 vols, Calcutta, 1864–69), I, pp.23–4; P.J. Marshall, 'The White Town of Calcutta Under the Rule of the East India Company', *Modern Asian Studies* 34 (2000), pp.326–7.

38 Clough, *Hartly House*, p.51. For an incisive discussion of European women in colonial spaces that focuses however on the nineteenth century, when female options and attitudes became in some respects more constricted, see A.L. Stoler, *Carnal Knowledge and Imperial Power: Race and the Intimate in Colonial Rule* (Berkeley, CA, 2002).

39 Marshall, 'White Town of Calcutta'.

40 J.M. Faragher, *Women and Men on the Overland Trail* (1979), passim.

41 P.J. Marshall, 'The Private Fortune of Marian Hastings', *Bulletin of the Institute of Historical Research* 37 (1964), pp.245–53.

42 A. Wright and W. Sclater (eds), *Sterne's Eliza* (1922), pp.85, 95–6; for Ross, see her will: *IOL*, P/154/57, fol. 77; on Cross and Persian trade: *IOL* G/29/20, fols 62 and 71.

43 *IOL*, MSS Photo Eur 32, I, fol. 89, and III, fol. 3.

44 J.S. Cotton *et al.*, *Catalogue of Manuscripts in European Languages Belonging to the Library of the India Office . . . The Mackenzie . . . Collections* (1992 edn), p.x; IJ, p.38.

45 F. Plowden, *An Investigation of the Native Rights of British Subjects* (1784), pp.108 and 159.

46 *IOL*, MSS Eur. E.4, fol. 157.

47 *IJ*, p.8; *Sterne's Eliza*, p.162.

48 See Francis Milbourne Marsh's will: *NA*, PROB 11/1095.

49 On Milbourne Warren's story, see *FB*, fols 35–7; and the papers regarding his divorce proceedings in *Lambeth Palace Library*, G139/114 and E41/65.

50 On Manila's expanding significance from the late sixteenth century, see D.O. Flynn and A. Giráldez, 'Born with a "Silver Spoon": The Origin of World Trade in 1571', *Journal of World History* 6 (1995), pp.201–21; N.P. Cushner (ed.), *Documents illustrating the British Conquest of Manila, 1762–1763* (1971).

51 *Lambeth Palace Library*, G139/114 and E41/65.

52 *IJ*, p.9.

53 Q. Craufurd, *Sketches Chiefly Relating to the History, Religion, Learning and Manners of the Hindoos* (1790), advertisement, and pp.8, 61; *IJ*, pp.9–10.

54 *IJ*, pp.10–11.

55 *IJ*, pp.7, 11, 13, 15, 17, 18, 24, 44, 62. The analogy is Edward Said's: see his *Culture and Imperialism* (New York, 1993).

56 See for instance JC's letter at *NA*, SP 46/151, fol. 5.

57 'Translation from the Persian Respecting Slavery', c.1774, printed in S. Islam (ed.), *Bangladesh District Records: Chittagong 1760–1787* (Dhaka, 1978), pp.227–8; for the East India Company and slavery in the subcontinent, see I. Chatterjee, *Gender, Slavery and Law in Colonial India* (Oxford, 1999), pp.176–224.

58 *IJ*, p.28; cf. E.A. Bohls, *Women Travel Writers and the Language of Aesthetics 1716–1818* (Cambridge, 1995), p.61.

59 *FCMS* (unfol), and see *infra*, p.152.

60 *FC*, pp.101, 106. It can only be speculated whether the description the *'fair Christian'* was in fact an assertion by EM or her publisher about her skin-colour as well as her religion. In the eighteenth century, 'fair' sometimes meant pale as distinct from dark; but the adjective was more commonly used to describe beauty in women. I suspect that the description in this case was intended as an allusion to Eliza Haywood's very popular *The Fair Captive* (1721).

61 *IJ*, pp.18, 20 and 51.

62 *Bodleian Library*, Dep.d.485, fol. 140 obverse; Kindersley, *Letters from the Island of Teneriffe*, p.72.

63 *Bodleian Library*, Dep. d.485, fol. 49; Kindersley, *Letters from the Island of Teneriffe*, frontispiece and pp.220–1; for Plowden, see Maya Jasanoff, *Edge of Empire: Conquest and Collecting in the East 1750–1850* (2005), pp.60–2.

64 *IJ*, pp.51–2.

65 J. Rennell, *Memoir of a Map*, p.57; for these and other early modern European writers on the subcontinent, see K. Teltscher, *India Inscribed: European and British Writing on India 1600–1800* (Delhi, 1997), pp.12–108.

66 *IJ*, pp.21–2.

67 *IJ*, pp.26, 28, 31.

68 *IJ*, pp.37–8, 41, 44.

69 *IJ*, p.44; *Guide to the Records of the Ganjam District*, pp.1, 93–107.

70 *IJ*, pp.42–3, 45–6.

71 It was a standard complaint among late-eighteenth-century incomers to the subcontinent that 'the Hindoos will not explain their tenets': see S. Chaudhuri (ed.), *Proceedings of the Asiatic Society* (Calcutta, 1980), pp.64–5; *IJ*, pp.46–7.

72 As a result, Elizabeth Marsh was also apparently ignorant of the persistent European superstition that pilgrims sometimes threw themselves under the wheels of Jagannath's chariot.

73 I am grateful to Susan Bayly for information on Puri. For an expert discussion of the cult, see H. Kulke and B. Schnepel, *Jagannath Revisited* (New Delhi, 2001).

74 There is an evocative and well-illustrated account of Puri festivals available online: see http://www.archaeologyonline.net/artifacts/british-view-india.htm.

75 *IJ*, pp.47–9, 56.

76 *IJ*, pp.50–2.

77 *IJ*, pp.54, 56–7; *cf.* C.A. Bayly, 'The Origins of *Swadeshi* (Home Industry): Cloth and Indian Society, 1700–1930', in A. Appadurai (ed.), *The Social Life of Things* (Cambridge, 1986).

78 *IJ*, pp.27, 57–8.

79 *IJ*, pp.60–1.

80 *IJ*, pp.24–5, 58–60, 64.

81 Though some British loyalists argued that royal and patriotic celebrations were sparse and badly neglected in East India Company enclaves in the subcontinent at this time: see H.E. Busteed, *Echoes from Old Calcutta* (1972 repr.), p.101.

82 For JC's 'bond debt' to Johanna Ross, negotiated before summer 1776, see *IOL*, L/AG/34/27/1, item 71.

83 I am grateful to Professor Om Prakash for confirming this likely identification (private communication); *IJ*, pp.1, 64–5.

84 *IJ*, pp.12, 15, 18–19, 28, 51.

85 B.S. Cohn, *Colonialism and its Forms of Knowledge* (Princeton, NJ, 1996), p.9.

86 *IJ*, p.19.

CHAPTER 6 : *World War and Family Revolutions*

1 On the global scale and repercussions of this conflict, see for instance C.A. Bayly, *The Birth of the Modern World 1780–1914* (2004), pp.86–96; D. Armitage, 'The Declaration of Independence and International Law', *William and Mary Quarterly* 59 (2002), pp.39–64; and Maya Jasanoff's forthcoming study of the worldwide loyalist diaspora after 1783.

2 M. Kurlansky, *Salt: A World History* (2002), p.347: and see *passim* for the mineral's human and commercial significance over time and distance.

3 P.J. Marshall, *East Indian Fortunes: The British in Bengal in the Eighteenth Century* (Oxford, 1976), pp.114–40; B. Barui, *The Salt Industry of Bengal, 1757–1800* (Calcutta, 1985).

4 JC's work as a salt agent – and the politics of salt in Bhulua – can be traced in his correspondence with Dhaka's Provincial Council: *IOL*, G/15/8–17, *passim*.

5 *IOL*, G/15/ 9, fol. 241.

6 *IOL*, P/49/61, fol. 321.

7 For one Company military officer's working list of Persian terms 'used in the collection of the revenue of Bengal', see *BL*, King's MS 197.

8 T.R.Travers, '"The Real Value of the Lands": The Nawabs, the British and the Land Tax in Eighteenth-Century Bengal', *Modern Asian Studies* 38 (2004), p.551; Edmund Burke's characterization of Company officials in

The Writings and Speeches of Edmund Burke, V, ed. P.J. Marshall (Oxford, 1981), p.430.

9 *IOL*, G/15/ 9, fol. 320; G/15/10, fols 646–50; G/15/12, fols 416–17.

10 *Lives of the Lindsays; or, A Memoir of the Houses of Crawford and Balcarres, by Lord Lindsay* (2nd edn, 3 vols, 1858), III, p.164; Marshall, *East Indian Fortunes*, p.140.

11 Kurlansky, *Salt*, pp.335–6.

12 *IOL*, G/15/9, fols 456, 610–11, 634–5.

13 *IOL*, G/15/12, fols 277–8.

14 M. Kwass, *Privilege and the Politics of Taxation in Eighteenth-Century France* (Cambridge, 2000), p.33; for this 'global crisis', see Bayly, *Birth of the Modern World*, pp.86–120.

15 *Infra*, pp.66–9.

16 Travers, '"The Real Value of the Lands"', *passim*.

17 P.J. Marshall, *The Making and Unmaking of Empires: Britain, India, and America c.1750–1783* (Oxford, 2005), pp.330–1.

18 *IOL*, G/15/12, fols 277–8; G/15/9, fol. 315; G/15/10, fol. 57.

19 *IOL*, G/15/ 9, fol. 197.

20 C.A. Bayly, *Rulers, Townsmen and Bazaars* (Cambridge, 1983), pp.144, 236.

21 H. Furber, *John Company at Work* (Cambridge, Mass., 1951), p.159.

22 Register of private trade outwards, 1772–5: *IOL*, H/21, fols 90 and 91; and *IOL*, P/49/62, fol. 754.

23 *IOL*, P/49/63, fols 643–51.

24 *IOL*, G/15/12, fols 243, 257; and see the correspondence on this matter in *IOL*, P/49/63.

25 *IOL*, H/224, fol. 81.

26 *IOL*, P/49/63, fols 647–59, *passim*.

27 *IOL*, P/49/63, fols 652–6.

28 This paragraph and the next draw heavily on a working paper by Dr Bishnupriya Gupta: 'Competition and Control in the Market for Textiles: The Indian Weavers and the East India Company'. I am grateful to Dr Gupta for allowing me to refer to it.

29 For one aspect of the Company's acute commercial difficulties at this time, see H. Bowen, 'Tea, Tribute and the East India Company', in S. Taylor, R. Connors and C. Jones (eds), *Hanoverian Britain and Empire: Essays in Memory of Philip Lawson* (Woodbridge, 1998), pp.158–76.

30 Gupta, 'Competition and Control'.

31 *An Inquiry into the Nature and Causes of the Wealth of Nations*, ed. R.H. Campbell and A.S. Skinner (2 vols, Oxford, 1976), II, pp. 636–41, 731–58.

32 It is possible that JC was pushed in the direction of Lakshmipur, as

distinct simply from jumping. There were complaints from private merchants in the Dhaka region in mid-1776 that, because of its economic difficulties, the East India Company was seeking to monopolize the cloth trade there. Its agents were reputedly stamping every length of fabric woven in the vicinity with the Company mark, for instance: see *IOL*, E/1/60, fols 421–2.

33 *IOL*, P/49/68, fol. 388.

34 Dhaka's Provincial Council was informed of JC's replacement on 3 December 1776: *IOL*, G/15/14, fol. 642; G/15/15, fols 106–7, 154.

35 Philip Francis to John Bourke, 21 November 1777: *IOL*, MSS Eur F5, fol. 266.

36 *IOL*, G/15/20, fol. 69.

37 *IOL*, P/154/57, fol. 77.

38 Though the range of married women's economic enterprise in early modern Britain, as elsewhere in the world, was far greater than the letter of the law or prescriptive literature suggested.

39 M. Hunt, 'Women and the Fiscal-Imperial State in the Late Seventeenth and Early Eighteenth Centuries', in K.Wilson (ed.), *A New Imperial History* (Cambridge, 2004), pp.29–47.

40 e.g. John Marsh to Baron Grantham, 5 March 1776, *Bedfordshire and Luton Archives and Record Service*, L30/14/243/5.

41 *FB* (unfol.).

42 *NA*, PROB 11/803.

43 *NA*, PROB 11/1095.

44 EM may have resorted to her navy connections once again and obtained a berth on one of the ships that Admiral Sir Edward Hughes (an old contact from her Asiatic progress) brought into Portsmouth from Calcutta in May 1778: the *Egmont*, the *Europa* or the *Stafford*.

45 *NA*, PROB 11/1053.

46 See the report on Chatham's victualling yard in 1773: *NA*, ADM 7/660, fol. 55.

47 e.g. *NA*, T77/5/5, fol. 104.

48 *FB* (unfol.); *NA*, WO 17/211.

49 John Marsh's account of his wartime service in his memoir, *NMM*, BGR/35; and see his regular intelligence reports in *NA*, CO 91/21–25, and *BL* Add. MSS 24168–24173. The role that consuls in port cities played in the information systems and cultural networking of states and empires, as well as in commerce, requires concentrated study.

50 See for instance '"That Historical Family": The Bakunin Archive and the Intimate Theater of History in Imperial Russia, 1780–1925', *Russian Review* 63 (2004), pp.574–93.

51 *CB*, I, fol. 53; *FB* (unfol.).

52 *Fifth Report of the . . . Several Public Officers Therein Mentioned. Commissioners of the Navy* (1793), p.5; D. Syrett, *Shipping and the American War 1775–83: A Study of British Transport* (1970), pp.24–35.

53 N.A.M. Rodger, *The Command of the Ocean: A Naval History of Britain, 1649–1815* (2004), p.615.

54 GM's memoir of his mission to Hamburg; *FB*, entries 18 February–4 June 1776.

55 *Ibid.*; Syrett, *Shipping and the American War*, pp.80–1.

56 *FB*, fol. 147.

57 *FB*, entries for 2 May 1778 and 15 March 1790.

58 I am grateful to Andrew Graciano for information about Benjamin Wilson.

59 For the *York*, see *FB* (unfol.) and the captain's log: *NA*, ADM 51/4402. I am grateful to Professor Roger Knight for his help in regard to identifying this ship. EM's transporting of 'wrought plate' is at *IOL*, B/94, fol. 538.

60 For these transcontinental sojourners, see M.H. Fisher, *Counterflows to Colonialism: Indian Travellers and Settlers in Britain, 1600–1857* (2003), pp.10, 57–61.

61 *IOL*, B/94, fol. 409.

62 T.A.J. Abdullah, *Merchants, Mamluks, and Murder: The Political Economy of Trade in Eighteenth-Century Basra* (New York, 2001); *IOL*, L/MAR/C/ 891, fol. 158.

63 H.V. Bowen, *The Business of Empire: The East India Company and Imperial Britain, 1756–1833* (Cambridge, 2006), 238–9; S. Conway, *The British Isles and the War of American Independence* (Oxford, 2000), pp.63–4.

64 *HMC: Report on the Palk Manuscripts* (1922), p.307; D.B. Mitra, *The Cotton Weavers of Bengal, 1757–1833* (Calcutta, 1978), pp.18–20; Marshall, *East Indian Fortunes*, p.56.

65 *FB* (unfol.).

66 For JC's association with Cator and Ross, see *IOL*, L/AG/34/27/1, item 71; and L/AG/34/29/1, fol. 11.

67 *IOL*, G/15/20, fol. 275; though see G/15/21, fol. 161.

68 *FB* (unfol.).

69 *IOL*, E/4/624, fols 13 and 359.

70 *IOL*, G/15/21, fols 315 and 374; P.J. Marshall, 'Warren Hastings as Scholar and Patron', in A. Whiteman *et al.* (eds), *Statesmen, Scholars and Merchants* (Oxford, 1973).

71 *IOL*, L/AG/34/29/1, fol. 11; *FB* (unfol.).

72 See the inventory of the sale: *IOL*, L/AG/34/27/2.

73 *IOL*, L/AG/34/27/1, fol. 70.

74 *Ibid.* There is no mention of JC's grave in the extant cemetery files for

Dhaka in the archives of the British Association for Cemeteries in South
Asia: *IOL*, MSS Eur F370.

75 *FB*, fol. 28 *et seq.*

76 *Ibid.*

77 *Travels of Mirza Abu Taleb Khan*, trans. C. Stewart (Delhi, 1972 repr.),
p.67; T.W. Copeland *et al.* (eds), *Correspondence of Edmund Burke* (10 vols,
Cambridge, 1958–78), VI, p.11.

78 *Hicky's Bengal Gazette*, 21–28 April 1781, 16–23 March 1782; H.E. Busteed,
Echoes from Old Calcutta (1972 repr.), p.210.

79 On Burke and Shee, see *Correspondence of Edmund Burke*, III, p.280; VI,
p.11; *IOL*, H/21, fol. 24.

80 GS's memorial c.1788, *BL* Add.MS 60338, fol. 25; *IOL*, MSS Eur E13C,
fol. 655.

81 The classic account of Philip Francis's political ideas, which was
formulated too early however to address how his attitudes to women's
place fitted crucially into his wider politics, is R. Guha, *A Rule of Property
for Bengal* (1996 edn).

82 S. Weitzman, *Warren Hastings and Philip Francis* (Manchester, 1929),
p.288.

83 *IOL*, MSS Eur E13C, fol. 654; MSS Eur E19, fol. 32.

84 J. Parkes and H. Merivale (eds), *Memoirs of Sir Philip Francis* (2 vols,
1867), II, p.16; *IOL*, MSS Eur E14, fols 415–16.

85 This paragraph and the next are based on Busteed, *Echoes from Old
Calcutta*, pp.242–59. This is the most comprehensive source available on
the Grand–Francis affair, but it contains inaccuracies as well as elements
of bias. I am grateful to Sadan Jha for also checking on my behalf the
rough notes on the trial made by Justice Hyde, who was one of the three
presiding judges in the Supreme Court. These are available on microfilm
in the Rare Books section of the National Library and at the Victoria
Memorial Library in Calcutta. Hyde also compiled a far more detailed
legal notebook, but this has been lost.

86 Busteed, *Echoes from Old Calcutta*, p.265.

87 *Ibid.*, p.260.

88 Before he left for the Cape, Grand took a Company position in Patna,
where 198 'distinct complaints from the inhabitants . . . of various
exactions and oppressions' were made against him: *IOL*, O/6/1, fols
200–1.

89 For what the city could be like for its disadvantaged, see D. Ghosh,
'Household Crimes and Domestic Order: Keeping the Peace in Colonial
Calcutta, c.1770–c.1840', *Modern Asian Studies* 38 (2004), pp.599–623.

90 Parkes and Merivale, *Memoirs*, I, 399. It was Francis's reactions to the
'corrupted' women of Italy that prompted these observations.

91 *IOL*, MSS Eur E 13A, fol. 15; *BL* Add.MS 47781, fol. 17.

92 *IOL*, P/2/28, fols 278–81; Busteed, *Echoes*, p.252.

93 Busteed, *Echoes*, pp.242–51, 259.

94 For the leading male actors in the trial – Francis, Grand, and their foremost judge – see Guha, *A Rule of Property*, pp.58–90; B.N. Pandey, *The Introduction of English Law into India: The Career of Elijah Impey in Bengal, 1774–1783* (Calcutta, 1967); and G.F. Grand, *Narrative of the Life of a Gentleman* (Cape of Good Hope, 1814). Catherine Grand merits, but has yet to receive, a transcontinental study to herself.

95 *IOL*, MSS Eur Photo Eur 175/2, fol. 201; Busteed, *Echoes*, pp.252–7.

96 *IOL*, MSS Eur E14, fol. 414; MSS Eur E23, fols 298 and 302.

97 *Hicky's Bengal Gazette*, 2–9 February 1782.

98 Syrett, *Shipping and the American War*, pp.44, 140–50; *Correspondence of Edmund Burke*, VI, p.11.

99 GS to EM, March 1783, *BL* Add.MS 60338, fols 54–5.

100 *Ibid*; for the marriage, see *IOL*, N/1/2, fol. 243, and MSS Eur E4, fols 231–8.

101 M.A. Shee, *The Life of Sir Martin Archer Shee* (2 vols, 1860), I, p.104; *Correspondence of Edmund Burke*, VI, p.11.

102 B. Francis and E. Keary (eds), *The Francis Letters* (2 vols, 1901), II, pp.368–9.

103 *BL* Add.MS 60338, fol. 164; for the scale of GS's commercial profits by the early 1780s, see his letters to G.G. Ducarel, *Gloucestershire RO*, D2091/F14/10, 16–17.

Ending – and Continuing

1 *FB*, fols 28–32; Burrish Crisp included some of the details of his mother's mortal illness in his epitaph for her: *The Complete Monumental Register* (Calcutta, 1815), p.34.

2 Thus in 1776 Mary Mustell of Chittagong left two hundred rupees in her will to her Indian physician: *IOL*, P/154/58, fol. 45.

3 Frances Burney, *Journals and Letters*, ed. P. Sabor and L.E. Troide (2001), pp.442–3; and for the medical procedures see J.S. Olson, *Bathsheba's Breast: Women, Cancer and History* (Baltimore, MD, 2002).

4 *FB*, fols 28–32; *Complete Monumental Register*, p.34.

5 GS to G. Ducarel, 27 November 1784, *Gloucestershire RO*, D2091/F14/10, 14; EM's death was announced in the *Calcutta Gazette* on 5 May 1785.

6 *Complete Monumental Register*, p.34. The original position of EM's grave, plot 1094, is shown in *South Park Street Cemetery, Calcutta: Register of Graves and Standing Tombs, from 1767* (BACSA, Putney, 1992). I am

grateful to Rosie Llewellyn Jones for information on the disappearance of EM's gravestone. Analyses of the imperial iconography and intent of South Park cemetery have sometimes failed to consider that many of the modest monuments that once made up the bulk of the tombs are now lost.

7 *FB, passim.* Later members of this family showed a similar concern to collect and deploy artifacts in order both to represent vast distances and to render them more intelligible. See, for instance, the list of James Milbourne Marsh's household contents in Australia in 1884: *Mitchell Library*, MSS. 1177.

8 JM's account of his career: *NMM*, BGR/35; JM is quoted in R. White, *The Case of the Agent to the Settlers on the Coast of Yucatan* (1793), pp.35–6.

9 See the account of this Marsh grandson on http://www.jjhc.info/marshgeorge1868.htm.

10 *FB*, entries for 1790–91; M. Gillen, *The Founders of Australia: A Biographical Dictionary of the First Fleet* (Sydney, 1989), p.236.

11 Note by JM, dated 20 September 1791, at the front of *IJ*.

12 For GS's support of the Union, see *BL* Add.MS 33106, fols 159–60; and D. Wilkinson, '"How Did They Pass the Union?": Secret Service Expenditure in Ireland, 1799–1804', *History* (1997), p. 240.

13 *Particulars of a Very Improvable Estate, Lockley House* (1812), Hertfordshire RO, D/EJnZ21.

14 The younger Shee's career and friendship with Palmerston can be traced in *BL* Add.MSS 60341–2; the contents of the Shees' London house are listed in *GL*, MS 11936/471/921679.

15 S. Bose, *A Hundred Horizons: The Indian Ocean in the Age of Global Empire* (Cambridge, Mass., 2006), p.7.

16 A possibly over-drawn report on the decay of Dhaka's textile industry by 1800 is in *IOL*, H/456f; for the mounting pressures on Sidi Muhammad, see N.A. Stillman, 'A New Source for Eighteenth-Century Moroccan History', *Bulletin of the John Rylands University Library* 57 (1975), pp. 463–86.

17 Slightly different chronologies for this decline are offered in J. Israel, *Diasporas Within a Diaspora: Jews, Crypto-Jews and the World Maritime Empires (1540–1740)* (Leiden, 2002), and F. Trivellato, 'Trading Diasporas and Trading Networks in the Early Modern Period: A Sephardic Partnership of Livorno in the Mediterranean, Europe and Portuguese India c.1700–50', Brown University Ph.D diss., 2004. Both scholars agree that, by the end of the eighteenth century, there had been a marked reduction in 'the general importance of the Sephardic trans-Atlantic and international trade network' (Israel, pp.38–9).

18 Most recently in N. Fergusson, *Empire: The Rise and Demise of the British*

World Order and the Lessons for Global Power (New York, 2003); for some interesting remarks by contrast on the tensions between empire and transcontinental economic linkages, see H. James, 'The Vulnerability of Globalization', *German Historical Institute Bulletin* 35 (2004), pp.1–11.

19 F.G. Dawson, *The First Latin American Debt Crisis: The City of London and the 1822–25 Loan Bubble* (New Haven, CT, 1990); I am grateful to J. Heath-Caldwell for information on William Marsh.

20 Galsworthy referred to 'that mysterious concrete tenacity which renders a family so formidable a unit of society, so clear a reproduction of society in miniature': *The Forsyte Saga* (New York, 1933), p.3.

21 C. Wright Mills, *The Sociological Imagination* (New York, 1959), pp.4–5. As Mary Midgley puts it, 'There can't be a single, comprehensive global story: all stories are partial': B. Mazlish and R. Buultjens (eds), *Conceptualizing Global History* (Boulder, Co., 1993), p.43.

22 By 1804 he was second judge of the court of appeal at Dhaka. His will is at *IOL*, L/AG/34/29/23.

23 *IOL*, N/1/4, fol.125; according to this register, John Henry had been born in 1789.

24 John Henry Crisp's career is summarized in *Historical Records of the Survey of India. Volume III: 1815 to 1830* (Dehra Dun, U.P., 1954), pp.434–5. His experiments on Sumatra, where he worked closely with Stamford Raffles, are detailed in *IOL*, MS Eur G51/30 and F/4/760, item 20656.

25 *IOL*, F/4/1855, item 78480; and see D.Ghosh, 'Making and Un-Making Loyal Subjects: Pensioning Widows and Educating Orphans in Early Colonial India', *Journal of Imperial and Commonwealth History* 31 (2003), pp.1–28.

CRIPT SOURCES

a) PUBLIC OWNERSHIP

AUSTRALIA

Mitchell Library, State Library of New South Wales, Sydney
   PXA 1012: Samuel Wallis sketchbook on *Dolphin*
   MS 1177: James Milbourne Marsh papers

ENGLAND

Bedfordshire and Luton Archives and Record Service, Bedford
   Wrest Park (Lucas) MSS

Gloucestershire RO, Gloucester
   Ducarel MSS

Hampshire RO, Winchester
   Wills

Hertfordshire RO, Hertford
   D/EJn/Z21: Lockleys sale particulars

National Maritime Museum, Greenwich
   ADM B: Board of Admiralty in-letters
   ADM/L/G and K: Lieutenants' logs
   BGR/35: Account of John Marsh
   HWK/1–7: Papers of Admiral Hawke
   JOD/7: John Stimson's Barbary narrative
   JOD/157/1–3: Journal of Admiral Sir Roger Curtis
   MRF/14: Journal of the siege of Menorca (microfilm)
   MS 83/135: John Russell papers
   VAU/2: Commissioner at Gibraltar letterbook

National Archives, Kew
   ADM 1: Records of the Admiralty

ADM 7: Admiralty miscellanea
ADM 33: Pay books
ADM 36: Ships' musters
ADM 42: Yard pay books
ADM 51: Captains' logs
ADM 106: Navy Board records
CO 91: Gibraltar original correspondence
CO 142: Jamaica miscellanea
CO 174: Minorca original correspondence
CO 389: Gibraltar and Minorca
FO 52: Morocco original correspondence
MPQ: Maps and plans
PC: Records of the Privy Council
PROB 11: Wills
SP 44: Entry books
SP 46: Supplementary domestic papers
SP 71: Barbary States original correspondence
SP 79: State papers, Genoa
SP 94: State papers, Spain
T1: Treasury Board papers
T77: East Florida Claims Commission

Liverpool RO, Liverpool
Earle papers

British Library, London

a) MANUSCRIPT ROOM
Additional Manuscripts
11643: Plan of Agent Victualler's house, Chatham
12427–35: Charles Long papers
23638: Minorca papers, 1721–56
24157–79: Papers of Lord Grantham, Ambassador to Madrid
35895: Minorca enquiry papers
47781–3: Philip Francis Papers
60337–42: Shee papers
King's MS 197: List of Persian vocabulary

b) INDIA OFFICE LIBRARY: RECORDS
Minutes of Court of Directors: B/84–B/94
Home correspondence: E/1/60

East India Company correspondence with India: E/4/304 and 624
Records of the Board of Commissioners for the affairs of India:
  F/4/760: Mission of Captain J.H.Crisp
  F/4/1855, item 78480: Madras Female Orphan Asylum papers
Factory records of Dacca: G/15/8–21
Home miscellaneous papers: H/21, 122, 224, 456
Biographical series: O/5/29
Bengal: Public consultations: P/2/9–11; P/2/28
Proceedings of Mayor's Court, Calcutta: P/154/57
Bengal Revenue consultations: P/49/61–68
Inventories and wills: L/AG/1/1/8–10; L/AG/34/27/1–2; L/AG/34/29/23
Marine Department records: L/MAR/C/891
Madras Army Lists: L/MIL/11/1
Madras returns: N/2/1

c) INDIA OFFICE LIBRARY: EUROPEAN MANUSCRIPTS
  Eur D. 1073: Papers of James Rennell
  Eur E 4: Papers of Margaret Fowke
  Eur D18, E 13–19, F5: Papers of Philip Francis
  Eur E 25: Papers of Alexander Mackrabie
  Eur G51/30: Madras Observatory papers
  Photo Eur 32: Memoir of Margaret Elizabeth Benn-Walsh, 6 vols
  Photo Eur 175: Memoirs of William Hickey, 4 vols
  MSS Eur/Orme OV.202

Guildhall Library, London
  Records of Sun Fire Office
  MS 05038: Churchwardens' accounts, Parish of All Hallows, Bread Street
  MSS 05396 and 5419: Rate books, Parish of St Botolph, Bishopsgate

Lambeth Palace Library, London
  Court of Arches records

Postal Museum and Archive, London
  Receiver General's entry book

Wellcome Library, London
  MSS. 7628–9: George Marsh MSS (CB)

Bodleian Library, Oxford
  MSS Eng.lett.c.81: Palmer MSS
  Dep.d.485: Mary Morgan MSS

INDIA

National Library, Kolkata
    Hyde MSS (microfilm)

Victoria Memorial Library, Rare Books Room, Kolkata
    Hyde MSS

ISLE OF MAN

Manx National Heritage Library, Douglas
    Goldie-Taubman papers
    Sir George Moore papers

JAMAICA

Island Records Office, Twickenham
    Parish registers
    Wills

Jamaica Archives, Spanish Town
    IB/11/1/1A: Patents to grants of land
    IB/11/3: Inventories
    IB/11/24: Powers of attorney
    IB/11/17: Letters of administration
    IB/5/9 to 11: House of Assembly journals
    2/19/1–4: Port Royal vestry minutes

SCOTLAND

National Archives of Scotland, Edinburgh
    CS226/5171: Kirkpatricks vs Crisp and Warren

National Library of Scotland, Edinburgh
    MS. 5599, 5619: Liston correspondence

SPAIN

Arxiu Històric de Protocols de Barcelona
    Sebastià Prats papers

UNITED STATES

William L. Clements Library, University of Michigan, Ann Arbor
Thomas Shadwell letterbook

Charles E.Young Research Library, Special Collections, University of California, Los Angeles
Bound manuscripts collection, 170/604:
[Elizabeth Marsh], 'Narrative of her Captivity in Barbary' (FCMS)
[Elizabeth Marsh], 'Journal of a Voyage by sea from Calcutta to Madras, and of a journey from there back to Dacca' (IJ)

Library of Congress, Washington
Microfilm 22671: Governor James Grant papers

b) PRIVATE OWNERSHIP

George Marsh Papers
Marsh Family Book (FB)
'A Journey to Hamburg'
Family Bible and Prayer Book
Miscellaneous papers

ACKNOWLEDGEMENTS

The global span of this book has made me more than usually indebted to the expertise, criticism and aid of very many friends, and to the kindness of even more learned and benevolent strangers.

For Elizabeth Marsh's Caribbean origins, I am grateful for the help of Vincent Carretta, Richard Drayton, Barry Higman, Nuala Zahedieh, and especially to James Robertson and Trevor Burnard.

For information on the Royal Navy and matters maritime, I thank Daniel Baugh, Jonathan Coad, Margaret Hunt, N.A.M. Rodger, and especially Roger Knight.

For Elizabeth's Mediterranean and Maghrebi worlds, I have benefited from the expertise of Amira Bennison, Khalid Bekkaoui, Wolfgang Kaiser, Frank Stewart and Madeline Zilfi.

For help in reconstructing James Crisp's European and trans-atlantic dealings, I wish to thank Michela D'Angelo, Josep Fradera, Christopher French, Derek Keene, Kenneth Morgan, Gigliola Pagano de Divitiis, Daniel Schafer, Francesca Trivellato, and above all James Amelang and David Hancock.

At different times, Susan Bayly, Anthony Farrington, Peter Marshall, Om Prakash, Giorgio Riello and John Styles have supplied me with valuable aid in the Asian portions of this book. I am particularly grateful in this regard to the close readings of Maya Jasanoff and Durba Ghosh.

Conversations with Natalie Zemon Davis, Hermione Lee, Felicity Nussbaum, Cassandra Pybus, Emma Rothschild and Jonathan Spence have helped me to think more clearly about biography, life-writings and history.

For encouraging me to think globally, I am grateful to Chris Bayly, Peter Coclanis, Paul Kennedy and Patrick O'Brien.

J.J. Heath-Caldwell has proved consistently generous in sharing his deep knowledge of the Marsh family and in introducing me to his remarkable family website: http://www.jjhc.info.

Acknowledgements

Benjamin Heller, Antonio Garcia, Sadan Jha, Katrina Olds, Suzanne Podhurst and Hannah Weiss have been invaluable researchers and proofreaders.

I began this project when I was Senior Leverhulme Research Professor and School Professor at the European Institute of the London School of Economics. I am most grateful to all my colleagues there, and especially to the generosity of Tony Giddens and Barry Supple. Crucial portions of this book were written when I was a Fellow at the Humanities Research Centre of ANU in Canberra in 2005, and I wish to thank Ian Donaldson and Iain McCalman for giving me the opportunity to spend time in that wonderful place. I benefited too from the award in 2006 of a GlaxoSmithKline Senior Fellowship at the National Humanities Center in North Carolina, where Geoffrey Harpham and Kent Mullikin and the rest of the staff and fellows provided me with a rich environment in which to think and write. My colleagues and students in the Department of History at Princeton, most civilized of universities, have afforded me boundless support and patience and ideas while I was completing this book.

As my list of manuscript sources consulted will make clear, it would be impossible for me to mention by name every archivist who has helped me in the ordeal of tracking Elizabeth Marsh. I am left, as ever, in awe of the enormous time, trouble and thought that the staff of records offices and libraries in different parts of the world willingly devote to people like myself.

For their sterling and inspired work in getting my ideas translated into print, I thank my literary agents in London and New York, Gill Coleridge and Michael Carlisle, and also Emma Parry. My editor Arabella Pike at HarperCollins, along with Helen Ellis, Robert Lacey, Alice Massey and Caroline Noonan, and Dan Frank, Fran Bigman and Katharine Freeman of Pantheon Books, have proved unfailingly enthusiastic, committed and professional.

David Cannadine though, and as always, deserves a category to himself.

LJC
Princeton, 2007

INDEX